PHYSICAL EDUCATION: FOUNDATIONS

CONTRIBUTORS

Robert W. Christina
James R. Ewers
Ellen W. Gerber
Robert Kaplan
Richard Kraus
Barry C. Pelton
Thomas J. Sheehan
Daryl Siedentop

PHYSICAL EDUCATION: FOUNDATIONS

ROBERT N. SINGER, Editor

The Florida State University

HOLT, RINEHART AND WINSTON   New York   Chicago   San Francisco   Atlanta
Dallas   Montreal   Toronto   London   Sydney

Copyright © 1976 by Holt, Rinehart and Winston

Library of Congress Cataloging in Publication Data
Main entry under title:

Physical education.

  Bibliography: p. 465
  1. Physical education and training. I. Singer,
Robert N. [DNLM: 1. Physical education and training QT255 P576]
GV341.P47   613.7'07   75-25582

ISBN 0-03-010386-X

Printed in the United States of America
9 8 7 6   032   1 2 3 4 5 6 7 8 9

PREFACE

This book was developed to orient the student and potential educator to physical education. Although several introductory texts exist on the subject, each having merits, we felt that a decade of significant change in the teaching and content of physical education justified a joint effort to produce a text grounded on those changes. Three fundamental concepts guided us.

First, the many dimensions of contemporary physical education required a team of specialists, each with an area of expertness, to present the varied material in an adequate and scholarly way. Each contributor has developed original materials for this book.

Second, development of physical education has been so rapid that the contents of the text not only had to be fully contemporary but also had to foresee the possibilities of the near future. Consequently, the latest trends, beliefs, and experiments are discussed for each area of concern to the student considering a career as a physical educator.

Third, the reader was constantly kept in the minds of the contributors, resulting in writing that is personal, informal, and easy to follow. The enthusiasm of the contributors for the work to which they are dedicated infuses each chapter.

Physical education, in our view, is far more than coaching or calisthenics, however worthwhile each may be. It is an integral part of the educational process. In this book, the multiple aspects of physical education are exhaustively explored; its numerous career possibilities are laid out for the reader. Not least, we emphasize its potential for personal commitment, community contribution, and self-realization.

Our primary concern has been to offer an all-encompassing work that will give the student a complete background in the field and will allow the instructor full freedom to concentrate as he chooses, because of the wealth and variety of material and approaches.

The first four chapters present the conceptual and historical background of modern physical education, not scanting controversy and clashing definitions. Chapters 5 through 7 discuss modern educational theory and practice in terms of the physical educator's responsibilities. The medical and scientific basis of physical education is presented in Chapters 8, 9, and 10. Growth, the psychology of learning, groups and leaders, performance psychology, testing, and research are the material of Chapters 11 through 15. The final four chapters, 16 through 19, make a thorough study of the several areas offering professional careers in physical education and the related fields of recreation and health education.

We wish to express our gratitude to the many professionals who reviewed the manuscript in its various stages and gave us helpful advice. They are Lonnie Clark, Drake University; Darrell Crase, Memphis State University; Curtis Decker, City College of San Francisco; Gary Dross, Orange County Community College; Ron Eastin, Phoenix College; Helen Fant, Louisiana State University; Richard Garber, University of Massachusetts; Walter Gregg, Northwestern University; Lawrence F. Locke, University of Massachusetts; John A. Lucas, Pennsylvania State University; Lincoln McClellan, Utah State University; Ken Parker, Joliet Junior College; Harold Ray, Western Michigan University; Dennis L. Swenson, Central Michigan University; and Homer Tolson, Texas A & M University.

Tallahassee, Florida   *Robert N. Singer*
November 1975

ABOUT THE EDITOR AND THE CONTRIBUTORS

Robert N. Singer, professor in the Movement Science Program and director of the Motor Learning Research Laboratory at the Florida State University, received his Ph.D. degree from Ohio State University. Dr. Singer is the author of several textbooks and has been a contributor to others; he has also contributed research, pedagogical, and general articles related to his area of interest, most notably motor learning and skill acquisition, sport psychology, and instructional design. He has addressed, nationally and internationally, teachers, researchers, sports groups, and the lay public. Dr. Singer is associate editor of *Research Quarterly* and *Journal of Motor Behavior* and a special reviewer for *Perceptual and Motor Skills, Journal of Applied Psychology,* and other professional journals.

Robert W. Christina, associate professor in the College of Health, Physical Education and Recreation at the Pennsylvania State University, received his B.S. degree from Ithaca College and his M.A. and Ph.D. degrees from the University of Maryland. Dr. Christina has coached several sports at the junior and senior high school levels as well as at the college level. He was voted Baseball Coach of the Year by the State University of New York Athletic Conference in 1972, when his team won the baseball championship. He has edited several books, has contributed to others, and has published research articles in *Research Quarterly, Journal of Experimental Psychology, Journal of Motor Behavior,* and *Perceptual and Motor Skills,* among other journals.

James R. Ewers, associate dean of the College of Health at the University of Utah, received his B.A. degree from the College of Wooster, his M.Ed. from Ohio University, and his Ph.D. from the Ohio State University. After teaching in the public schools, the College of Wooster, the Ohio State University, and the University of Akron, Dr. Ewers joined the faculty at the University of Utah. He is a member of AAHPER, NCPEAM, Southwest District AAHPER, UAHPER, and is a Danforth Associate. Dr. Ewers has contributed to several professional publications; outstanding among his contributions are "Move Over Men, the Women Are Coming" and "Try It, You'll Like It," both of which have appeared in the NCPEAM Proceedings.

Ellen W. Gerber, a law student at the University of North Carolina, Chapel Hill, received her Ph.D. degree from the University of Southern California. Dr. Gerber, formerly associate professor in the School of Physical Education at the University of Massachusetts, is the author of *Innovators and Institutions in Physical Education,* editor of *Sport and the Body: A Philosophical Symposium,* and coauthor of *The American Woman in Sport;* has lectured on matters in the physical education field; and has contributed chapters and articles in professional books, compilations, and journals.

Robert Kaplan, chairman and professor of health education in the School of Health, Physical Education and Recreation at the Ohio State University, received his B.S. and his M.A. degrees from New York University and his Ph.D. degree from the Ohio State University. Dr. Kaplan helped develop and teaches the first required television course in health education at Ohio State. He is the author of *Aspects of Human Sexuality* and *Drug Abuse: Perspectives on Drugs,* is the coauthor of *Positive Health,* has written numerous professional articles, is a contributing editor of *Journal of School Health,* and is a consulting editor for William C. Brown, Publishers. Dr. Kaplan is a Fellow, an office holder, and an active committeeman of several professional education, health, and family organizations; has been vice-president of the School Health Division of AAHPER; and was chairman of the NCAA Fencing Rules Committee.

Richard Kraus, professor and coordinator of the Recreation Division of Herbert H. Lehman College of the City University of New York, received his Ed.D. degree from Teachers College, Columbia University. Dr. Kraus is the author and coauthor of several texts, among them *Recreation Today: Program Planning and Leadership, Recreation and Leisure in Modern Society, Therapeutic Recreation Service, Creative Administration in Recreation and Parks* (with Joseph Curtis), and *Recreation Leadership and Supervision* (with Barbara Bates). Dr. Kraus has also published research reports on leisure education, recreation for minority groups and in urban settings, and recreation in psychiatric care.

Barry C. Pelton, coordinator of graduate studies and associate professor of physical education at the University of Houston, received his Ed.D. degree from the University of Southern California. His major publications are the following textbooks: *New Curriculum Perspectives for Collegiate Physical Education, Tennis,* and *Badminton.*

Thomas J. Sheehan, professor and head of the Department of Physical Education at the University of Connecticut, received his B.A. degree from the University of Notre Dame and his M.A. and Ph.D. degrees from the Ohio State University. Dr. Sheehan has been vice-president of the General Division of the Midwest Association for Health, Physical Education, and Recreation; is the author of the textbook *An Introduction to the Evaluation of Measurement Data in Physical Education;* and has contributed the article "Sport: The Focal Point of Physical Education" included in the *Quest* monographs.

Daryl Siedentop, associate professor of physical education at the Ohio State University, received his P.E.D. degree from Indiana University. Dr. Siedentop is the author of the widely used text *Physical Education: Introductory Analysis* and of *Developing Teaching Skills in Physical Education* and is the coauthor, with Brent Rushall, of *The Development and Control of Behavior in Sport and Physical Education.* He is editor of *Quest.*

CONTENTS

OBJECTIVES OF PHYSICAL EDUCATION, MOVEMENT EDUCATION, AND SCIENCE EDUCATION   43

HISTORY OF ORGANIZED PHYSICAL ACTIVITY   59

TEACHING AND LEARNING—INFORMAL EDUCATION   101

INSTRUCTIONAL MATERIALS   127

15

RESEARCH 299

16

PROFESSIONAL RECREATIONAL SERVICE   309

17

HEALTH EDUCATION   351

18

SCHOOL AND COLLEGE PROGRAMS OF PHYSICAL EDUCATION   377

19

CAREERS IN PHYSICAL EDUCATION   437

1

WHAT IS PHYSICAL EDUCATION?

Physical education today encompasses many concepts that may not be new but are receiving new emphases. To identify the interrelationships among sport, games, play, physical education, and physical recreation while distinguishing each from the other is part of the complexity. The impact of sport on a society appears to be far greater than most coaches and physical educators have realized. The growth of competitive athletic programs for women has created changes more rapidly than schools and colleges are prepared for. The attempts to replace the term *physical education* with a more accurate one are continuous.

Such developments illustrate that physical education is a complex phenomenon undergoing constant changes. To understand the subject is most important, because all of your future study and professional activity will depend upon your conclusions: You must be able to distinguish physical education from nonphysical education. Unless you know what physical education is, how do you know what you are studying, and how do you know what you may

Benefits of activity in participation

eventually practice? Unless all physical educators (within a society or an institution of higher education) can define the distinguishing characteristics of physical education, how can a college curriculum enable students to learn the properties of physical education?

Interpretations of physical education have changed as new directions have been taken or old controversies have been solved. Generally, historical definitions of physical education have centered around two opposed concepts—that is, education *for* the physical and education *through* the physical. Vigorous physical activity has always been at least a part of the total physical education experience in or out of schools; both views of the field have capitalized on this. Education *for* the physical was operative in the schools that provided information and techniques concerned with body exercises. Its purpose was to promote organic health and all its beneficial side effects. Education *through* the physical saw physical activity as a means to the total education of the individual rather than an end in itself.

Education **for** *the physical*

After physical education began to gain some impetus in school programs in the United States, leadership was provided primarily by medical people. At the end of the nineteenth century, they saw physical education programs as a significant contribution to the physical well-being of the youth of this country, that is, education *for* the physical.

The early promoters of what eventually became physical education were not concerned with a definitive statement about its nature. For the most part, they believed in the beneficial aspects of gross motor activities. If physical activity was so rewarding, should it not be a part of the school day so that teachers could involve all children? Physical training, therefore, was interpreted as a system of exercises or calisthenics, and this sufficed for the school program. Today physical culturists also see exercises and calisthenics as activities that should become a part of everyone's daily living pattern.

Early leaders in physical education made exercise and its benefits the reason for physical education. This idea was not transitory. Education for the physical is still the basis of programs in many schools and colleges in this country. In the past this interpretation of physical education enjoyed much currency during and immediately following national military crises, or following the publication of studies that allegedly compare the physical fitness levels of American children with those of children from other countries.

Of course, those physical educators who uphold the viewpoint of education for the physical are better prepared to justify their contentions in the 1970s than were their counterparts at the turn of the century. During the past fifty years a wealth of sophisticated information about the effects of exercise on the human organism has become available. One does not need to be conversant with professional literature to realize the benefits of controlled physical exercise with regard to longevity, weight control, psychological balance, and general health. Exercise and physical conditioning programs are at the disposal of every literate person in the United States. Many contemporary physical educators maintain that because physical exertion is so rewarding, they should be responsible for making certain that this vigorous activity is supervised and performed within certain limits. They feel that the school is where this supervision and instruction should take place; that every school child should be knowledgeable about and possess skills which will lead to a more active life.

As asserted by a popular magazine a few years ago, the "best" physical education program in this country contained tasks for children that were exercise-oriented only. Children progressed through various stages of the program by virtue of the levels of muscular strength and cardiovascular endurance they attained. As children passed from one level to another, they were entitled to wear a particular costume that identified the level of achievement. What criteria were used to evaluate this program as the "best" were not discussed, but obviously the prevailing concept was education for the physical. Nor is this type of physical education program rare in this country, because so many people believe this to be physical education, including those on school boards which control the financial support that physical education programs receive.

What are a few recent opinions about this type of physical education? In 1963, Arthur H. Steinhaus, a scholarly and well-respected figure in physical education, presented some of his basic beliefs about physical education:

If I may dare pose for a brief second as an interpreter of current history, I would say that in Germany there has always been a greater emphasis on education of the physical while in America we have, in the last decade or two, taken a very strong swing toward education through the physical and very often, unfortunately, neglected education of the physical. . . There are, however, now many positive signs on our horizon which indicate that we in America are returning to a stronger emphasis on "physique education," or education of the physical—really the primary and distinctive though not the sole function of physical education. All forms of education may develop the mind and spirit of man but only physical education can develop his body.[1]

Although actually part of a 1936 speech of Steinhaus, this view received enthusiastic support in 1963 throughout the physical education world. Steinhaus isolates the function of physical education from other forms of education by stating that "We who professionally represent the fields of health and physical education, and recreation are responsible more than any other group for the development in all persons of this general fitness—this positive physical and mental health."[2]

More recently Jerome C. Weber defined physical education as "education in its application to the development and care of the body."[3] He acknowledged the necessity of founding physical education on scientific knowledge about the effects of exercise on physiological function. He concluded that these effects constitute the body of knowledge we call physical education and which distinguishes it as an academic discipline. He thus implied that unless physical education has "unique" knowledge it is doomed to extinction.

[1] A. H. Steinhaus. *Toward an Understanding of Health and Physical Education.* Dubuque, Iowa: William C. Brown Company, Publishers, 1963, p. 19.

[2] *Ibid.,* p. 3.

[3] J. C. Weber. "Physical Education: The Science of Exercise." *The Physical Educator.* March 1968, p. 5.

A discussion of education for the physical would not be complete without reference to the concept of physical fitness. In fact, education for the physical has today become education for physical fitness. Wynn F. Updyke and Perry B. Johnson, for example, caution that "if we are to survive as an effective, contributing, educational agency, we must accept the obligation to become experts in the unique subject matter of our profession: human physical activity."[4] They suggest that human physical activity and/or physical fitness can be divided into two parts: (1) health and fitness parameters of circulorespiratory capacity, flexibility, muscular endurance, and strength; and (2) motor performance parameters of coordination, agility, power, balance, reaction time, and speed. These parameters or qualities of the human system, they believe, should be the disciplinary and professional concern of physical educators.

Education through *the physical*

Although tentatively formulated in the latter part of the nineteenth century, the concept that physical educators were involved in education through the physical was not well received until the beginning of the twentieth century. The idea that educational aims and objectives could be realized *through* a properly conducted physical education program maintained the existence of the field for approximately fifty years. Its early proponents took advantage of the opportunity to maintain physical education in the schools. Their view was not necessarily a protest against the dominant concept and method of teaching physical education; it served the field well by adding a function to the programs of the day. We can surmise from the writings of Dudley Sargent, Edward Hitchcock, and E. M. Hartwell, early respected leaders in physical education, that physical education was struggling for a place in the school curriculum. The identification of an additional role that physical education might play in the schools made this struggle much easier.

This new approach to physical education was a significant contribution toward arriving at a definition of the field. From our present vantage point we can conclude that this early inclusion of function in the definition of the field was not a panacea. It did, we must stress, serve a vital need of the day. The concept did not gain immediate approval by the physical educators of that day. A great communicational effort was required. One of these communicators, Luther H. Gulick, is credited with the foresight and ability to bridge the gap

---

[4]W. F. Updyke and P. B. Johnson. *Principles of Modern Physical Education.* New York: Holt, Rinehart and Winston, Inc., 1970, p. 22.

between the old and the new. In 1890, Gulick commented on the misinterpretation of the role of physical educators. He concluded that many thought that physical education was a subspecialty of the medical profession, or that it was part of a department of athletics, or, worse, that physical educators devoted their time and enthusiasm to building muscle tissue.

Gulick, classifying physical education as a profession, went on to attempt a definition of this "profession" by stating its objectives. He first divided exercises into three purposes: educative, curative, and recreative. Physical education was concerned with the category of educative exercises. The purpose of educative exercises became Gulick's definition of physical education: "To lead out and train the physical powers; to prepare and fit the body for any calling or business, or for activity and usefulness in life."[5] This goal would be accomplished by a system of exercise activities designed to develop:

1. Muscular strength
2. Endurance
3. Agility
4. Muscular control
5. Physical judgment
6. Self-control
7. Physical courage
8. Body symmetry
9. Grace
10. Expression

These objectives, surprisingly, are still the underpinning of many elementary and secondary school physical education programs in this country, although they were devised over eight decades ago.

In 1932, Thomas Wood stated that "The great thought in physical education is not the education of the physical nature, but the relation of physical training to complete education, and then the effort to make the physical contribute its full share to the life of the individual, in environment, training, and culture.[6]

Clark W. Hetherington, following Wood and Gulick, also helped define the "new physical education" or education through the physical. One of Hetherington's main theses was that the "education" in the term physical education was the primary concern, a somewhat different emphasis from Wood, who stressed the benefits to health of education through the physical. In Hetherington's scheme, the "physical" in physical education meant only that the activities practiced affect the total organism.

Hetherington did think that physical education was the basis for all education, and that the mind and the body functioned in concert. Organic education,

[5]L. H. Gulick. "A New Profession," in A. Weston, ed., *The Making of American Physical Education*. New York: Appleton-Century-Crofts, 1962, pp. 145–149.

[6]Thomas D. Wood. "The New Physical Education," in A. Weston, ed., *The Making of American Physical Education*. New York: Appleton-Century-Crofts, 1962, p. 154.

Education through and for the physical.

psychomotor education, character education, and intellectual education he termed "fundamental education," to be achieved by physical education.[7]

This concept of physical education had a decided impact on the field when it was introduced, and has been the single idea that has shaped most modern practices. Professionalization of the area of study, establishment of undergraduate curricula, development of teaching methodology in the schools, and justification of the program for the past six decades have been based on the contention that educational aims and objectives could be realized through a properly conducted physical education program of instruction. As we have shown, Gulick, Wood, and Hetherington had insisted that physical education should be an integral phase of the educational process, but it was Jesse Feiring Williams, a lifetime proponent of this view, who actually coined the phrase "education through the physical." His interpretation of physical education was really a protest movement against the advocates of physical education as education for the physical.

Williams declared that physical education "is the sum of man's physical activities selected as to kind, and conducted as to outcomes."[8] The activities that should be selected are those which contribute to the democratic way of life and present opportunities for individuals to become tolerant, kind, self-reliant, friendly, generous, and eventually possess strong personalities. By "outcomes" Williams meant those learned characteristics which are so necessary to the strength of America.

Advocates of education through the physical have been materially reinforced

[7] Clark W. Hetherington. "Fundamental Education," in A. Weston, ed., *The Making of American Physical Education.* New York: Appleton-Century-Crofts, 1962, pp. 159–165.

[8] J. F. Williams. *The Principles of Physical Education,* 6th ed. Philadelphia: W. B. Saunders Company, 1954, p. 3.

Table 1.1.   Purposes of education

1918	1938	1961
1. Command of the fundamental processes 2. Health 3. Worthy home membership 4. Ethical character 5. Vocational competence 6. Effective citizenship 7. Worthy use of leisure time	1. Human relationships 2. Civic responsibility 3. Economic efficiency 4. Self-realization	Development of creative thinking process in individuals

by committees of the National Education Association. In 1918, the Association published a list of seven desirable objectives for the schools in this country, striving to encompass the total potential of the secondary school curriculum. Considered too general, they were replaced in 1938 by four goals by the Educational Policies Commission. In 1961, this same committee reduced the four goals to one pervasive objective of American education. Although the committee was dissolved a few years later, the objectives had a decided effect upon physical education. Table 1.1 is an account of these objectives.

During the twenty-year life of the seven cardinal principles, physical educators believed that their school program could contribute measureably to health, worthy use of leisure time, and ethical character objectives. Some also believed that vocational competence could be realized because of the growing numbers of people involved in professional sports as both participants and managers. When the seven objectives were reduced to four, most physical educators thought that the physical education program could achieve all four. Since 1961, there have not been many references to the relationship between physical education programs and the stated purpose of American education. While the Commission was operating, however, those who supported education through the physical relied heavily upon its principles.

Delbert Oberteuffer, also an advocate of education through the physical, contributed much to the maintenance of physical education during the years between 1930 and 1965. He was, in addition, one of the first to focus attention on the concept of human movement in physical education. Although human movement advocates have significantly broadened the Oberteuffer approach, he interpreted education through the physical as education through movement experiences.

We have, to this point, briefly surveyed initial efforts to justify physical education. These ideas have persisted and are reflected in contemporary analyses of physical education. Is it now possible for you to justify physical education on the basis of these concepts? Will these arguments satisfy the criticisms you have heard leveled against physical education today? It is very important that you begin to ask yourself these questions; you may be assured that eventually you will be obliged to address this problem. Your defense will be based primarily on what physical education is to you or to your colleagues, and should be as strong and as well thought out as possible.

To summarize our two important concepts in physical education, we can say that education *for* the physical is:

A system or program of vigorous large muscle activities designed to stimulate the physical organism in order that the healthful benefits accrued from such activities may be realized by the participants.

Education *through* the physical we can describe as:

A program of physical activities in which the medium of physical movement is designed to produce a variety of experiences and outcomes, among them learning, social, intellectual, aesthetic, and health related.

Human movement

A new approach to physical education, human movement, arose in the United States in the 1950s, grew rapidly in the 1960s, and is now the concept supported by most writers in the field because physical educators need to define their work both as academicians and as professionals. In 1964, a scholarly justification of physical education was imperative. By then, the concept of human movement, and movement education as its practical application, was very well developed. Human movement as a directing concept in physical education is not an American invention. Following World War II, the use of movement experiences as educational tools became well established in Britain, where it had been introduced in the 1930s by Rudolph von Laban, a German dance advocate. Laban's ideas gained enthusiastic support for the movement concept from many physical educators in Britain, and it was subsequently translated into a system for American physical education.

A large number of American physical educators view human movement as a panacea for all of our ills, as well as a point on which to focus our scholarly attention. Through it, physical education can become an academic discipline, and physical educators can function in the schools, using a scholarly and theoretical base. Many movement advocates would like to change the name of physical education to "human movement" or some analogous term.

9

Human movement related to culture and society; folk dancing

Human movement and aesthetic experience: ballet dancing

Matthew C. Resick and Beverly L. Seidel have written that "physical education is the art and science of human movement."[9] The "science" of human movement resembles the academic disciplinary approach mentioned earlier. The "art" aspect could be interpreted as teaching physical education or relating to the professional structure. Resick and Seidel, however, explain in an interesting fashion that:

When the art of movement is considered, the aesthetic quality of any skilled, graceful movement is involved—whether it is the dancer executing leaps and turns, the football player blocking an opponent, or the youngster skipping rope. The science of movement is employed by the track coach when he explains to a discus thrower the role of the body's center of gravity in relation to force and body levers, by the research professor as he measures maximum oxygen uptake during strenuous exercise, or by the swimming teacher as he applies Newton's third law of motion to an analysis of the flutter kick.[10]

They caution further that they are not equating physical education as human movement with movement education, since movement education is but one phase of the entire physical education program.

A series of position papers developed by physical educators and sponsored by the American Alliance (formerly Association; all references in this text will show the present name) for Health, Physical Education, and Recreation supported the assertion that human movement is the preeminent focus of physical education. These papers concerned physical education in elementary and secondary schools, and offered guidance to excellence for physical

[9]B. L. Seidel and M. C. Resick. *Physical Education: An Overview*. Reading, Mass.: Addison-Wesley Publishing Company, Inc., 1972, p. 4.

[10]*Ibid.*, p. 4.

education in colleges and universities. Without defining the term physical education, the elementary school paper stated that "it aids in the realization of those objectives concerned with the development of favorable self-image, creative expression, motor skills, physical fitness, knowledge and understanding of human movement."[11] The secondary school paper insisted that "physical education is that integral part of total education which contributes to the development of the individual through the natural medium of physical activity—human movement."[12] The third paper, for colleges and universities, presented the definition that "physical education is the study and practice of the science and art of human movement. It is concerned with why man moves, how he moves; the physiological, sociological, and psychological consequences of his movements; and the skills and motor patterns which comprise his movement repertoire."[13] The elementary and secondary school papers alluded to the professional possibilities of human movement in the school; the college guideline stated that human movement could be a legitimate "study" and "practice." These position papers have had a decided influence on the definition and interpretation of physical education in this country by physical educators and nonphysical educators alike.

Jan Felshin, in a summary of the total concept of human movement in physical education, insists that "the primary focus of physical education has been identified as the study of human movement. Throughout the 1960s, many individuals, faculties, and groups within the profession sought to develop and refine a concept of physical education that transcended its functions and expressed its bases in knowledge. Although there are a variety of qualified definitions being used and developed, it is fairly generally agreed that physical education is concerned with man and his movement."[14] Felshin distinguishes the task of the discipline from the function of the profession. She categorizes the academic disciplinary body of knowledge derived from the study of movement under five headings:

1. Human movement as basic to human functioning and performance. As a person moves, he/she is affected in terms of physiological and/or biological function.
2. Human movement as related to culture and society. The assumption here is that

[11] AAHPER. *Essentials of a Quality Elementary School Physical Education Program.* Washington, D.C.: American Alliance for Health, Physical Education, and Recreation, 1970.

[12] AAHPER. *Guidelines for Secondary School Physical Education.* Washington, D.C.: American Alliance for Health, Physical Education, and Recreation, 1970.

[13] AAHPER. *Guide to Excellence for Physical Education in Colleges and Universities.* Washington, D.C.: American Alliance for Health, Physical Education, and Recreation, 1970.

[14] J. Felshin. "Physical Education: An Introduction," in R. N. Singer et al., eds., *Physical Education: An Interdisciplinary Approach.* New York: Macmillan Publishing Co., 1972, p. 4.

human movement affects the culture of particular societies, as well as being affected by this culture. In addition human movement forms have social significance as illustrated by the form of dance and/or sport.

3. Human movement as an aesthetic experience. There is a high degree of beauty expressed in certain human movement forms. How and why this beauty is interpreted is a source of investigation and resultant knowledge for the field.

4. Human movement as a source of human meaning and significance. Movement has meaning and people are motivated to move in characteristic ways. There is knowledge to be gained with reference to movement behavior.

5. Human movement as persistent and dynamic forms. Much evidence could be gained by studying how people have maintained certain movement forms and have discarded others. Some sport and dance forms have existed down through the ages but others have been fads and have subsequently disappeared. Why this occurs is a subject for study.[15]

Felshin goes on to explain that only as students master the body of knowledge pertaining to human movement are they then prepared to function as teachers of this discipline in the schools. As teachers function in the school using human movement concepts, they are evaluated on the manifest strength of being able to express significant ideas contained in the body of knowledge, and to realize the relationship between these ideas and the function of school.

The terms *movement education* and *movement exploration* in practice mean the same thing. They identify the human movement concept as it applies to the school or the professional setting. Movement education and/or movement exploration are distinct from the disciplinary study in our colleges and universities. *Movement exploration,* according to Elizabeth Halsey and Lorena Porter, is defined as "planned problem-solving experiences, progressing in difficulty, through which the child learns to understand and control the many ways in which his body may move and thus to improve many skills."[16] *Movement education* is similarly defined as "an individualized approach or system of teaching children to become aware of their physical abilities and to use them effectively in their daily activities involving play, work, and creative expression . . . movement education incorporates the natural inclinations of children, such as the desire to move freely, to be creative, and to test their own abilities through a variety of stunts, games, and play apparatus,"[17] Finally, Joan Tillotson identifies movement education as "that phase of the total education

[15] *Ibid.,* pp. 5–6.

[16] Elizabeth Halsey and Lorena Porter. "Movement Exploration," in R. T. Sweeney, ed., *Selected Readings in Movement Education.* Reading, Mass.: Addison-Wesley Publishing Company, Inc., 1970, p. 72.

[17] G. Kirchner, J. Cunningham, and E. Warrell. *Introduction to Movement Education.* Dubuque, Iowa: William C. Brown Company, Publishers, 1970, pp. 4–5.

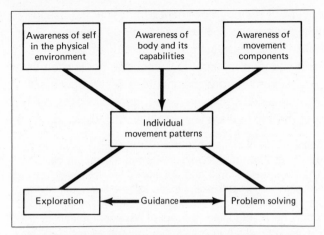

Figure 1.1   Relationship of exploration and problem solving
Source: J. Tillotson, "A Brief Theory of Movement Education," in R. T. Sweeney, ed., *Selected Readings in Movement Education.* Reading, Mass.: Addison-Wesley Publishing Co., 1970, p. 36.

program which has as its contribution the development of effective, efficient, and expressive movement responses in a thinking, feeling, and sharing human being."[18]

Tillotson defines exploration as "a 'child-centered' approach or method of teaching which allows for individuality, creativity, spontaneity, and self-discovery." Problem solving is a teacher-guided method that involves procedures for "(1) presenting the problem; (2) providing time for exploration with guidance; (3) refining and selecting solutions to the original problem; and (4) demonstrating for evaluation, analysis, and discussion."[19] Schematically, Tillotson explains the interrelationship of the terms as represented in Figure 1.1. Thus we can see the relationship between the tasks imposed on the child and the function of the teacher in a movement education program for the schools. It should also be clear that movement education is closely connected to a theoretically oriented academic discipline—human movement. In order to perform their responsibilities in the school, teachers must amass much knowledge about movement behavior. In this context we can answer the question "What do physical educators (movement educators) study?" They study the characteristics of human movement as manifested in sports, games, aquatics, gymnastics, exercise, and dance

[18] J. Tillotson. "A Brief Theory of Movement Education," in L. T. Sweeney, ed., *Selected Readings in Movement Education.* Reading, Mass.: Addison-Wesley Publishing Company, Inc., 1970, p. 33.

[19] *Ibid.,* pp. 33, 34.

13

The application of the concept of human movement to physical education cannot be criticized as avoiding reference to the disciplinary as well as professional features of the field. The discipline criteria have been fairly well met through an appeal to study general human movement; the application of this, movement education, well covers the professional role. Some issues still remain. Lawrence F. Locke[20] has asked some interesting questions about the movement education phase of the total idea, synopsized as follows:

1. "Movement education emphasizes an ultimate objective that may be impossible to attain." Movement educators claim that through experiences in movement children develop a readiness to learn all types of simple and complex motor behavior. In other words, if children learn basic locomotor skills, these skills will transfer to the future learning of dance and sport skills or any subsequent motor skill that must be learned. Unfortunately, this may be an outdated concept in physical education. No valid and reliable evidence is at hand which indicates that there is such a thing as general motor ability. It seems that learning a motor skill is specific to the activity that is being learned. If you wish to learn to perform in the sport of badminton, learn the skills of badminton and not some other set of skills that you may think will be directly transferable. As of this date the movement educators have not provided evidence which would contradict these contentions.
2. "Understanding movement is neither as useful nor as desirable as movement educators sometimes insist." If a child or an adult is to gain so much pleasure from the movement experience, teaching these individuals how and why they move may detract from this pleasure.
3. "In focusing upon the superiority of their method when contrasted with traditional procedures, movement educators have seriously misidentified and underestimated the central problems in physical education." Locke asserts that movement educators have misrepresented a basic problem by concluding that the *methods* employed in traditional physical education have been the cause of the inability to gain desirable results. Movement educators claim that their method is superior. The real cause of the problem, however, may be the teaching or the user of the method, and there is no reason to suspect that a teacher will not misuse the methods invented by the movement educator also.
4. "The teacher's role in movement education is deceptively simple." Movement educators have contended that their method is easily learned by the prospective teacher and can be used in the classroom or gymnasium with little effort. This may not be the truth, as many physical educators who have previously used traditional methods and changed to movement education methods conclude that the latter system is much more difficult.
5. "Movement education may not be the best method of instruction for all students." The teacher meets students who have a wide range of interests and many individual differences. The methods used in movement education may not appeal to all of

[20] L. F. Locke. "Movement Education—A Description and Critique," in R. C. Brown and B. J. Cratty, eds., *New Perspectives of Man in Action*. Englewood Cliffs, N.J.: Prentice-Hall, Inc., 1969, pp. 216, 219, 220, 221, 222, 223.

these interests and differences. In addition, advanced age groups may not be able to see the necessity of constantly learning basic skills or being asked to solve problems in space, time, and force using the body.

6. "Some movement educators have made physical education seem only an accessory to academic learning." It is the belief of many movement educators that their system will complement achievement in other academic areas of the school. This announcement only serves to compound the difficulty of arriving at the nature of physical education.

7. "Sequences of good movement problems are difficult to produce."

8. "The kinesthetic element to which much attention is directed in movement education is not always the best focus for the learner." Focusing upon that part of feedback from movement which is available to conscious centers is of limited value in learning a complex skill. As any golfer knows, kinesthesis is inaccurate and can often mislead. The acquisition of motor skills is the gradual placement of control into automatic circuits to which consciousness is no longer adjunct. Any continuing stress on awareness defeats this process. In the final analysis, skill, from the learner's standpoint, is concerned with results in the environment and not with process in the performer.

9. "The range of ability and past experience to be found in a typical class often creates irritating problems for the teacher." It is obvious to the observer of a room or gymnasium filled with students learning specific skills that some learn faster than others, and some are stimulated to learn from environmental situations that do not affect other students. If the teacher assumes that the rapid learner's response is the general response of the class and moves on to the next movement problem, this may negate the effectiveness of an entire learning section.

Locke's critical comments concerning movement education were not all negative, however. He pointed out that, among other strengths, the process of movement education stresses teaching method which is directed to children, as well as encourages appropriate self-directed introductory experiences.

Physical education: an academic discipline or a profession?

During the 1950s and early 1960s, many educational experts and a large number of self-proclaimed experts made a concentrated effort to improve the curricula in our schools and colleges. Some of their criticisms were valid and led especially to new methods in teaching mathematics and the sciences. Some were not, but served at least to reinforce the principle that something constructive and decisive would have to occur in the schools if we were to sustain any type of national direction or international leadership. As you may imagine, physical education did not escape this period unscathed. Generally, the program of physical education, per se, was not a direct object of this intense criticism. However, if the sciences should demand more of the pupils' time, something would have to be pushed from the already overcrowded curriculum. Physical education, considered by many as merely a frill subject, was marked the first to go.

School programs at the elementary and secondary levels were not the only physical education offerings that received criticism. In suggesting that physical education did not realize society's expectations, analysts moved for its exclusion, stating that not only is it unimportant for schools but that the education of teachers of physical education was not in the best interest of colleges and universities.

Such negative comments about physical education demanded new answers, because, if the traditional defense had been sound, physical education would not be susceptible to this criticism and would not be in danger of exclusion from the curriculum.

At that point, physical educators might have concluded that if physical education were considered at best an extracurricular function of the school, it should not be a part of the school day. Had they agreed with the educational critics of the day, they would not have arrived at a more rational justification. But this was not the case. Most physical educators have a visceral feeling that what they do is important and extremely valuable in the total educational scheme. Until very recently, except for a relative few, physical educators were not prone to make a concerted effort to justify their work. Professional introspection about teaching had not been needed. At this time in our history, however, it became obvious that if physical educators were of value to the school and society, they would have to communicate exactly how and why their labors had merit. Physical educators met the challenge and brought about the most significant change in physical education since its inception in the United States.

The change began in 1964, when Franklin M. Henry published a critically important article, in which he tackled the question of why physical educators had not been sufficiently concerned with the identification of their subject matter.

Since most of the present senior generation of physical educators received doctorates in education, it is understandable that their orientation has been toward the profession of education rather than the development of a subject field of knowledge. In fact physical education has the doubtful distinction of being a school subject for which colleges prepare teachers but do not recognize as a subject field, since the typical physical education department is unique in being under the jurisdiction of or closely related to the school or department of education.[21]

Thus Henry arrived at the nub of a problem that had plagued physical

[21]Franklin M. Henry. "Physical Education: An Academic Discipline," *Journal of Physical Education and Recreation,* September 1964. pp. 32–33. (*Note:* The former title of this journal was *Journal of Health, Physical Education, and Recreation;* all references to the journal will show the present title.)

educators for decades. As a consequence of continually justifying physical education on the basis that children receive some educational benefit from it, the identification of subject matter or acquired knowledge of the field had been overlooked.

The importance of this discovery may be illustrated by a question that could be addressed to any physical educator: "What do you teach?" A satisfactory answer a number of years ago might have been, "I teach physical education." For those more concerned with the educational significance of physical activities, this was obviously not a sufficient statement. They would have preferred "I teach children." Following the advice of Henry and others, a more adequate response to this question today would be, "I teach children physical education." At this point, of course, exactly what *physical* means becomes paramount. By imposing on the field of physical education the rigor of an academic discipline, we come much closer to identifying its nature. If this task can be accomplished, we can answer such a question as "What does the physical educator study and do that is not studied and done by someone other than the physical educator?"

Academic discipline

If we are to determine whether physical education is an academic discipline, what criteria must it meet? "Academic" is defined as a theoretical contention or statement about the nature of something apart from its practical value. This is not to say that theories are divorced from practical applications, because there are very few practical operations of merit that are not based upon theoretical knowledge. Theories are, in a sense, well-founded general principles that explain the nature of phenomena. It would be very difficult, for example, to apply anything practically without knowing how it works generally or not knowing how its parts are interrelated. It would be virtually impossible to practice physical education in the schools if the nature and function of physical education were not known. "Discipline" may be interpreted as a system of rules applicable to conduct. So, an academic discipline in a literal sense is a system of rules that conditions the conduct of theoretical statements about the nature of phenomena. Henry concluded that "An academic discipline is an organized body of knowledge collectively embraced in a formal cause of learning. The acquisition of such knowledge is assumed to be an adequate and worthy objective as such, without any demonstration or requirement of practical application. The content is theoretical and scholarly as distinguished from technical and professional."[22]

[22] *Ibid.*, p. 32.

What are examples of avowed academic disciplines? As you are probably aware, you have been involved with academic disciplines since beginning your formal education. Languages, chemistry, history, physics, psychology, and sociology, to mention but a few, are all examples of areas of study that have been identified as academic disciplines.

What are the characteristics of an academic discipline? If we are to determine whether physical education is an academic discipline, we must have standards against which to judge this possibility. Generally, there are four characteristics indigenous to a discipline:

1. *An academic discipline has a focus.* Members of a discipline concentrate their investigatory efforts upon a single phenomenon. The focus is unique to the particular discipline. Again, this focus must be of sufficient value to demand the efforts of individuals who are studying and analyzing.
2. *An academic discipline necessitates structure.* Members of a discipline arrive at definitions about the phenomenon in focus and establish what they will seek as true representations of its operations, interactions, and organizations.
3. *An academic discipline necessitates a body of knowledge.* From observations of the phenomenon, data are collected leading to information concerning the operations of the object in varying conditions and settings.
4. *An academic discipline necessitates distinctive modes of inquiry.* Members of a discipline establish and communicate methods of observation which are possible to employ when their phenomenon is under investigation.

As you can see, these characteristics are interdependent. Analysis can occur only after the phenomenon is identified and defined. Through various methods of inquiry the body of knowledge is amassed and more is known concerning the structure of the discipline.

By comparing a field of study with the qualities of an academic discipline, we can achieve two things. First, if the traditional "subjects" housed within the school maintain credence because they are academic disciplines, it is rational to conclude that any "new" field of study would have a much better chance for inclusion in the school curriculum if it also could qualify as a discipline. Second, by comparing an emerging field of study with the characteristics above, organization of the study becomes much clearer.

Is physical education an academic discipline? Is it possible so to formulate the nature of physical education that it can assume a position equal to other academic disciplines? Many contemporary opinion leaders in our field think this is possible. Since 1964, volumes have been produced arguing the pros and cons of this issue, and wrestling with the problems of focus, structure, and the body of knowledge particular to the field. Prior to 1964, a basic problem in the field was the identification of "the unique contribution of physical education." Many of us now think that perhaps the field would have progressed much more rapidly if the basic problem had been identified as "What is the unique phenomenon that physical educators study?"

Profession

Whether physical education is an academic discipline is a recent issue, but whether physical education is a profession is not. A cursory glance at the bulk of the literature in the field, historical and contemporary, will show that professional status has been granted. Article after article refers to "the profession of physical education." In the final analysis this reference to our field may prove to have been a bit too hasty and slightly misinterpreted.

What is a profession? In everyday usage we usually single out engineering, the practice of law, and the practice of medicine as prime examples of activities classified as professional. But why is an electrical engineer a professional and the electrician a craftsman? This argument may be solved by identifying the necessary characteristics that distinguish a profession from a nonprofession.

1. A profession encompasses activities that are beneficial to mankind. These services are not random aids but assigned functions that can be used by the major portion of a society.
2. A profession demands intensive training and education of its membership. Those who seek to become professionals must adhere to a rigid sequence of experiences designed to assure that they have the necessary skills to become a member of a specific profession. The education received by the preprofessional is broad-based and theoretical so that the novel and unique problem may be solved whenever it occurs.
3. A profession is structured to control its membership, characteristically giving a series of tests leading to a license. Not only must preprofessionals be subjected to educational tasks, but the fact that they have mastered the necessary skills must be ascertained through this licensing practice. The governing body of a profession also maintains a current register of those who qualify as skilled and licensed members of the profession.
4. A profession maintains a code of ethics or standards of conduct to which individual professionals must adhere in order to sustain continuous membership.
5. The membership of a profession assumes responsibility for the manner in which the professional task is conducted.
6. The membership of a profession imposes a self-monitoring system. Following licensing, the members of a profession are constantly accountable for their professional conduct. If this conduct violates the standards imposed by the profession, dismissal from the profession can result.
7. A profession is centered around an organized association to administer the varied ethical systems, educational requirements, and monitory methods. Usually, professional organizations are limited geographically to a particular country, but it is not uncommon to find international professional associations. International associations are not usually effective in licensing, but do serve well one additional function of an association, that of providing professional communication through meetings and informational journals.

Professions are not established and do not grow simply because a group of people get together and arrive at the conclusion that they should be professionals and in the process invent a governing organization. Professions develop as a result of the needs of a particular society for service crucial to its maintenance and, hence, must be performed only by those who are eminently qualified.

Relationship between a discipline and a profession

One of the characteristics of a profession, as we mentioned earlier, is that its members have, prior to their acceptance, gone through an extensive and intensive period of training and education. Those who wish to devote all or a portion of their lives to functions which are of some benefit to mankind are going to accomplish this either through an identified medium or by direct application of what is known about some phase of reality. For example, a good public school teacher helps people to understand themselves and their environment through the medium of particular subject matter. A civil engineer helps people by direct application of what he has learned, and may be instrumental in designing and constructing a superhighway. Both the teacher and the civil engineer belong to groups classified as professional. Both have been involved in a specific educational experience. In order to become members of their professional groups, they had to demonstrate that they had mastered their fields, which are nothing more or less than academic disciplines. In other words, teachers and engineers, in order to practice their profession, are required to study and comprehend what they profess. All professions are intimately linked to academic disciplines. Usually people will study some important phase of reality in college and then after graduation join a profession through which they may use the knowledge gained as a result of the study. Diagrammatically this concept may appear as shown (see Figure 1.2).

In Figure 1.2 the thick line separates the academic discipline from the professional practice. Although professions are related to disciplines, their functions are independent. The function of a discipline is to provide for people an environment where a specific subject can be described and investigated. An academic discipline is said to be value-free, because it concentrates on where its object of study is found and how it operates or behaves, not whether it is good or bad for people. When people are involved above the thick line in the figure, they ask the question "What is it?" or "What is the nature of the particular object?"

The function of a professional practice, on the other hand, is service to mankind. A profession is value-laden: it makes a judgment that certain

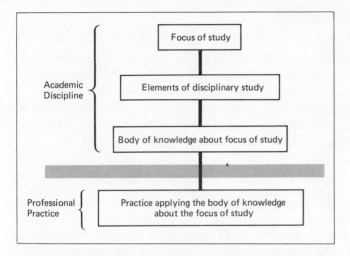

Figure 1.2 Moving from an academic discipline to professional practice

practices, using certain objects, can appreciably improve the conditions of humans. As one functions below the thick line in Figure 1.2 one asks the question "What does it do?"

This brief analysis should point out the difference between an electrical engineer and an electrician, for example. As a result of his disciplinary studies, the electrical engineer has a broad-based theoretical knowledge about the properties of electricity that enable him to design an electrical system for a large manufacturing complex. In these terms he acts as a professional. The electrician is a craftsman, not a professional, building a product using the plans and specifications put together by the electrical engineer. This does not imply that the professional is any more important than the craftsman; both are needed to make a product.

Most physical educators consider themselves members of a profession. In the light of our discussion in this section, this may be an error, but an understandable one. With few exceptions those who have studied physical education pursue teaching careers. Certainly, some work for community agencies, but there their work does not differ substantially from teaching. In addition, at this writing our national service organization, the American Alliance for Health, Physical Education, and Recreation, is no longer a department of the National Education Association. Perhaps we can assume that when physical educators talk of their profession, they really mean the teaching profession.

Physical education as a title

Currently, physical educators are not only progressing toward an unmistakable identification of their field but, as a result of that effort, are also deliberating about its name. Very few members are content with the term "physical education." Those who are satisfied hold to the concept of education *for* the physical. A name should denote ideological or functional structure, and, in view of the contemporary concepts we have explored, "physical education" is not an apt term. Marlin M. Mackenzie has concluded that:

any attempt to evaluate physical education encounters a major difficulty because of the term *physical education,* which is both limiting and confusing—It is limiting because it implies that physical activities can be taught in a vacuum, without giving consideration to thought and feeling. The concept of the totality and integrated nature of the human being negates the notion that education is a fractioned process of *mental* education on the one hand and *physical* education on the other. Education is concerned with the whole being, and consists of learning modes that are based upon the interrelated cognitive, affective, and motor behaviors of man. There just cannot be a process called *physical education.*[23]

Many names to replace the term "physical education" have been suggested over the past few years. It is refreshing to note that these names have all sought to stress the disciplinary aspect and not the professional function, showing awareness of the importance of identifying the field. Human movement, sport science, sport studies, exercise science, activity sciences, kinesiology,

Figure 1.3   Can physical education withstand the challenge?

kinanthropology, and movement science are some recent suggestions. In fact, some progressive colleges retitled their former physical education departments with one of these terms.

[23] M. M. Mackenzie. *Toward a New Curriculum in Physical Education.* New York: McGraw-Hill, Inc., 1969, pp. 8–9.

Renaming physical education is not, however, the most pressing problem in the field today. Someone has aptly put it: "We can name the baby after he is born." The most difficult problem is bearing the baby and this is the task which we, the involved and concerned, face during the next decade. Some physical educators maintain that we should not only forget about renaming the field, but also should concentrate on producing more competent teachers and better educational objectives for the field. This is a direction which is very difficult to comprehend, much as in Lewis Carroll's *Alice's Adventures in Wonderland.*

"Would you tell me, please, which way I ought to go from here?" asked Alice.
"That depends a good deal on where you want to get to," said the cat.
"I don't care much where," said Alice.
"Then it doesn't matter which way you go," said the cat.

Physical education, or whatever the name becomes, is an emerging field of study. Problems of definition always beset members of developing disciplines. Introspection, dialogue, and even argument are inevitable and healthful—but healthful only to the point where discussion ceases to be productive and threatens to fragment the members of the field. This has not yet occurred in physical education, but we must constantly be on guard against this possibility. In any discipline there are different theoretical views concerning how something should be studied—but this *something* is always common to members of the field regardless of the approach taken to observe it.

At the present time, you can choose the answer to our opening question, What is physical education? Is it education *for* the physical, education *through* the physical, human movement, sport, play, none of these, or all of these? As a student in the field, you should seek the definition with which you feel most comfortable. As you progress through your studies, you will gather information which supports your decision, and thus find the excitement and self-fulfillment of this search. Your professional achievement, whether in the schools or in some other career associated with the discipline, will be much increased as a result of your effort.

Summary

1. Students study physical education for numerous reasons: (1) Some feel that the professional life of a physical educator may be rewarding. (2) Some desire to coach a competitive sports team. (3) Some enjoy the physical activity associated with physical education. (4) Some enjoy the beauty associated with the body in motion. (5) Some enjoy the relaxed feeling that

accompanies participation in vigorous sports. (6) Some want to help boys and girls attain a significant degree of social and emotional development.

2. Historically, physical education has been centered around two opposed concepts: education *for* the physical and education *through* the physical. Education *for* the physical is a system or program of vigorous large-muscle activities designed to stimulate the physical organism and bring the healthful benefits of such activities to the participants. Education *through* the physical is a program of physical activities designed to produce, in addition to healthful benefits, the mental, moral, and social discipline and learning that are outgrowths of these experiences.

3. Descriptions and definitions of physical education: *Weber*—Education in its application to the development and care of the body.

   Updyke and Johnson—If we are to survive as an effective, contributing, educational agency, we must accept the obligation to become experts in the unique subject of our profession: human physical activity.

   Gulick—To lead out and train the physical powers; to prepare and fit the body for any calling or business, or for activity and usefulness in life.

   Oberteuffer—We may speak of one's physical education as the sum of those experiences which come to him through movement.

   Resick and Seidel—Physical education is the art and science of human movement.

4. Felshin categorized human movement under five headings: (1) human movement as basic to human functioning and performance; (2) human movement as related to culture and society; (3) human movement as an aesthetic experience; (4) human movement as a source of human meaning and significance; (5) human movement as persistent and dynamic forms.

5. Movement exploration is defined by Halsey and Porter as planned problem-solving experiences, progressing in difficulty, through which the child learns to understand and control the many ways in which his body may move and thus to improve many skills.

6. Halsey and Porter define movement education as an individualized approach or system of teaching children to become aware of their physical abilities and to use them effectively in their daily activities involving play, work, and creative expression.

7. Many names to replace the term "physical education" have been suggested over the past few years. Among these terms are: human movement, sport science, sport studies, exercise science, activity sciences, kinesiology, kinanthropology, and movement science.

Questions

1. Before you entered college, what did you think physical education was? What did you expect to learn as a physical education student?
2. What led you to consider physical education as a career?
3. Do you favor the idea of education *for* the physical over education *through* the physical? Document your statements.
4. Gulick, Wood, and Hetherington, early notable educational philosophers, presented their ideas about physical education. Identify the common thread(s) and the main difference(s) among them.
5. Who was Jesse Feiring Williams? Jay B. Nash? What were their unique contributions to physical education?
6. Differentiate physical education, human movement, and movement education.
7. Obtain a copy of the three position papers published by the AAHPER on what should be the focus of physical education at the elementary, secondary, and college levels. State your own understanding of these three papers in terms of definitions and objectives.
8. Movement education and movement exploration have been popular terms over the last few years. Who were or are the advocates of these concepts? Do these concepts say the same thing?
9. Why would you agree or disagree with Locke on the questions and critical comments that he raised about movement education?
10. Identify the intrinsic elements of an academic discipline? a profession?
11. What difference does it make whether physical education be a discipline, a profession, or both?
12. Draw a parallel between history and physical education in terms of academic discipline. History is not a profession per se, but history teachers are professional practitioners. Can you explain this seemingly complex situation?
13. Considering physical education only as a profession is like building a two-story building without a first floor. Why is this so?

2

WHAT IS SPORT AND SPORT SCIENCE?

Physical education has had an important part to play in the American educational dream. Since time immemorial, athletes have demonstrated that for them the importance of sport lies in its deep personal significance. Many physical educators have become aware of the contribution they can make toward the development of the individual by providing opportunities for him or her for good, sport experiences. Once, the aim of physical education was to build the body through sport and exercise; then it became even more instrumental as the profession sought to meet social-adjustment objectives and attain intellectual strength *through* the medium of physical activities. Now it is understood by many that the experience per se of sports can be a valued end in itself. It is comparable to teaching Shakespeare because the beauty and perfection of his writings bring the reader pleasure, rather than because he presents great moral truths and values. Because of the potential values to the individual of the sport experience, many people now believe that sport should be the central focus of physical education, as you will see in later pages.

Terminology

Sport is not a simple, unitary phenomenon. First, there are many levels of sport itself, each of which can be a different entity. It is difficult, for instance, to generalize about the sport experience if one is simultaneously talking about a professional football team and an intramural match between representatives of two dormitories. Second, many terms often used interchangeably with sport make it difficult to understand what kind of activity is being discussed. These terms include play, games, recreation, athletics, and sometimes physical education, leisure-time or carry-over activities, and even gymnastics. These terms, while part of a family of concepts, can be defined in distinctive ways so as to increase the communication of ideas. The following working definitions reflect common usage in the physical education literature.

Sport

Sport is probably the central concept to be dealt with, because it is the term most frequently applied to a large body of activities. It may be defined in the following way:

Sport is a human activity that involves specific administrative organization and a historical background of rules which define the objective and limit the pattern of human behavior; it involves competition or challenge and a definite outcome primarily determined by physical skill.

Because it involves specific organization and a historical background of rules, spontaneous activities or those modified to meet the situation are not considered to be sport. For example, a pickup game of one-on-one basketball would not be sport. Two students, inspired by a beautiful spring day to race to the physical education building, are not taking part in sport. Some organized activities that are sport are all sorts of league games from the Lassie League to the American League, as well as intramural, interscholastic, and intercollegiate competition. The professional tennis tour and the tournament at the local tennis or golf club are both sport. The NASTAR ski races are sport, but picking one's way down the slope is not. Competition in parachuting, surfing, and white-water canoeing (or kayaking) are obvious examples of sport. Street games with their local rules are not sport but may, under certain circumstances, be raised to that level. For instance, the New York City street game of punchball became an intramural tournament activity in many high schools.

Our definition used the terms "competition or challenge." Many people think all sport is competitive; that this is, in fact, its major characteristic. However, a case can be made for the idea that *natural sport* (taking place out of doors in

Which is sport?

accordance with the laws of nature rather than the rules of the contest) is a form of sport. The goal of basketball is to win the game; the goal of mountain climbing is to reach the top. The rules limit the basketball player from running with the ball in order to score goals. The rules limit the mountain climber from riding up the other side in a car to reach the top. The key to natural sport is that a challenge is set which must be met with the exercise of physical skill. A simple walk up a local hill would not be sport. An attempt to scale the southeast face of El Capitan in Yosemite National Park is a good example of natural sport.

An obvious example of an activity commonly called sport, which does not fit our definition, is chess. The results of chess tournaments and those of other board and card games are often reported on the sports' pages of newspapers or magazines, such as *Sports Illustrated.* However, their outcome is not affected by physical skill. A case might be made that the physical-skill requirement is arbitrary and conflicts with the common concept of chess as a sport. However, these working definitions are intended for use by physical educators, sport theorists, and others who are dealing with people engaging in activity that requires physical skill. Chess is not included in physical education programs. In fact, were the definition not to be limited, physical educators would have no way of making logical choices of activities for their programs. Thus for *us*, sport activities must have an important component of physical skills. Contests *determined* by chance, as roulette, are not sport. Contests primarily determined by physical skill are sport even if they include a chance factor—as all things do.

Some theorists[1] have proposed that the term *athletics* represents the serious, highly competitive type of activity usually found in intercollegiate or professional contests. They would reserve the term *sport* for contests more diversionary in nature. Admittedly, it would be useful to separate the two types of endeavors. However, the term athletics, derived from the Greek *athleter,* or winner of prizes, has unfortunately been preempted. In the rest of the world, and to some extent in the United States, the term means track and field activities. For example, the Olympic program includes athletics, meaning the track and field events; British books on athletics deal solely with track and field. But a more important reason for not using this term is that the criterion of seriousness as opposed to diversion is not a properly distinguishing factor. Children on a neighborhood softball team may be as serious and as highly competitive as any major league baseball player. Conversely, intercollegiate athletes may find diversion through their participation.

[1] This idea was first proposed in an article by J. W. Keating, "Sportsmanship as a Moral Category," *Ethics,* LXXXV, October 1964, pp. 25–35. Harold J. VanderZwaag provided an amplified discussion of the concept in his book *Toward a Philosophy of Sport.* Reading, Mass.: Addison-Wesley Publishing Company, Inc., 1972, pp. 66–69.

It seems that the best way to separate sport into various categories to increase communication or to analyze it is to use modifiers such as intercollegiate, professional, natural, or intramural. The term athletics, then, can be used in its traditional meaning of track and field events.

Games

The term *game* is often interchanged with sport, because games are the predominant form of sport. Nevertheless, there are some major definitional differences:

Games are activities with an agreed-upon organization of time, space and terrain, and rules that define the objective and limit the pattern of human behavior; the outcome, which is to determine a winner and a loser, is achieved by totaling or accumulating objectively scored points or successes.

A historical background of rules is not a requisite component of games, as it is for sport. That is, a game may be a single occurrence or a temporary version of an activity played by a particular group. Various children's games are good examples of this, and a child moving to a new neighborhood must learn the local rules for familiar activities. Because of this, games per se are more flexible than sport.

Many sports are games in that points are objectively scored to determine the victor. Some, such as aquatics, gymnastics, and figure skating, are not, because points are awarded on a subjectively judged basis. In track and field activities points are not scored during the event but are awarded by the judges for the rankings achieved. Thus running the 100-yard dash or throwing the discus are not games. Natural sport, whose outcome is the accomplishment of reaching a set objective, is another sport form which is not gamelike.

Moreover, some games are not sports, because their outcomes are primarily determined by chance or strategy rather than physical skill. Thus bridge, checkers, and monopoly are games but not sports.

It can be understood, therefore, that games and sports may often overlap and may be one and the same, as basketball. But some sports may not be games, as diving, and some games may not be sports, as checkers or running bases.

Play

It is impossible to define play as a class of activities, because its most notable quality is its lack of formal, predetermined structure. Many theorists[2] have

[2] J. Huizinga. *Homo Ludens*. Boston: The Beacon Press, 1955. (The most comprehensive book on play.)

viewed it as outside ordinary or real life and have thus found a way to set it apart from other activities. However, that appears to be a philosophical absurdity, since everything a human being does is part of that person's ordinary or real life.

Another complexity in defining play is that it is viewed as a behavior of animals and infants, as well as of adults, and therefore terms such as rules must be viewed in such broad contexts that only a vague resemblance exists to the idea of compliance to external designated factors. With this in mind, the following definition is offered:

Play is an enjoyable experience deriving from behavior which is self-initiated in accordance with personal goals or expressive impulses; it tolerates all ranges of movement abilities; its rules are spontaneous; it has a temporal sequence but no predetermined ending; it results in no tangible outcome, victory, or reward.

The relation of play to sport is a matter of some controversy. Some authorities believe that play is a generic concept and that sport is a more specific and refined version of play. After all, the term sport itself derives from the Middle English word *disporten,* which includes the concept of frolic or amusing oneself. Such an approach envisions a continuum with play and sport on different points. This theory has the advantage of paralleling the human process of growth and development from the simple to the more complex activity, from spontaneity to formal structure. However, the essence and the outcome of both activities are so different that nothing can be developed from this idea.

Another approach is to consider play an attitude rather than a phenomenon, so that one might engage in sport with or without a playful attitude. This concept is favored by theorists who would like to see sport played more for fun and less for victory. However, since sport by definition must have an outcome, it is difficult to understand why one would participate without wanting to achieve the prescribed goal. The playful attitude conflicts with this purpose. However, the intrinsic satisfaction always associated with play may also be found in sport, though the material rewards of sport, by definition, are not a part of play.

Recreation

Recreational activities, now called leisure-time activities because they are done during an individual's nonworking hours, may consist of almost any activity known to humans. The English tend to use the term physical recreation to refer to activities that demand a primary component of physical effort or bodily movement. In this way, hiking, swimming, skiing, and ice skating can be distinguished from reading, sewing, or watching television. It seems useful for our purposes to adopt this distinction, because that is our primary interest, and define physical recreation in the following manner:

Physical recreation encompasses identifiable activities different from those by which the individual earns a living and which require physical effort or bodily movement; it is undertaken voluntarily in accordance with personal interests and goals.

Sport can be a form of physical recreation provided it meets the criteria of the definition. Remember that what is work for one person may be recreation for another: the professional tennis player works, while the weekend player recreates on the same courts. One should also note that sport has a tendency to lose its voluntary quality. To meet adequately the challenge of competition, one generally must be willing to train and subject oneself to discipline both from the self and from others. Furthermore, sport usually involves teams and organizations; once a commitment is made to these groups, one is no longer free not to participate. Scholarship players and professional athletes must play when told to do so. Sport *may* be a form of recreation and vice versa; as with games there is an area of overlap.

Physical education

Physical education may be the hardest entity of all to define, as we saw in Chapter 1. Looking at curriculums past and present, one is prompted to recall the story of the five blind men who tried to describe an elephant. One standing near the trunk said it was a long narrow beast; another felt the legs and decided it resembled the trunk of a tree; still a third felt the tusks and said it was made of a very hard substance with a sharp point; the fourth felt its side and thought it like a wall; and the fifth held its tail and thought the elephant to be small and whiplike. On the premise that physical education is what each individual teacher says it is, it might be defined as the school-centered program of physical activities. Such a definition in effect says that any physical activities in an educational institution are part of physical education. It was probably this kind of definition that led to the inclusion of cheerleading and driver training in the physical education program. It also means that intramural, interscholastic, and intercollegiate sport contests are considered part of the physical education program, a concept ardently supported by many people. Another definition with a somewhat different focus can be stated this way:

Physical education is a program in which skills used in sport, dance, and exercise are taught and practiced. This definition includes many situations which are nonschool centered, such as community centers, YMCAs, camps, and day-care centers. Its principal component is that activities of a certain nature are presented in a situation *designed for learning.*

Many people prefer to generalize the nature of these activities as movement activities and the skills taught as movement skills, such as throwing and catching, running, striking, and gauging the spin and bounce of balls. However, since most skills are specific to the task, and should result in the ability to participate in specific sports, dances, and exercises, it seems appropriate to delineate the activities more precisely. Besides, movement forms include a wide range of activities, such as ploughing a field, scrubbing a floor, and building a cottage—none of which are considered to be part of physical education.

Our definition says that the organized sport activities connected with institutions are not part of the physical education program. However, there is a relationship that springs from the nature of the activities. Since participation on a sport team requires the learning and practice of certain skills, physical education is part of sport programs and vice versa. As with games and play, there is both overlap and separateness.

Related activities model

We can summarize and abstract this discussion by visual model, Figure 2.1, which depicts the relationship of the various terms. It should be remembered that this is only one possible model, based on one set of definitions. Other definitions and related models can have equal validity.[3] Students are

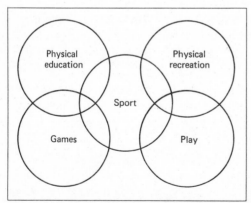

Figure 2.1 Relationships of physical activities

[3] An excellent definition of sport, which differs substantially from the one used here, is given in J. W. Loy, Jr., "The Nature of Sport: A Definitional Effort," *Quest,* X, May 1968, pp. 1–15. That article and numerous others on the subject are reprinted in E. W. Gerber, ed., *Sport and the Body: A Philosophical Symposium.* Philadelphia: Lea & Febiger, 1972.

encouraged to try to develop their own taxonomy with accompanying schematic drawings.

From this look at terminology, it should be easy for you to understand the logic of selecting sport as the focal point for study by those who are preparing to be physical education teachers. As the related activities model suggests, those people who are interested in careers related to physical activity will want to have a clear understanding of the central phenomenon: sport. This need, then, has led to the development of the discipline of sport science, which enables people to study sport in a formal, academic setting.

The formal study of sport

Gerald S. Kenyon, in a paper "A Sociology of Sport: On Becoming a Sub-Discipline," presented a classic statement:

To be a discipline implies among other things, having as an objective *the understanding of some portion of reality*—that is, *its description, its explanation, and sometimes its prediction.* A profession, on the other hand, has as its fundamental goal the altering of some aspects of reality with a view to improving the lot of mankind. . . . It follows, therefore, that arguing that a given field can be simultaneously a profession and a discipline is little else save a logical contradiction of terms. The only solution to this dilemma would be to recognize that, while it is possible for the same phenomenon to serve as the focal point of both the profession and a discipline (subject matter for one, a medium for the other), it is there the similarity ends. Thus, the expression "physical education," with its obvious professional connotations, is not a suitable label for both the professional and disciplinary aspects of human physical activity. However, because of its widespread currency, and despite the semantic difficulties long alluded to, the term might be retained, but in a restricted sense. Those who would use physical activity to change behavior—whether it be cognitive, affective, or psychomotor—we may term physical educators. On the other hand, those whose objective is to understand the phenomenon, we may consider members of a discipline, the name of which is still a topic of much debate.

Regardless of the nomenclature that meets with the greatest favor, there is no logical reason why the study of all the various manifestations of sport, exercise, and dance cannot be put under a single umbrella, one that could include the traditional approaches, whether they be scientific or humanistic. It is conceivable that certain subfields would emerge, based primarily on different approaches to truth, and perhaps, to some extent, on interest in particular forms of physical activity. Thus, one major classification may be the *sport sciences,* which in turn could be subdivided into the physical science of sport, the biological science of sport, and the social science of sport.[4]

[4]G. S. Kenyon. "A Sociology of Sport: On Becoming a Sub-Discipline," in R. C. Brown and B. J. Cratty, eds., *New Perspectives of Man in Action.* Englewood Cliffs, N.J.: Prentice-Hall, 1969, pp. 164–165.

Kenyon, in one fell swoop, justifies the need for the existence of a sociology of sport, as well as other subdisciplines of sport, within a broad disciplinary interpretation with some undetermined name. This led Thomas Sheehan to conclude that since sport has been a part of physical education at least since its American inception, we can eliminate most of our problems by restructuring physical education to include *only* the study of sport. Thus, we could concentrate, rather than scatter our attention, especially on subjects that are too broad or are included in other academic disciplines.[5] As Kenyon has concluded, it is possible to study the characteristics of sport (as a discipline) and it is also possible to use sport to benefit people (as a profession). With this concept, although it does not conflict with the history of physical education, the term physical education is not defined as anything, but simply discarded. The disciplinary title would be "sport science" or "sport studies," denotating more accurately the kinds of studies and professional practices carried on. For many, a "sport science" may be a presumptuous title, but if there can be a political science, why not a sport science? Whether sport science or sport studies, the structure of the discipline is the same.

Clark V. Whited writes about the concept of sport science that:

For more than a decade, various leaders have recognized the desirability of securing recognition for physical education as a separate discipline and of encouraging broader and more intensive investigation of man in our culture. The task has been to devise a conceptual model of an academic discipline for physical education that would be true to our heritage, clear and decisive enough to give direction and vigor to our efforts, and relevant to today's modern cultural patterns. If our field is to continue to develop and provide effective leadership for our society, it must accept the responsibilities for a broader portion of the study of man in an area as yet unclaimed by other disciplines.

The concept of sport science, the modern academic discipline for physical education in the 1970s, fulfills the task requirement in every respect. This is not just a visionary, theoretical concept under lengthy philosophical discussion to be attempted some time in the future, but is an actuality for one of the largest undergraduate programs in the country.[6]

Whited here refers to the curriculum at the State University College at Brockport, New York—the first undergraduate program of sport science in the United States; West Virginia University had presented one at the graduate level.

Harold J. VanderZwaag, a physical educator, contended that sport studies and exercise science go hand in hand as the focus of physical education and would eventually replace the concept of human movement:

---

[5] T. J. Sheehan. "Sport: The Focal Point of Physical Education."*Quest,* May 1963, pp. 59–67.

[6] C. V. Whited. "Sport Science." *Journal of Physical Education and Recreation,* May 1971, p. 21.

. . . physical education should not and will not be replaced by the concept of human movement. There has been a tendency to contrast the profession of physical education with the discipline of human movement. The net result is a comparison of one abstract entity with another. Both abstractions have risen from the search for appropriate umbrellas. In this search, concrete components have been overlooked. These components are sport and exercise.[7]

John W. Loy, Jr., also emphasizes the fact that sport science is an alternative to human movement. He stated that

. . . several leading physical educators have suggested that human movement provides a particular focus of attention for physical education; and they have indicated that the study of human movement using different modes of inquiry can result in the establishment of a unique body of knowledge. One may legitimately ask, however, whether human movement is the only viable focal point for a discipline-oriented physical education. We contend that sport provides an equally viable focal point and strongly suggest that the study of sport is more likely to result in a body of knowledge related to physical education than is the study of human movement.[8]

Is sport an important human activity to study? Sociologists tell us that sport is a social institution; it solves, or aids in the solution of, certain problems in society. If problems such as maintaining the cultural behavorial patterns, reducing tensions, adapting to the environment, and racial integration, for example, are not taken care of, the social system will soon collapse. Sport is said to help solve the problem of integration and thus becomes very meaningful to any society. Other social institutions such as power structures, religion, schools, economic systems, and the family—all are studied, but sport has not been, at least not until very recently. In addition, all social systems on record have had some form of sport.

Contemporary physical educators have proposed that sport be studied by first compartmentalizing certain characteristics for separate study. For example, the functional elements of sport consist of the rules, boundaries, and tasks indigenous to all existing forms. Further, (1) sport has a history; (2) groups interact in sport (sociology of sport); (3) individuals are motivated to enter and leave sport and something happens to them as they engage in this activity (psychology of sport); (4) in order to participate actively, people must possess a certain degree of motor skill (sport-skill acquisition and/or motor learning,

[7]H. J. VanderZwaag. "Historical Relationships Between Concepts of Sport and Physical Education." *Proceedings of the National College Physical Education Association for Men.* Minneapolis, Minn.: The Association, December 1969, p. 88.

[8]J. W. Loy, Jr. "Sport Science: The Academic Dimension of Physical Education," in R. N. Singer et al., *Physical Education: An Interdisciplinary Approach.* New York: The Macmillan Co., 1972, p. 173.

and sport biomechanics); (5) individuals are affected organically (sport physiology); and (6) sport has meaning (sport philosophy). Investigating these characteristics will yield a body of knowledge that, in turn, will make possible questions of interrelationships, such as, "What is the effect upon physiological efficiency of varying degrees of aggressive behaviors in sport?" Any questions the sport scientist asks as an academic disciplinarian are limited to how, when, where, and with whom sport functions. Whether sport is beneficial or nonbeneficial to a particular social group or whether it should be an environment for personal involvement are questions related to the function of the professional.

The professional, or practitioner of sport-science studies, must comprehend the many components of sport through a college or university program. It is absolutely necessary that people who anticipate a career in sport have a deep understanding of *all* the sport forms of their society. This is slightly different from the traditional physical education curriculum, which teaches the student a certain degree of skill and knowledge about the rules, boundaries, and tasks of only a few selected sport forms. A traditional physical educator may have a fairly good background in badminton, for example, but be totally ignorant of the sport form of skiing. Just as it is expected that a literature major know and understand all literary forms, so it is also expected that a sport scientist know and understand all sport forms. In addition, the professional sport scientist should have significant knowledge about the biomechanics, history, sociology, psychology, physiology, and philosophy of sport. So prepared, the sport scientist is then ready to begin a career. This career *may* be teaching, but there are others. Sport scientists who master an undergraduate program have a choice of the following career areas:

1. Sport equipment manufacturing
2. Sport equipment design
3. Sport equipment research
4. Sport radio and television broadcasting and operations
5. Sport journalism
6. Sport costume design
7. Sport facilities management
8. Sport facilities planning
9. Sport facilities construction
10. Sport equipment sales
11. Sport law
12. Sport publicity
13. Sport information direction
14. Sport teams management
15. Community sport recreational supervision
16. Sport for the handicapped and disadvantaged

17. Sport nutrition research
18. Sport training or paramedical practice
19. Sport promotion
20. Sport medicine
21. Sport art
22. Sport insurance
23. Sport safety
24. Sport publications and training in film production

It is felt that these and perhaps many other career patterns are at the disposal of the sport scientist. At the undergraduate level the student is exposed to three different educational concentrations: (1) general education; (2) the curriculum in sport science which is concerned only with the body of knowledge about sport (and not how to teach it); and (3) special or professionally oriented experiences. This latter category could be educational methodology courses if one wishes to teach, or courses in journalism, business management, and so forth, to prepare for a selected career. This scheme also includes the possibility of graduate study in sport history, psychology of sport, and so forth, enabling the person to teach at a college or university and to perform needed research in the area of specialization.

This, then, is a brief analysis of the potential for sport science, or sport studies, to replace the traditional physical education program. In keeping with

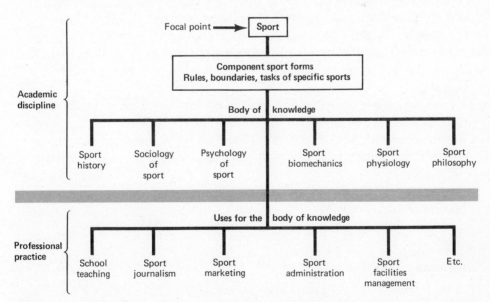

Figure 2.2 Structure of the potential of sport science as an academic discipline and as a profession

the concept of human movement, sport science does distinguish between disciplinary and professional aspects. Diagrammatically the structure of these two complementary functions would appear as shown in Figure 2.2.

Summary

1. *Sport* is a human activity that involves specific administrative organization and a historical background of rules which define the objective and limit the pattern of human behavior; it involves competition and/or challenge and a definite outcome primarily determined by physical skill.
2. *Games* are activities with an agreed-on organization of time, space, and terrain, with rules that define the objective and limit the pattern of human behavior; the outcome, which is to determine a winner and a loser, is achieved by totaling or accumulating objectively scored points or successes.
3. *Play* is an enjoyable experience deriving from behavior which is self-initiated in accordance with personal goals or expressive impulses; it tolerates all ranges of movement abilities; its rules are spontaneous; it has a temporal sequence but no predetermined ending; it results in no tangible outcome, victory, or reward.
4. *Physical recreation* encompasses identifiable activities different from those by which the individual earns a living and which require physical effort and/or bodily movement; it is undertaken voluntarily in accordance with personal interests and goals.
5. *Physical education* is a program in which skills used in sport, dance, and exercise activities are taught and practiced in a situation designed for learning.
6. *Sport science* is a discipline that enables the formal, academic study of sport.
7. Various characteristics of sport, including its history, sociology, psychology, skill acquisition, biomechanics, physiology, and philosophy, can be studied separately.
8. Numerous career opportunities are open to people who study to become sport scientists.

Questions

1. What is the essential component of a sport activity?
2. How do you compare the British understanding of the term athletics with the North American?

3. How similar and different are the terms play and sport?
4. Is physical recreation part of physical education or of recreation? Support your answer.
5. Explain the differences between physical education and recreation to a neophyte in these two areas.
6. Would you consider a basketball lesson offered in a YMCA program to be physical education?
7. Enumerate some of the central issues that sport scientists should address themselves to.
8. Which aspects of sport are important to study in preparing for the profession of physical education?
9. Enumerate existing social institutions and compare the influence and role of sport in the power structure.
10. What advantages and disadvantages would you envision if the term physical education became a sport science?
11. Many undergraduates are not really interested in teaching, but take a teaching certification to feel more secure. In terms of career patterns in sport science, would you encourage this kind of thinking?
12. Design a course of study (a) for a physical education major interested in sport journalism and (b) for a journalism major interested in sport science.

OBJECTIVES OF PHYSICAL EDUCATION, MOVEMENT EDUCATION, AND SPORT SCIENCE EDUCATION

Function of the school

Frequently, people use the terms *school* and *education* synonymously. *School,* however, refers to the social institution, and *education* refers to the process and the product that takes place in or out of the school. The school is responsible for a particular kind of education. Being a social institution, it is designed to solve a functional social difficulty, such as we discussed in Chapter 2, when we considered sport as a social institution. In every society, confusion would result if each new member had to learn its values and behavior patterns by a trial-and-error method. These values and behavior patterns constitute the society's culture. Each society assimilates new members by teaching the culture in the most expeditious fashion. For centuries in our society, this task has been the responsibility of the school, the place where the old pass on to the young knowledge about how to function in society. Or put another way, the school is responsible for the perpetuation of the culture—enculturation.

At first glance, this passing on of the culture may seem a not too difficult task. After all, you may say, I have gone through twelve or fourteen years of schooling without finding the process so confusing or mysterious. In a few years, if you become a teacher, you will be on the other side of the desk and will see the school as considerably more complex.

The school, as a social institution, developed through specialization. As civilization found more efficient ways to control the environment, individuals realized that by grouping together, they could implement these controls more easily. One person or one family performed more specialized tasks. Rather than build a shelter, make protective clothes, and grow or hunt and process food, people performed one of these activities for themselves and others. In this way they became proficient in specific tasks and saved valuable time. As the single person, or the family group, became more specialized, the responsibility of enculturation of offspring became more difficult to bear. This job was then entrusted to another group within the social system—the teachers—eventuating in the institution of the school. In effect the teacher concludes that "if some people build my house, others attend to my nutritional needs, and still others perform other tasks for me, I will enculturate the new members of our society."

Establishing the process and norms of enculturation, however, has posed perennial problems. How does one define the characteristics of a particular culture? You have been enculturated to a measurable extent—what is your answer? Discuss this with your classmates and see if you can arrive at a representative list of the behavior patterns expected in your society. If it is extremely taxing to agree, and it is, even in such a small group as your class, think how much more difficult it would be if you included more people in the discussion.

The school as a social institution receives its mission from the needs of the society; if those needs change, those responsible for the mission of the school must be sensitive to the changes and flexible enough to make certain that these needs are being met. In fact, this is the responsibility of the teacher. Teachers are licensed to interpret the culture and pass it on to those in their charge.

The discipline of physical education in the school

Physical educators have an equal responsibility with their colleagues in other disciplines to be aware of society's needs. If physical educators are to play a role in the school, what they teach must have sufficient value in the enculturation of society's children and young adults, or physical education should be stricken from the curriculum. Physical educators must impress upon society that their subject matter is indispensable to enculturation. It may seem easier for language arts teachers, physical science teachers, or reading teachers to justify their role in the educational process. But physical educators must attain this same level of justification, pointing to the significant contribution they can make.

As we pointed out in Chapter 1, justification requires a clear definition of physical education. Whether physical education aids and abets enculturation is dependent upon whether youths need to study to function in their social system. Is the body of knowledge constituting physical education a necessary part of contemporary education? You must come to grips with this question at this stage of your academic development. The knowledge and skill you are now acquiring is what you will probably be teaching in the near future. Ultimately, this is what you will be asked to justify as a viable part of your total education.

The inclusion of physical education, and its accompanying body of knowledge, in the school curriculum places the burden of accomplishment on you as a prospective physical education teacher. It is through teaching that youths emerge armed with these desirable skills and necessary knowledge.

Generally, when the physical educator functions in the classroom or gymnasium, three interrelated processes are involved: planning, teaching, and evaluation. These can be shown diagrammatically as:

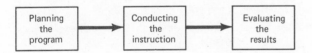

Of course, there are many techniques and methods in each of the above processes, but the teacher will have to work out his or her own instructional behavior in at least planning, teaching, and evaluating. The first thing a teacher does in preparing a program of instruction is to plan. This planning must be detailed and exact so that the activity selected, physical or verbal, can bring about the desired results. These results are commonly called *objectives,* statements about the learning possibilities inherent in the selected activities.

Next, the teacher introduces the students to the activities or instructional program, explaining to the students what they are doing and supervising their practice. The next phase, one frequently overlooked by teachers of all disciplines, is *evaluation.* Having planned experiences and learning objectives and conducted the students' practice, the teacher now seeks to determine whether the program has been successful. Through testing, the teacher receives measurements, or data, which indicate whether the student really has a degree of mastery of the intended objectives. To justify to others that real learning takes place in a physical education program, this third step is absolutely necessary. If little or no learning actually occurred, the teacher has a number of alternatives. In the diagram shown on page 45 the lines leading from the evaluating phase back to the teaching and planning steps illustrate these alternatives. If the teaching has been ineffective, the teacher can restructure the actual instructional phase or revert to the planning stage and readjust the objectives to make them more realistic.

Objectives of physical education programs

What are the possible outcomes of physical education? What does the physical educator intend to accomplish in planning a program? What are the objectives of the program in physical education? Physical education cannot and will not accomplish the total school education of youth. Its objectives, therefore, are conditioned and limited by exactly what is possible, given a specific focus for the field of physical education. For example, the objectives of a sport science program would be different from a movement education program. Before we enumerate these differences, let us look at more traditional objectives of physical education in the school.

At one time it seemed desirable to establish both an aim and an objective for school-oriented programs in physical education. An aim is broader than an objective, a very general statement of the ultimate, desired ends of the physical

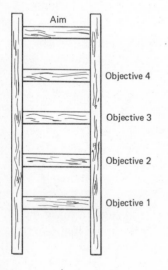

Figure 3.1 The ladder of the aim and the objectives

education program. Although an aim has some utility, it is by definition so encompassing that realizing it is improbable. Objectives, on the other hand, are attainable, and are steps in the direction of an aim. We can liken these two ideas to a ladder of which the top rung is the idea. From Figure 3.1 it can be seen that as students realize each objective, they come closer to fulfilling the stated aim. Karl W. Bookwalter and Harold J. VanderZwaag have stated that the aim of physical education "is the optimum development, integration, and adjustment physically, mentally, and socially of the individual through guided instruction and participation in selected total-body sports, rhythmic, and gymnastic activities conducted according to social and hygienic standards."[1]

To gain some insight into traditional objectives in physical education we should review the conclusions of a sample of authoritative analysts. Helen Fabricius has presented objectives for an elementary school program which are quite similar to the objectives for a physical education program at any school-age level. She classifies the objectives in five areas:

I. Physical Development
   This is the unique contribution of physical education to the school program. No other subject in the curriculum is primarily concerned with the development of physical endurance, strength, and coordination.
   A. To develop strength of muscle groups—primarily those of the shoulder area, trunk, legs, and feet.
   B. To develop endurance—ability to perform physical activity for increasingly longer periods of time without undue strain or fatigue.
   C. Through strength and endurance to increase control of the body so that it will assure the individual's health and safety.
   D. To understand the value of exercise to health, and to develop pride in one's physical accomplishments and the development of the body.
II. Physical Skills—Basic and Recreational
   A. To learn the basic skills correctly—walking, running, bending, lifting, climbing, dodging, falling, relaxation; for efficient, fatigueless, creative, and safe use of the body.
   B. To learn sport and rhythmic or dance skills—for ability to participate in such activities with confidence and security.
   C. To explore one's physical capacity—and limitations—in relation to the environment, including one's own body.
III. Individual Emotional Development
   A. To gradually, but consistently, improve in self-control, self-discipline, and self-direction; to do what is right and/or acceptable without threats or help from others; to control self in "stress" situations.
   B. To play according to the rules, whether observed or not; to be honest.

[1] K. W. Bookwalter and H. J. VanderZwaag. *Foundations and Principles of Physical Education.* Philadelphia: W. B. Saunders Company, 1969, p. 4.

    C. To grow in self-confidence, courage, initiative and poise, willing to try new things.

    D. To recognize one's strengths and limitations, and to accept them as part of "knowing thyself."

IV. Social Development—Human-relations Skills

    A. To learn to be a contributing group member; to listen to and follow directions; to cooperate with the group for the welfare of all; to carry responsibilities as a team member or a leader. The playground is a laboratory for learning how to get along with others.

    B. To begin to learn that life is governed and made more pleasant and fruitful for all by adherence to certain unwritten social customs, rules, and traditions.

    C. To try to be a good sport; to win without gloating or razzing the loser; to lose without griping, arguing, or making alibis.

    D. To be courteous to and thoughtful of one's playmates and peers.

    E. To learn "to take it" gracefully.

V. Fun

    A. To participate in physical activities with joy and enthusiasm.

    B. To achieve release of physical and mental tension through activity.

    C. By successful and enjoyable participation in activity, to use physical activities as after-school and leisure-time activities.

    D. To become aware of the role of sports in American life, and to enjoy participating as a player and/or as a spectator.[2]

Beverly L. Seidel and Matthew C. Resick have also concluded that the objectives of the school program fall into five categories:

1. Organic development and physical fitness
2. Skill development
3. Emotional health
4. Mental development
5. Social development[3]

The slight variation between these two sets of objectives arises because the first was developed for the elementary school level and the second for physical education programs at any level. Seidel and Resick add that the development of a positive self-concept, acceptance as a member of a team, increased enjoyment of sports activities, and the ability to relax and forget study pressures can also be considered worthwhile objectives.

Many physical educators agree that Jesse F. Williams does justice to combining, in schematic form, the idea of an aim and objectives in physical education, as shown in Figure 3.2. Williams' objectives are development of organic systems, development of neuromuscular skills, development of interest

[2] H. Fabricius. *Physical Education for the Classroom Teacher.* Dubuque, Iowa: William C. Brown Company, 1971, pp. 9–11.

[3] B. L. Seidel and M. C. Resick. *Physical Education: An Overview.* Reading, Mass.: Addison-Wesley Publishing Company, Inc., 1972, pp. 41–42.

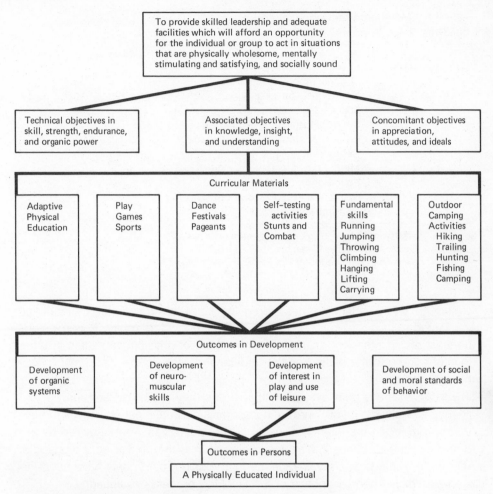

Figure 3.2 Williams' analysis of the aim of physical education
Source: Reproduced by permission from J. F. Williams, *The Principles of Physical Education,*
8th Ed., Philadelphia: W. B. Saunders Company, 1964.

in play and use of leisure, and development of social and moral standards of behavior.

In 1969, Joel Rosentswieg asked 100 physical educators in Texas to rank ten objectives. His findings are shown in Table 3.1.

In 1970, Anthony A. Annarino provided an outstanding analysis of what he terms "the five traditional objectives of physical education," shown in Table 3.2. You will observe that Annarino's five objectives are organic, neuromuscular, interpretive, social, and emotional, which serves to sum up the lists of objectives we have considered above.

Table 3.1.   Most important physical education
objectives, listed in priority order

Rank	Objective
1	Organic vigor
2	Neuromuscular skills
3	Leisure-time activities
4	Self-realization
5	Emotional stability
6	Democratic values
7	Mental development
8	Social competency
9	Spiritual and moral strength
10	Cultural appreciation

Source: J. Rosentswieg, "A Ranking of the Objectives of Physical
Education," *Research Quarterly,* December 1969, p. 785. By
permission of American Alliance for Health, Physical Education,
& Recreation.

Although we have labeled these foregoing objectives traditional, they are still
considered valid by a large number of physical educators today. Regardless of
the most recent pleas for change, most teachers of physical education in our
country adhere to the belief that the traditional objectives are being met
through participation in their program. The question you might entertain at this
time is: "Can these objectives be realized? Are they too broad and too
all-encompassing?" If you were to incorporate the traditional objectives in your
future program, in the interest of being accountable, you would have to be able
to measure the student's achievement to show that the objectives are possible.
After all, providing conclusive evidence that your program goals have been met
is an extremely important phase of the teaching process—*evaluation.*

Objectives of movement education

Advocates of the human-movement theory in physical education maintain that
movement education in the schools requires new physical educational
objectives. This is reasonable because of the changes in the activities and,
ultimately, the learning objectives of these activities. The physical educator must
not impose on the program objectives that are impossible to obtain. Only
certain learning can come from certain school activities; through physical
education the individual consumer cannot become "totally educated."

John E. Nixon and Ann E. Jewett have extended the interpretation of the aims and objectives of movement educators. They assert that "organized physical education should aim to make the maximal contribution to the optimal development of the individual's potentialities in all phases of life, by placing him in an environment which will promote the movement and related responses or activities that will best contribute to this purpose."[4] They go on to caution us that to attain this aim only those objectives should be selected which will reflect a consistent change in the behavior of our students. Their choice of objectives is outlined in five sections.

1. To develop a basic understanding and appreciation of human movement. This broad objective involves (a) the development of understanding and appreciation of the deeper, more significant human meanings and values acquired through idea-directed movement experience; (b) an appreciation of human movement as an essential nonverbal mode of human expression; (c) the development of a positive self-concept and body image through appropriate movement experience; and (d) the development of key concepts through volitional movements and closely related nonverbal learning activities.
2. To develop and maintain optimal individual muscular strength, muscular endurance, and cardiovascular endurance. It is customary to refer to this purpose as the "physical fitness" objective. Many authors expand it to include such factors as flexibility, balance, agility, power, and speed. It is essential to develop not only skills, but also knowledge and understanding relevant to physical fitness.
3. To develop individual movement potentialities to the optimal level for each individual. Physical education instruction concentrates on the development of selected neuromuscular skills, and on the refinement of fundamental movement patterns basic to specific skills.
4. To develop skills, knowledges, and attitudes essential to satisfying, enjoyable physical recreation experiences engaged in voluntarily throughout one's lifetime. Normal mental and emotional health are enhanced by participation in voluntary physical recreation.
5. To develop socially acceptable and personally rewarding behaviors through participation in movement activities. Physical education instruction seeks to develop desirable social habits, attitudes, and personal characteristics essential to citizens in a free, democratic society.[5]

Joan Tillotson, with a more specific aim of movement education, stated that "the *aim* of movement education is to develop an awareness of the self in the physical environment, the body and its capabilities, and the components of movement responses of each child in every class."[6] Although she has not

[4] J. E. Nixon and A. E. Jewett. *An Introduction to Physical Education,* 8th ed. Philadelphia: W. B. Saunders Company, 1974, p. 86.

[5] *Ibid.,* p. 90.

[6] J. Tillotson. "A Brief Theory of Movement Education," in R. T. Sweeney, ed. *Selected Readings in Movement Education.* Reading, Mass. Addison-Wesley Publishing Company, Inc., 1970, p. 34.

Table 3.2. Developmental objectives of physical education

Organic	Neuromuscular	Interpretive
Proper functioning of the body systems so that the individual may adequately meet the demands placed upon him by his environment. A foundation for skill development.	A harmonious functioning of the nervous and muscular systems to produce desired movements.	The ability to explore, to discover, to understand, to acquire knowledge, and to make value judgments.
Muscle Strength	Locomotor Skills	A knowledge of game rules, safety measures, and etiquette.
The maximum amount of force exerted by a muscle or muscle group.	Walking; Skipping; Sliding; Leaping; Pushing; Running; Galloping; Hopping; Rolling; Pulling	The use of strategies and techniques involved in organized activities.
Muscle Endurance	Nonlocomotor Skills	A knowledge of how the body functions and its relationship to physical activity.
The ability of a muscle or muscle group to sustain effort for a prolonged period of time.	Swaying; Twisting; Shaking; Stretching; Bending; Handing; Stooping	A development of appreciation for personal performance. The use of judgment related to distance, time, space, force, speed, and direction in the use of activity implements, balls, and self.
Cardiovascular Endurance	Game-type Fundamental Skills	
The capacity of an individual to persist in strenuous activity for periods of some duration. This is dependent upon the combined efficiency of the blood vessels, heart, and lungs.	Striking; Catching; Kicking; Stopping; Throwing; Batting; Starting; Changing direction	
	Motor Factors	An understanding of growth and developmental factors affected by movement.
Flexibility	Accuracy; Rhythm; Kinesthetic awareness; Power; Balance; Reaction time; Agility	The ability to solve developmental problems through movement.
The range of motion in joints needed to produce efficient movement and to minimize injury.	Sport Skills	
	Soccer; Softball; Volleyball; Wrestling; Track & Field; Football; Baseball; Basketball; Archery; Speedball; Hockey; Fencing; Golf; Bowling; Tennis	
	Recreational Skills	
	Shuffleboard; Croquet; Deck tennis; Hiking; Table tennis; Swimming; Horseshoes; Boating	

Social	Emotional
An adjustment to both self and others by an integration of the individual into society and his environment.	A healthy response to physical activity through a fulfillment of basic needs.
The ability to make judgments in a group situation.	The development of positive reactions in spectatorship and participation through either success or failure.
Learning to communicate with others.	The release of tension through suitable physical activities.
The ability to exchange and evaluate ideas within a group.	An outlet for self-expression and creativity.
The development of the social phases of personality, attitudes, and values in order to become a functioning member of society.	An appreciation of the aesthetic experiences derived from correlated activities.
The development of a sense of belonging and acceptance by society.	The ability to have fun.
The development of positive personality traits.	
Learnings for constructive use of leisure time.	
A development of attitude that reflects good moral character.	

Source: A. A. Annarino, "The Five Traditional Objectives of Physical Education," *Journal of Physical Education and Recreation,* June 1970, p. 25. By permission of American Alliance of Health, Physical Education, & Recreation.

stated them as objectives Tillotson does list guidelines for evaluating desirable outcomes of a program in movement education.

1. Is respect for individual's worth instilled through your methodology?
2. Is respect for equipment instilled?
3. Are self-respect and self-control fostered?
4. Is alertness gained through listening, moving, and thinking?
5. Is there a carry-over of movement practices evident from problem solving of individual problems, into game, rhythmic, and stunt activities?
6. Is there a keener sense of kinesthetic awareness apparent through movement practice?
7. Are the children conscious of safety actions?
8. Do individuals think for themselves?
9. Do children recognize qualities of movement in other children?
10. Can a child take an idea given by one child and use it so that his movement pattern is improved?[7]

Objectives of sport science education

Because sport science education often leads to teaching, advocates of this approach have postulated learning outcomes for their program in the schools. As this concept is purposely more restrictive than others about physical education, the objectives of its school program are less involved. It seeks to provide students with an environment wherein they may assimilate the knowledge and skills associated with sport as a sociocultural phenomenon. The student is consciously enculturated only to the extent possible through the phenomenon of sport. Part of enculturation is accomplished through a knowledge and understanding of the historical heritage, the prevailing economic system, or the existing government structure, among the many disciplines offered in the schools. Because sport is a product of the social system and is related to the culture, the student should have an opportunity to become conversant with it. Whether or not people are going to be active participants, sport will affect directly or indirectly the way they live.

Sport as a disciplinary study in colleges and universities is dependent on what teachers present in the school; they must become totally involved with how, what, when, where, and why sport exists in particular societies. They must know the components or elements of how sport operates. Just as social science teachers know about social systems and literature teachers know the form and content of literature, sport science teachers know the characteristics of sport.

[7] *Ibid.,* pp. 37–38.

The sport science teacher has two general objectives:

1. Providing knowledge and skills related to sport and various sport forms.
2. Modifying social behavior through participation in sport forms.

More specifically, the types of learning particular to the school have been differentiated as cognitive, affective, and psychomotor. Cognitive learning is related to knowledge, affective learning to value and attitude internalization, and psychomotor learning to motor-skill acquisition. In terms of the objectives of sport science education, knowledge of the rules, boundaries, and tasks of sport forms (for example, football, field hockey), and an understanding of why sport exists in social systems, individual motivation for participation, physiological benefits, and so forth, are cognitive aspects of the program. Psychomotor aspects include the actual motor skills involved in actual sport participation. Familiarizing students with the cognitive knowledge and psychomotor skills associated with sport forms (for example, badminton, bowling, and so forth) is the first general objective for the sport science teacher.

Affective learning aspects of sport science education are a bit more complex. Because traditional physical education has always devoted some concentration on the knowledge and skills required for sports, teachers in the field have recorded great success in these areas. Physical educators, however, have not been as proficient at modifying social behavior, even though sport activities do contain structural characteristics that lend themselves to this kind of learning. There is conclusive evidence that sport reflects the values, norms, and social structure of the social system in which it is found. We also know that youths do learn social behavior. Why is it not possible, then, for the sport curriculum to teach, or to reinforce, those social patterns particular to our society? As a matter of fact, the sport curriculum is the only phase of the school where this is possible. The sport program, one for all students, is the only school environment that is a direct imitation of social life outside the school, although it avoids some of the real consequences. What better environment could there be for students to learn the principles of social processes (competition, cooperation, social conflict, assimilation, and accommodation) and practice them in a situation where they would not be severely penalized if they make a mistake? To accomplish this, much more expertness will be demanded of the teacher of sport, and much more information and skill about group dynamics and about the techniques of behavior modification will have to be acquired by the teacher.

Summary

1. The school is the social institution, and education is the process and the product that takes place in the school and out of the school.
2. Seidel and Resick have concluded that the objectives of the school physical education program are (1) organic development and physical fitness; (2) skill development; (3) emotional health; (4) mental development; and (5) social development.
3. Nixon and Jewett state that organized physical education should aim to make the maximal contribution to the optimal development of the individual's potentialities in all phases of life by placing him in an environment which will promote the movement and related responses or activities that will best contribute to this purpose.
4. Nixon and Jewett express the objective of human movement as (1) to develop a basic understanding and appreciation of human movement; (2) to develop and maintain optimal individual muscular strength, muscular endurance, and cardiovascular endurance; (3) to develop individual movement potentialities to the optimal level for each individual; (4) to develop skills, knowledges, and attitudes essential to satisfying, enjoyable physical recreation experiences engaged in voluntarily throughout one's lifetime; and (5) to develop socially acceptable and personally rewarding behaviors through participation in movement activities.
5. The sport science teacher has two general objectives: (1) providing knowledge and skills related to sport and various sport forms, and (2) modifying social behavior through participation in sport forms.

Questions

1. What is the unique contribution of physical education to the enculturation of new members of society?
2. Why must physical educators strive harder than their fellow teachers to justify their role in the school educational process?
3. Let's assume that many of your fellow teachers in areas other than physical education have misconceptions of and prejudices against physical education. Could you explain simply and effectively why you are as important as any other teacher in that school?
4. Identify the three most important steps a teacher must take into account when preparing a program of instruction.
5. In what ways would the objectives of a sport science program be different from those of a movement education program?
6. In view of your previous exposure to physical education in elementary and

      secondary schools, discuss the desirability of developing new objectives and/or retaining traditional objectives.

7. How do you relate the accountability of the teacher to program objectives?
8. Select a specific grade level and design a set of objectives (a) for a movement education-oriented program; (b) for a sport science-oriented program.
9. What is meant exactly by the cognitive, affective, and psychomotor learning domains? How do you relate them (a) to a specific game situation? (b) to your undergraduate education?
10. Eventually you will have to develop and change attitudes toward physical education. What kind of knowledge and skill will be required of you?

HISTORY OF ORGANIZED PHYSICAL ACTIVITY

Evidence of organized physical activity—games, sports, simulated work, exercise, and dance—is found in archeological artifacts, literature, and art from the earliest societies to the most modern ones. These activities were simple recreational pursuits as well as spontaneous and formal contests and tournaments; they were promoted in schools and other social institutions. Physical education, or a learning-centered program of physical activity, has been thought necessary by many societies. It has ranged from the informal one-to-one instruction given by parents to their children to the highly structured course of study offered in schools today.

Popular physical activities, such as ball playing, wrestling, swimming, dancing, hurling warlike implements, racing, have shown a remarkable similarity across time and cultures. Somewhat more variable than the kinds of activities have been the motivations behind them. Societies in different times and places seemed to have planned their activities with different ends in view, depending, of course, upon what were conceived to be the most pressing needs. Writers and artists in those societies set forth rationales for physical activity emphasizing these different purposes, which were often logically associated with the kinds of activity favored.

We will examine the history of organized physical activity in terms of the three primary motifs in undertaking programs of sport and exercise. It must be understood, however, that although a single motif—survival, competition and reward, or social development—may have been *foremost* in a given society's hierarchy of purposes, other ideas certainly coexisted with it. Furthermore, humans have shown a remarkable capacity to do their own thing and maintain their private motivations no matter what the prevailing social purpose. Through this thematic approach, you will understand how certain activity forms lend themselves to various purposes and comprehend more clearly the relationship and continuity of certain modes of activity and rationales through many centuries.

Physical activity for survival

The most fundamental requirement for all living beings and for all social groups is physical survival. Like the politician whose first duty is to get elected, only a live individual or a going society can attempt to deal with other, seemingly more significant issues. The fact that physical survival is inherently related to the quality of an individual's existence means that survival is directly related to good health and/or physical fitness. Individuals must be able to defend themselves against the "enemy"—disease, deterioration of physical capacity, and literal threats from other humans or natural forces in the environment. Individuals must also have the strength and physical capacity to perform the tasks required and/or chosen for daily living. Since a society is composed of individuals, it is obvious that the health and fitness of its citizens is of first concern for collective survival.

In order to ensure physical survival, individuals and social groups have devised activities, methods, and programs designed to "up the odds." These techniques in some places have enabled humans to double their life span compared to that of early tribes. Examples of aids to survival have been advances in the field of medicine, invention of laborsaving devices and protective equipment, better understanding of human physical needs, increased world agricultural productivity, and, of course, the development of weaponry.

Concomitantly, physical activity—primarily exercise and sport—has been designed to enhance personal and, by extension, group survival in two distinct ways. First in chronological development, sport became a vehicle for learning and practicing skills necessary for survival. For example, the skills necessary to throw a rock or a spear to bring down an animal during the hunt or an enemy warrior were abstracted into sports forms such as the shotput or javelin throw. Children and adults played and competed at shotputting and javelin throwing with the expectation that these skills would be transformed at the proper moment into rock- and spear-throwing abilities. Second, when human societies became more specialized, those people freed from physical labor learned to do exercise and sport activities to maintain physical capacities sufficient to respond to both ordinary and emergency demands.

The problem of learning the physical skills necessary for survival and of keeping oneself in a state of fitness and readiness for action has not been the same throughout all history. In some societies, such as our own contemporary American one, skills necessary for survival cannot be learned through sport. Emergencies are met by specially trained groups, for example, police, fire fighters, soldiers.

But in some societies—both ancient and modern—survival has been a primary problem and children *must* be educated in the means of survival. Therefore other interests and values must be subjugated to those which ensure personal health and military efficiency. In such circumstances skill in physical activities which contribute to survival has a high priority. For example, when the philosopher Plato was a young man (in the late fifth century B.C.), he advocated in *The Republic* a wide program of sport activities. But by the time he was 70 years old and the survival of Athens was severely threatened by the Persians, he wrote in *The Laws:* "Those [athletic contests] which provide a training for war should be encouraged and prizes instituted for success in them; those which do not may be dismissed."[1]

Activities particularly useful for survival purposes included hunting, paramilitary events, exercise systems, and other fitness programs. Although permitting a choice among activities, societies faced with a survival problem tended to be authoritarian about physical activity for all. As in armies, the assumption has been that there is no room for discussion when one's life is literally at stake, nor for experimentation, for there is no room for mistakes or failure when one is living at a marginal level. A society which faced a survival crisis tended to ignore the wishes of its individual citizens and promulgated legislation that forced all to have the requisite skills.

The societies described here each had reason to be intensely concerned about their survival—either collectively or individually. Thus their physical activities were designed to *emphasize* that which lent to health, fitness, and

[1] Plato. *The Laws,* trans. by A. E. Taylor. New York: Everyman's Library, 1960, p. 219.

military preparedness. Physical education was an important subject which, from the time of the Roman Empire, consisted in these societies of various programs of exercise.

Early societies

The earliest societies are sometimes called primitive, because they lacked the sophisticated development of later civilizations. Around 10,000 B.C. humans moved from their natural shelters in caves to huts which they learned to construct. According to a famous archeologist, "history, as such, begins in the Negev during the latter part of the Chalcolithic period, near the end of the fourth millennium B.C., when people lived in mud-brick villages, tilled the soil, wove cloth, made fired pottery, carved ivory images, and forged copper tools and weapons."[2] From that quotation it is obvious that life was physically demanding; it surely involved numerous skills of hunting and fighting.

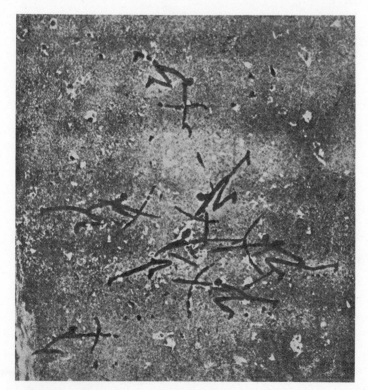

A battle of archers, from a prehistoric Spanish cave painting

[2] N. Glueck. *Rivers in the Desert*. New York: Farrar, Straus & Giroux, 1959, p. xi.

There is evidence to show that popular physical activities in early cultures included simple running, throwing, and wrestling contests, archery, spear or boomerang throwing, paddling a boat or canoe, swimming, ball playing, and dancing. Presumably, children played with replicas of adult tools and weapons or toys in the form of animals.

The responsibility for teaching the children the requisite skills devolved on all members of the social unit, but were sex differentiated. Little boys were taught the skills of hunting, fishing, and making war, while little girls learned to grow, preserve, and cook food, as well as weave, make pottery, and construct shelters. Education was informal in the sense that there were no schools, but it was a rigid passing down of acquired knowledge from one generation to the next.

Testing the skills learned by the youths was generally a formal affair. Initiation ceremonies to mark passage to adult status in the group gave youths opportunity to display their skills, endurance, and courage. Sport contests were one means of proving oneself and establishing one's relative status in the group. Sometimes a real task was put to young men, such as killing a wild animal or even a human enemy.

Sport in the early societies was serious business. Without certain skills the society would cease to exist. Sport afforded a pleasant medium for the learning and practice of these skills.

Sparta

Sparta was one of the two most powerful Greek city-states; Athens was the other. Its period of greatness extended from about the middle of the eighth century B.C., when its territory of Laconia was conquered by Dorians, till the battle of Leuctra (371 B.C.), when Sparta was conquered by Thebes.

In order to survive threats to its existence from both within and without, Sparta became a totally militaristic state. All citizens—men and women—were soldiers in the sense that iron discipline was considered necessary to maintain the requisite control. Actually, Sparta became a totalitarian state in that the will of the state was supreme.

To accomplish its militaristic goals, the Spartan state directed the education of boys and girls almost totally toward physical conditioning and the acquisition of physical skills. From the age of seven, a young male child was required to live in state barracks. The male children were grouped in "herds" according to age, were given one garment a year, no shoes, a bed of reeds, and a diet so sparse and distasteful that it was mocked by the civilized world. In fact, the term "Spartan" still describes a highly disciplined lifestyle with no softening comforts. Public beatings were common, even for being too fat or too lazy.

The day was spent practicing sports, including boxing and wrestling, pancration, archery, running, riding, hunting, stone or javelin throwing, ball playing, and dancing. Specialization was discouraged, because each sport had a purpose that related to conditioning or preparation for warrior duties. All exercising was performed naked under the supervision of older citizens who taught skills, evaluated performance, inspected the physical condition of the youths, and meted out punishment when necessary.

The adolescent boys were called "ballplayers," because this was their chief activity. Yearly tournaments among teams of about fifteen players were rough-and-tumble affairs. Another team game that helped train Spartan boys for their future occupation involved two teams playing on an island. The object seemed to have been to hit, kick, or bite the opponents till they were driven into the water.

Girls in Sparta also took part in these exercises, because it was believed that only a fit and trained woman could bear healthy children for the state. A famous statue from ancient times is that of a Spartan woman runner.

Spartan athletes proved the superiority of their training in competition with other Greeks. They took part in the Olympics and from the fifteenth to the

Girl running. Probably Spartan, about 500 b.c. Found in Albania
Source: The British Museum

fiftieth Olympiad won most of the events. They did not, however, take part in the boxing or pancratic contests, because those required the loser to give up by stretching out his hand as a signal. Spartan men were never permitted to acknowledge defeat in contest against other Hellenes.

In Sparta we find a society that epitomized the concept of physical training for survival purposes. All efforts were bent toward this end and were successful to the extent that Spartan warriors were famous for their courage and ability and Sparta was able to dominate its region for over 400 years.

Rome

Beginning in the third century B.C., the Roman Republic began the process of building what later became the Roman Empire. The citizen-soldiers who fought for Rome during these wars had more sophisticated skills and weapons than the earlier Spartans. Furthermore, the Romans disliked Greek athletics, because they thought naked exercising by boys was effeminate and led to homosexual practices (which were, in fact, common in the Greek city-states).

Consequently, their battle training was different. Roman youths trained on Campus Martius (Field of Mars, the god of war), supervised by their fathers in fencing, javelin throwing, sword play, vaulting, riding, swimming, and the use of every kind of weapon. These were not necessarily sportlike activities, because they were not competitive. The Roman term for games, *ludus,* meant "training" and the derivative term *ludiones* described actors, indicating a relation to performance rather than contest. In fact, performances were very much a part of Roman training: gladiatorial combats and fights against wild animals were originally undertaken by young men from the best families, testing and exhibiting their skill and courage before large crowds in the amphitheater.

During the Empire (31 B.C. to 455 A.D.—the fall of Rome) both soldiers and athletes were professionals. Guilds (unions) of athletes achieved sufficient power during the second century to win for their members wealth and privileges. For instance, a winner in an important festival might receive free sustenance or a pension, and exemption from taxation and from both civil and military service. These professional athletes became highly specialized and devoted their lives to being ready for competition. Under those circumstances, what emerged was not the beautiful lithe warrior of the Spartans, but ugly, misproportioned men. Claudius Galen, a physician, expressed the prevailing opinion:

That athletes have never shared in even a dream of mental blessings is clear to anyone. . . . From the standpoint of bodily health . . . it is evident that no other class is more miserable than the athletes. . . . Many with well-proportioned limbs are totally

65

changed by the coaches who take them in hand, overfatten them, and gorge them with flesh and blood.[3]

Besides watching professional athletes, the Romans also enjoyed performances in the Circus Maximus. These became increasingly enormous and gory spectacles. The Emperor Augustus records that during his reign he had eight gladiatorial shows in which about 10,000 gladiators fought—often to death. The Colosseum was inaugurated in 80 A.D. with a show during which 5000 beasts were killed in one day.

The tradition of sport completely disappeared in the wake of the circus performances and the professional athletes and soldiers. The populace no longer had any need in their daily lives for the skills and qualities developed through sport. Sport had deteriorated to mass entertainment.

The Roman people, having little else to do, spent a great deal of their time at the public *thermae,* or baths. Such sport or exercise as they took there was motivated by the need to maintain personal health. Galen became the first to attempt to set forth a series of classified and graded health exercises. He defined exercise as vigorous movement and said that "the criterion of vigorousness is change of respiration. . . ."[4] Galen's ideas were a sort of bridge between the concepts of exercise and sport, because he equated the two. His exercises, which recommended the use of a small ball, were generally performed in company with others, although not competitively, in rooms provided for the purpose at the baths.

The Roman baths were enormous structures with hot, cold, warm, and steam baths; swimming pools; exercise, dressing, massage, and lounging rooms, as well as restaurants, shops, libraries, and even museums located within the walls. Thus the need to find a means of maintaining health in a society where the citizens had no usual form of physical activity and where sport was exclusively professional caused the development of medical gymnastics or exercises for the purpose of personal health survival.

[3]Galen. "Exhortation to the Arts," in R. S. Robinson, *Sources for the History of Greek Athletics.* Cincinnati, Ohio: published by the author, 1955, pp. 192, 194.

[4]Galen in R. M. Green, *A Translation of Galen's Hygiene.* Springfield, Illinois: Charles C Thomas, 1951, p. 53. This is not far removed from today's belief that the main component of fitness is good cardiovascular functioning and that exercise for fitness purposes, therefore, should revolve around increasing the efficiency of the cardiovascular system.

Roman baths
Source: Mercurialis *De Arte Gymnastica*

Germany

In Roman society, the survival problem that had motivated the people to exercise as a means of maintaining health was largely a personal one. In nineteenth-century Germany the problem was one of state survival, of achieving much-delayed national unification. In this political setting, the *Turnen* arose, a form of gymnastics originally developed by Frederich Ludwig Jahn and later systematized by Adolph Spiess. Jahn, a teacher and ardent German nationalist, had taken his students to an outdoor area in the woods to play. Using natural objects such as tree branches and streams, they learned to walk a balance beam, vault, climb, and wrestle. Later, at this *Turnplatz* (place for gymnastics) they built structures on which to exercise and which they finally brought indoors to a *Turnhalle* (indoor gymnasium). By this time the apparatus had grown to include vaulting horses (complete with tails), parallel bars, and climbing ladders. Students practiced on the equipment and invented new moves, which they taught to others. After practice Jahn told the students stories of German heroes, German songs were sung, and all non-German foods

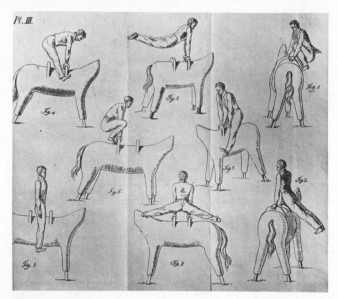

Vaulting the horse
Source: Beck, tr., *Die Deutsche Tumkunst*

and clothes were prohibited. Jahn deliberately intended to prepare the youth both physically and psychologically for the task of unifying the homeland.

Turnen caught on among the young male adults too. In fact, the heavy apparatus was more congenial to their strength than to the younger boys'. A political group associated especially with university students, the *Burschenschaft,* adopted *Turnen* as a regular part of its program, preparing their strength for the day when they would fight for Germany. Because of this political connection, *Turnen* was outlawed for a period. Nevertheless, the movement continued to grow and attract thousands of members. (Some of these later emigrated to the United States and started the gymnastics movement which today flourishes in schools and colleges.)

Gymnastics became the basis for the German school physical education program. Adolf Spiess collected, analyzed, and classified descriptions of the possible movements of the body and enabled large groups of children to use the apparatus. To facilitate this process, he developed an authoritarian system in which one teacher commanded the whole group, which performed simultaneously. To move the students around the gym and to promote group discipline, he added marching to this process—a connection that still lingers today as gymnasts, in contrast to other sport teams, march into place for their performances.

Because Spiess graded the exercises in order of difficulty, he made it possible for girls to do them. As such, he was one of the early sponsors of physical education for girls.

German gymnastics, or *Turnen,* has since become a popular sport, with competition on all levels. But in the nineteenth century it was an exercise system designed to ensure the survival of Germany. Youths and young adults prepared their bodies in a conscious patriotic endeavor to prepare to fight for the fatherland.

Sweden

Sweden, whose defeat during the Napoleonic Wars cost her the loss of much territory, faced a problem similar to Germany's. A Swedish nationalist, Per Henrik Ling, had studied in Denmark and observed the training of gymnastic teachers for the army. Like Jahn, he believed that training in fencing and gymnastics would help to restore the physical health and military power of the country. King Charles XIV (Bernadotte), convinced of the validity of Ling's plan, provided government support for the founding of the Royal Gymnastics Central Institute (RGCI), which opened in 1814 with young military officers as students.

There Ling developed the world-famous system of Swedish gymnastics, organized around four components: pedagogical, military, medical, and aesthetic. The pedagogical exercises were done in schools to maintain normal fitness; the military exercises were specially designed to meet the needs of soldiers; the medical were designed to correct orthopedic defects (corrective exercises in today's terminology); the aesthetic were never developed.

Unlike German gymnastics, where heavy apparatus demanded the development of upper-arm strength, the Swedish free-standing exercises

Swedish gymnastic exercises
Source: Posse, *Handbook of School Gymnastics*

emphasized development of the chest and lungs. All of Ling's exercises were done with an expanded chest, because it was believed (erroneously) that this would provide more room for the lungs and would increase vital capacity. Furthermore, Swedish gymnastics emphasized positions rather than movements; the precision of the performance was the precision of each successive body position. When apparatus was used (the Swedish boom, the stall bars, the Swedish box) the movements and exercises were simple. Jahn had selected apparatus, and students had learned to do movements on them. Ling had in mind certain results, and he invented apparatus that would help to bring about these results.

This approach led Ling to claim that his system was scientifically based. Stressing anatomy and physiology, he designed exercises in accord with the best available information in those areas. His aim was to afford the human body the best overall training and exercise that science could devise.

Accordingly, it became necessary to grade and classify the exercises in some progressive order of difficulty. This was also of assistance to the teachers who, being ex-military men, did not have the knowledge necessary to make adequate selections. Hjalmar Ling, Per's son, tabled the exercises in a *Day's Order,* which placed movements in a sequence of difficulty; each day's table grouped exercises to affect different parts of the body. Exercises were executed at least three times to each side and for, say, a week.

The teachers would memorize the day's order and give commands to the students such as: "To right angles, arms—bend!" or "Arms upward—fling!" Students would then hold the position until the teacher had checked that the back was properly arched, the chest expanded, the arms in exactly the right place, and the legs at the prescribed angle. It was very boring for the students, but teachers liked it, because memorizing the day's order and barking commands was something they could easily learn to do. Furthermore, the exercises demanded no equipment and little space; they were therefore especially suitable for use in schools. Since Ling claimed scientific validity for the Swedish exercise system, there was also good philosophical rationale for choosing it. For all these reasons, Swedish gymnastics became a mainstay of physical educational programs the world over. Even in the twentieth century it is still being taught in large numbers of American and European schools.

The Swedish and the German gymnastic systems originally were designed to build up the strength of individual males in order to better ensure national security. Ultimately, German gymnastics became transformed into sport with its own inherent purposes, while Swedish exercises were used primarily in educational and therapeutic situations where the maintenance of health and the correction of postural defects were the paramount concern.

United States

In early nineteenth-century America, a stylish gentleman or gentlewoman did not have a robust complexion or obvious physical strength; strenuous physical activity was considered vulgar. Even walking was not considered a pursuit for gentlepeople, and sports were out altogether. Clothing, especially for women, was tight and cumbersome and not adaptable to activity. The rise of industrialism and the move to the cities bred unsanitary conditions, and diseases such as tuberculosis were common. The workers suffered long hours, often in cramped positions that caused orthopedic deformities. School children sat at their desks without moving for many hours a day.

A number of prominent figures—including Benjamin Franklin and Thomas Jefferson—began to advocate physical activity and even physical education. A few schools included some form of physical training in their curriculums. Catharine Beecher, an outspoken woman whose chief concern was that women be physically capable of fulfilling their duties as wives and mothers, developed a system of exercises that became popular for young girls especially. Called calisthenics—from *kalos,* the Greek for beautiful, and *sthenos,* strength—they consisted of light exercises sometimes performed to music. Unfortunately, the exercises were so gentle as to be almost useless; nevertheless it may be said that Beecher helped to popularize the idea of calisthenics as important and suitable, even for fashionable women.

Light gymnastic exercises
Source: Lewis, *The New Gymnastics for Men, Women and Children*

The time was ripe for Dio Lewis when, in the 1860s, he introduced his system of light gymnastics (as opposed to the heavy apparatus gymnastics of the Germans or the weight lifting that popular George Windship was advocating). It consisted of free exercises such as hopping in place or circular arm movements, and also exercises with light hand apparatus such as two-pound wooden dumbbells, wands, and bean bags. Unlike the European systems, which sought to build up male strength for nationalistic purposes, Lewis' system aimed at overcoming the poor health of Americans, including women and children. It was logical, therefore, that the light gymnastics be designed differently from the heavy ones. As Lewis acknowledged:

The only question which remains is that which lies between all heavy and light gymnastics, viz: whether strength or flexibility is to be preferred. . . . Men, women and children should be strong, but it should be the strength of grace, flexibility, agility and endurance; it should not be the strength of a great lifter. . . . The principal object of all physical training is an elastic, vigorous condition of the nervous system. . . .[5]

Since that purpose seemed to meet the needs of the American people, Lewis' system became very popular. His book, *The New Gymnastics for Men, Women and Children,* went through ten editions from 1862 to 1868. Finding the exercises easy to do and easy to teach, the American Institute of Instruction, composed of leading educators from the whole country, passed a resolution stating that the exercises were "eminently worthy of general introduction into all our schools, and into general use."[6] In 1866, when California passed the nation's first law requiring physical exercise in grades 1 through 6, Lewis' handbook was suggested as a guide. The new gymnastics were, in fact, widely used until the advent of the Sargent system in the 1880s.

Dudley Allen Sargent was a leading physical educator, director of the gymnasium at Harvard College and founder of the Sargent School for Physical Education, one of the foremost institutions for the training of female physical educators. Sargent's system of exercises, sometimes called the American system, was different from all others in major ways. First, it eschewed group performance, fitting the exercises to the needs of the individual through a medical examination and a written prescription of exercises. Measurements of all parts of the body were taken, including such mundane measures as the girth of the upper arm and leg and such quixotic ones as the height to the navel. The strength of various muscle groups was tested with dynamometers, and other tests recorded the lung capacity and the condition of the skin. A

[5] D. Lewis. *The New Gymnastics for Men, Women, and Children,* 8th ed. Boston: Ticknor and Fields, 1864, pp. 61–63.

[6] F. E. Leonard. *Pioneers of Modern Physical Training.* The Physical Directors' Society of the Young Man's Christian Association of North America, New York: (n.d.) pp. 47–48.

medical history was taken. After six months the examination was repeated and the prescription changed accordingly.

Some of the exercises were adapted from other systems, but with the major difference that they involved the use of developing apparatus invented by Sargent. His apparatus included chest expanders and developers, quarter circles, high pulleys, inclined planes, leg machines, finger machines, traveling parallels, and hydraulic rowing machines, as well as a system of chest weights and pulleys. In all there were more than 80 machines; students could work out for an hour by going from machine to machine, adjusting each to suit the prescription geared to their own strength and endurance. The session was then completed with a mild run and a good bath.

Despite the cost of these machines and the knowledge needed to prescribe properly,[7] the Sargent system became a popular form of physical education in the United States prior to the twentieth century. In 1889 Sargent claimed more than 350 institutions, with a membership of over 100,000 people using his apparatus. These included colleges, YMCAs, private schools, athletic clubs, and even an insane asylum.[8] However, it was rarely used in the public schools. The process was probably too complicated and too expensive; furthermore, prior to the twentieth century there was much less concern for the health of children, who were presumed to have all the activity they needed in the course of their playing. When the public schools included exercises, they used either the Lewis system or, late in the century, the Swedish system.

The concern for survival then began to diminish somewhat. More people were taking part in sports, the horrible conditions in factories and cities were being alleviated through legislation sponsored by reformers and unions, restrictive clothing styles changed, attitudes toward physical activity changed, and hundreds of thousands of people were bicycling, bowling, and playing croquet, baseball, basketball, tennis, and golf.

The next survival-related crisis took place around World War I. Draft examinations showed that the physical condition of one-third of the men was too poor for military service. The shock of this helped to persuade state legislators to pass laws requiring physical education in the public schools. Prior to 1900, only five states had passed such laws; three more states enacted them before 1914. By 1921, twenty-five additional states had "signed on."

Sports and games were by then the mainstay of the curriculum. It was assumed that health and fitness could be gained through a variety of physical

[7] This was the main reason for including anatomy and kinesiology in the early professional preparation curriculums.

[8] *Physical Training, A Full Report of the Papers and Discussion of the Conference Held in Boston in November, 1889.* Reported and edited by Isabel C. Barrows. Boston: Geo. H. Ellis, 1890, p. 65.

activities that were more natural to children than the formal exercise systems. Some prominent physical educators such as Charles Harold McCloy disagreed, however, and sought to remind the profession of its responsibilities: "We need better-developed muscular systems than most of the current literature in our profession is demanding. . . . Therefore, I should like to propose that as a profession we rethink the whole problem of our more purely *physical* objectives, and that we emphasize them more."[9]

Nevertheless, physical fitness through exercises kept a low profile until the World War II draft again revealed a low level of physical conditioning. "Selective service statistics for World War II showed that out of 4 million men rejected for military service, about 700,000 had remediable defects which had not been corrected."[10] The Secretary of War, Henry L. Stimson, prevailed upon physical educators to focus on physical conditioning (primarily because some professionals were advocating a return to military drill). A joint committee of physical educators and representatives of the armed forces prepared a booklet called *Physical Fitness through Physical Education for the High School Victory Corps,* recommending a program of calisthenics and other fitness activities, with tests and norms for male students. McCloy's "back to the body" aim was then very much in evidence in the schools.

After World War II, the concern for survival again diminished and programs of physical education returned to sports and dance activities. However, in 1953, a study was published[11] on the lack of fitness of American youths. Using tests developed by Hans Kraus and Sonya Weber, almost 2000 European and 4500 American children were tested for what purported to be a "Minimum Muscular Fitness Test."[12] Since 56.6 percent of the American children between the ages of six and nineteen years, as compared with 8.3 percent of the European children, failed the test, the American people were shocked into again worrying about their personal physical survival. This episode set off a wave of interest in physical fitness comparable to the stimulus which Sputnik provided American scientific education. This concern still persists, not only in the school physical

[9]C. H. McCloy. *Philosophical Bases for Physical Education.* New York: Appleton-Century-Crofts, 1940, p. 80.

[10]D. B. Van Dalen and B. L. Bennett. *A World History of Physical Education,* 2d ed. Englewood Cliffs, N. J.: Prentice-Hall, Inc., 1971, p. 484.

[11]H. Kraus and R. P. Hirschland (Bonnie Prudden). "Muscular Fitness and Health." *Journal of Physical Education and Recreation,* 24, December 1953, pp. 17–19; "Minimum Muscular Tests in School Children." *Research Quarterly,* XXV, May 1954, pp. 178–188.

[12]The six component parts tested abdominal and psoas muscle strength, upper and lower back strength, and hamstring flexibility. Failure on one item was interpreted as failure of the whole test. The flexibility test (touching the floor without bending the knees) produced the greatest number of failures for American school children.

education programs, but also in an increased interest in adult exercise packages; programs of isometrics, aerobics, and jogging; health foods; strength-building gadgets; and increased sports participation for health purposes.

Following the report of the Kraus-Weber tests, President Eisenhower convened the President's Conference on Fitness of American Youth (1956), to determine procedures for improving the physical status of the youth of our country. The President's Council on Youth Fitness resulted. (The name was later changed to the President's Council on Physical Fitness and then to the President's Council on Physical Fitness and Sports—reflecting a somewhat different emphasis.) The AAHPER contributed the *Youth Fitness Test,* a manual with norms for boys and girls from grades 5 to 12. Schools and colleges began to reemphasize fitness in their curriculums and test programs. Certificates and rewards encouraged students to strive for excellence in their physical performances.

Thus the concept of exercise for personal health and survival has had a long history in the United States. During national crises it has emerged as a paramount goal of individuals and physical education programs. But when these crises passed, this interest faded: exercise for fitness gave way to sport and dance activities.

Sport for competition and reward

Citius, Altius, Fortius ("Swifter, Higher, Stronger"), the Olympic motto, expresses the essence of the challenge of competition. Since the earliest days, to surpass oneself or one's peers or even to beat an abstract record in contests of strength, endurance, speed, or skill appears as a human ambition.

Although sport has been used to prepare for combat, it often has been simply "sport for sport's sake." In other words, humans have played for the joy of the competition and the resultant demonstration of personal prowess rather than for any instrumental reasons. A third factor motivating sport participation has been the possibility of earning substantial material rewards.

Sport competition can be as local as individual challenge, but most societies have generated various levels of sport organization, including international tournaments.

Although sport forms were said to have originally stemmed from an abstraction of hunting or warrior skills, these were soon removed from usefulness. For instance, when throwing the spear at an animal or an enemy was abstracted into throwing a javelin as far into space as it could be thrown, the careful aiming inherent in the spear-throwing task was eliminated. It was thus far less useful for future combat than the practice of throwing at a target.

Furthermore, most sport contests do not seem to relate to hunting and warrior activities. The numerous types of ball games, for instance, are remote from these skills, although there is evidence of ball play in even the earliest societies. Modern sports such as diving, skating, and gymnastics obviously do not stem from such functions. They are rationally created or evolved activities, which may bear some symbolic relationships to other social forms, but in essence were constructed for the purpose of finding new and pleasurable ways in which humans could test their abilities against each other. A good example of this is basketball, a game designed to meet a certain purpose—namely, the need of YMCAs for an indoor, wintertime activity that young people could enjoy.

Of course, even though a sport may in fact have had utilitarian purpose, individuals probably choose to engage in competition for their own personal reasons. Thus it is assumed that for the contests described here, the primary motivating factor was the joy of competition or the expectation of reward.

Sporting events—even as far back as the Homeric games—exhibit a high level of social organization in that certain rules are agreed upon and obviously understood by participants from many countries; officials with the concomitant notions of fairness and equality of opportunity; material rewards; a sense of ceremony; and a cross-cultural persistence of activity forms in many important sports and contests.

Homeric funeral games

Homer's description of the Funeral Games commemorating the death of Patroclus, beloved friend of Achilles, in the *Iliad,* provides evidence that at the time of the Trojan War (circa 1200 B.C.) diversified forms of sport were an important part of the culture. Games to commemorate an important event—such as, in this case, the funeral of a warrior-hero—were common. The contests included chariot racing, boxing, wrestling, footracing, armed combat, archery, and discus and javelin throwing. Also described in the Homeric epics, though not part of the funeral games, were long jumping and rhythmic ball tossing.

The general atmosphere of the funeral games was one of good-humored competition. The contestants boasted of their abilities, bragged of past victories, and blamed the gods for their failures. The arena for competition was a dirt ring with a naturally sloped hillside for the spectators. The contestants used an old monument as a turning-post for the chariot race. The ground dust was choking, and when one runner tripped, his mouth and nostrils were filled with cattle dung.

That the games were partially for the amusement of the spectators is reflected in the description of the wrestling match. The wrestlers, who were evenly matched, perceived that they were boring the troops and one said, therefore: "Either you or I must let the other try a throw." Even so, neither succeeded in quickly pinning the other, so Achilles, who ran the games, told them to "take equal prizes and withdraw." The spectators also figured in the decision of the armed combat contest, similar to a fencing match. "The spectators were so terrified for Aias that they called upon the combatants to stop and share the prizes."[13]

The funeral games are a fascinating account of early sport—the more so since almost all the events are still held today. Those day-long games were the root of later festivals such as the Olympics. The description revealed the importance of competitive sport in this early society, which highly valued the *athleter* (winner of prizes).

Ancient Olympics

The first recorded Olympics took place in 776 B.C. Only one of several festivals that eventually became a regular part of life in the ancient Hellenic world, the Olympic festival was singularly important, however. The Greeks marked time by the Olympiads (a four-year period), dating important events by saying, for example, that such-and-such took place in the second year of the sixty-third Olympiad. Furthermore, the Olympics was dedicated to Zeus, the father of the gods and the most important deity.

The athletes were required to arrive in Elis (the territory in which Olympia was located) a month before the games to train in front of the Hellanodikai, the ten official judges chosen by lot from the ten tribes of Elis. This rule probably gave the judges time to check on the athletes' eligibility. All athletes had to be free-born Greeks who had never committed a crime. They also had to swear that they had trained for the required ten months and would obey the rules of the games. The judges, for their part, had to swear that their decisions would be honest and that they would not reveal the reasons for them.

From 776 to 708 B.C. the contests consisted only of footraces. Wrestling and the pentathlon were added later, boxing in 688 B.C., the four-horse chariot race in 680 B.C., and horse races and the pancration in 648 B.C. In succeeding centuries other forms of races were added, but it is evident that the basic adult program was completed by the end of the seventh century. Contests for boys, including footracing and wrestling, the pentathlon, and

---

[13] Homer. *The Iliad,* trans. by E. V. Rieu. Baltimore: Penguin Books, Inc., pp. 431, 432, 434.

Greek stadium at Delphi

boxing, were also added late in the seventh century. Girls and women did not participate in the regular events but were permitted to enter teams in the equestrian contests; three women were recorded as winners at Olympia, the first between 390 and 380 B.C. However, separate footraces dedicated to Hera, the wife of Zeus, were held at Olympia for the girls.

The most important event of the Olympics was a footrace, the *stade,* which was about 200 yards. Olympiads were often named after the winner of the *stade.* Other footraces included the *diaulos* (400 yards), the race in armor (400 yards), and the *dolichos* (about 20 *stades* or 4000 yards).

The pentathalon had five parts: long jump, discus, javelin, footrace, and wrestling. Probably the winner was the athlete who won three events. The long jump may have resembled today's hop, step, and jump. The jumper held weights (*halteres*) in his hand while jumping to the music of a flute player who helped set the complicated rhythm. The discuses were made of stone but otherwise did not differ much from contemporary ones; the method of throwing was also similar. The javelin had a thong that was looped over the first finger, or the first two fingers, of the throwing hand to give additional leverage and to add spin to the flight.

Wrestling was the most popular of the Greek sports, because it epitomized the all-around athlete; it was similar in form to today's sport. Boxing, on the other hand, was different in that it had no rounds. The match ended when a boxer conceded by raising his hand. The boxer's hands and forearm were wrapped with a long leather thong for protection. The pancration was a kind of combination of wrestling and boxing—an all-out, no-holds-barred sport whose aim was to get an opponent to raise his hand in defeat. Biting and gouging were the only acts not allowed, but even these were sometimes committed. It was a very rough activity for which there is no modern parallel.

The Olympic festival took five days, the first for ceremonies, the second for the equestrian events and the pentathalon, the third for the boys' matches, the fourth for the major events including the races, boxing, wrestling, and pancration, and the last day for ceremonies and feasting.

Perhaps because of both the high honor and the possible lucrativeness of winning, athletes became more and more specialized and less and less the exemplification of the private citizen demonstrating his excellence. Cheating took place as demonstrated by statues, the *Zanes,* paid for by the fines of athletes caught violating their oaths. The *Zanes* were lined up just outside the entrance to the stadium as a last reminder to the athletes.

In later years, under the Romans, the festivals took on political significance and prominent people even had themselves declared winners. The significance of the games naturally declined under such conditions. Furthermore, the contests were of less interest, because they were not gory enough for the Romans. Finally, the rise of Christianity affected the Olympics; Christians reviled it as a festival dedicated to a pagan god and considered it immoral to compete naked before a crowd. The last games took place in 393 A.D., after which they were abolished by a decree of the Roman Emperor Theodosius.

Middle Ages

After the fall of Rome, Europe was left in a weak and disintegrated state. With the exception of the Church, most social institutions, including state systems of education and international sporting events, disappeared. The feudal system, the new organization of society, produced an upper class of knights and clergymen and a lower class of peasants. By the late Middle Ages, the eleventh to fourteenth centuries, these groups had created new forms of sports.

The medieval tournaments were associated with the knights. Events included the joust, or tilt, during which two horsemen, using blunt lances, charged at full speed trying to unseat one another. Sometimes, if one or both were dismounted, the knights continued on foot, battling with the short sword until defeat was acknowledged or the judges called a halt. The main and most exciting event of the tournament, however, was the mêlée, in which groups of knights fought each other on the list (field) as in an actual battle. Because of the choking dust from the lists, the large numbers of trampling horses, and in later days, sometimes the use of real instead of blunt swords, many knights were killed in the tournaments. In the tourney at Neuss (1240) some sixty were killed.[14]

The risk was well worth it, however, because in addition to the prize money offered by the sponsor, prisoners were taken and ransoms exacted as in war; also, the victors kept the armor and the horses of the defeated. Thus it was possible to earn one's living participating in the tournaments, as well as to prove one's courage and ability.

Like the Olympics, the original chivalric ideal that motivated the knights vanished in increasing professionalism and malpractice. The many fatalities caused the Church to ban the tournaments, and knights who died as a result of their enlistment were forbidden burial in sacred ground. Kings outlawed tournaments, not wishing to lose their manpower; also the knightly skills exemplified were becoming anachronistic. However, the tournaments lingered in some places until the sixteenth century.

Other sports arose during this period. Football was established by 1100 A.D. as a rough free-for-all; it was played in England by peasants, with the whole town out to get the Dane's Head (a skull or later a cow's bladder) through the town's gate. In medieval Italy, it became *calcio,* somewhat like Rugby, played by noblemen with 45 players on one side. So many men were hurt and killed playing some version of football that it too was outlawed by many rulers.

Tennis players in 1664
Source: Comenius *Visible World*

14Will Durant. *"The Age of Faith,"* Vol. IV, *The Story of Civilization,* 10 vols. New York: Simon and Schuster, Inc., 1950, p. 574.

Court tennis was first popular with the monks, who spent so much time at it that in 1245 the Archbishop of Rouen issued an edict forbidding clergy to play. It became a favorite sport of kings especially in France, where, by 1400, a Guild of Tennis Masters controlled play and the manufacture of racquets and balls.

Bowling originated in the churches of Germany, where peasants rolled stones down a passageway at a club (*kegel*); success proved their virtue.

Golf originated in Scotland in the fifteenth century and became so popular that in 1457 the Scottish Parliament, fearing that golf would interfere with the practice of archery, proclaimed that it be "utterly cryit down, and nacht usit."

Other sports and games were also played; peasants celebrated holidays with fairs which included races and contests, and variations of the sports described above were common too. The late Middle Ages is marked as a period during which sport for competition and reward flourished despite bans placed on it. Today's societies thus are provided with early forms of some popular activities.

Modern Olympics

In 1896, thanks to the hard work of the French Baron Pierre de Coubertin and others, the Olympic festival was revived. It has continued to take place every four years, but unlike the ancient Olympics, whose occurrence caused wars to cease, the modern Olympics ceased for war in 1916, 1940, and 1944. De Coubertin had hoped that the Olympics would help bring universal peace. "To attain this end [peace], what better means than to bring the youth of all countries periodically together for amicable trials of muscular strength and agility?"[15] He also hoped to purify sport by fostering amateur competition instead of the professional sport then rampant. And, he thought that by getting countries to agree on rules for the purposes of the international competition, the Olympics would put an end to the constant squabbles. Finally, de Coubertin hoped to kindle an interest in sport in France, because he believed it had done so much good for the English.

Delegates to a conference in Paris in 1894 agreed on the formation of an International Olympic Committee and on the idea of rotating the host countries for each Olympiad. For obvious reasons Greece was chosen as the site of the first modern Olympics.

Competitors included athletes from Austria, Denmark, England, France,

[15] P. de Coubertin. "The Olympic Games of 1896." *The Century Magazine,* LIII, November 1896–April 1897, p. 53.

Germany, Greece, Hungary, Switzerland, and the United States. The unofficial team of the United States consisted of thirteen athletes; there were ten track men, five sent by the Boston Athletic Association, and four Princeton men and one Harvard man who paid their own way; the ten won nine events. To these ten men were added a swimmer (who came in second in the 100-meter freestyle) and two military revolver shooters (who took first and second in their event). The most surprising American victory was in the discus throw, which was won by Robert Garrett. His winning throw was made with a borrowed discus—the first real one he had ever seen!

The most sentimental victory, however, was that achieved by the Greek, Spiridon Loues, in winning the marathon. The event commemorated a famous military victory in ancient Greek history and the Greeks intensely desired to win this event. Loues was rewarded with numerous gifts, including a gold watch set with pearls and a certificate good for a year's free meals at a local inn; he did, however, refuse a gift of 10,000 francs.

The 1896 program had twelve track and field events, four swimming races, wrestling, weight lifting, six cycle races, three fencing matches, eight gymnastics events, four shooting matches, and tennis singles and doubles. In 1900, several water events—rowing, yachting, water polo—in addition to golf, archery, and a tug-of-war were added to the program. New, too, were the events for women: tennis and golf. In the latter event, Margaret Abbot won the first women's gold medal for the United States. Although the American women also took gold medals for archery in 1904, it was 1920 before they participated in any great numbers. In those Olympics the U.S. women swimmers and divers were phenomenally successful, sweeping three events and taking a gold in the

1946 Olympics: United States women sweep springboard diving

fourth. Some other important additions to the women's program include equestrian events (1912), basketball (1936), swimming (1912), fencing (1924), track and field (1928), modern gymnastics (1952), and volleyball (1964). In 1924 the Winter Olympics was started.

The traditions revived from the ancient Olympics include the opening and closing processions, led always by Greece with the host country marching last, and the Olympic oath. In 1920 the Olympic flag, its five rings symbolizing the five participant continents, was created. The torch-lighting ceremony, which brings the sacred flame from Olympia, where it burned during the ancient games, originated in 1936.

The Olympic games are the epitome of the concept of sport for competition. They have become an event in which not only individuals but also nations demonstrate their prowess.

United States

Sport activity in the United States did not really take root until the middle of the nineteenth century. Prior to that time, Puritan inhibitions against wasting time by playing, in addition to the general lack of wealth and free time, hindered the development of sport.

In the 1860s croquet became the first mass sport. The game was so popular that manufacturers placed candle sockets on the wickets so that it could be played at night. One of the reasons for the game's popularity was undoubtedly the fact that men and women could enjoy playing together. Baseball, track, roller skating, archery, bowling, gymnastics, and, later in the century, tennis, golf, and bicycling, all became popular activities in the latter half of the nineteenth century.

For most sports, national organizations were founded and competitions organized for men and for women. The technological revolution enabled greater participation and spectatorship: factories could manufacture cheap equipment and uniforms; railroad and steamship could bring people to attend distant contests; the telegraph and sport journalism helped to promote an interest in the competitions.

The 1930s saw more growth in sport, first, because of increased leisure time (thanks in part to the unions, workers gained a five-day work week and paid vacations in this period). Second, the Depression forced the creation of public-works programs, resulting in public recreation facilities such as tennis and handball courts, swimming pools, and golf courses.

Spectator sports have a long history in this country, beginning with horse racing and boxing soon after the Revolution. In 1876, the National League of

Baseball Clubs was organized, but baseball had been attracting paid spectators since the 1850s. In the same period, intercollegiate sports, including rowing, track and field, football, and baseball, began to attract crowds. For instance, Harvard College sent a baseball team on tour in 1870, and more than 10,000 spectators gathered to watch a Harvard-Yale crew match.

In the next few decades, intercollegiate sport for men developed quite rapidly, at first under the control of the students. But when colleges realized the value of the publicity, they placed control of the sports in the hands of athletic councils composed of students, faculty, and alumni.

Often blatant malpractices such as the use of "ringers" (students not regularly enrolled) aroused many educators and physical educators to vigorous protest. However, they had no authority to make changes, because athletics were conducted outside the physical education departments. The first attempt to place athletics under faculty control was made in 1891 at the University of Chicago under Amos Alonzo Stagg. However, not till the 1930s did most colleges move to this type of organization and professional control.

Women's sport programs were also student organized at the beginning, in the 1860s, but quickly came under the purview of the physical educators. Their sport programs were primarily on a club basis until the advent of basketball. The first intercollegiate basketball match took place between the University of California (Berkeley) and Stanford University in 1896. Favorite collegiate sports for women have been basketball, tennis, field hockey, and swimming.

Interscholastic sports for both boys and girls were organized early in the twentieth century in activities such as track and field and basketball. Baseball and football were also favorites.

The growth of intercollegiate and interscholastic sports inevitably led to a need for organizations both to promote and to control the activities. Football in colleges was particularly criticized for its abuses of rules and its brutality. In 1905, when a student was killed in a game, the story made the front page of the New York Times. The public outcry resulted in a meeting of university representatives, who formed the Intercollegiate Athletic Association of the United States in 1906. In 1910, this became the National Collegiate Athletic Association (NCAA). The formation of athletic conferences, beginning in 1906 and encouraged by the NCAA, was even more helpful in regulating sport. The NCAA also formed rules committees to standardize the various sports, thus making it possible to hold national championships, which began in 1921 with track and field.

Physical educators put their efforts into the Athletic Research Society, which focused on amateurism and athletic administration and which attempted to persuade colleges to emphasize the educational values of athletics. They eventually succeeded in organizing the National Amateur Athletic Federation (NAAF) but, partly because of the opposition of the Amateur Athletic Union (AAU), this group was unable to take hold.

However, in 1923, a Women's Division of the NAAF was formed, with great influence over the development of sport programs for women. Opposed to high-level competition for girls and women, they preferred the concept of "a sport for every girl and every girl in a sport." Thanks to the efforts of this group, intercollegiate and interscholastic competition for women largely ceased by the end of the 1920s. In its place, the women developed a strong program of intramural activities and conducted play days and sports days in which competition was minimized. The Women's Division of the NAAF worked very closely with the Section on Women's Athletics of the American Physical Education Association, now the National Association for Girls' and Women's Sports (NAGWS), and finally merged with that group in 1940. In 1971, the Association for Intercollegiate Athletics for Women (AIAW) was formed to promote competitive women's sports and now sponsors national championships in seven sports.

The National Intramural Association was founded in 1950, but even before World War I, intramurals were popular activities. Women were not invited to be members until 1971, perhaps because they had such strong programs of their own.

The National Junior College Athletic Association (NJCAA) started in 1938 with only thirteen members. It has become an important element in college sport, conducting national tournaments for its member institutions. It is now allied with the National Federation of State High School Athletic Associations and the National Association of Intercollegiate Athletics.

Outside of the schools and colleges, over 400 sport organizations have been founded for the promotion of their own activities and have been greatly responsible for the growth of sport in the United States.

Other factors important to the development of sport include the advent of television, which greatly increased the already large spectator interest and provided financing for professional sport. The integration of black athletes both in professional and in collegiate sports has opened doors in society as a whole. Synthetic surfaces and improved equipment, such as the fiberglass vaulting pole, changed the face of sport and helped new records to be set. The making of artificial snow and indoor ice made winter sports more available to the masses. The general prosperity that included more ready cash and increased leisure time made it possible for more Americans to take part. The increased acceptability of competition for women brought hundreds of thousands of new sportswomen into the picture. In short, from its first spurt in the half century between 1860 and 1910, sport for competition and reward has become an American way of life.

Physical education for personal and social development

Education has always been a primary means for transmitting to the young the cultural values of a society. Because schools often have been created for the express purpose of preparing the children to be good citizens as adults, a socialization process has been built into the curriculum in diverse ways. One of the most amenable ways of doing this has been through the physical education program. The primary reason for this choice is that the physical education subject matter per se has rarely been considered important. Rather, the by-products or qualities learned as a result of participation, primarily in sport and dance activities, have been seen as the really significant outcomes of physical education.

At some points in history, for example, ancient Athens or contemporary America, the emphasis has been on the development of personal qualities that bring the individual respect and enable him or her to live a more satisfying life. These qualities include body control, self-knowledge, skill, courage, endurance, and the ability to find pleasure in sport and dance activities. At other times, such as renaissance Italy or America in the 1930s and 1940s, the emphasis has been on training in social skills expected of a young man or woman (for example, dancing, fencing, riding) and the appreciation of teamwork, cooperation, good sportsmanship, and fair play. Of course, both sets of purposes are generally operative, though in differing proportions. In fact, as stated earlier, *all* purposes, including survival and the desire for competition and reward, are generally present in a given society's conduct of sport, exercise, and dance activities. But in the examples described here, the curriculum, methods of teaching, and, above all, the spoken rationale, were designed to optimize the idea of physical education for social development.

Ancient Athens

Physical education in ancient Athens of the fourth and fifth centuries B.C. is often the conceptual model for contemporary programs. Respect for what occurred there is so high that it is sometimes referred to as the golden age of sport.

The great enthusiasm for Athenian physical education is primarily owing to its integration with the general education curriculum. Plato, writing in *The*

Republic, set forth the rationale for this position:

And as there are two principles of human nature, one the spirited and the other the philosophical, some God . . . has given mankind two arts answering to them (and only indirectly to the soul and body), in order that these two principles (like the strings of an instrument) may be relaxed or drawn tighter until they are duly harmonized. . . . And he who mingles music with gymnastics in the fairest proportions, and best attempers them to the soul, may be rightly called the true musician and harmonist. . . .
Such, then are our principles of nurture and education. . . .[16]

Thus the basis of the Athenian system was the belief that the education of a citizen necessitated consideration of the *whole* person. Plato was afraid that exclusive devotion to music would produce a soft and effeminate spirit, while exclusive devotion to gymnastics would cause a person to be hard and ferocious. In Plato's terms, then, *all* elements of education were devoted to developing the character of the person. In fact, somewhat in anticipation of later dualistic ideas *mens sana en corpore sano* ("a sound mind in a sound body"), he warned against that interpretation:

Neither are the two arts of music and gymnastic really designed, as is often supposed, the one for the training of the soul, and the other for the training of the body.
    . . . The teachers of both have in view chiefly the improvement of the soul [character].[17]

Athenian boys began school at about age seven, spending half their time in the music school and half in the *palaestra,* a building equipped for wrestling, boxing, changing clothes, bathing, massaging, and scraping. Outside was a sports ground and a running track. The children's[18] activities in the *palaestra* included games, wrestling, boxing, running, jumping, javelin and discus throwing, and possibly swimming. Some of the games were ball games, including a form of field hockey which is depicted on an ancient frieze; also played were leap frog and tug-of-war. Recognizing their socializing potential, Plato made an interesting comment about children's games when he advocated in *The Laws* that children should not be permitted to vary them or change the rules:

They all suppose . . . that innovation in children's play is itself a piece of play and

[16] Plato. *The Republic,* trans. by B. Jowett. New York: The Modern Library, n.d., p. 120.

[17] *Ibid.,* p. 118.

[18] Men of all ages used the *palaestra.* In fact, it was the center of activity; men usually paid it a daily visit to take part in sport and discuss politics and so forth with their friends. In a later period, hot baths were added and these became the most popular area. Eventually, as in Rome, the baths became the main focus and the exercise rooms an auxiliary function.

nothing more, not as it is in fact, a source of most serious and grievous harm; . . . they never reflect that these boys who introduce innovations into their games must inevitably grow to be men of a different stamp from the boys of an earlier time, that the change in themselves leads to the quest for a different manner of life, and this to a craving for different institutions and laws. . . .[19]

One of the guiding principles behind the choice or span of activities was the ability to produce a well-developed, beautifully proportioned body. A harmony of appearance was as essential as a harmony of soul, so students were discouraged from specializing in any one sport. Wrestling was the favorite activity, however, because it required and developed all-round skill and physique.

At age fifteen the boys left the *palaestra* and were relatively free to spend their time in the gymnasium (from *gymnazein:* to exercise naked). There they continued, more strenuously, the activities of the *palaestra* and added racing in armor and horse and chariot racing. At age eighteen they entered the Ephebic College, where they studied the liberal arts of grammar, rhetoric, philosophy, and mathematics, and also military gymnastics, the term referring to all activities associated with a gymnasium, which some authorities consider to be the *palaestra* and outdoor areas.

The physical education of the youths was under the direction of the *paidotribe,* who, like the modern physical educator, was expected to have a knowledge of the body and its requisites and the rules of health, and to be able to teach the activities. The professional trainers, who were more like coaches, were called *gymnastes.* Generally, gymnastes were ex-athletes who primarily trained youths for specific contests.

The beauty of the Athenian system of physical education is that it was founded on a sound philosophical rationale reflecting its activities. Owing in part to the solid training of the *palaestra,* participation in sport was a way of life for adult male Athenians.

European reform movement

By the eighteenth century in Europe the sixteenth-century renaissance of Greek ideas had degenerated into dreary and dark schools where children sat all day memorizing Greek and Latin. There was no physical education to relieve their day. Reform of this system began with the neo-humanist philanthropic movement in Germany, destined to have wide influence on the practice of education both in Europe and in the United States. The movement was named after the Philanthropinum, a school at Dessau founded in 1774. In addition to

[19] Plato. *The Laws,* p. 181.

the liberal arts studies, three hours a day were allotted to instruction in fencing, riding, dancing, and vaulting a live horse. These so-called knightly exercises were considered essential for a young man about to enter the world of gentlemen. A teacher at the school, Johann Friedrich Simon, regarded as the first modern teacher of physical education, introduced his students to what he termed "Greek gymnastics"—the running, wrestling, throwing, and jumping activities of the *palaestra*. He also devised and used a crude high-jump bar and a balance beam, and taught the children games such as tennis and shuttlecock (badminton).

The Philanthropinum was a deliberate attempt at putting into practice the principles of education enunciated by Jean Jacques Rousseau in his famous treatise *Émile*. Rousseau was a naturalist—a believer in nature and in an education that harmonized with the natural instincts. He stated that since the child "is perpetually in motion, he is obliged to observe much and to note a variety of effects. . . ."[20] Because he believed that sensations are the raw materials of ideas, he advocated training the senses through physical activities. He believed further that through games one could learn to make judgments as well as "discipline, equality, fraternity and co-operation."[21]

In Switzerland, the reformer Johann Heinrich Pestalozzi utilized the ideas of Rousseau in his own famous educational institution at Yverdon. He, too, saw more to physical education than the benefits of physical activity:

If the physical advantage of gymnastics is great and uncontrovertible, I would contend that the moral advantage resulting from them is as valuable. . . . Gymnastics, well conducted, essentially contributes not only to render children cheerful and healthy . . . but also to promote among them a certain spirit of union and brotherly feeling . . . habits of industry, openness and frankness of character, personal courage, and a manly conduct in suffering pain, are also among the natural and constant consequences of an early and a continued practice of exercises on the gymnastic system.[22]

Another equally important educator of the time, Friedrich Froebel (creator of the kindergarten) extended the ideas of both Rousseau and Pestalozzi. He termed play the highest phase of child development, "the independent, outward expression of inward action and life." He thought that play with simple geometric forms such as a ball could lead to important understandings.

The ball itself, being the representative of all objects, is the unity and union of the essential properties of all objects. Thus the ball shows contents, mass, matter, space,

[20] J. J. Rousseau. *Émile, Julie and Other Writings,* R. L. Archer, ed. Woodbury, N.Y.: Barron's Educational Series, Inc., 1964, p. 123.

[21] *Ibid.,* p. 67.

[22] In L. F. Anderson, *Pestalozzi.* New York: McGraw-Hill, Inc., 1931, p. 172.

form, size, and figure; it bears within itself an independent power (elasticity), and hence it has rest and movement, and consequently stability and spontaneity; it offers even color, and at least calls forth sound. . . . Therefore the ball . . . leads to the consideration of the most important phenomena and laws of earth-life and the life of Nature. . . .[23]

The most successful school to epitomize the reformers' ideas was the Schnepfenthal Educational Institute. Modeled along the lines of the Philanthropinum, it was founded in 1784 and exists today. In addition to a liberal academic curriculum and some practical experiences in manual labor (also a feature of the reform movement), Schnepfenthal was characterized by a well-designed physical education program developed under Johann Christoph Friedrich Guts Muths. As at the Philanthropinum, the activities were based on Greek sport and were done outside in a natural setting in accord with Rousseauan precepts.

One of the important concepts for physical education practiced by Guts Muths was that "A genuine theory of gymnastics should be constructed on physiological principles, and the practice of each exercise be regulated by the physical qualities of each individual."[24] This attention to individual differences was essential if the activities were truly to be educational. He bolstered this idea by keeping a record of each student's performance in order to understand his needs and progress.

Guts Muths earned enduring fame as a physical educator, not only for his program at the school which was, in fact, much admired and imitated, but also for his book *Gymnastics for Youth*. This book was translated and published in at least eight countries, including the United States. Written in 1793, it was the first modern manual on the subject and had direct influence on a number of European and American physical educators.

Guts Muths divided gymnastics into three classes: (1) exercises intended for improvement of the body, (2) manual labors, and (3) games for youth. Thus he recognized the educative value of certain activities.

On a small scale games imitate in a lively way the numerous and various ways of the course of life, which cannot be reached by any other activity or situation of youth. . . . Here is a small insult to endure, a rashness, unfairness, boasting, cheating, disappointment . . . superiority of mental and physical strength; here is cause for pain

[23]F. Froebel. *Pedagogics of the Kindergarten,* trans. by J. Jarvis. New York: Meredith Publishing Company, 1900, pp. 29, 53–54.

[24]J. C. F. Guts Muths. *Gymnastics for Youth.* London: J. Johnson, 1800, p. 8 (On the title page, authorship is incorrectly attributed to C. G. Salzmann.)

and sorrow as well as cheerfulness and unhappiness, here is an opportunity for evaluation of courtesy, ability, kindness, etc., in fellow man.[25]

The reform movement taught educators to treat children as children. It firmly reestablished the importance of physical education *within* the curriculum because it contended that children learn through sense experiences. Like the Athenians, the reformers contended that sport could promote the development of skills and personal qualities that were important to the socialization of the child.

British public schools

In England, physical education for social development reached its height during the nineteenth century. Used with great effectiveness by the British public schools (by U.S. standards, boarding schools) and attended by the sons of gentlemen, usually from ages eight to eighteen, it became a model system.

Some team games, including cricket and football, were played; rowing was a favorite activity where possible, and tennis and fives were occasional sports. The sport activities were not highly organized and, except for cricket, no formal rules were written down. While there were interschool cricket matches,

Schoolboys playing football, 1886
Source: Routledge *Every Boy's Annual*

[25] Guts Muths quoted in N. J. Moolenijzer, "The Concept of 'Natural' in Physical Education: Johann Guts Muths—Margarte Streicher." Unpublished Ph.D. dissertation, University of Southern California, 1966, pp. 92–93.

football rules differed so from school to school that it would have been difficult to schedule contests. Besides, football was regarded with great skepticism; because it was a rough game and was played by common people, the masters considered it inappropriate for young gentlemen. Some headmasters took a neutral stance, but many were actively opposed to sports, probably in part as a hangover from Puritan ideas.

In 1828, Thomas Arnold became the headmaster of Rugby School, a public school immortalized in the novel *Tom Brown's School Days,* by Thomas Hughes. Arnold is generally credited with catalyzing a reform movement which helped make the schools the shaping institution of the English ruling class. Sport played a major role in these reforms.

Arnold's general aim was to make Christian men of the Rugby students, to teach them virtue, manliness, honor, and responsibility. In order to accomplish this, he instituted a number of reforms which were so successful that they were copied by most of the other public schools. He set up a system of self-government in which the younger boys were officially placed in the charge of the older ones. He prohibited riding to hounds and various other diversions which had been destructive of the local environment, and, to replace them, encouraged participation in sports.

The sports served the purposes of the reform movement in a number of ways. Most importantly, they were organized and conducted by the boys themselves, who scheduled fields and matches, assessed and collected fees to finance the activities, chose teams and captains, made awards, and also supervised the matches. Not until after midcentury did games committees composed of both masters and boys become commonplace. Even the coaching in the earlier part of the century had been done by the older boys, though masters first volunteered and then were hired to assist. Occasionally a professional coach was hired for a cricket season. Because responsibility was placed in the hands of the boys, they were able to learn invaluable social skills of leadership, which they later applied as British army officers and in other official positions.

The rewards for playing were also an important part of the socialization process. To be chosen for the house team gave a boy the right to wear the house crest and colors on his cap and jersey; making the school team entitled him to wear the school blazer. Naturally, boys who had earned these honors were looked up to by the younger students. This helped develop a sense of solidarity and school spirit, a sense of pride in oneself and one's teammates, a spirit notably lacking in other social institutions of the time.

The sports themselves were often demanding and very rough. Younger and older boys played together on teams, and in the case of football, this demanded some amount of physical hardiness and courage. Thus the development of these qualities was attributed to sports.

The custom of fagging—having the little boys do chores for the older ones—was also part of the public school system. In the reform movement it was brought under control and used in sports as well. The younger boys served to shag ball for cricketers, tend goal in football, and in general serve an apprenticeship for their teams.

The use of sports by the public school authorities to help accomplish their social development aims was much admired by observers. Pierre de Coubertin pressed the French authorities to institute such a system in France. The Germans introduced the British games to their own schools, where they were welcomed by many as a substitute for the more formal *Turnen.* But it was in America that the British games had their largest impact. They were eagerly adopted by American colleges and later became a part of the American public school system.

United States

The concept of physical education for social development grew slowly in the United States. In the early part of the twentieth century the curriculum continued to center around exercises for the purpose of health and survival. The first break with this tradition was the introduction of play and games into the curriculum, and sports into the after-school program of activities.

However, although the activities changed, the rationale did not. An early advocate of play as part of physical education, Luther Halsey Gulick reasoned: "Through these plays, bodily skill as well as vigor of heart and lungs is gained and the muscles are called upon for constant and varied activity." He also supported sports, because "they represent the supreme form of muscular exercise." [26] To this end he created the first Public School Athletic League (1903) in New York City. For the Girls Branch of the PSAL (1905), he recommended folk dancing as an activity that could accomplish ends similar to those promoted by sports.

The play, games, sport, and dance curriculum continued to expand and become established during the first decade of the century. In 1910, Thomas Denison Wood set forth the philosophical cornerstone for what came to be called "the new physical education." It was a rationale for the educational as opposed to the physical values of physical education.

[26] L. H. Gulick. *Physical Education by Muscular Exercise.* Philadelphia: P. Blakiston's Son, 1904, pp. 45, 46–47.

It is most desirable that physical education should occupy itself with a program of activities for the young which would secure these physical aspects of health without fail, as by-products, as it were, while the pupil is being guided in the doing of things which will result in the acquirement of mental, moral and social benefits.[27]

American physical educators believed that the important element in accomplishing these goals was the complete rejection of the formal exercise systems and the embracing of activities more "natural" to children. Play and sport were now viewed as developmental activities inherent in the normal growth patterns of children.

Like the European reformers, well-known psychologists such as G. Stanley Hall claimed that play was the best kind of education. They viewed play as part of the natural social process. Darwin's theory of evolution was applied to education and to physical education, including the concept that "ontogeny recapitulates phylogeny" (the life history of the individual repeats the life history of the race). It was interpreted to mean that the elemental drives necessary for hunting and living in primitive societies had survived in the individuals and had manifested themselves in play instincts. Games books, for instance, classified games in categories such as "chasing and fleeing," suggesting the old tribal lifestyle.

The importance of play in the social development of the child was recognized by many authorities. A play movement grew up, particularly in American cities, and municipal money was allocated to build playground facilities. Often these were adjacent to the school yard, thus providing a handy place to carry out the new physical education curriculum. Unfortunately, these playgrounds were sometimes little more than fenced-in concrete areas with a sandbox.

Building good physical education facilities with adequate gymnasiums, pools, and playing fields was most apparent in the 1920s, after the concept had taken hold that the school program of physical education was a basis for the recreation of children and adults. Theorists such as Clark Wilson Hetherington and his protege, Jay Bryan Nash, who led, successively, a dynasty in graduate physical education at New York University, were convinced that play was of paramount importance not only to the child but to the adult as well. The social development of the individual required an ability to take part in leisure-time activities. Furthermore, as Nash argued, the physical education of a child could not be confined to the gym period but must extend to after-school and vacation programs. On the basis of these ideas, schools were designed to function as community recreation centers, and teachers of physical education prepared themselves for the additional role of community recreation specialists.

[27]T. D. Wood. *Health and Education, The Ninth Yearbook of the National Society for the Study of Education,* Part I. Chicago: University of Chicago Press, 1910, pp. 80–81.

At the same time the concept of physical education for social development was becoming an established professional belief. People advocated distinguishing between health and physical education to enable them to preserve both the aims of health and fitness and the new aims. In 1927 Thomas Wood of Teachers College, Columbia University, became the first professor of health education. Departments began to be termed "Health and Physical Education."

The profession recognized these trends in 1937, when the American Physical Education Association (APEA) merged with the Department of School Health and Physical Education of the National Education Association (NEA), creating the American Association for Health and Physical Education. Only one year later "Recreation" was added to the name. Its present title, American Alliance for Health, Physical Education, and Recreation (AAHPER), represents all the professional personnel involved in school and agency programs in these areas.

During the next thirty years, from 1930 to 1960, the concept of physical education for social development became well established in this country. Curriculum and teaching methods were developed in accord with the idea.

The person most responsible for enunciating the basic rationale of this new program was Jesse Feiring Williams. A colleague of John Dewey at Columbia University, he absorbed the ideas of this famous "father of progressive education" and applied them to physical education. Dewey helped to establish the principle that the "whole child" went to school and that educators were concerned not with a mind or a body, but with a whole person. *All* aspects of the school program, therefore, dealt with the education of the whole child. This fit right in with the new physical education, which had renounced bodily fitness and health as its major objective in favor of the social development of the child.

Dewey also helped to shape the purposes of education into a firm commitment to social development. He said: "I believe that the school is primarily a social institution. Education being a social process . . . in which all those agencies are concentrated that will be most effective in bringing the child to share in the inherited resources of the race, and to use his own powers for social ends."[28] Williams, in proclaiming that physical education was education through the physical, was saying, therefore, that physical education, *through* the medium of sports, dance, and other related activities, was aiming to fulfill the social aims of education. In a democratic society, education included teaching the child the principles of cooperation, teamwork, sharing, good sportsmanship, and individual worth. The good citizen of a democracy would also be physically "fit to serve," and would have mastered the skills and

[28] John Dewey. "My Pedagogic Creed," in W. Baskin, ed., *Classics in Education. New York:* Philosophical Library, Inc., 1966, p. 180.

knowledge necessary not only for productive work but also for the ''worthy use of leisure time.''

The curricular program developed to meet these aims assumed that young people preferred group sports; more importantly, it was believed that team sports, which demanded cooperative endeavor, best inculcated social skills. At the same time, since students were being prepared for future leisure-time pursuits, the program also advocated individual sports and recreational activities. Because aesthetic sensibilities were also considered an important cultural value, dance was given a place in the curriculum. Other social needs identified and met through the physical education curriculum were emergency health care (first aid and safety education) and road safety (driver education). Unfortunately, in the desire to meet *all* the designated social needs of the young through physical education, the curriculum became an unwieldy hodgepodge of activities, many only distantly related to sports, dance, and exercise.

This affected professional preparation programs that tried to graduate teachers able to meet any eventuality. With so many skills deemed necessary, it became impossible to learn each of them well enough. This problem touched off, in the late 1960s, a movement away from the generalist and toward the specialist. Certification was given in specific areas such as elementary physical education, driver education, health education, or coaching, and some curriculums even began to develop activity specialists in aquatics, dance, gymnastics, or team sports.

The focus on social development also brought a change in teaching methods. Originally, when the curriculum began to emphasize sport over exercise, the authoritarian teaching approach appropriate to the European exercise systems had been retained. The new physical education tried to be more democratic, advocating that the felt needs of students be taken into account. To develop leaders, squad organizations were set up; student assistants or captains were elected and were given responsibilities. Girls' physical education programs made particular use of this technique and leader clubs became common in the high schools. Discussion time was increased, Williams (and his colleagues) reminded the profession:

The time is past when a physical education period is adjudged good or bad depending upon the amount of physical activity obtained during the period. A period is good or bad to the extent of desirable, useful, and pertinent intellectual knowledges, skills, and control obtained.[29]

[29] J. F. Williams, J. I. Dambach, and N. Schwendener. *Methods in Physical Education.* Philadelphia: W. B. Saunders Company, 1932, p. 81.

In fact, this emphasis became so important that pleasure in physical activity for its own sake was denigrated.

What then, is to be said of the efforts of certain persons to develop large and bulging muscles or to pursue certain odd skills that have no useful function in life? The satisfactions derived from such exercises serve only whimsical values such as exhibitionism; at times they are outlets for maladjusted personalities. For example, the yoga devotees may finally acquire unilateral control over the *rectus abdominus,* but the evidence is lacking that this has in any way deepened spirituality.[30]

From 1930 to the present, education *through* the physical became a goal of physical educators, despite some sporadic attempts to return to education *for* the physical, as discussed in Chapter 1. It was translated into a curricular emphasis on team sports and on an advocacy of lifetime sports. It was the rationale for increasingly expanded and expensive programs of intercollegiate and interscholastic sport. It was used to persuade state legislatures that physical education served an important role in meeting the schools' aim—to prepare the citizen for American life. During this period virtually all states that had not already done so passed legislation requiring physical education for public school children. Most colleges and universities (all but about 6 percent) required a course in physical education.

To sum up, the development of the socializing objectives of physical education helped to establish the subject as an integral part of the American educational system. From that vantage point, the profession was able to expand its programs—its curricular activities, extracurricular sports and dance, membership, facilities, and existence in most of the nation's schools and colleges.

Summary

1. The fact that physical survival is inherently related to the quality of an individual's existence means that survival is directly related to good health and/or physical fitness.
2. In most ancient societies, learning and practicing of sports skills was first developed for survival alone. Then children and adults played and competed in skills that could be transformed to self-protection and survival skills.
3. Evidence abounds that the earliest societies participated in running, throwing, wrestling, archery, spear and boomerang throwing, paddling a boat, swimming, ball playing, and dancing.

[30] J. F. Williams. *The Principles of Physical Education,* 8th ed. Philadelphia: W. B. Saunders Company, 1964, pp. 186–187.

4. In Sparta, we find a society that epitomized the concept of physical training for survival purposes. All efforts were bent toward this end and were successful to the extent that Spartan warriors were famous for their courage and ability. Sparta dominated its region for over 400 years.

5. During the time of the Roman Empire (31 B.C. to 455 A.D.) soldiers and athletes were professionals. Sport participation as part of the daily lives of individuals disappeared in the wake of the circus performances and professional athletic exhibitions. The Roman people spent much of their time in the public baths to exercise and relax.

6. Frederick Ludwig Jahn, an ardent German nationalist, originally developed a form of gymnastics called *Turnen*. This program was designed to develop strength in young men for the day when they would fight for Germany. Gymnastics became the basis for the German school physical education.

7. A Swedish nationalist, Per Henrik Ling, believed that training in fencing and gymnastics would help restore the physical health and military power of the country. Unlike German gymnastics, which used heavy apparatus, Swedish gymnastics emphasized free-standing exercises and positions.

8. The Swedish and the German gymnastic systems were originally designed to build up the strength of individual males in order better to ensure national security.

9. In the 1860s, Dio Lewis introduced his system of light gymnastics to the United States. In the 1880s, Dudley Sargent initiated his system of anthropometric measurements and prescribed individual exercise programs.

10. Although the European influence was prominent in the development of physical education in this country, the philosophy of sports and games became the mainstay of curriculums in the early 1900s.

11. Selective-service statistics from World War II revealed that a large number of men were not physically capable for military service. A study by Hans Kraus and Sonya Weber reported that American children were less physically fit than European children. These findings were instrumental in the development of The President's Council on Physical Fitness and Sports.

12. The Homeric Funeral Games (1700 B.C.–1000 B.C.) revealed the importance of competitive sport in this early society.

13. During the Middle Ages, the feudal system of social organization developed, with an upper class of knights and clergymen and a lower class of peasants. This period witnessed the initiation of such events as two horsemen challenging each other with blunt lances, and the sports of football, tennis, bowling, and golf.

14. The modern Olympics were revived by the French Baron Pierre de

Coubertin in 1896. They have continued every four years except for the war years of 1916, 1940, and 1944.

15. The first intercollegiate contest in the United States was a boat race between Harvard and Yale in 1852. Baseball was started in 1859 and football in 1869.

16. The Intercollegiate Athletic Association of the United States was founded in 1906; in 1910 it became the National Collegiate Athletic Association.

17. In 1971, the Association for Intercollegiate Athletics for Women was formed.

18. Sports have served many purposes in different countries during different historical periods. Following the Athenians, many have felt that such characteristics as virtue, manliness, honor, responsibility, and sportsmanship could be taught through sports. The socializing objective of physical education helped to establish the subject as an integral part of the American educational system. In the United States this philosophy has been credited to such leaders as Luther Gulick, Thomas Wood, Clark Hetherington, J. B. Nash, and Jesse Williams.

Questions

1. Of what did physical education consist for the Spartans?
2. How would you differentiate the Roman physical education program from the Spartan approach?
3. Who were the German pioneers of physical activity? What were their respective contributions?
4. What were the most important characteristics of the Swedish system?
5. Document the fact that the political climate of the United States has been a determining influence upon organized physical activity.
6. Reconstitute the major elements of the ancient Olympics.
7. Are there any similarities between ancient Olympics and modern Olympics?
8. Describe some of the events that led to the founding of the NCAA.
9. Compare the original concept of the development of sport programs for women with today's trends.
10. Plato had a decisive influence on physical activity as part of total education. Who was Plato? What were his philosophical ideas about education and physical activity?
11. Identify these early leaders and make a brief statement about their main achievements: Pestalozzi, Rousseau, Froebel, Guts Muths.
12. What roles did theorists like Jesse Feiring Williams, G. Stanley Hall, and Jay B. Nash play in the promotion of physical activity as an agent of social development?
13. The development of the socializing objectives of physical education helped to establish the subject as an integral part of the American educational system. Document this statement.

5

TEACHING AND LEARNING—
INFORMAL EDUCATION

One of the most important factors responsible for humanity's dominant position on earth is its capacity to learn. In the broadest sense, people learn by interacting with the environment. In a somewhat more restricted sense, they learn the traditions, customs, and skills of the culture and society in which they grow and develop. The informal physical and social environment has always been and still is the most general educational agency responsible for much of what we learn. Highly specialized organizations, staffed by well-trained specialists, are not necessary for people to learn.

Children learn many things through informal play. Young girls and boys can learn what fair play means in their particular subculture as they learn the games common to that subculture. They also learn, at the same time and in the same manner, how to cheat and bend the rules to gain an advantage. No teacher is present—children learn how to behave just by interacting in their social environment.

Any child, adolescent, young adult, or adult can learn a sport skill without

Informal play

anything remotely resembling formal instruction. A young girl can purchase a tennis racket and some balls, go out to the local tennis court, and learn to play the game of tennis. All the necessary factors for learning are present. If she needs an idea of what a skill looks like, she can find someone to watch who is fairly skilled and then attempt to imitate this model by hitting the ball. The ball will go into or over the net and into or outside the boundaries of the court, thus providing the feedback necessary for her to modify her subsequent efforts. Through repetitive practice under these conditions, and assuming proper motivation, she can probably become a fairly competent tennis player. We all know people who have learned golf, tennis, bowling, and a host of other sport activities in this manner.

We also know that much can be learned about health, fitness, and recreation by reading books, seeing films, and gathering information through various other media. Through these means people have learned simply by being properly motivated and by interacting with the environment. The culture provides the necessary environments (tennis courts and libraries) and tools (tennis equipment and books) for substantial learning to occur in informal learning environments.

The nature of teaching

What is the nature of teaching? Obviously, many societies for many centuries have thought teaching to be of such importance that they have trained

The educational environment

specialists for this function, and have developed facilities to carry it out. As pointed out in earlier chapters, an increasing complexity of society requires vocational specialization. A society's rules, customs, skills, habits, traditions, art, literature, and music demand specialists to pass on this culture to the young. Without viewing the historical role of the teacher too romantically, it appears that the *teacher* has generally commanded substantial respect within any given culture.

However, to describe teaching as a specialized function within a complex culture, with the specific role of passing on that culture to the young, does not fully differentiate teaching from informal education as described earlier. Teaching emphasizes the acquisition of behavior in a formal setting. This is a valid description even of the "open classroom" or of "independent study," modes within the boundaries of formal education as opposed to the informal learning environments. The question then might be raised: "If behavior can be acquired in informal learning environments, why have schools and teachers?" This is not a frivolous question; many critics of current educational practices ask it or similar ones. The answer is twofold. First, teaching should ensure that people acquire behaviors they might not if left to the whims of informal educational environments. Second, teaching should make the acquisition of behaviors quicker and more enjoyable than an informal environment.

Possible roles for teachers

Teachers have viewed their roles in the learning process in many ways.[1] Some see themselves as "lamplighters," illuminating the minds of children and penetrating the darkness of ignorance. Others view their role much as a gardener, in terms of cultivation, planting, fertilization, and even a good plowing now and then. Far too often we have met busy little teachers who act like personnel managers, aiming at efficient minds and industrious bodies. Then there are the muscle builders who strengthen flabby minds and bodies through regimentation, discipline, and hard work, and, finally, teachers who simply try to pour into students endless amounts of materials and who are best described as bucket fillers. These descriptions are all caricatures, but like all caricatures they developed because in the past they have too often been true. Fortunately these descriptions are probably less applicable today than at any other time in history. The role of the teacher is changing as we begin to find out more about teaching. Teachers are beginning to demand a status within society that recognizes their basic importance to its ongoing well-being.

The basic role of the teacher is to change the behavior of students, to have them learn, learn efficiently, and enjoy the process. The day is past when teachers can avoid their responsibilities by suggesting that a student was lazy or just plain dumb. The teacher can no longer say: "I taught them, but they did not learn the material." Teaching without learning, without demonstrable changes in students' behavior, is simply not teaching.

Specific teacher roles

The ordinary teacher plays many roles at different times of the day, in different situations, and with different groups. These roles are highly specific, but it is possible to identify several generalized roles which many teachers are called on to perform.

1. *The role of manager.* Teachers in physical education, health, and recreation programs must plan programs, make time schedules, and maintain reasonable order within the classroom, camp, gymnasium, and on the playing fields. These are managerial tasks that require managerial skills to fulfill adequately.
2. *The role of instructor.* Teachers impart skills, knowledge, and social behaviors, among other things. Many students recognize this as the primary role of the teacher, and, indeed, it may be the role that evokes the greatest amount of teacher effort, being most directly related to the learning process.
3. *The clerical role.* Teachers keep records, make out reports, administer tests to

[1] N. Postman and C. Weingartner. *Teaching as a Subversive Activity.* New York: Delacorte Press, 1969.

students, score and analyze those tests, and report progress to students, administrators, and parents. To fulfill this role properly, the teacher needs to possess testing, analyzing, recording, and reporting skills.

4. *The role of professional.* Teachers, including physical educators, health educators, and recreation workers, are professionals in the sense that they belong to professional organizations and have responsibilities within those organizations. Their professional role may conflict with some other role, as when a teacher takes several days off from the job in order to attend a professional convention. The greater number of roles a teacher has, the greater the possibility for conflict requiring resolution through setting priorities, either by the teacher or by his superior.

5. *The role as student.* Teachers in many states are required to attend school periodically to maintain their teaching credentials. Often, pay increases are at least partly dependent on advanced graduate work. However, this formal educational experience is not the only way that the teacher functions as a student. Reading professional journals, watching other teachers use new methods, and simply being an observer of the current educational scene allow the teacher continually to refine and upgrade his program and practices. The good teacher is a student all his professional life.

6. *The role of model citizen.* Teachers cannot escape the fact that they are models for their students; that is, students may tend to emulate the behavior of the teacher. Throughout history, teachers have been required to be model citizens beyond reproach in morals and ethics. Currently we are more realistic and students realize that teachers are human beings with human frailties. However, this does not relieve the teacher of his special obligation as a model for students. In the long run, if a student identifies with a teacher, he will do as the teacher *does,* not as the teacher *says.* A coach can talk about sportsmanship for hours, but if he is unsportsmanlike during games, that is the way his students will tend to behave. Likewise, teachers can promote the values of cardiovascular fitness, but if they are known to be smokers (and students inevitably find this out), then lecture, demonstration, and persuasion are much less effective.

7. *The role of counselor.* Physical educators have served as unappointed school counselors for many years. The less formal nature of the physical education environment seems to encourage student-teacher interaction, and often students feel that the "phys ed" teacher is a person with whom they can discuss school-related and personal problems. Many physical educators and coaches have performed a vital service to students in this sensitive area. Of course, many students feel that the physical educator might be the last teacher in the school they would consider going to with a personal problem; being a physical educator does not automatically cast you as counselor. However, if students perceive that you are receptive to them as individuals, you might spend a substantial portion of your time counseling students. Unfortunately very few undergraduate physical education programs help to prepare students for this very sensitive and vital role by including counseling skills and strategies in the undergraduate major program.

8. *The public-relations role.* Teachers exist outside the school as part of a community. If teachers are interested in the development of their programs or the general level of community support for education, they inevitably assume a public-relations role. This can range from making speeches at local service clubs or parents

The physical educator as a counselor

organizations to giving demonstrations during half times at basketball games, writing articles for local newspapers, or having a physical education open house during the evening. Note that in each example the teacher interacts with the public, directly or indirectly, to promote the program. The undeniable importance of the public-relations role can be overemphasized if teachers fall into the trap of describing a program in more glowing terms than the realities warrant, and spending time in public relations that might conflict with roles more directly related to the learning process.

A new role for teachers

We are now apparently redefining the role of the teacher. While some teachers of the future will probably still function in these roles, others may receive greater emphasis. Newly emerging is the role of team leader. More and more teachers are identified as leaders, administrators, or directors of a total educational team, directing the activities of each member to provide the most effective and efficient educational experience for the student. Some possible members of such an educational team are defined below.

1. *The paraprofessional.* This person may be a specialist in a specific area—a golf professional, a lifeguard, or a testing specialist—who will work under the supervision of the teacher while providing specific instructional, testing, or supervisory skills for the educational team.
2. *The teaching intern.* Professional preparation programs are increasingly emphasizing field experience. Future teacher trainees will more and more use the schools as training environments. The teaching intern might be a sophomore gaining an early field experience, a junior doing some small-group teaching or working as an assistant coach or trainer, or a full-fledged student teacher fulfilling the certification requirements of his undergraduate major.

The teaching intern

3. *The teacher aide.* Basically a record keeper, this person relieves teachers of some of the tedious but necessary clerical duties associated with teaching, thus enabling them to direct more attention to program and instructional roles. Two noteworthy trends are (1) hiring part-time teacher aides on a contract basis and (2) using parents as aides, thus bridging the gap between the school and the home.

Because teachers will guide and direct the team and perform the vital planning and supervisory functions, they will have to develop administrative skills as well as the ability to work in small groups with other adults and young adults. Again, these skills can be taught and need eventually to be included in the professional preparation of the teacher. The teaching-team concept, it is hoped, will free the teacher of certain tasks to devote more time to others that demand the expertness of a highly trained educational specialist.

Obviously the physical education, health education, and recreation specialists of tomorrow will need a number of highly developed skills in addition to the traditional sport skills. Administrative, supervisory, curricular, public relations, and counseling skills will enable the teacher to function effectively in roles necessary both in and out of school. The effectiveness of teachers in any given situation will depend on how properly they fulfill the specified role function. Thus, the answer to the ever-present question, "What is a good teacher?" can be found only by examining the degree to which the teacher can effect change by functioning effectively in a role. If an administrator measures good teaching primarily by how well the physical education class is managed, then the effectiveness of the teacher will be determined by how well he functions in his role as class manager. Likewise, if students or parents make judgments about teachers in their instructional or counseling roles, their success or failure will be determined by their effectiveness in these roles. Obviously, each teacher will not display a high degree of competency in all role functions: some will be good counselors but less than able instructors. It is important, however, that you recognize that teachers are called on to perform numerous and diverse roles. This is the first step in developing skills necessary to perform well within a role function.

Classifications of learning

What do students learn in physical education, health, and recreation? At one level, the answer is easy: They learn physical skills, game rules and strategy, how to play fair, and about fitness, safety skills, and other important outcomes. Traditionally, as we have discussed previously, learning outcomes have been classified as:

1. physical or physiological development
2. motor skill development
3. acquisition of self-knowledge
4. emotional and social development

This classificatory scheme, popular physical education for over 60 years, has the advantage of being familiar to professionals within the field. However, it does have some disadvantages, especially that it promotes a simplistic approach to what might well be complex learning problems.

The disadvantage of developing a more specific and complex method of examining what is learned in physical education, health, and recreation is the difficulty of mastering and teaching it. However, as education progresses, those preparing to teach physical education should begin to examine learning phenomena in a more sophisticated and precise framework.

Bloom's taxonomy of educational objectives

In the past two decades, attempts have been made to classify educational goals within the context of a taxonomy, that is, according to logical relationships.[2] It is now standard practice to classify educational objectives into three domains:

1. cognitive
2. affective
3. motor

The cognitive domain deals with knowledge and the development of intellectual skills and abilities. The affective domain deals with interests, attitudes, values, appreciations, and social-emotional adjustment. The motor domain includes all motor-skill development.

Obviously, skills within the cognitive and motor domains are much easier to define than those in the affective domain. This is true because the affective domain includes learnings which are internal, and it is difficult to write precise educational objectives for covert feelings. Instruments normally used to measure variables within the affective domain are still quite primitive, and they may remain so because covert feelings may never be open to reliable and valid measurement. Then, too, there is the problem of the relationship between overt behavior and covert feelings. What does it mean to appreciate the importance of fitness? Does this mean that you maintain adequate levels of fitness? Is it possible both to *appreciate* fitness and to *be* unfit? This is just one example of the difficulty of defining learning phenomena within the affective domain.

Bloom's taxonomic approach is an improvement over the traditional method of classifying learning outcomes, because it allows for a classification based on the type of learning involved. For example, students do not learn volleyball in the sense that volleyball is a unitary element to be learned. In playing volleyball, a student learns motor skills (spiking, bumping, and setting), rules, basic and complex offensive and defensive strategies, social behaviors specific to playing volleyball, and perhaps some general behaviors involved in task-persistence and emotional control. The taxonomic approach has the advantage of revealing that knowledge of rules or court markings is one particular level of learning within the cognitive domain, while learning strategies is a different level within the same domain. These cognitive learnings have motor correlates within the motor domain that may demand different kinds of learning situations. To learn a strategy in the cognitive sense is different from performing the strategy in the motor domain, and each learning problem may require a different strategy.

[2] B. Bloom, ed. *Taxonomy of Educational Objectives.* New York: David McKay Company, Inc., 1956.

Certain strategies may be more common to the cognitive domain; others may be more effective within the affective domain; still others, in the motor domain. By classifying what is learned within the framework of such a taxonomy, the teacher has the immediate advantage of recognizing what kind of teaching strategy may be most appropriate to the learning problem.

Gagné's learning hierarchy

Another approach to a better understanding of the teaching-learning process is classifying types of learning rather than categories of objectives. This view derives more directly from the experimental study of learning within the field of psychology. Rather than focus on cognitive, affective, and motor learning, this view examines learning problems that cut across all three domains. It allows the educator to delve more deeply into the nature of learning, regardless of the educational category within which the learning may be logically classified. For example, *discrimination learning* may be defined as learning to behave differently in different situations; it is found in cognitive, affective, and motor domains.

Gagné[3] has proposed a hierarchical approach which has been widely discussed in education. In learning hierarchy, types of learning grow progressively more complex. Mastering a complex learning problem depends partially on having previously mastered the less complex forms of learning on which the new problem is built. Gagné has identified eight learning levels within the hierarchy.

Teachers in physical education, health, and recreation are confronted with all the learning situations shown in Table 5.1, although it is unlikely that they are accustomed to dealing with them within this kind of hierarchical framework. It might prove useful at this point to translate these levels of learning into situations ordinarily confronted by teachers.

Signal learning might be encountered if a student had developed a fear of water, or if an adolescent student had undue anxiety concerning physical development. Many emotional behaviors are encountered in physical education and athletics, and dealing with emotional behaviors is within this learning type.

Stimulus-response, chaining, and verbal association deal with the simple kinds of learning encountered primarily in elementary schools. Ball skills, rope skills, learning to listen when a teacher talks, learning words, and other responses are covered in these three learning types. It should be remembered

---

[3] R. Gagné. *The Conditions of Learning,* 2d ed. New York: Holt, Rinehart and Winston, Inc., 1970.

Table 5.1   Hierarchical model for understanding learning

Gaǵne's eight types of learning

1. Signal learning	Reflex behavior including emotional responses.
2. Stimulus-response	Learning a single motor or verbal response to a specific stimulus situation.
3. Chaining	Motor responses linked together to form a motor skill.
4. Verbal association	Verbal responses linked together to form more complex verbal skills.
5. Multiple discrimination	Making appropriate motor or verbal responses to different stimulus situations.
6. Concept learning	Making a proper motor or verbal response in an unfamiliar situation.
7. Principle learning	Linking two or more concepts to perform an act in an unfamiliar situation.
8. Problem solving	Combining principles to provide solution to unfamiliar problem.

Source: R. M. Gagné, *The Conditions of Learning, 2d ed.* New York: Holt, Rinehart & Winston, Inc., 1970, pp. 63–64. (Adapted)

that the particular behavior taught is for a specific situation, what is normally called discrimination learning in psychology.

Multiple discrimination learning begins the more complex levels of the hierarchy. Learning to hit a straight pitch is one thing, but learning to discriminate among fast balls, curves, change-ups, and knuckleballs, and learning to make the proper batting response to each, is an exceedingly more complex learning problem. Most high-level sport skills are based on multiple discrimination learning, as are all important cognitive skills.

Concept learning can be motor or verbal. When a child who has never seen a Toyota nevertheless recognizes it as a car and is able to label it as such, the child has demonstrated the acquisition of a simple concept, that of an automobile. Baseball players learn the concept of the strike zone. Health educators learn the concept of sprain.

Principle learning and problem solving are the highest levels and draw heavily on previously learned multiple discriminations and concepts. A basketball player learns the principles of attacking a zone defense. Most strategy teaching in any sport involves learning concepts and putting them together to form principles. It should be noted that there is a substantial difference between stating a principle, which is simply a long verbal chain (level 4), and actually demonstrating the principle by performing it in an unfamiliar situation. Problem solving is yet one step higher. Features of the problem must be identified (levels 5 and 6 particularly), relevant principles must be selected, and finally they must be put together so that the problem is solved. A familiar situation is, of course, no longer a problem. Solutions to familiar situations become verbal or motor chains (levels 3 and 4). Again, problem-solving abilities can be demonstrated only by confronting the learner with an unfamiliar situation.

The essence of Gagné's approach to learning is based on the teacher's understanding both the *external* and the *internal* conditions necessary to learning. The internal conditions are the previous learnings necessary for the student to encounter the new learning problem; that is, the student cannot learn a principle if he has not learned the relevant concepts. He could not have learned the concepts unless he had made the necessary discriminations. The internal condition necessary to learning at any level is mastery of the previous level. This is Gagné's unique contribution. Once the concept of internal conditions is understood, Gagné's advice for setting external conditions for learning is fairly standard. You confront a learner with a proper situation, the learner makes a response, and the consequences of the response become feedback for evaluating the response.

A behavioral focus

More recently, the problem of defining educational objectives has been resolved somewhat differently by focusing on actual student behavior, which can be defined, observed, and measured. Students' attitudes toward fitness are defined by how fit they are. The degree to which students value the importance of leisure-time sports is defined by how regularly they participate in them. Obviously, their cognitive and motor behaviors are more easily measured and lend themselves well to the behavioral approach.

Critics of the behavioral approach insist that the most important outcomes of education cannot be measured in precise behavioral terms. They also argue that to focus on measuring behavior creates an unhealthy educational atmosphere.

Proponents of the behavioral approach suggest that the clarification of behavioral goals benefits both teacher and student. They also suggest that the success or failure of teaching and of the educational process itself can be evaluated only by reference to changes in student behavior, which carries particular weight in light of the current emphasis on accountability in education.

The behavioral approach can define the basic behavioral situations encountered in teaching by focusing on combinations of the three basic learning variables, stimulus–response–stimulus (S-R-S, see Chapter 6). Behavior can be taught—or, in the language of research—a student can be taught to

Table 5.2 Basic behavioral learning situations

1. Free operant	A behavior is developed and maintained generally by positively reinforcing it in different situations.
2. Discriminated operant	A behavior is developed and maintained by reinforcing it only in specific situations. The behavior then tends to occur only in those situations.
3. Punishment	A behavior is suppressed generally by punishing it in different situations. The behavior tends not to reoccur independent of situation.
4. Discriminated punishment	A behavior is suppressed by punishing it in specific situations. The behavior tends not to recur in those specific situations.
5. Escape	The presence of a punishing event is terminated by emitting a behavior. That behavior tends to recur because the removal of punishment is rewarding.
6. Avoidance	A behavior is emitted in a situation in which a punishment has previously been encountered, thus avoiding the punishment. The behavior tends to recur in that situation.
7. Omission	Not emitting a particular behavior is reinforced in different situations. The behavior tends not to be emitted independent of situation.
8. Discriminated omission	Not emitting a particular behavior in a specific situation is reinforced. The behavior tends not to be emitted in that specific situation.

Source: Based on B. Rushall and D. Siedentop, *The Development and Control of Behavior in Sport and Physical Education.* Philadelphia: Lea & Febiger, 1972, p. 81.

emit a behavior or not to emit a behavior with positive or negative consequences. Rushall and Siedentop[4] have used some of the logical combinations of these three factors to define basic learning situations from the behavioral points of view.

The behavioral point of view is based on operant psychology. An operant can be defined simply as a class of behaviors. These may be motor-skill behaviors, strategy behaviors, social behaviors, rule-following behaviors, or any other observable, definable behavior. Table 5.2 contains the learning situations applicable to any of the traditional educational objectives associated with physical education, health, and recreation.

[4]B. Rushall and D. Siedentop. *The Development and Control of Behavior in Sport and Physical Education.* Philadelphia: Lea & Febiger, 1972.

Perhaps an example of the different ways to develop a simple behavior would prove helpful in understanding these behavioral learning situations. When teachers are lecturing, giving instructions about a skill, explaining a game, or discussing issues with a group of students, they want the students to be quiet and pay attention to them so that the information can be passed on efficiently. Learning to pay attention is a simple social skill. However, it can be taught in a number of different ways, and if students are not paying attention regularly, their behavior can be modified in several different ways.

One way to develop the behavior of paying attention is to yell at students or otherwise punish them when they are not paying attention. This would be *discriminated punishment training.* The situation is specific (the teacher is talking), the behavior is "not paying attention," and the consequence is some form of punishment. Another method would be to say something nice to a student who was attentive while you were talking. This would be *discriminated operant training.* Still another way would be to reward a student for omitting the behavior of not paying attention, that is, you might say "Jim, I appreciate it that you didn't talk and fool around while I was explaining that game to the class." This would be *discriminated omission training.* Thus, the same behavior can be developed in several different ways—the essence of the behavioral focus. This material provides a brief overview of what is most commonly referred to as *behavior modification* or the *applied behavior analysis* movement in education.

The learner as an individual

Information regarding the biological, psychological, and sociological development of the human being (as found in later chapters) is of great importance in helping the teacher set and achieve realistic and meaningful goals. We emphasize here that the teacher must integrate all this important information so that it has meaning for the student as a living, behaving individual. Teachers can never deal with students as if they were caricatures of physical development stages, psychosocial stages, or cultural types. The student is always an individual—a human being whose behavior is often very complex and highly individualistic.

The concept of the nuclear self

One helpful way of understanding the student's individuality is through the concept of the nuclear self, which developmental psychology divides into five factors. A teacher who is cognizant of the history of any individual student in these five areas has a good chance of understanding where that student is at any given moment and in any particular situation. These five factors are:

1. *Physical temperament.* This may be partially determined by genetic inheritance but is more probably affected by environmental factors. It refers most directly to a student's style of behaving.
2. *Sense of security.* This aspect of behavior is most directly related to the way the student has been treated by parents. It involves his growth toward becoming an independent human being, and may be particularly evident in the student's willingness to take social, physical, and academic risks.
3. *Linguistic and educational stimulation.* Students live in an academic environment, and their language skills are of crucial importance. Students differ greatly in the degree to which they have been exposed to linguistic and educational stimulation in nonschool environments.
4. *Cultural patterns.* Even within a relatively homogeneous student population there will be important individual behavioral differences resulting from ethnic, religious, and family influences.
5. *Defense mechanisms.* Almost all students have learned methods of defending themselves psychologically. It is human to attempt to escape from punishing situations and to avoid them in the future. All students have learned methods of escaping from and avoiding physical, social, and academic situations that might threaten them.

Any given instance of student behavior will somehow reflect aspects of the nuclear self. Obviously, no teacher can take time to examine the situation from these points of view in the midst of a behavioral interaction. However, as teachers develop long-term relationships with students, it is helpful to make efforts to understand their individual styles of behavior in terms of these important factors. Once a teacher discovers how a particular student defends himself psychologically, how willing he is to take social risks, how his particular religious or ethnic background affects his behavior, and what his physical style of behavior is, then he can interpret the student's behavior, attempt to effect change if so desired, and begin to predict how the student might react to new situations. This will particularly help the teacher in his roles as instructor and counselor.

The phenomenon of the self-fulfilling prophecy

The interaction of teacher and student affects the future behavior of both of them. Recent experiments[5] have shown that student performance in educational situations can be greatly affected by how the teacher *expects* the student to perform. Experimenters went into a normal classroom and administered aptitude

[5] R. Rosenthal and L. Jacobson. *Pygmalion in the Classroom: Teacher Expectation and Pupils' Intellectual Development.* New York: Holt, Rinehart and Winston, Inc., 1968.

tests to the students. After test results were analyzed, the experimenters (in the guise of school psychologists) picked several students at random and told the teacher that their aptitude scores were high and that hence they were underachievers. Of course, because of the random selection, this was not true. Nevertheless, by the end of the school year, the students originally designated as underachievers had indeed made great advances in their academic performances, far more than the other students in the class. Naturally, there are limits to the extent to which teacher expectation can affect student behavior, but it does appear to be an important variable.

Brophy and Good[6] have suggested a behavioral explanation for this, which has come to be known as the phenomenon of the self-fulfilling prophecy.

1. The teacher forms differential expectations for student performance based on early observations or outside information.
2. The teacher begins to treat the child differentially in terms of this early expectation.
3. The student begins to perform differentially, owing to the differential treatment by the teacher.
4. The performance direction of the student reinforces the teacher's early expectation.

This circular process continues to repeat itself. Student behavior and performance is enhanced in certain cases and depressed in others. The effects show up in the academic or skill performance of the student, in his behavior within the instructional setting, and in his attitude toward school in general.

The point is that teachers should not form unmodifiable opinions about

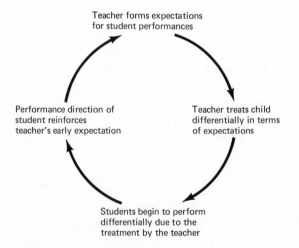

Teacher forms expectations
for student performances

Performance direction of
student reinforces
teacher's early expectation

Teacher treats child
differentially in terms
of expectations

Students begin to perform
differentially due to the
treatment by the teacher

Figure 5.1   Self-fulfilling prophecy cycle

[6] J. Brophy and T. Good. "Teachers' Communication of Differential Expectations for Childrens' Performance: Some Behavioral Data." *Journal of Educational Psychology,* 61, 1970, pp. 365–374.

students, especially from early experiences with them or from information from other, even supposedly "expert," sources. Teachers should be open to viewing students as individuals whose behavior can be maintained or changed. No student should be written off for any reason—pegged and then forever treated on the basis of that estimation. Students, as individuals, may behave differently at different times, and differently in gym than in math class. They can be "good guys" at home and "bad guys" at school (or vice versa). Your job is first of all to be responsible for their performance in your class, and then to attempt to know them as the complex individuals they are. Never be guilty of helping a student become a "loser" because another teacher or student or school psychologist told you he was going to be a "loser." Your job is to do everything you can to make him a "winner" in your class.

Teacher behavior

If it is productive to examine students as individuals who behave in different ways, then it is also of value to view teaching from the standpoint of the behavior of the teacher. After all, what teachers do when they teach is emit behaviors that supposedly fulfill whatever role in which they find themselves. Much research examining the characteristics of good teachers has a place, but the research is limited because of its focus on personality traits and such descriptions as "dominant" or "has a high need for achievement." The teacher in the gymnasium, locker room, or classroom is behaving, and it is therefore valuable to focus directly on the actual behaviors of teachers as they function in instructional settings. Recently, it has become more popular to examine the instructional environment from the standpoint of how teacher behavior affects the behavior of students. This is an important step forward in trying to understand the teaching/learning process. Two such systems will be examined: one used in many educational settings and one designed specifically to measure the behavior of physical education teachers.

Flanders' interaction analysis

Flanders[7] has developed seven categories of verbal teaching behavior, two categories of student behavior, and a final category in which are lumped periods of silence or confusion. Research with this system has used five scales

[7] N. Flanders. "Some Relationships among Teacher Influence, Pupil Attitudes, and Achievement," in B. Biddle and W. Ellena, eds., *Contemporary Research on Teacher Effectiveness.* New York: Holt, Rinehart and Winston, Inc., 1964.

Table 5.3   Categories for interaction analysis

Teacher Talk	1. *Accepts feeling:* Accepts and clarifies the feeling tone of the students in a nonthreatening manner. Feelings may be positive or negative. Predicting or recording feelings included.
	2. *Praises or encourages:* Praises or encourages student action or behavior, jokes that release tension, but not at the expense of another individual; nodding head or saying "um hum?" or "go on" are included.
	3. *Accepts or uses ideas of students:* Clarifying, building, or developing ideas suggested by a student; as teacher brings more of his own ideas into play, shift to category 5.
	4. *Asks questions:* Asking a question about content or procedure with the intent that a student answer.
	5. *Lecturing:* Giving facts or opinions about content or procedures; expressing his own ideas, asking rhetorical questions.
	6. *Giving directions:* Directions, commands, or orders with which a student is expected to comply.
	7. *Criticizing or. justifying authority:* Statements intended to change student behavior from nonacceptable to acceptable pattern; bawling someone out; stating why the teacher is doing what he is doing; extreme self-reference.
Student Talk	8. *Student-talk-response:* Talk by students in response to teacher. Teacher initiates contact or solicits student statement.
	9. *Student-talk-initiation:* Talk by students which they initiate. If calling on student is only to indicate who may talk next, observer must decide whether student wanted to talk. If he did, use this category.
	10. *Silence or confusion:* Pauses, short periods of silence, and periods of confusion in which communication cannot be understood by the observer.
	11. *Meaningful nonverbal activity:* Periods of silence in which the student is engaged in meaningful productive activity.

Source: After N. Dougherty, "A Plan for the Analysis of Teacher-Pupil Interaction in Physical Education Classes," *Quest,* XV, 1971, p. 50.

to measure the attitude of students toward the learning environment. These five scales are designed to measure the degree to which students:

1. like the teacher;
2. find the material interesting;
3. feel the rewards and punishments are fair;
4. feel free to make decisions and work independently;
5. feel anxious about the teacher's authority.

Research results indicate that pupils achieve more and have better attitudes when a larger proportion of the teacher's statements with regard to expanding activities are encouraging rather than restrictive and authoritarian.

The Ohio State University Teacher Behavior Scale

A teacher behavior scale for use in research and in training of physical education teachers presents opportunities for examining behaviors more specific to physical education environments. The scale has eight behavior categories as shown in Table 5.4. The scale is designed to use with a behavior-modification approach to training physical education teachers, but provides a useful categorization of the important behaviors emitted by teachers in physical education environments.

Table 5.4   A behavior scale for modifying the teaching behaviors of student teachers in physical education

Parameters of behavior categories

Behavior category	Behavioral parameters
1. Input teaching arts	Includes all teacher behaviors that provide a discriminative stimulus function directly related to learning. This includes questioning (teacher asks a question), explaining (teacher elaborates or summarizes previous material or clarifies a problem for better understanding), informing (answering a question), and providing guidance (including verbal guidance, demonstration, forced-responding, and physical restriction) (B. Rushall and D. Siedentop, 1972).
2. Managerial	Refers to teacher behaviors that provide a discriminative stimulus function indirectly related to learning. This includes establishing and maintaining order, directing the class to change activities, and giving directions for equipment, and so forth. Also includes role taking, marking down performance scores, and other forms of record keeping directly related to current behavior of students. These behaviors are primarily teacher initiated (discriminative function) and are not teacher reactions to student disturbances (consequential function).
3. Monitoring	Refers to watching the class as a whole, a subset of the class, or an individual student. No verbal or nonverbal interaction occurs.

119

4. No activity	Refers to all teacher behaviors in which visual contact is broken and no verbal or nonverbal interaction occurs. Includes looking out the window, being out of the room, talking to another teacher, and record keeping not directly related to immediate behavior of students.
5. Skill attempt— Positive IF	Refers to all positive verbal and nonverbal teacher reactions to an appropriate skill attempt by a student.
6. Skill attempt— Negative IF	Refers to all negative verbal and nonverbal teacher reactions to an inappropriate skill attempt by a student, including corrective feedback. Does not necessarily imply a punishing or menacing tone.
7. Positive reaction to on-task behavior	Refers to all positive verbal and nonverbal teacher reactions to on-task student behaviors other than skill attempts.
8. Negative reaction to off-task behavior	Refers to all negative verbal and nonverbal teacher reactions to off-task student behavior.

Source: D. Siedentop and C. Hughley, "O. S. U. Teacher Behavior Rating Scale," *Journal of Physical Education and Recreation,* February 1975, p. 45.

The following goals are sought when using the scale for modification purposes.

1. *Gradually decrease the rate of managerial behaviors.* This means that the student teacher gradually teaches students how to organize for activity, how to change activities, how to handle equipment, and how to perform other managerial tasks. As students become more self-directed in these tasks, there should be a reduction in the rate at which teachers need to emit managerial behaviors.
2. *Decrease rates of monitoring and no activity.* If teachers engage in these behaviors too frequently during an instructional period, they are simply neglecting their responsibilities as teachers.
3. *Increase the general level of information feedback.* An important way to improve teaching is to increase the rates of feedback, particularly of a positive nature. Research[8] indicates that physical education student teachers emit very low rates of these behaviors (approximately one every 2 minutes is an average rate of positive feedback).
4. *Maintain control of general student behavior while shifting from negative to positive forms of control.* Teachers must have control of general student behavior if they are to teach effectively. Students need not be in neat lines and always quiet; indeed, they may be very boisterous and seemingly moving in every direction. However,

[8] C. Hughley. *Modifying Teacher Behavior.* Unpublished Ph.D. dissertation, The Ohio State University, 1973.

students should listen when a teacher gives some instruction or direction, and should attempt to engage in the activity in an appropriate manner. They should not kick and hit classmates. Most physical education teachers maintain control by reacting in a negative manner when students misbehave (category 8 of the behavior scale). As will become clear in the following two chapters, it is far better to control student behavior by reacting in a positive manner (category 7 on the scale). When a student follows directions immediately, the teacher can compliment him. When a student is quiet while the teacher explains an activity, the teacher can thank him. Research[9] indicates that student teachers emit virtually no category 7 behaviors until an experimenter or supervisor intervenes to modify the behavior of the student teacher.

This behavior scale, covering virtually all the behaviors of teachers in an instructional setting, constitutes an important advance in understanding the teaching-learning process. Its main advantage is that it provides a framework within which student-teacher behavior can be measurably changed.

In-depth analysis of a specific teacher behavior

The behavior rating scale shown in Table 5.4 is general, with broad categories for a wide range of teacher behaviors. It is possible to describe and analyze any one of the behavior categories in more specific detail, as was done by W. Anderson[10] and his colleagues. An example of a highly specific teacher-behavior analysis is presented in Table 5.5. The behavior is augmented or artificial feedback, which is not normally a part of a task, but brought in for purposes of enhancing the learning environment during the training period.

Specific methods are needed to change student-teacher behavior so that student teachers will become better teachers. It does little good to tell prospective teachers that they can secure good discipline by simply being good teachers, presenting interesting material to the students, or utilizing efficient classroom management. While true in an abstract, formalistic sense, this advice remains insubstantial, failing to tell the prospective teacher *how* these goals are to be achieved. What techniques can be used and what evidence is there that the techniques are valid? We will now look at some techniques that are specific, have been substantiated by research, and can be used in most teaching situations.

[9] *Ibid.*

[10] W. Anderson. "Descriptive-analytic Research on Teaching." *Quest,* XV, 1971, pp. 1–8.

Table 5.5 Example of categories used for in-depth analysis of a specific teacher behavior

Classification of augmented feedback

1.0 *Form*
1.1 auditory: feedback provided orally.
1.2 auditory-tactile: feedback provided orally and with manual assistance.
1.3 auditory-visual: feedback provided orally and by demonstration.

2.0 *Direction*
2.1 single student: feedback directed to one student even though it may be seen or heard by others.
2.2 group of students: feedback directed to more than one student but fewer than all students.
2.3 entire class: feedback directed toward class as a whole.

3.0 *Time*
3.1 concurrent: feedback provided during performance of skill.
3.2 terminal: feedback provided after response is completed.

4.0 *Intent*
4.1 evaluation: feedback to provide an appraisal of the performance.
4.2 descriptive: feedback to provide an account of the performance.
4.3 comparative: feedback providing an analogy related to performance.
4.4 explicative: feedback to provide an interpretation of the performance.
4.5 prescriptive: feedback to provide instructions for a subsequent attempt.
4.6 affective: feedback to provide an attitudinal or motivational set.

5.0 *General Referent*
5.1 whole movement: feedback directed to movement as a whole or to multiple components.
5.2 part of the movement: feedback directed to one component.
5.3 outcome or goal: feedback directed toward outcome or goal of performance.

6.0 *Specific Referent*
6.1 rate: feedback about time or duration of the movement.
6.2 force: feedback about strength or power expended in movement.
6.3 space: feedback provided about the direction, level, or magnitude of the movement.

Source: After S. Fishman and W. Anderson, "Developing a System for Describing Teaching," *Quest,* XV, 1971.

The control/teaching dichotomy

We have already suggested that a teacher may play many different roles while fulfilling his total role as a teacher, whether in a school or a nonschool setting. Obviously, the teacher's major role is that of instructor. When a teacher begins to spend more time administering, counseling, or doing public relations, his title is usually changed to counselor, athletic director, department chairman, or sports information director. Those whom we still call teachers spend most of their time in the primary teaching role (manager, instructor, and clerical roles in the previous role distinctions).

Within this framework it is useful to distinguish between two basic and different functions: (1) controlling student behavior (managing) and (2) teaching or instructing. Students will not learn anything if their behavior is so disruptive that they never engage in the learning process designed for them, be it a movement education problem-solving session or a varsity basketball practice. Learners first of all must attend the learning session where they have to pay attention and receive instructions, take care of the equipment, and refrain from doing harm to fellow students. In the broadest sense, they have to "try" to learn. All of this must occur *before* any learning can take place. These are what we refer to as "control" or "management" functions. An important part of teaching is finding efficient and useful ways that enable students to behave so that they can maximize their potential for learning.

Once the teacher has established control over the general behavior of the students, learning can proceed. Students can learn new motor skills, new ways to move, new methods of health education, new facts about cardiovascular fitness, new ways to behave in games, and new ways to have a great deal of fun doing it only after establishment of control. Teachers cannot escape this fact. This does not mean that we have to become authoritarian teachers, exerting strict punitive control over students. Indeed, the teacher behavior scale (Table 5.4) indicates that control methods can be positive as well as negative. In the important question of positive versus negative control, many strongly support the use of positive control methods. On the other hand, the question of control versus no control is a false issue. With no control over student behavior, learning will occur only by chance, and even then usually in spite of, rather than because of, the teacher's role.

The development of a total learning environment

Whether in a gymnasium, classroom, recreation center, or summer camp, the teacher of physical education, health, and recreation must come to view the situation as a total learning environment. Within this environment students will learn, to some extent at least, what the teacher has specifically intended they learn, be it a sport skill, a new fact or principle, or a piece of complex strategy. They will learn these things efficiently to the extent that the teacher arranges the learning environment to expedite their acquisition. This will be accomplished to the extent that the teacher can set up imaginative and relevant learning situations (the first S in our S-R-S formula), provide for maximum learner involvement (the R in the S-R-S formula), and provide relevant, meaningful feedback and reinforcement (the final S in the S-R-S formula).

However, the student will also learn what the environment tells him about what he is learning and how he is learning it. This is what Marshall McLuhan meant in his now famous "medium is the message" thesis. The student will learn whether learning is an active or a passive pastime, whether he can speak his own mind or should just follow instructions, whether risk taking is approved, or whether being a good student means obeying the teacher. On the other hand, the student may learn that being a good student means taking stands, defending them, and helping others. The total learning environment conveys a message to the learner far beyond the specific skills or knowledges being taught. This is precisely why teachers must be cognizant that they operate in total learning environments, and must ensure that the message the environment conveys to the student is the message that the teacher wants it to convey.

The cult of the personality in teaching

It is probable that a teacher with a pleasant personality, who really cares about students, is a better teacher than one with a dull personality who doesn't care. A point of caution: It is too easy for prospective teachers to fall into the trap of viewing their personalities and their relationships with students as matters of overriding importance in their careers as teachers.

A recent survey[11] asked students and teachers to rank order what they felt was most important in the educational experience. The teachers ranked such items as (1) commitment to students, (2) ability to communicate, and (3) closeness of teacher-student relationships as the most important factors. They ranked "specific learning objectives" last. The students, on the other hand, ranked "specific learning objectives" first on their lists. Even though the research was carried out at the college level and generalizations to other levels of education are not warranted, the implication is rather clear. While warmth, understanding, and close teacher-student relationships are important goals, they do not supersede the more specifically educational goals. The first responsibility of the teacher is to help students learn: to learn skills, knowledges, and social behaviors that the educational institution deems worthy and important. Fulfilling the more personal objectives of warm teacher-student relationships should not

[11] A. Cohen. "Technology: Thee or Me? Behavioral Objectives and the College Teacher." *Educational Technology*, 10, 1970, pp. 57–60.

take precedence over learning. The teacher who attempts to win students with his personality and whose reputation is based on being a "nice guy" does not fulfill his primary function of being responsible for student learning. The ideal, of course, is for a student to come to the end of an educational experience not only having learned a great deal, but also having come to know the joy of learning and having developed a warm and lasting relationship with another human being who happens to be a teacher.

Summary

This chapter introduced the reader to the general nature of the teaching-learning process, emphasizing the following points.

1. Human beings can learn motor, cognitive, and social skills without the formal guidance of a teacher; that is, the necessary conditions for learning exist in informal learning environments.
2. Creating a specialized teaching function ensures that people acquire behaviors they might not otherwise acquire and do so efficiently and enjoyably. Teaching can be meaningfully defined only by referring to changes in learner behavior.
3. Teachers have specialized role functions, including those of manager, instructor, clerk, professional, student, model citizen, counselor, and in public relations. A new role involves managing a team including paraprofessionals, interns, and teacher aides.
4. Learning may be classified in terms of educational outcomes (Bloom's taxonomy), hierarchies of learning types (Gagné), or categories of behavioral situations (Rushall and Siedentop).
5. The learner is an individual whose behavior is always a function of a complex history. Teacher expectation is an important variable affecting student achievement.
6. Teacher behavior is an important variable in the learning process. Teacher behavior can be analyzed by different methods (Flanders, O.S.U. Behavior Scale, and others).
7. The primary role of the teacher is as manager-instructor. This involves managing the behavior of students so as to create an environment in which learning and instruction can take place. The management-teaching functions involve different problems and require different strategies.
8. The student will learn what the teacher has prescribed, but will also learn what the environment tells him about the nature of learning. The role of the teacher is to develop a total learning environment.

125

Questions

1. Explain the S-R-S nature of learning variables. Find examples of antecedent stimulus situations and consequential stimulus variables.
2. One important role of a teacher is to serve as a catalyst for a more efficient acquisition of behaviors. Do you see any relationship between the objectives of a program and the type of behaviors a teacher wants to instill in the students?
3. Characterize emerging roles of a teacher. How different are these new roles from traditional ones?
4. Identify Bloom's taxonomy of educational objectives and Gagné's learning hierarchy. Compare them.
5. Use Gagné's eight types of learning and give an example of your own for each type.
6. Explain in your own words Gagné's unique contribution to learning theory. What are the implications of this approach?
7. Do you see any practicality to Rushall and Siedentop's development and control of behavior approach?
8. What would you suggest to replace the punishment-oriented method to develop the behavior of paying attention?
9. What are the five most important factors that describe the nuclear self?
10. What does the literature say about the teacher's early expectation and student performance?
11. Try to remember the best physical education teacher you have had. Could you associate his or her behavior with the schematic parameters of behavior categories used at the Ohio State University?
12. How important is a teacher's personality in the teacher-learning process?
13. Identify different types of feedback and construct an example for each one.

INSTRUCTIONAL MATERIALS

Necessary conditions for learning

The fact that people can learn in informal learning environments indicates that the important variables that contribute to learning are present. At the most basic level, the conditions necessary for a student to acquire a skill or to learn any material are (1) an antecedent stimulus situation (S), which we might label a learning situation; (2) a response (R) from the learner (most often overt, but occasionally covert); and (3) a consequential stimulus (S) in the form of feedback/reward. *Stimulus* is simply the psychological term for classifying environmental events. Thus, our basic learning formula is of the S-R-S nature.

The art and science of teaching is involved mostly with the manipulation of antecedent and consequential stimuli, that is, with setting up learning situations and manipulating feedback/reward. For example, if you use a loop-film to demonstrate a skill, you are setting up an antecedent stimulus situation. If you tell a student to straighten his arm in the backswing, you have used a consequential stimulus variable (feedback). If you tell your students that running

127

a mile in less than 6 minutes earns them an "A" for fitness, then you are manipulating reinforcement, another consequential stimulus variable. Throughout this section it will be helpful to keep in mind the importance of the S-R-S nature of learning variables.

The variables affecting learning do not change when the learning is cognitive or social rather than motor. Learning to follow rules in games, or to play fair in general, requires a clear definition of the situation, a response by the learner, and some feedback/reward from the teacher (or the environment). The S-R-S formula still holds. A close call by a referee or umpire is a learning situation (an antecedent stimulus situation). The learner makes a response to that situation (he might swear, argue, or accept the decision), and the appropriateness of that reaction is approved or disapproved of by coach, teacher, peer, or fans (feedback and/or reward from various sources). Again, the S-R-S formula provides the basic framework for understanding the learning process.

Anyone associated with schools at any level during the past two decades can give first-hand evidence of the media revolution. Special instructional materials once meant a 16 mm film, a slide projector, or a flannel graph. Today, overhead and opaque projectors are commonplace, as is the computer terminal in the classroom and imaginative combinations of slide projectors, film loops, videotapes, and programmed machines.

As we examine current instructional materials, it will be helpful to pinpoint what aspect of instruction each is designed to enhance. This is best accomplished by always keeping in mind the basic S-R-S model, shown in Table 6.1. A film loop, for example, is clearly designed to set a situation and provide information that is antecedent (the first S in S-R-S). An immediate videotape replay of your own attempt at high jumping is just as clearly consequential (the last S in S-R-S). Some materials, such as behavioral objectives and programmed instruction, will include all the elements of the basic learning model.

Table 6.1   Basic conditions for learning

S	R	S
Antecedent stimulus	Response	Consequential stimulus
Learning situation	A behavior	Feedback-reward
Demonstration	Skill attempt	Feedback
Question	Answer	Right-wrong

Types of communication

Teaching involves communication. Communication in the broadest sense is any form of interaction between individuals, between an individual and a group, between groups, or among any combination of individuals and groups. From a teacher's point of view, there are several criteria by which communication between teacher and student can be judged. First, the communication should convey the intended message; that is, the communication should be *accurate.* This accuracy can be judged only by the reaction of the recipient. Second, the communication should be *efficient*—it should not take any more learner time than necessary. Teachers who spend fifteen minutes demonstrating and explaining a skill that could have been better done in five minutes through another method of communication violate this criterion badly. Third, the communication should contribute to rather than detract from the *motivational* level of the learning environment. A particular film or lecture may be so boringly presented or a textbook so badly written that the information contained does not get communicated because the audience lacks motivation to absorb it. If the form of communication between teacher and student is accurate, efficient, and appealing, then the learning potential is optimized.

Verbal communication

Communication is both verbal and nonverbal. Instructions, orders, pep talks, verbal feedback, and lectures are all forms of verbal communication. The teacher behavior scales described in the preceding chapter focused primarily on the verbal behavior of the teacher.

Several basic types of verbal communication are widely used by teachers. Each has its proper place in teaching, and the good teacher knows when to utilize the proper form.

1. *Informational communication*—where the goal is simply to pass on information, such as in explaining the rules of a game or the mechanics of a skill.
2. *Persuasive communication*—where the goal is to talk an individual or a group into doing something (or not doing something) without resorting to direct authority, as in a pep talk with a team or in an individual counseling session with a student.
3. *Authoritative communication*—where the goal is to utilize the authority vested in the position (teacher-coach) to direct the behavior of students, assuming immediate compliance, as in telling your team to change to a zone defense, or in creating order by threatening punishment.
4. *Collaborative communication*—where the goal is to provide direction to students without supplying direct information concerning answers or goal attainment, as in suggesting a book or a new way of performing a skill.

Teachers' verbal behavior can also be considered in terms of its consequential nature, that is, as a reaction to student behavior. Verbal feedback can be positive ("you really set a good screen"), negative ("that was a lousy screen"), or correctional ("your feet were not wide enough when you set the screen"). Teachers also provide verbal feedback in terms of the general behavior of the class. This too can be negative ("you guys at that mat—quit fooling around") or positive ("I'd like to thank Squad 3 for following my directions so quickly").

Although the lecture—verbal communication—has been the standard American method of teaching, it has been considered for many years a basically inefficient method of communication and of limited value as a motivational device. Students often misinterpret the lecturer and write down the misinformation, study it, and learn it. They later find, on a midterm or unit test, that it was not the correct interpretation. Without taking notes, it is almost impossible to remember more than a few points made in a standard fifty-minute lecture. Powell[1] suggests the following points for developing good lectures:

1. A fifty-minute lecture contains approximately 5000 words, at a pace of 110 words per minute.
2. To be useful, lectures should be accompanied by a lecture outline or lecture notes emphasizing the important points.
3. Vocabulary should be simplified and not above the level of the audience.
4. Visual aids can enhance interest, focus attention, and clarify meanings that are difficult to transmit with words alone.
5. Visual and auditory explanations should reach the audience simultaneously.
6. Feedback from audience should always be obtained to improve the lecture for its next use.

Adherence to these guidelines would optimize the usefulness of lectures.

Nonverbal communication

Nonverbal communication is much more important than most teacher trainees realize, because much of the information we convey to students is by nonverbal means. The most obvious form of nonverbal communication in physical education is the demonstration of a skill. However, nonverbal communication goes far beyond skill demonstrations. We are all familiar with the meaning of a finger to the lips, a teacher standing with hands on hips staring down a class in order to get them quiet, the menacing look that tells us we have done

[1] L. Powell, *Communication and Learning.* New York: American Elsevier Publishing Company, Inc., 1969.

something inappropriate, and the smile, wink, or pat on the back that is a strong form of positive feedback.

How you dress and look as a teacher is a form of nonverbal communication. How you wear your hair, whether or not you smoke, and even the way you stand, sit, and walk may convey important messages to students.

There are two important reasons why nonverbal communication is of special interest to the teacher. First, the teacher is almost always aware of any message communicated verbally, but many times totally unaware of a message communicated nonverbally. A look of displeasure may disappoint a student without the teacher's having intended this. Second, students feel that the message conveyed nonverbally is the *real* message.

Pupils assume that nonverbal cues are more consonant with the actual feelings and thoughts of a teacher; therefore, those detecting a contradiction between a teacher's verbal and nonverbal behavior will accept the nonverbal as being more valid.[2]

Awareness of your own verbal and nonverbal types of communication can help you become a better teacher.

Verbal and nonverbal methods are the direct lines of communication between teacher and student. Naturally, the teacher also communicates in indirect ways, ranging from an announcement on a bulletin board to a mimeographed handout diagraming a defense, films, and even more sophisticated communication via computers.

The lesson plan

In traditional forms of teaching it is suggested that teachers develop yearly, unit, and individual lesson plans. Although the traditional methods of teaching physical education are often maligned, the idea of specific planning for yearly, unit, and daily learning experiences is educationally sound, and can, in some modified form, be recommended for almost every teaching system.

The traditional lesson plan usually includes the following elements:

1. The specific objectives of the lesson and how the lesson relates to the objectives of the overall unit.
2. The specific subject matter content to be practiced that day and how it relates to total content of the unit.
3. A fairly detailed time sequence for the lesson.
4. Patterns of organization, and teaching methods to be used for each aspect of the lesson.

[2]Charles Galloway, "Teaching Is More Than Words," *Quest,* XV, 1971, p. 70.

Table 6.2 Lesson plan for a ninth-grade volleyball class

Date: December 2   Unit: Volleyball (5th lesson)
Equipment: 2 courts, 10 balls   Class: 9th (boys)

Objectives:

1. To introduce bump pass.
2. To integrate bump pass return of overhead serve.
3. To integrate bump pass return of overhead serve into game situation.

Time Schedule:

10:00–10:05	Take attendance and explain objectives of lesson.
10:05–10:10	Explain bump pass/demonstrate/use students to model.
10:10–10:20	Use all balls/attempt to bump ball to yourself 10 times in a row.
10:20–10:35	Half of class on each side of nets/one side serve overhead/other side use bump return/alternate every 3 minutes.
10:35–10:45	Modified game conditions using overhead serve and bump return.
10:50	Class dismissed.

COMMENTS:

5. The equipment necessary to fulfill the objectives of the lesson.
6. A space for evaluation of how the lesson went.

Over a period of years, lesson plans are modified on the basis of such daily evaluation. These lesson plans can be stored in a central location, or even become part of a syllabus for teachers and/or students. An example of a standard lesson plan is presented in Table 6.2.

The traditional lesson plan can be a valuable instructional aid. Its obvious advantage lies in its careful planning of objectives and methods and in time distribution to meet these objectives. Its disadvantages lie in its obvious group orientation and in absence of individualization of instruction.

Behavioral objectives

During recent years the utilization of precisely defined behavioral objectives has grown rapidly. Today one is likely to find them being used not only for elementary school reading but also for music education, political science, and physical education. The behavioral objectives movement has grown out of the application of principles of behavioral psychology to educational endeavors.

Educational objectives too often have been vaguely stated. The teacher does not always understand what specific goals are to be attained, and the student is left even more in the dark. The student is told that he is expected to know, appreciate, understand, or be aware of some content or experience, but he does not know exactly what those verbs mean in terms of his performance in the classroom or gymnasium.

Behavioral objectives are also called instructional or performance objectives. They have enormous potential as instructional aids in physical education, in health education, and in recreation. They can be used in programmed instruction and in teaching systems to optimize the potential of any learning environment.

There are three main parts of any well-written behavioral objective:

1. a behavior stated in observable, measurable terms;
2. the conditions under which the behavior is to occur;
3. the criterion stating when the objective has been achieved.

The behavior

Stating a behavior correctly depends primarily on the kind of verb used in the objective. If the verb requires inferences, then it is inadequate. The verbs *to know, to learn, to appreciate,* and *to understand* are examples of verbs requiring inferences because they do not describe what the learner actually is to do. Verbs such as *to dribble* a basketball, *to underline, to fill in* a blank, *to do* a head stand, and *to tape* an ankle require no further inferences about what the learner is to do.

The conditions

A well-formulated behavioral objective will make explicit the conditions under which the behavior will occur. This part of the objective tells what is and is not imposed upon the learner. If the behavior is the forehand stroke in tennis, the conditions will make clear under what circumstances the student will perform the forehand stroke. Will he bounce the ball to himself? Will he have it thrown to him by a classmate? Will it come from a machine? Will it be hit to him by an opponent? As you can see, by changing the conditions, you can change the degree of difficulty of the objective. The important point is to recognize that the learner should understand the conditions.

The criterion

The criterion sets the level of performance needed to meet the objective and probably to move on to the next objective. Again, the difficulty of any behavioral objective can be changed by changing the criterion. The criterion for a forehand serve might be:

1. three out of five that land in the opposite court;
2. three out of five that pass between the net and a line stretched parallel to and four feet above the net and land in the opponent's court;
3. three out of five that pass between the net and the line and land within a designated target area within the opponent's court.

The first criterion can be fulfilled just by getting the ball across the net and into the opponent's court; the second requires that the forehand stroke have sufficient velocity (it avoids the lob stroke); and the third adds a measure of accuracy.

By manipulating the conditions and the criteria for objectives, the teacher can develop a set of progressively more difficult objectives. The criterion for the objective can be left open-ended so that the student can continually attempt to improve performance. Examples of such objectives for first-grade physical education were presented by Frederickson.[3] For example, one such objective was "I can jump rope _____ times without tripping or stopping," or "I can juggle two beanbags _____ times without dropping either of them." Sometimes a criterion of duration is implied in the objective. For example, the objective "when on the pool deck, the student will walk" implies that the student will always walk and will never run when on the deck.

The advantages of behavioral objectives as instructional aids are numerous:

1. The learner knows exactly what is expected of him.
2. The learner competes against a standard.
3. The learner has many chances to achieve the objective.
4. Explanation time is decreased owing to the preciseness of the objective.
5. The student can move through a program at his own pace.
6. The student knows exactly when an objective is completed.
7. The intrinsic and augmented feedback within the objective aids learning.

Behavioral objectives can be of great use in programmed instruction and are an integral aspect of the teaching system called *contingency management.* Some examples of behavioral objectives are presented in Table 6.3.

In developing good behavioral objectives, the teacher must make sure that the objective excludes skills that the teacher does not want developed. For example, if the criterion for the overhand serve in volleyball simply states that the student will serve the ball into the opponent's court, it leaves open the possibility that the student will hit a high lob-type serve (a *dink*). To exclude this possibility, the teacher can write a criterion for the serve to pass between

[3]V. Frederickson, "I Can!" *Journal of Physical Education and Recreation,* May 1972, p. 33.

Table 6.3   Development of some behavioral objectives

Conditions	Behavior	Criterion
Standing in legal service position, the student will serve 4 out of 5 overhand serves that pass between the net and a string stretched parallel to and 4 ft. above the net.		
Standing in legal service position	overhand serve	4 of 5 that pass between the net and a string stretched parallel to and 4 ft. above the net
Standing behind a line drawn 12 ft. from the wall, the student will make 8 consecutive overhead passes that hit the wall above the 10 ft. line.		
Standing behind a line 12 ft. from wall	overhead pass	8 continuous that hit wall above a 10 ft. line
Given diagrams of 4 zone defenses, the student will correctly label each one.		
Diagrams of 4 zone defenses	label	each one
Given a written description of a golf situation, the student will correctly identify the rule involved and the penalty imposed.		
Written description of a golf situation	identify rule and penalty	each one
When mounting the trampoline, the student will initiate the mount when 4 spotters are in place.		
Trampoline practice	mounting	when 4 spotters are in place
Given a list of 10 communicable diseases, the learner will identify, in two minutes or less, these diseases that develop immunity.		
List of 10 communicable diseases	identify those which develop immunity	correct identification within two minutes

the net and a string stretched parallel to and 4 feet above the net. In order to meet this criterion, the student would have to serve the ball with sufficient velocity to develop the actual serve the teacher wants developed. Behavioral objectives can be judged in the following ways:

1. Is the behavior stated in observable terms or does it require further inference?
2. Are the conditions under which the behavior is to occur explicitly stated?

Table 6.4 Examples of behavioral objectives for developing balance and volleyball skills

Static and Dynamic Balance Objectives

1. Sitting on the floor with arms at his side and legs extended forward, the child will maintain balance for 1 min.
2. Lying on his right side, with underarm extended above the head and top arm placed against his side, the child will maintain balance for 1 min.
3. In hands and knees position (4 points touching mat), the child will raise his right arm and hold it up for 20 sec.
4. In hands and knees position, the child will raise his right arm and left leg simultaneously for 20 sec.
5. In a one-leg kneeling position (3 points touching mat), the child will maintain balance for 30 sec.
6. With arms at his side and body upright, the child will maintain balance for 15 sec, on knees only.
7. With arms folded across body and knee held high, the child will maintain balance on one foot for 10 sec.
8. The child as in position 7 will hold balance for 10 sec. with eyes closed.
9. The child will walk forward 10 ft. on a walking board without losing balance and without stopping.
10. The child will walk backward 10 ft. on a walking board without losing balance, stopping, or looking behind him.
11. The child will hop on one foot for 10 ft. without losing balance.

Volleyball Objectives

1. By throwing the ball to herself, the student will make 4 consecutive legal sets that reach a height of 10 ft.
2. By throwing the ball to herself, the student will set the ball so that it passes over a 12-ft.-high rope and lands within a target circle 3 out of 4 times.
3. By receiving a ball thrown by a teammate, the student will set the ball over a 12-ft. rope and have it land in a target 3 out of 4 times.
4. By throwing the ball to herself, the student will make 4 consecutive bump passes that reach a minimum height of 10 ft.
5. By receiving a ball thrown below the waist from 15 ft. away, the student will execute 3 out of 4 bump passes that pass over a 12-ft.-high rope.
6. By receiving a thrown ball, the student will execute 3 out of 4 bump passes that pass over a 12-ft.-high rope and land within a target area.
7. Standing behind the end line, the student will make 3 out of 4 legal overhand serves that pass between the net and a line stretched parallel to and 4 ft. above the net.
8. Standing 15 ft. from a wall, the student will throw the ball to herself and spike it so that it hits the floor and rebounds from the wall so that it can be spiked in this manner 4 consecutive times.
9. Given a setup pass 4 ft. above and 1 ft. away from the net, the student will use a 3-step approach and 2-foot takeoff to execute a successful spike 3 out of 4 times.

3. Is the criterion for achieving the objective clear?
4. Does the objective exclude skills not intended to be developed?

Table 6.4 details two examples of behavioral objectives. The first is a set of objectives for developing static and dynamic balance in a perceptual motor development program for children. The second set is from an instructional volleyball class for college women.

Books as instructional aids

The growth of professional physical education, health education, and recreation has been accompanied by a phenomenal increase in the number of books in these fields that can serve as instructional aids for the teacher. Many are textbooks; a number cover many sport rules, history, skills, and strategies; activity series books perform the same service in greater depth for individual activities. These have proved to be especially popular at the college level for physical education instruction.

An increasing number of books cover the entire range of physical education, describing the *why* of physical education and physical fitness. These are less activity-oriented and more academic, and can be used in either high school or college.

The considerable number of books on health education range from general books encompassing all aspects of health education to smaller, more specifically oriented books on particular health education subjects, such as drugs or sex education.

In recreation education there are perhaps an even wider range of books from which the professional can choose. Books on games, handicrafts, and other recreational pursuits abound and are readily available for both school and nonschool settings.

The availability of books as instructional aids can be of great potential to the teacher. Much information and material formerly communicated by a lecture can now be communicated out of class by reading assignments. The student can read at his own pace and is less likely to be misinformed. The major disadvantage of books is quite simply their cost. Education costs have soared in recent years, and adding more and more reading requirements makes necessary the purchase of more books, thus further increasing the cost of education. This is especially important if the outlay for books might have gone to equipment, facilities, or other instructional materials.

Nevertheless, the proper use of books as instructional aids can greatly increase the amount of actual practice time the teacher has available. If students read about a game, learning rules and strategy from a book, then the class time can be spent actually playing the game, which cannot help but be more sound educationally.

Television as an instructional aid

Television has probably influenced growing up in the modern era more than any other single factor. There are more television sets per capita in the United States than there are bathrooms or automobiles. Children are said to watch on the average of 4 to 6 hours of television per day.

"Educational" television is a common designation without precise meaning. Much television is educational in the sense that we may learn things by watching it. Hixson[4] has made a very useful distinction between educational television and instructional television. Instructional television is designed to be an integral aspect of the formal educational environment. It may be educational for a student to watch a golf tournament on a Saturday afternoon or a program on heart disease some evening, but these programs are not instructional.

The "Shape-up" series of movement-education programs in New York is an example of instructional television. So too are the 30 lessons of elementary physical education developed by the National Instructional Television Center. These lessons are based on the newest concepts in content and techniques for elementary physical education and are entitled "Ready, Set . . . Go!"

Television taping has many instructional advantages. Assuming that the school has a video camera, many homemade videotapes can be useful as instructional aids. Videotape allows for editing, splicing, updating, and storage. While it is true that television is an expensive instructional aid, it is not uncommon to find a videotape system in many high schools and elementary schools today. Hixson[5] has suggested the following potential uses for television as an aid in instructional settings:

1. providing expert instruction to groups when expert live demonstrations are not available;
2. providing demonstrations by teams and individuals not ordinarily available;
3. providing augmented feedback (slow motion, stop action, and so forth);
4. self-instructional tapes for in-class and independent study use;
5. recording and replaying athletic contests or physical education classes;
6. recording student performance for later assessment when there are too many students to assess on the spot;

[4] C. Hixson, "Television in Physical Education," *Quest,* XV, 1971.

[5] *Ibid.*

7. evaluating the performances of teachers, coaches, and referees;
8. evaluating student-teacher performance;
9. research.

Much research on videotape as a form of artificial feedback has shown it to be a valuable tool in teaching motor skills. However, even if experimentally verified, it has yet to be demonstrated as a practical system for ordinary teaching situations. Videotape replay is time-consuming and is usually limited to one performer or one group, as in team play. It may well prove to be more useful in providing feedback for group action rather than for individual skill training. For example, a physical education teacher might tape a volleyball game in a regular class and use the replay to point out skill and strategy mistakes and also to provide positive reinforcement for good individual and team performances.

Instructional television can be used in many ways: to set up the learning situation by providing an expert demonstration on video tape; to record individual or group responses of students; and to supply a feedback source. Additionally, television can provide interaction among people from different geographical regions. Kalakian[6] has described a *telelecture* system that allows a speaker from any region to deliver a lecture and, with the help of a telephone hookup, interact with the distant audience in a question-and-answer session. Visual aids such as slides can be sent ahead of time and cued into the lecture presentation. With the permission of the lecturer, the host institution can record the entire event and have a permanent teaching aid. All of this can be

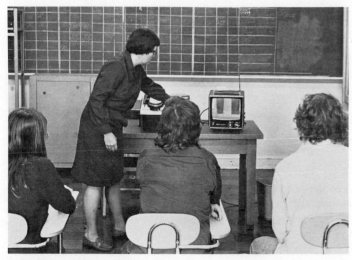

Teaching with video tape

[6]L. Kalakian, "Telelecture," *JOPER,* May 1970, p. 40.

accomplished at a fraction of the cost of bringing a speaker to a school from afar.

Television has also been used for interregional athletic competition in sports such as gymnastics, thus saving traveling expenses and student time. Naturally, this has limitations, and it should also be recognized that traveling and face-to-face interaction in educational or competitive situations have added educational significance.

Programmed instruction

Programmed instruction is one of the more important innovations in education during this century. Sidney Pressey of The Ohio State University is thought to have created the first teaching machine in 1915. However, the immense growth of programmed instruction followed B. F. Skinner's article of 1954, "The Science of Learning and the Art of Teaching," published in the *Harvard Educational Review.* Most of what we know as programmed instruction today is a direct outgrowth of Skinner's work in behavioral psychology. Most people conjure up images of a teaching machine when they think of programmed instruction and, indeed, so-called teaching machines are an important element in the programmed instruction movement. However, programmed instruction can also be packaged in the form of books, audio tapes, television tapes, films, records, or computer terminals.

Programmed instruction need not be thought of as some terribly difficult product of twentieth-century technology. Many teachers have informally programmed their instructional settings for years. Many of the instructional aids discussed here and some of the teaching systems described make use of some or all of the basic features of programmed instruction.

Basic features

All programmed instructional materials have certain features in common:

1. Students are required to focus their attention on a limited amount of material at a time. The extent to which the material is broken down into small units (the unit is usually called a "frame") depends upon the difficulty of the material, the age of the learner, and the stage of learning involved.
2. The student is required to respond to each segment of the material. Perhaps the most distinguishing characteristic of programmed instruction is that it directly involves the learner by requiring verbal or motor responses to each of the steps in the program.

3. The student is given immediate knowledge of results. Whenever the student makes a response, the correctness or error in the response is made immediately available to the student.

These three features (limited amounts of material, student responses, and immediate knowledge of results) form what is called a *learning cycle*. You will notice that the learning cycle is the basic S-R-S format we have strongly emphasized. This cycle is repeated many times, and forms the basis of all programmed instruction. Because the material is programmed, the student can move through the material at a fast or slow pace. Individual pacing is a general characteristic of programmed learning cycles.

Not all programs are good programs. Programmed instruction is not the only means by which educational objectives can be achieved. Badly prepared programs can be devastatingly boring and produce little if any learning. However, the basic value of programmed instruction cannot be denied. Well-designed programs have been demonstrated, in various settings with various kinds of learning, to be of significant educational value as compared to other kinds of instructional materials.

Programmed instruction works because it adheres to sound educational principles and applies as much as possible what has been discovered about human learning. Material is effectively presented in sequence and in well-ordered progression. Material is mastered in steps so that the learner is not confused by a host of information. The learner is actively involved in the process. The learner receives feedback immediately, and can correct mistakes before they become habits. The individual pacing allows the learner to move at his own rate of learning. The small steps and immediate feedback ensure an optimum of success in learning and a minimum of failure. Taken together, these features constitute a sound instructional format, and that is precisely why programmed instruction has been widely accepted as an important instructional aid.

Steps in developing programs

Developing good programs is a skill learned by attempting to follow some model, trying it out, and revising on the basis of feedback. The following steps are necessary to begin to develop programs for teaching:

1. Decide what material is to be programmed. This means specifying precisely the goals for learning, such as a motor skill, a knowledge of rules, a knowledge of strategy, or the performance of strategy.
2. Break the material down into small units. These can be thought of as tasks to be accomplished, and they may be in the form of behavioral objectives. In the language

of programmed instruction, the unit is called a *frame*. The size of the unit (frame) should be such that it can be learned with optimum motivation. The unit should not be so easy that it bores the learner, but at the same time not so difficult that it cannot be achieved with sufficient effort by the student.

3. Try out the program by administering it to a class. Use the program in a unit for six, eight, or ten weeks. You will find out many things by getting feedback from students. Was the material presented clearly? Were certain steps too hard or too easy?

4. Validate by measuring how much the students have learned. This can be a formal evaluation, by comparing with other classes or with previous classes, or an informal evaluation based on your previous experiences in teaching. You might also gather opinions from your students on how well they liked the program.

After trying out and revising programs several times, you should have a good idea about the size of unit (task, frame, and so forth) that will best accomplish your goals. The question of error rate is much discussed in the programmed instruction literature. Originally, it was assumed that units of material would be so small that learning would proceed without errors. However, research indicates that certain kinds of programs built on very small units (and thus low error rates) can be very boring and thus lead to less learning. With no other motivational technique than the program itself, it has been found[7] that an error rate of 50 percent produced best learning; that is, in the absence of other sources of motivation such as grades, students seem to learn best when they have about a 50-50 chance of making a correct response to each unit.

Linear and branching programs

There are two basic types of programmed instruction. *Linear* programmed instruction breaks the material into fairly small units and each student progresses through all the material in the same sequence, although at different rates owing to the individual pacing feature. Linear programming is based on the concept of gradually *shaping* behavior until a desired terminal behavior is achieved. The student is helped along with each small step by *prompts,* which are really partial answers. The prompts are gradually faded out until the student has learned the proper response. The response is then presented in different situations so that the learned response becomes *generalized* rather than tied to a specific situation. There is no necessity for remedial work, because the units are usually small enough to make the error rate very low.

Branching programs usually involve larger units of material. The student goes through the program until an error is made. At this point, the student is directed

[7]W. Gay and B. Stephenson, "A New View of Reinforcement In Learning," *Educational Technology,* 12, 1972, pp. 48–49.

to another part of the program to correct the error just made. Once the error is corrected, the student is returned to the mainstream of the program. Branching programs allow faster movement through the program for abler students, while the students who need more detailed work are led through those remedial branches necessary to make corrections.

Branching programs have a positive as well as a remedial educational function. The material is programmed so that the more able student can skip material, while the average student tends to go through the program in a linear way and the slower student has the benefit of remedial branches. Thus, branches can accelerate or slow down, depending upon the individual needs of each learner.

For motor skill, using a behavioral objectives format, a branching program might be developed as shown in Table 6.5.

Locke and Jensen[8] have reviewed research attempts at programming sports skills instruction and concluded that in all cases the programmed method was equal to or better than traditional methods of instruction. Certainly content aspects dealing with rules, history, strategy, and mechanics can be programmed easily and would free the teacher from utilizing valuable practice time for these learning problems.

Whether motor skills can be adequately taught using a programmed instruction approach is a more difficult question. Given *only* programmed instruction, the learner may have difficulty getting a good idea of what the skill should look like. Words, pictures, and drawings simply do not convey movement information as well as demonstrations can.

The physical education teacher, fortunately, does not have to face this

Table 6.5 A branching program

Task # 15:

Given a ball thrown by a teammate. The student will make a legal bump pass that reaches a minimum height of 15 ft. and lands in the center-forward target area.

Student performance:

a. less than 5 out of 10. Proceed to task number 12 (a remedial branch for bump passing).
b. 5–7 out of 10. Proceed to task # 16 (a further bump-pass task) (normal progression).
c. 8–10 out of 10. Proceed to task # 17 (skips a task because of high level of proficiency).

[8] L. Locke and M. Jensen, "Prepackaged Sports Skills Instruction: A Review of Selected Research," *JOPER,* September 1971, pp. 57–59.

situation. Given the demonstrable benefits of programmed instruction, coupled with having demonstrations (models) provided by teachers, and other kinds of artificial feedback, the possibilities for programmed instruction in physical education would seem unlimited. Certain issues, such as the best size for a frame, need to be worked out, but programmed instruction offers the physical education, health education, and recreation teacher a viable instructional aid for optimizing the learning process. Several of the teaching systems mentioned in the next chapter will utilize programmed instruction techniques either directly or indirectly.

Table 6.6 shows frames from a program for teaching golf. The first frame is an introductory frame for teaching the golf swing with the iron. The next frame is a test frame for iron shots. On the basis of performance at this frame, the student is directed to the proper branch that will enable the learner to correct his errors or proceed with learning. The following frames are remedial frames. One of the frames is designed to remedy the problem of not being able to hit an iron shot in the air consistently. Another frame is designed to correct iron shots that slice.

In regular instruction, programmed materials are important instructional aids that, combined with the other elements of a good learning environment, should account for substantial learner progress. Programs can also be used outside the regular instructional format, in independent study options, enrichment courses for students who need accelerated or remedial work, and in-service training of personnel.

Visual aids

Visual aids of various kinds have been used for centuries in teaching, because the human being learns very well through the visual sensory system. While visual aids can be utilized in all aspects of the learning process, they are most often utilized in the antecedent stimulus portion of the basic S-R-S learning formula we have stressed; that is, visual aids are most useful in setting up a learning situation.

Visual aids are particularly useful in presenting material that is difficult to convey with words. A teacher demonstrates a skill in far less time and conveys the important information to the learner far better than he would explain it verbally. In this sense, a demonstration is worth a thousand words. Visual aids can help teachers communicate information that they cannot readily demonstrate themselves. When a team learns a new defense in basketball, the teacher/coach can convey information about the defense through

Table 6.6. Four frames from a branching program to teach golf

You are now ready to start work on the iron swing. The basic purpose of an iron shot is to get the ball onto the green so your next shot will be a putt. This, of course, entails accuracy in both direction and distance. There is no need for maximum distance because you can pick an iron that will get you the desired distance with a firm, controlled swing. However, to get a consistent result with your irons, it is essential that you get the ball *up into the air* every time.

There are certain basic fundamentals that are necessary before you embark on the details of a good iron swing. Your grip and stance must be correct. Remember to keep the "V's" of both hands pointing toward the right shoulder and to work the hands together as a single unit. Your stance should be comfortable with the knees bent slightly and the back fairly straight. The knees and elbows should be squeezing toward each other, and the weight evenly distributed between the feet.

During the swing, the body coils as if it were a spring. As it turns back to the right on the backswing, the weight should shift toward the right foot. As your body turns back to the left, your weight should shift to your left foot. When the swing is completed, you should always have the major portion of your weight on your left foot. Simply coil and uncoil, letting the weight flow easily in the direction you are turning.

The basic rhythm of an iron swing is a pendulum rhythm. That is, slow at the top and fastest at the bottom. The essential thing to remember is never to hurry the swing from the top. Let the club start down with a natural ease, and accelerate it only at the bottom. You can help yourself set this rhythm up by always starting the backswing low and slow.

Once again, the basic rhythm of the golf swing is a _____ rhythm.

Pendulum. Start the backswing *low and slow,* and don't accelerate the clubhead until you are in the hitting area.

The weight should shift from _____ to _____ during the downswing.

Right to left. The weight should shift to the right during the backswing, then back to the left during the downswing.

To get consistent results with your irons, it is essential that you get the ball _____ every time.

You have turned to this page because you have difficulty getting the ball in the air with an iron, and you feel that part of the difficulty may be your inability to keep your left arm straight during the backswing.

Have you tried to analyze the problem?

I would hope so, but if not, let's do it together and see if the system works well enough to convince you of the necessity for thinking your way through the fundamentals of the golf swing.

What is the anatomical problem that limits the length of the backswing when the left arm is straight?

Did you try it and see? Basically it is that the upper arm comes into contact with the chest, and the only way to keep the clubhead going in the direction of the backswing is to bend the arm at the elbow.

The way to get a longer backswing with a straight left arm is to turn the shoulders so the arm can go back farther without being stopped by the chest. In fact, the shoulders should always rotate to the point where you are *looking down at the ball* over the tip of your *left shoulder.*

If you can now keep the left arm straight and turn to the point where you are looking at the ball over your left shoulder, skip to the end of this lesson and follow instructions. If you are having difficulty yet, work on.

The problem now is that you have difficulty turning your shoulders far enough to look down over your left shoulder at the ball. Let's take another anatomical test. What action will free the shoulders to turn farther?

I am sure you recognized the fact you must turn your hips in the same direction to free the shoulders for greater turn. This is correct. The hips should turn about 45° to the right during the backswing. The hip turn is accomplished by bending the left knee toward a point behind the ball and letting the left heel come up about an inch off the ground. No more than an inch please!

In summary, the body turn starts at the feet and works its way up to allow a 90° rotation of the shoulders and a straight left arm. When you have accomplished this movement, hit some golf balls with your iron.

A. If you are now consistent in getting the ball in the air, turn to page 11.*

B. If you are still having trouble getting your iron shots into the air, turn to page 4.

Now hit twenty shots.
A. If the majority of the shots are slicing, turn to page 18.
B. If the majority of the shots are hooking, turn to page 20.
C. If you are satisfied that the shots are straight enough, turn to page 24.
D. If the ball is not getting up into the air so you can tell if it is slicing or hooking, turn to page 3.
E. If the shots are going in a straight line but left or right of the target, turn to page 28.

At least one of the causes of your slice iron shots is an outside-in swing arc that imparts a left to right spin on the ball, and thus a curving flight. In this lesson we will work on correcting the swing arc. You may still slice the ball when we are finished, but don't worry about that. If you can get the arc straightened out, there is only one problem left to lick.

Basically, your swing arc in the hitting area will be aligned with a straight line through your shoulders. If, when you contact the ball, your shoulders are pointing to the left of the target your swing will be going from right of the intended line to the left of the intended line, or outside-in. This is the swing arc you have indicated by coming to this lesson, so our problem is to square those shoulders at contact. To do this you must be sure you have turned back fully. That is, you are looking down at the ball over your left shoulder at the top of your backswing and your chin is lightly touching the shoulder. Next, you must be sure that the shoulders are turning in an over-and-under pattern, especially that the right shoulder turns under your chin during the swing. One way of checking this is to see where your hands finish on the follow-through. If your right shoulder is going under as it should, your hands will finish above your head. If your hands finish about shoulder level, you know your shoulder turn is too flat. Finally, it may help if you imagine someone is holding a pointed stick against the front of your right shoulder at address. Now swing through without impaling yourself on the stick. The *only* way you could do this would be to turn that right shoulder under in the hitting area.

When you are sure you are keeping your shoulders square in the hitting area and have a square stance, hit a few iron shots from the grass.
A. If the divots still indicate an outside-in swing arc, turn to page 21.
B. If you are now successful in hitting the ball straight, turn to page 24.
C. If you now have a straight swing arc but are still slicing your shots, turn to page 16.

---

*The page numbers shown refer to the page numbers of the dissertation.
Source: J. Adler, "The Use of Programmed Lessons in Teaching a Complex Perceptual Motor Skill," unpublished doctoral dissertation, The University of Oregon, 1967. Used by permission of the author.

mimeographed diagrams, blackboard diagrams, magnetic boards, films, and other aids to impart a large amount of complex information quickly and efficiently. The teacher/coach may even want to outline with colored tape the basic moves of the defense right on the basketball floor. Each of these methods is a visual aid, and the primary function of each is to set a stimulus situation so that the learner can respond and improve through feedback/reinforcement.

Charts and diagrams

Charts and diagrams have been used as teaching aids for years. Coaches systematically incorporate them into *playbooks*. Often charts and diagrams are enlarged to be mounted on a gymnasium or classroom wall to give a group a full view of the particular information at all times. Gymnastics teachers have

Communicating with charts and
diagrams

made particularly imaginative use of stick figures on charts to provide a visual
model of a gymnastics skill that is permanently available at the teaching station
where the skill is practiced. Commercial firms have also been helpful in
producing professionally prepared and attractive charts and diagrams, thus
optimizing the motivational quality of the visual aid as well as its capacity to
convey information to the learner.

Photographs

Photographs can provide visual input information for skill learning. Often, a
particular aspect of a skill can be emphasized with a photograph. For example,
the precise relationship of body parts in a skiing maneuver might be best
conveyed through a photograph that captures the crucial moment of the skill.
Photographs may also have some feedback/reinforcement value; to have one's
own picture on the wall of a gym is no doubt highly rewarding. Polaroid film
allows a teacher to provide fairly immediate feedback about a skill performance,
although the cost factor may prohibit its use in normal teaching situations.

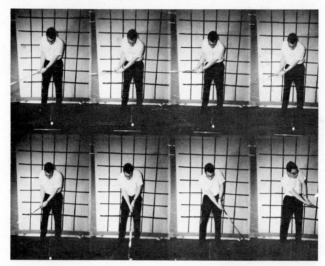

Sequence photographs

Series photographs

Series photographs are a sequence of individual photographs that demonstrate the sequence of a skill performance. They permit studying individual aspects of the skill while also giving a good idea of the sequence of the movements involved. Many books reproduce sequence photographs that are individually selected frames from a 35 mm movie camera. These can be blown up and presented in chart form to provide excellent teaching aids.

Sequence photography can also be a feedback device. A graphcheck camera is a Polaroid-type camera that photographs eight sequence pictures. The timing of the sequence can be altered from 1 to 10 seconds. The film develops in 1 minute. This type of instant feedback is particularly helpful at the high-skill level where slight changes in form need to be made. Again, the cost of this kind of feedback aid is prohibitive for most normal teaching situations.

Magnetic boards

In recent years, magnetic boards have become very popular teaching aids, particularly for team sports. The board is usually in the shape of a particular playing field or court, with bright color lines marking the boundaries of the playing area. Small figures, either representing players or just X's and O's, are attached magnetically to the board. Teachers can manipulate the figures to show the various strategies involved in the game. This can be used as a basic teaching device to provide new information, and also as a feedback device during competition to show a team what is happening on the field or court.

Communicating with the magnetic board

Slide projectors

Slide projectors are particularly useful in imparting information during lectures. Slides can be bought already prepared or can be made from photographs and diagrams. Modern slide projectors lend themselves well to efficient presentation of material. Projectors fitted with slide magazines can be focused and operated by remote control, making an assistant or a projectionist unnecessary and allowing the teacher to move aröund the learning space. Naturally, the degree to which the slides aid the learning process is dependent upon (1) the degree to which the learners attend to the slides, and (2) how well the slides convey the information intended. Audio tapes can accompany the use of slides and make for a very stimulating multimedia presentation. These presentations can be updated and revised with minimal expense and time.

The fact that slides can now be made at a fairly reasonable cost should encourage teachers to make better use of this medium for communication. Diagrams, photographs, charts, and almost anything else can be reproduced as slides. Slides are permanent, easily stored, and lend themselves to a variety of learning situations.

Filmstrips

Filmstrips are sequences of transparencies on 35 mm film. They are used much in the same fashion as slides. Most filmstrips consist of from 20 to 40 frames. Commercially produced filmstrips are often accompanied by an audio tape that includes either a sound signal for moving the filmstrip up a frame or notes that give cues for moving the strip forward.

Opaque projectors

Opaque pictures, graphs, and material from books can be projected with an opaque projector. Unlike most projectors, recent versions of this projector allow the instructor to project the material while the room is partially lit. The second advantage of the opaque projector is that the materials need not be specially prepared but can be projected as is.

Overhead projector

The overhead projector is a box with a window on top. Light passes upward through the window, reflecting material from a transparency through a lens and onto a screen. Many teachers feel that the overhead projector is the most versatile and useful of all projector-type teaching aids, because it can be so well utilized as an extension of the teacher. Almost any kind of information can be made into an overhead transparency. Also a teacher can use a pointer or a special pen to point out material at the projector rather than at the screen. By fitting an acetate roll to the projector, the teacher can draw diagrams and continually move the roll to present a new surface for presenting information. The overhead projector can be used in a fully lit room, thus permitting students to take notes.

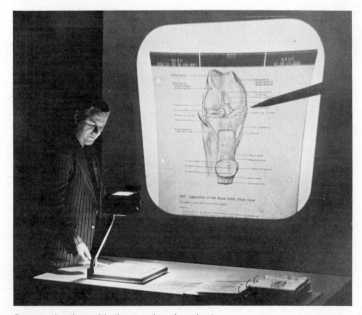

Communicating with the overhead projector

Overhead transparencies can be specially made to emphasize special types of drawing or writing. Expense for this depends primarily upon the availability and cost of visual aid service. Overhead transparencies can also now be copied, much as one makes a copy of a letter or of a page of a book on a Xerox or IBM copier, thus considerably reducing the cost of transparencies.

Films

Motion picture film has been used extensively as an instructional aid for many years. Three kinds of film are utilized in educational films. Thirty-five millimeter film results in the best quality product, but is also quite expensive and most often beyond the reach of the normal school situation in terms of making films. However, high-quality, professionally photographed 35 mm films are readily rented.

Many educational films that are sold or rented are produced on 16 mm film, the cost of 16 mm equipment and film placing it within reach of many schools. The audiovisual aids section of the *Journal of Physical Education and Recreation* typically lists 16 mm films (rental and sale) on subjects that range from movement education to West African tribal dances, and from introductory archery films to highly specialized films on wrestling takedowns.

A recent innovation in filming is the use of 8 mm film. Eight millimeter equipment and film is very reasonably priced and should be within the budgetary reach of most schools. While this allows for the production of homemade films, a remarkable number of 8 mm films are commercially produced for physical education, health education, and recreation.

Commercially produced films have the significant advantage of professional production techniques. Homemade films have the significant advantage of content specific to the needs of the individual situation. A combination of the two would seem to provide for the best use of film as an instructional aid. It should be pointed out that films, for the most part, are used to set up learning situations (the first S in the S-R-S formula). The use of films as a feedback device has certain disadvantages. The feedback is delayed while the film is processed, and the expense of using film for feedback would be substantial. Although many athletic teams have used films as feedback for team and individual play for many years, such funds are not usually available for instructional purposes.

Film loops

Film loops are simply lengths of 8 mm film with their two ends spliced together to form a continuous loop and present the particular sequence over and over again. Film loops now also come in cassettes, which makes the technical aspects of setting up the film considerably less time-consuming. The Athletic Institute[9] produces a wide range of film loops on sports skills. Also available are series such as the four-part Ealing[10] elementary physical education models. These include six loops on basic movement, five on movement awareness, seven on basic manipulative activities, and six on functional fitness.

Teachers should see that their local resource center has current copies of *Educators' Guide to Free Films, Educators' Guide to Free Tapes, Scripts, Transcriptions,* and *Educators' Guide to Filmstrips.*[11] These, along with commercial catalogs, will provide a wide range of possibilities for utilizing film as an instructional aid.

Models

Models can be used for a variety of instructional purposes, although their most common use is in health education. Models of the human skeleton, the heart, the knee joint, and other anatomical subjects have long been utilized. Many students learn mouth-to-mouth resuscitation from a lifelike model of the human being. Often models can be taken apart and put back together, thus acting as a feedback variable as well as an input variable.

Obviously, the contemporary teacher has a number of instructional aids on

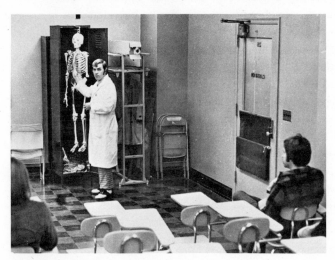

Communicating with a model

[9] The Athletic Institute, Chicago, Illinois.

[10] Ealing Film-Loops, 2225 Massachusetts Avenue, Cambridge, Massachusetts 02138.

[11] Educators Profess-Service Inc., Randolph, Wisconsin 53956.

which to draw, and visual aids are among the most useful and plentiful. Visual aids tend to attract attention; indeed, the better they are constructed and produced, the more attention they will attract. Their primary use is in helping the teacher to set the stimulus situation for learning by providing information and demonstrations efficiently and in ways that would not be possible without them. If well done, visual aids can consolidate information and communicate it to the student quickly and efficiently, and will increase the motivational level of the system. However, we ought also to recognize that poor visual aids will not only fail as communication instruments but will also lower the motivational level of the environment. The difference is in careful selection and use of visual aids, and this too is a skill that can be taught as part of the student's professional preparation.

Media centers

Media resource centers are being developed around the country. A media resource center serves several purposes, among them the collection, storage, and distribution of aids such as video tapes, audio tapes, and special media materials. A recent example is the National Center on Education Media and Materials for the Handicapped, being developed by the Curriculum and Foundations Faculty in the College of Education at The Ohio State University. All disciplines and professions working with special education will contribute to and profit from the development of this media center.

In 1970 the Executive Council of the Physical Education Division of The American Alliance for Health, Physical Education, and Recreation established a resource center on media in physical education. The primary functions of the center are:

1. duplication of video and audio tapes;
2. distribution of conference reports and bibliographies;
3. collection and storage of unpublished manuscripts, teachers' guides, and so forth;
4. collection and storage of master tapes of speeches, conference proceedings, and so forth;
5. provision for limited taping service for conferences and speeches.

The resource center is currently housed in the Physical Education Department at Wayne State University, Detroit, Michigan.

Instructional devices

An instructional device can be defined as apparatus additional to the normal environment within which an activity is performed. Its purpose is to improve the learning environment during the period of training so that the student or player may actually perform better in the normal environment even though the instructional device is not present.

An instructional device can be as simple as an extra line chalked on a badminton court to provide a target for practicing the long serve. It can also be a commercially manufactured machine such as those that pitch baseballs or tennis balls for players to practice hitting or stroking. Some instructional devices may cost thousands of dollars and therefore be prohibitive except for learning environments for training highly skilled athletes. However, many instructional devices can be homemade, especially if the physical educator or coach can develop a good working relationship with the custodian or shop teacher.

Instructional devices can aid the learning process in several ways. Perhaps the most important principle to remember is that the learning environment is relatively inefficient if it becomes too teacher-dependent. For example, the teacher can only hit tennis balls to one student at a time, spot for one tumbler at a time, provide artificial feedback (artificial feedback is feedback not normally present in the performance environment) to one student at a time. Instructional devices can help to make the learning environment optimally efficient. They can also help to free the teacher to provide the very expert services that teachers should render.

In our basic S-R-S learning formula, instructional devices can play important roles both in setting up the learning situation (antecedent stimulus function) and in providing feedback/reinforcement (consequential stimulus function).

Helping to set the learning situation

Instructional devices can help in many ways in setting up the learning situation. One way is to arrange the learning environment so as to restrict the kind of response the student can make. When a teacher hangs a tennis ball from a bamboo pole for students to practice their serving stroke, he is setting up a situation in which the response (hitting the ball) has to be within certain acceptable limits. Track coaches put up a string or hurdle in the jumping pit so that long jumpers have to achieve a certain height in their jump for it to be successful. When you mark an X on the wall for children to watch while dribbling a basketball, you are restricting the kind of response they make in that you force them to dribble without watching the ball. Basketball coaches have used special glasses for the same purpose.

Another use of instructional devices is to set up the learning situation so that cues are provided for the student as he performs the skill. Setting up an obstacle course of chairs or pins and having children dribble (soccer or

Teaching with instructional devices

basketball dribble) in and around the course is a common example. Each obstacle encountered tells the student something to do, that is, change direction, change hands, or both. A much more sophisticated example of this is the *flying ball* apparatus developed by Russian sport specialists for training volleyball players in the volleyball smash. The player approaches the net, but hits the proper ball on command from the teacher or coach. The apparatus develops timing and split-second decision making required for high-level smashing ability in volleyball.

A third use of instructional devices in setting up the learning situation is simply to provide more practice in shorter periods. A pitching machine can deliver more strikes per unit of time than can most batting practice pitchers. A badminton player can practice overhead clears and smashes on shuttlecocks

Teaching with instructional devices

155

The soccer board

suspended from a rafter or rope without having to waste time retrieving the shuttlecocks. Tennis players regularly practice against practice boards so that the ball rebounds to them, thus permitting more strokes per unit of time. The same function is played by the soccer board shown here. In each of these examples, students can increase the amount of practice they get even though the practice is conducted in an artificial setting. Naturally, the student will also have to spend time practicing in the real setting, but with many students needing practice and with short practice periods, instructional devices can substantially improve the potential of the learning situation.

To sum up, instructional devices can help to set up the learning situation:

1. by restricting the limits of acceptable form of response;
2. by providing cues for the learner to alter his response;
3. by increasing the amount of practice per unit of time.

Providing feedback/reinforcement

It has already been suggested that feedback/reinforcement is perhaps the most important variable in the learning process. All activity environments have feedback that is intrinsic to the environment (for a classification of feedback see page 122). The lines on a court tell the performer whether the shot was in bounds or out of bounds. A basketball player knows whether the shot went in or missed. A balance beam performer knows when he has lost his balance.

The teacher is a primary source of artificial feedback. By providing verbal comments, the teacher points out facets of the performance that either were well done or need correction. However, the teacher cannot focus on more than one performer at a time if he is to provide expert feedback. Instructional devices can be of much help in establishing extra feedback to the learning

Teaching with instructional device

environment. When a teacher puts a string above a badminton net and tells the student that a good short serve will pass between the net and the string, the teacher has provided a built-in source of artificial feedback that the student can use to improve his skill even when the teacher is not present.

The mirrors that are almost always found in dance studios provide artificial feedback for the dancer about his form that would not be possible without them. The dance teacher cannot provide verbal feedback for all the students at the same time. Video tape can also provide artificial feedback.

Again, a more sophisticated example of an artificial feedback device is a volleyball apparatus designed to develop accuracy in the set-up pass by requiring a certain height and trajectory to go through the goal. Several players can practice at the same time with this device, and the feedback from it is both immediate and very precise.

The extent to which an instructor can build in artificial feedback devices is really limited only by the instructor's imagination and willingness to use some lumber and string. Most of the devices mentioned in this section could be easily built without undue expense. There is no doubt that their use would greatly improve the potential of the learning environment.

The proper use of instructional materials

It should be clear that instructional materials can contribute greatly to learning and motivation, whether extremely sophisticated, commercially produced materials or relatively inexpensive, homemade materials. However, it is important to note that instructional materials may be used in ways that seem to improve the learning environment, but actually worsen it in the long run. In the preceding chapter (see page 123), it was suggested that a total learning environment conveyed a message to the student about the learning process. If multimedia presentations in classrooms make it unnecessary for the student to make an actual response, then the student will receive the message that learning means being entertained by bright lights and a good show.

Hinkemeyer and Langenbach[12] have warned about this phenomenon by suggesting that we ought to be wary of the *good teacher.* Imagine, for example, a teacher who uses good films, overhead transparencies, video tapes, and audio tapes for a total media approach to teaching. The students enter the room, sit back, and enjoy the show. The students do enjoy the show, and they may even learn somewhat better because of the motivating quality of the media presentation. However, we must also recognize that the students may be learning that education is a passive phenomenon, that to be educated is somehow equated with being entertained, and that learning depends upon and centers around the teacher. This kind of teaching will eventually disable the students from any kind of self-generated learning capacity.

Fortunately, this danger is probably minimal in physical education. The learner is most often required to make responses. The learning environment may be set up with media aids and instructional devices that help him get necessary information quickly and efficiently, but this is done to allow him more opportunity for practice. The learning environment may be infused with a maximum of artificial feedback, but this feedback is not available until he has made a response. Thus, the entire environment is set up so as to optimize the opportunity for the student to make response and to learn from the environment while he is responding. Such an environment will not produce a passive learner.

Summary

1. Communication can be judged in terms of its accuracy, efficiency, and motivational qualities.
2. Verbal communication can be informative, persuasive, authoritative, or collaborative.
3. Nonverbal communication conveys important information of which the teacher is not always aware.
4. The traditional lesson plan is still a useful instructional aid.

[12] M. Hinkemeyer and M. Langenbach, "Beware the 'Good Teacher'," *Educational Technology,* 12, May 1972.

5. Behavioral objectives state observable behavior, the conditions under which the behavior is to occur, and the criterion for achieving the objective.
6. By manipulating the conditions and criteria, progression in behavioral objectives can be developed.
7. The growing availability of books aids both the teacher and the student.
8. Television has also been used as an input and feedback source.
9. Commercial television is producing a growing number of packaged physical education, health education, and recreation programs.
10. Video-tape systems allow schools to produce homemade programs.
11. Programmed instruction structures material in progressions of learning cycles.
12. Linear programming utilizes shaping and prompts.
13. Branching formats allow for more flexible programming.
14. Visual aids can be used to improve communication of input materials.
15. Visual aids can also be used to improve quantity and precision of feedback.
16. Instructional devices can help set the learning situation by restricting the form of response, providing cues, and increasing the amount of practice per unit of time.
17. Artificial feedback devices can greatly improve the quantity and precision of feedback built into the learning environment.

Questions

1. Make a list of possible instructional materials. How could you maximize the use of these aids in different teaching situations?
2. In a school setting, whom should you talk to in order to have the appropriate instructional materials available and accessible? What is your responsibility in this matter?
3. In verbal communication, can you enumerate ten situations in which you could use effectively instructional materials?
4. Design a lesson plan model and exchange it with a classmate. Consider the strengths and weaknesses of your classmate's model.
5. Could you define precisely instructional objectives, behavioral objectives, and performance objectives? Do you observe any similarities and differences?
6. What are the three main components of a well-written behavioral objective?
7. Select a group of students and a specific activity, and write the performance objective.
8. Do you consider instructional television identical with educational television? Explain.
9. As pointed out in this chapter, television is an extremely valuable teaching aid. What would be some of its limitations?

10. How do you relate the so-called learning cycle to programmed instructional materials?
11. What steps are necessary for developing programmed instructional materials?
12. Linear and branching programs are the two basic approaches to instructional programming. Give examples of both.
13. Obtain the names of five companies from which you can order visual aid materials.
14. List instructional devices that are likely to improve your teaching effectiveness if properly used.
15. In light of the S-R-S learning theory, why is it important to use as often as possible instructional devices that will produce feedback/reinforcement?
16. Describe situations in which you could use instructional materials that will produce immediate and precise artificial feedback.

7

TEACHING SYSTEMS AND METHODOLOGIES

If we were asked to observe teachers over a period and to record the kinds of tasks they perform, the kinds of behaviors emitted, and the ways in which they interact with students, we probably could summarize what we have seen as a teaching system. Within any given teaching system, a teacher will no doubt utilize several teaching methods. Some of the methods described in this chapter actually could be adopted as total approaches to teaching, and thus be teaching systems. However, most teaching systems will incorporate several teaching methods—at different times, in different ways, and to greater or lesser degrees. Teachers will discover, on the basis of the feedback/reinforcement in the learning environment, which combinations of methods produce what they consider to be the best results.

It should be understood that the adoption of a teaching system by a teacher is governed by the feedback/reinforcement contingencies in the school or nonschool setting. A teacher most highly rewarded by student-skill progress will eventually adopt the teaching system that optimizes skill development. The teacher most concerned with the development of social behavior will adopt a system that allows for maximum interaction and growth in this domain. A teacher who wants the student to know and understand the *whys* of physical education will adopt a system that produces learning in the cognitive domain. Classes that reflect these different goals would appear to the observer to be very different kinds of experiences, as indeed they would. Some systems could be used for each of the above examples. Some systems will lend themselves better to development in one domain than in another.

It should be pointed out that other kinds of feedback/reinforcement also affect the choice of a teaching system adopted by a teacher over the years. If a school principal or camp director is most concerned with *order* and *discipline,* then a teacher working under this kind of supervision will eventually adopt a style and system of teaching that produces these outcomes. The point is that the teaching system adopted is affected by many factors, some of which do not have a great deal to do with the educational progress of the student. For example, a teacher might be strongly rewarded by exerting authority, and thus allow an authoritarian atmosphere to develop, not because it is educationally sound but because of factors in the teacher's background. In this sense, a teaching method may be used not because of student needs but because of teacher needs. Or, over a period of years many teachers tend to adopt a teaching system that requires the smallest effort on their part. Or, administrators may favor systems of teaching that create the illusion but not the reality of order and learning. Thus, many factors may affect the choice of a teaching system, and you should recognize that certain of these noneducational factors are actually very powerful influences on the job.

The traditional model

It seems fair to suggest that there has been a standard model of teaching physical education activities, even though individual teachers may deviate from the model in several aspects of their teaching. The traditional model has received substantial support by professionals and is taught in methods courses at the university level. It is the way that most of us learned physical education, and therefore seems a natural model to adopt. Unfortunately, it is not possible to suggest that the traditional model has developed through the applications of knowledge from motor learning and psychology. The bridge to permit crossing the gap theoretically separating research from teaching practice has really never been built. The fault lies partially with researchers whose investigations are laboratory oriented, a method for which there is no application to the teaching world. It also lies partially with teachers who, because of the comfort and ease of using the traditional model, make no effort to translate into practice the meaningful research that has been done.

The traditional model can be characterized colloquially as:

1. "explain it to them";
2. "demonstrate it for them";
3. "let them practice it";
4. "correct their errors."

It should be emphasized that we are not here equating the traditional model with the "throw the balls out and let them play" attitude, which amounts to noninstruction. Hoffman[1] has described the traditional model as follows:

1. emphasis on delivery of the message to the group particularly through demonstration and explanation;
2. organizational efficiency;
3. neatness and order;
4. discipline and control;
5. little emphasis on skill analysis.

This description is probably familiar to each of us. A short lecture and demonstration about a skill or strategy is followed by a well-organized dispersion of the students into lines for drills and practice. Much has been made of uniforms and straight lines, and even of a quiet gymnasium. Too often the discipline and control have been military in style, and exercised for its own sake rather than for any potential contribution to the efficiency of the learning environment. On the other hand, overcrowded classes and emphasis on the importance of discipline and order have greatly encouraged this method of teaching; given those conditions, it is probably a reasonable model. Supporters of new systems should not assume that their models will automatically work better, in the sense that "anything is better than the old way of doing things."

The methods and systems presented in this chapter allow for changes in the traditional model of teaching. While maintaining a certain respect for the traditional model, we are clearly on the side of change. Incorporation of certain new methodologies into a teaching system for physical education can create more efficient learning environments that not only produce more learning, but motivate the student more highly. More learning is not the only goal; students should enjoy their learning experience. We want students to have the desire to learn to like physical education.

The traditional method of teaching physical education probably was acceptable for its day, but for some time we have recognized that it is no

[1]S. Hoffman, "Traditional Methodology: Prospects for Change," *Quest,* XV, 1971, *pp.* 51–57.

longer acceptable. What Mosston[2] has called the *command style* of teaching needs to be changed. The remainder of this chapter describes a variety of methods that can improve the teaching of physical education.

Behavior shaping

When you teach the novice student the golf swing, trampoline skills, or even basic throwing and catching skills, he does not yet possess the necessary skill to perform. As a teacher, you have a good idea of how you would like the student to be able to perform. The problem is to help the student get from where he is to where you would like him to be. In behavioral psychology, the method used to accomplish this task is called *shaping*. Rushall and Siedentop have described the shaping procedure as follows:

Shaping consists of reinforcing closer and closer approximations of a desired terminal behavior. It is unlikely that a correct response will be emitted on a first attempt so a behavior short of the final behavior form must be reinforced. With subsequent emissions of the behavior, the requirements for reinforcement are made more strict and reinforcement is only provided as the behavior more closely approximates the desired act.[3]

Teachers have always used behavior shaping in a crude way, but enough is known about the intricacies of shaping to use it in a systematic way. The steps in the shaping process are:

1. A final performance goal is defined. This is referred to as the terminal behavior.
2. An initial behavior of the student is found that is as close as possible to the terminal performance desired.
3. A set of steps is developed to move from the initial to the terminal behavior. Each step should have a criterion which defines when the step is completed and the student can then move on to the next step in the sequence.
4. A significant feedback/reinforcement signal is found so that each response of the performer can receive immediate feedback/reinforcement.
5. Each step should then be primed. A *prime* is simply a signal that gives the student an idea about how to perform the particular step. This can be done by demonstration, explanation, or even manual manipulation.
6. Each step is reinforced until the criterion for the step is met.
7. The sequence of steps is followed until the terminal performance is achieved.

Ideally, of course, behavior shaping works best when it is applied individually,

[2] M. Mosston, *Teaching Physical Education.* Columbus, Ohio: Charles E. Merrill Books, Inc., 1966.

[3] B. S. Rushall and D. Siedentop, *The Development and Control of Behavior in Sport and Physical Education.* Philadelphia: Lea & Febiger, 1972, p. 138.

because the step sequences can then be developed in terms of the performer's specific capabilities. However, a good approximation of shaping can be achieved by developing a series of behavioral objectives that lead a student along the path toward a terminal performance objective. For example, the bump pass in volleyball might be taught by developing a series of from four to eight behavioral objectives, each progressively more difficult, and leading up to a terminal objective of being able to return a serve with a bump pass that reaches a desired height and accuracy criterion.

You will notice that behavior shaping appears quite similar to programmed instruction, which we discussed in Chapter 6. Linear programmed instruction is a direct application of behavior-shaping strategies developed in the laboratory.

Behavior shaping can be utilized with any kind of behavior. Even though our examples have focused on sport skills, shaping can be used to develop social and cognitive skills. Behaviors as seemingly obscure and complex as "making a good competitive effort" or "displaying good sportsmanship" can be shaped by the method described. If a teacher can define the terminal behavior goal, then step sequences can be developed, and through the use of feedback/reinforcement, successive approximations of this terminal goal can gradually be shaped. A programmed textbook uses shaping procedures to develop knowledge skills.

Behavior modification

Behavior modification changes the rate of occurrence of a defined class of behavior or behaviors. Like behavior shaping, it is an application of the principles of behavioral psychology. Behavior shaping seeks to develop behaviors the student did not previously possess. Behavior modification changes behaviors already possessed by the student. For example, most students know how to take care of equipment, listen to a teacher when he is explaining material, follow directions, and treat classmates with respect and decency. However, students know equally well how to mistreat equipment, be inattentive, do everything but what you intended, and be abusive to their classmates. Both sets of behaviors have been learned. The problem is to make one class of behaviors more likely to occur than the other. Again, behavior modification, like behavior shaping, can be applied to learning in the cognitive, social, or motor domains.

Rushall[4] has provided an excellent example of modifying the motor behavior,

[4]B. S. Rushall, "Some Applications of Psychology to Swimming," *Swimming Technique,* 7, 1970, pp. 71–82. Used by permission of the author.

the butterfly stroke, of a highly skilled young swimmer. Inefficient aspects of the stroke were analyzed as follows, and changes made accordingly:

1. The hand entry was to be no less than shoulder width apart.
2. A longer push back was needed.
3. The arms were to be stretched forward for a wide hand entry.
4. The forearms and elbows were to be pronated on contact with the water.
5. The hips and shoulders were to be stabilized.
6. A low flat arm recovery with pronated hands was needed.
7. The breathing action was to occur at the end of the effort phase of the stroke.

Like all behavior modification, the single most important variable is the feedback/reinforcement. Because this modification was for a highly motivated athlete, all that was needed was a feedback signal that could be presented after each response (in this case, after each stroke). The coach stood at the end of the pool and held a flashlight that could be seen during the breathing phase of each stroke. When the flashlight was not turned on, the swimmer knew that the particular aspect of the stroke had been performed correctly; the light-on condition indicated an error. This procedure quickly brought about the desired changes.

Basic principles

Behavior-modification techniques are now commonly used by teachers in school and nonschool settings. They are particularly effective for increasing rates of appropriate student behaviors like attending to work, listening to teachers, helping others, being polite to others, and other social and academic behaviors. They are equally effective in decreasing the occurrence of behaviors that are incompatible with effective social and educational environments. The basic principles involve:

1. defining the behavior class very clearly;
2. finding a reinforcer or punisher that will be effective within the particular environment;
3. determining the precise relationship between the behavior and the consequence, called establishing a contingency;
4. applying the contingency;
5. noting the resultant change.

Methods for increasing a behavior

Although our examples are of individual behaviors of students, behavior-modification procedures can be effective with groups, as shown in the following section on contingency management.

1. *Positively reinforce the behavior:* A student is verbally praised when he helps another child; a player is praised for making a good pass.
2. *Remove any punishment previously associated with the behavior:* A group is instructed not to make fun of the attempts of a clumsy student; a player is not yelled at for failing if he has made a good effort.
3. *Provide a model and reinforce the target behavior of the model:* A student who follows directions quickly earns the right to be a teacher's aid. A student who acts in a sportsmanlike manner is respectfully congratulated by a coach. The other students observe the interaction and tend to imitate the behavior of the student who was reinforced.

Each of these methods will increase the behavior described. The reinforcement may be social (praise or attention), material (candy, a comic book, a letter, an award), a privilege (helping the teacher, being a leader), or the chance to take part in a well-liked activity (extra gym time, time on a trampoline, and so forth). The basic principle is that positive reinforcement or the removal of a punishment will tend to increase the behavior upon which it is contingent.

Methods for decreasing a behavior

Many times teachers encounter individual students who behave in ways that not only jeopardize their own educational chances, but seriously disrupt the learning environment so that other students are affected. Many times coaches encounter players who behave in ways that harm the team. Whether these are social or motor-skill behaviors, they need to be reduced in frequency.

1. *Extinguish the behavior by withholding reinforcement:* A class is told not to pay attention to the *showoff* antics of a child. A teacher ignores *attention-getting* behavior.
2. *Withdraw reinforcement for an amount of time:* A child has to sit out for 5 minutes whenever he verbally abuses a classmate. A player is taken out of a game for making a strategy error. This is called *time out* in behavioral psychology.
3. *Withdraw a certain amount of reinforcement:* A child loses privileges for misbehaving.
4. *Present a punishment:* A child is spoken harshly to when he misbehaves. A player is yelled at when he makes a mistake.
5. *Positively reinforce the student for not emitting the behavior:* A student is given extra privileges if he does not engage in fighting for seven consecutive days. A player is given extra playing time for shooting less. In behavioral psychology this is called *omission training,* since it is the omission of the target behavior that earns the reinforcement.

These are the primary methods of increasing or decreasing the frequency of occurrence of a behavior. Certain points are worth emphasizing. First, to be effective the reinforcer must have sufficient strength to change the behavior.

The *only* way that a teacher can be sure of the reinforcer's effectiveness is to apply a contingency and note the resultant change. If the behavior has not changed, then the reinforcer was not effective. Second, you need to recognize that behavior does not occur in a vacuum. A child may be positively reinforced by his peers for behaving inappropriately in the educational environment. You must recognize that reinforcement from peers can be very strong, and take this into account when attempting to modify the behavior. We might label this the · problem of *competing reinforcers.*

Changing a behavior in one situation does not mean that you have changed it in all situations. You might arrange contingencies so that children behave very well in the gym, but when they return to the classroom they behave poorly because the contingencies in the gymnasium are different from those in the classroom. Different sets of contingencies will develop and control different sets of behaviors. For example, a player may learn to behave differently in the presence of an assistant coach than in the presence of the head coach. If a behavior is to change *generally,* then it must be treated similarly in different environments, by receiving uniform reinforcement contingencies. If it does not, then a *discriminated* set of behaviors will develop, that is, the behavior will be different in different situations.

The final stage of behavior modification should be characterized by (1) infrequent reinforcement; (2) naturally occurring reinforcers. When a behavior is first modified, it should be reinforced each time it occurs (as in shaping). After the behavior is occurring at a desirable rate, the reinforcement should *gradually* become less and less frequent. Often, in order to modify a behavior, it is necessary to use a contrived reinforcer such as candy, toys, or special privileges. As soon as possible, it is important to switch control of the behavior from the contrived reinforcer to whatever reinforcement occurs naturally in the specific environment. Social attention, praise, approval of peers, privileges natural to the environment, and access to naturally occurring activities can all be used as long-term reinforcers.

Contingency management

Contingency management, along with behavior shaping and behavior modification, is an outgrowth of behavioral psychology. Although the basic principles of behavioral psychology were derived from nonhuman subjects, extensive analysis and documentation of human behavior has now been made in medical, therapeutic, correctional, educational, industrial, and home settings.

A contingency is simply the relationship between a task and a consequence.

As with all outgrowths of behavioral psychology, contingency management is a system of managing reinforcers (consequential events) to produce desired educational outcomes. It is a teaching system in which behaviors are clearly specified and clearly related to available consequences. The student understands what performances are required, under what conditions the performances must occur, the criteria for evaluating the performances, and the reinforcers earned when the performance standards are achieved. Contingency management is now used at all levels of education from preschool to college.

Developing a contingency management program

The first step in developing such a program is to begin to focus on student behavior. Teachers for many years have viewed teaching primarily from the input side of the S-R-S formula (see page 127), assuming that certain lectures, drills, demonstrations, and discussions will result in certain outcomes. These input variables are prepared with great care, but then less attention is paid to what is learned. A contingency manager, on the other hand, uses available motivational techniques (mostly reinforcers) to maximize the probability that students will learn the material.

The second step is to write behavioral objectives (see page 132), which become the primary guidelines for the student to move through the program. The objectives can be programmed in either a linear or a branching format (see discussion of programmed instruction on page 140).

The third step in developing a contingency management system is to select consequences (reinforcers), ranging from contrived to naturally occurring reinforcers. At higher levels of education, grades have often been the back-up reinforcers, but are not the only nor necessarily the most effective reinforcers. Consequences must be of sufficient strength to produce the desired results, and not readily available outside the system. A particularly fruitful way of establishing a set of naturally occurring consequences is to find out the student's favorite activities around school (or camp or recreation center) and then use these as reinforcers. Using the chance to engage in a favorite activity as a motivational device to improve the learning environment is known as the *Premack Principle,* from the experimental work of psychologist David Premack.[5]

The fourth step in developing the system is to specify the actual contingencies between the learning tasks and the consequences. You must decide whether reinforcement will be contingent upon the amount or the quality of work output, or some combination of the two. You must also decide if the

[5] D. Premack, "Reinforcement of Drinking by Running: Effects of Fixed Ratio and Reinforcement Time," *Journal of the Experimental Analysis of Behavior,* 5, 1964, pp. 91–96.

Table 7.1   A reinforcement menu for an elementary physical education program

Points	Reinforcing Activity
5	5 minutes use of jump ropes
5	5 minutes use of tumbling tube
5	5 minutes use of mini tramp
5	Entry into one dodgeball game
5	5 minutes shooting baskets
25	Extra physical education period
20	Choose and lead one group activity during class
50	Serve as teacher's aid for younger group for 1 week

contingencies will focus only on skill and knowledge tasks, or whether other behaviors will also be included. If the available reinforcers are of sufficient strength, contingency management systems will produce a very highly motivated learning environment.

The motivation is built into the system, as Table 7.1 shows. Students know beforehand what performance is required in order to earn a particular reward. They can try to achieve the performance as often as they want. They proceed through the system at their own pace. If they fail to pass a task, they simply practice some more and try again. The punishing aspects of school failure are minimized. At any time during the sequence, the student knows where he has been, what he can do, and what remains to be done. The teacher knows that the student has learned, because the student has had to demonstrate the learning in order to pass the task.

Contingency-management guidelines[6]

1. Behaviors must be defined in observable terms. Contingency managers do not talk about physical fitness. They are more likely to talk about "40 bent-leg sit ups in two minutes," or "a mile run in less than 6:30."
2. Terminal behaviors must be specified clearly. The student must understand beforehand what is expected of him, in terms of tasks completed or levels of performance within tasks.
3. The target performance is the one that should be reinforced. If a task such as dribbling a soccer ball is stated only in terms of a speed criterion, then speed will be developed perhaps to the detriment of control. If speed and control are both desired, then task completion must be contingent on both.
4. The contingency must be clearly stated. "Two minutes of trampoline time" states both the reinforcing activity (trampoline) and the amount of time (two minutes) to engage in the activity.

[6] Rushall and Siedentop.

5. At the outset, tasks should be small and reinforcement frequent. If a child cannot do three push-ups, he should be rewarded for supporting his weight on extended arms for increasing lengths of time. In other words, his behavior needs to be shaped. Frequent reinforcement at the outset establishes the motivation.

Types of contingency-management systems

Contingency management can be used in any type of physical education activity course, lecture courses, summer camps, health education courses, and recreation centers. The system utilized depends upon what behaviors are to be developed and the general motivational level of the students. If you start with a group of highly motivated students, it is often enough to develop a set of tasks and give the students feedback on their progress through the sequence. This is reinforcing in itself. Often, it is sufficient to mark on a wall chart the performance of each student through the program. This generates some intragroup competition as well as personal effort to meet the standards of each task. However, if the group is not highly motivated or if there are serious behavior problems, then some specific consequences will need to be developed and applied to the program. Table 7.2 shows a contingency-management plan for badminton.

Alternating periods of work with periods of reinforcement is called a *task-reward system* and is particularly useful in lower elementary grades. Its serious drawbacks are that it does not teach the student task persistence or to work for deferred rewards, a goal for which all contingency managers strive.

Using points (or physical tokens such as poker chips) to mark the completion of a task is called a *token system.* Tokens (points) can be saved up, allowing for longer periods of practice. Tokens can be exchanged for a variety of back-up reinforcers, thus ensuring each student's individual motivation. Token systems allow large reinforcers such as a special field trip, a letter award, a grade, or a special privilege like being a teacher's aid.

Formalizing a token system by having students choose beforehand what rewards they will work toward is a *contract* form of contingency management. In a high-school class, you might have various ways of earning a "C" contract, a "B" contract, or an "A" contract. Lloyd Homme[7] has shown that elementary-age students can learn to make up their own contracts, selecting what is to be learned and what rewards will be earned. Even though you might start with a totally teacher-controlled system, you can gradually shift to the student the responsibility for contracting. This form of self-management is considered a highly valuable educational outcome.

[7]L. Homme, *How To Use Contingency Contracting in the Classroom.* Champaign, Ill.: Research Press Co., 1970.

Table 7.2   A badminton contingency-management plan (senior high school or college)

Core Requirements

1. Low Serve: hit 3 of 5, under 2-ft. rope and within 18-in. area from short service line (*1 point*).
2. Long Serve: hit 3 of 5 at least 9 ft. high and within a 3-ft. area from back boundary line (*1 point*).
3. Underhand Clear: receive bird hit 3 of 5 from your forecourt, contact below the waist, return over 9 ft. to opponent's backcourt (*1 point*).
4. Overhead Dropshot: receive a high shot in your backcourt, drop bird to opponent's forecourt under 2-ft. rope. 3 of 5 times (*1 point*).
5. Rally 10 consecutive times with instructor (*1 point*).
6. Participate in 5 matches (*1 point*).
7. Receive bird and overhead clear from 6 ft. from your back boundary line to opponent's back 6 ft. (*1 point*).
8. Make 90 percent or better on rules test (*1 point*).

Optional Requirements

1. Forehand Overhead Clear: stand in your backcourt, hit 3 of 5 over 9 ft. to the back 5 ft. of your opponent's court (*1 point*).
2. High Doubles Serve: hit 3 of 5 over opponent's racket to a 2-ft. area from long doubles service line (*1 point*).
3. Smash: receive a high shot at your midcourt and smash 3 of 5 to opponent's midcourt (*1 point*).
4. Underhand Dropshot: from midcourt, receive a shot and return 3 of 5 under 2-ft. rope to opponent's forecourt (*1 point*).
5. Play doubles or mixed doubles (*1 point/3 games, up to 5 points*).
6. Backhand Clear: stand in your backcourt, receive bird hit 3 of 5 over 9 ft. to back 5 ft. of your opponent's court (*1 point*).
7. Backhand Clear: same as #6 but from back 3 ft. to opponent's back 3 ft. (*2 points*).
8. Round the Head: receive a high shot to your backhand side, hit 3 of 5 to same side on opponent's court (*2 points*).
9. Clear: For Men: hit 3 of 5 over 9 ft. from back 3 ft. to opponent's court 3 ft. from back boundary line (*2 points*). For Women: hit 3 of 5 over 9 ft from back 4 ft from your backcourt boundary to opponent's court, 4 ft from back boundary (*2 points*).
10. Net Shot: 2 people hitting consistently 5 in a row for each, under 2-ft. rope (*1 point*).
11. Perform the drive serve 3 of 5 times in appropriate service area (*1 point*).
12. Perform the push shot 3 of 5 times from your midcourt under 2-ft. rope to appropriate area (*1 point*).
13. Attacking Clear and Dropshot Combination: you and your partner hitting 5 consecutive clears and drops for both of you (*2 points*).

Contingencies

C grade = 8 core points + any 5 optional points.
B grade = 8 core points + any 12 optional points.
A grade = 8 core points + any 18 optional points.

Source: F. Rife, *Contingency Management Plan for Badminton.* Unpublished material. Columbus, Ohio: The Ohio State University, 1973. Used by permission of the author.

Contingency management is essentially a system for managing motivation, a crucial variable in the educational process. Contingency management utilizes elements of programmed instruction and other principles from behavioral psychology. Along with behavior shaping and behavior modification, it forms a viable teaching system for physical education, health education, and recreation.

Computer-assisted instruction

It might seem premature to include a section on a computer system of instruction since, owing to the enormous expense of the systems, very few are available in schools. However, costs will go down as more systems are installed, and it would appear almost certain that computer instruction will play a vital role in education in the future.

The computer is transforming government, industry, and education. Primarily for noninstructional support services thus far, its instructional uses are increasing steadily. Your school may use a computer to schedule classes, catalog the library books, or do much of the accounting. It is less likely that you have experienced the computer in an instructional setting.

In computer-assisted instruction, a computer terminal (like a big electric typewriter) is hooked up to a computer. The terminal may be in a learning center, library, dormitory, or wherever it can receive maximum use with adequate supervision. A telephone circuit links the student terminal to the computer. The student can then interact with the teacher through the computer. Note that we do not say "the student interacts with the computer." Too often, we assume that the computer is a living organism. It is not! It is a highly sophisticated, very quick machine, but still a machine. The student actually interacts with a *program* that has been coded into the computer by the teacher with the help of a computer programmer. Computer-assisted instruction is useful to the extent that the programs in the computer are well prepared. Poorly planned computerized programs are no better than poorly prepared teachers. However, the process a teacher must go through to develop an instructional program for computer use would no doubt optimize the probability of its being an excellent instructional unit.

Computer-assisted instruction, one of the most sophisticated applications of programmed instruction (see page 140), tends to absorb the interest of those who use it, be they second-graders or graduate students. All the elements of programmed instruction are present. The feedback not only helps the learner, but the computer can be programmed to provide feedback for the teacher to help monitor student progress through a program and modify the program where necessary. The ultimate uses of computer-assisted instruction have yet to be explored. It is now possible to combine administrative and instructional operations to provide a totally individualized program for each student. The computer program integrates information about the student, his abilities, aptitudes, progress through the course, and individual responses in order to determine the next sequence of steps that will most benefit him individually.

Models for computer-assisted instruction

Four basic instructional formats have been widely utilized in computer-assisted instruction programs:

1. *Drill and test format.* In this format the program provides for practice and drill in areas already covered in other instructional programs (a lecture, for example). The student is then tested and assigned to the next block or sent back to the teacher for further work.
2. *Tutorial format.* In this format the teacher acts through the program as a tutor. The branching format is used extensively (see page 142). Questions are asked by the program. The student answers, and feedback/discussion follows. In this format, the program does all of the teaching, rather than act as an auxiliary aid, as in the drill and test format.
3. *Dialogue format.* This format is an extension of the tutorial. The student can ask the program for more information, some calculations, or answers to specific questions. The program also asks questions, provides feedback, and tests the student. This format would be extremely useful in teaching material such as first aid or basketball strategy.
4. *Simulation-diagnosis format.* In this format, the student is provided with information, can ask for further information, for calculations, and so forth. At some point, the student makes a decision on the problem. The computer program then verifies the accuracy of the decision and also provides feedback on the appropriateness of information that the student requested. For example, a student might play the role of a coach who has a problem with an individual or a team. The student would make a decision after asking questions. Feedback would inform the student about (a) which questions were proper, (b) which were irrelevant to the problem, and (c) which questions were not asked that should have been asked. The medical profession uses this format in developing the abilities of young physicians to make proper diagnoses and utilize medical information properly.

Although these four are the most frequently used, the format utilized is limited only by the ability of the teacher and programmer to provide the kind of instructional format that will best meet the specific needs of the educational situation.

The computer as an aid in counseling

The computer can help individual teachers solve problems for individual students. Information about the student is fed into the computer, and the program uses this information to provide a diagnosis of the problem and several alternative solutions that the teacher might use to remedy the problem. Learning problems, perceptual-motor development problems, and common behavior problems might be treated with the help of a computer diagnosis. Long-term educational problems also could be usefully treated in this manner.

Rushall[8] has provided an example of using the computer in this format to help coaches know their players better so they can help them to achieve their full potential as athletes. Certain questions from the Cattell 16 Personality Factors Test and the IPAT Anxiety Scale Questionnaire are administered by the coach to his team or to certain individuals on the team. The test results are sent to Dr. Rushall, who has developed a program to analyze athletic motivation problems using these instruments. The computer printout forecasts: (1) a diagnosis of the specific behavior strengths and weaknesses of an individual, and (2) suggestions on how the individual might be treated so as to achieve his full athletic potential.

The computer is fast, accurate, and totally stupid. The human is incredibly intelligent, but very slow and inaccurate. The combination of man and machine produces programs showing human intelligence in a very fast, accurate, highly individualized teaching system. Computers tend to breed fears of depersonalization in the minds of many educators, and certainly we must constantly safeguard against their improper use, but at least in its beginning stages computer-assisted instruction appears to be a very absorbing and useful way to learn.

Guided discovery and problem solving

In the 1940s and 1950s, a methodological revolution in elementary school physical education in England centered around the concept of human movement and the teachings of Rudolph Laban. This educational revolution changed some emphases in the content of physical education but, most importantly, it fundamentally changed teaching methodology. In the late 1950s and early 1960s, this new approach to physical education was imported by the

[8]B. Rushall, "A Psychological Consultation Service for Sporting Environments," paper delivered at Atlantic Provinces Health, Physical Education and Recreation Conference, November 1972.

United States, where it found great acceptance and became immediately popular.

The "old" physical education methodologies tended to be militaristic, as we mentioned at the beginning of this chapter. It was against this way of dealing with children that physical educators began to rebel. The names most often associated with the new methodologies have been *guided discovery* and *problem solving.*

Guided discovery

As should be clear by this stage, the acquisition of motor skills and associated learnings occurs primarily through the S-R-S formula. In most cases the learning situation is set for the student: he is *told* what to do or *shown* what to do, and is then expected to approximate the model. Feedback/reinforcement gradually brings those approximations closer to the original model. However, the S-R-S formula does not require the student to imitate a demonstration or verbal explanation. Many people feel that this kind of learning stifles the creativity and higher mental processes of the student, and also inhibits his ability to meet and solve problems.

Guided discovery creates a learning situation that requires the student to find an answer (that is, a proper response) on his own, with the teacher acting as a resource person instead of directly controlling the learning act. Mosston[9] has suggested that the learning situation (the first S in the S-R-S formula) should present the student with a problem for which there is no obvious answer. With no immediate solution in sight, an attitude of inquiry is aroused in the learner. As the learner inquires into possible problem solutions, he gradually discovers the solution or solutions.

The most fundamental difference between guided discovery and other teaching methods is that in guided discovery the instructor never reveals the solution, never tells the answer, and never shows how the skill is done or the problem solved. This rule is simple, but of enormous importance, because once the solution is known, then all inquiry stops and the process is destroyed.

Mosston[10] has suggested three important variables in developing and utilizing this teaching method.

1. Subject matter is broken down into a sequence of steps consisting of clues or questions used by the teacher to gradually guide the student toward the solution of the problem. The steps should be small enough so that the student can experience

[9] Mosston, p. 149.

[10] *Ibid.,* pp. 149–151.

success and feel secure in further efforts. You will note the similarity to the basic principles of behavior shaping (see page 164).

2. During actual practice sessions the teacher follows three basic rules: (a) never reveal the goal or answer; (b) always wait for the student to respond; (c) reinforce the appropriate response when it occurs. If inappropriate responses occur, the teacher merely encourages further attempts and perhaps has an additional set of clues or questions that will further guide the learner.

3. The solution of each small step acts as a strong motivation for the individual and the entire class. Students feel more secure in making efforts of their own, and the evaluation process is immediate, personal, and individualized.

Guided discovery is a teaching method that could be utilized with any subject matter and at any age level. The nature of the questions and clues would change to accommodate the level of the student, but the basic process would remain the same.

It is important to recognize that guided discovery is a good teaching method because it involves the learner mentally. The clear implication is that this teaching method will produce a more creative, independent thinker. Mosston[11] describes this as breaking the *cognitive barrier.* No evidence, however, shows it to be the best way to produce a highly skilled athlete. Obviously, guided discovery and problem solving are intended to contribute to cognitive and emotional objectives.

Table 7.3 is an example of guided discovery in soccer.

Table 7.3   Example of guided discovery in soccer

Specific Purpose:	To discover the use of the toe kick in long and high-flying kicks.
Question 1:	"What kind of kick is needed when you want to pass the ball to a player who is far from you?"
Anticipated Answer:	"A long kick!" (teacher response: "Good!")
Question 2:	"Suppose there is a player from the opposing team between you and your teammate?"
Anticipated Answer:	"Then the ball must fly high!" (teacher response: "Right!")
Question 3:	"Where should the force produced by the foot be applied on the ball in order to raise it off the ground?"
Anticipated Answer:	"As low as possible!" (teacher response: "Yes!")
Question 4:	"Which part of the foot can comfortably get to the lowest part of the ball without interference with the direction of the run and its momentum?"
Anticipated Answer:	"The toes!" (teacher response: "Very good!")
Question 5:	"Would you like to try it?"

Source: Reprinted by permission from M. Mosston, *Teaching Physical Education,* Columbus, Ohio: Charles E. Merrill Books, Inc., 1966, p. 153.

[11] *Ibid.*

Problem solving

Problem solving is the logical extension of guided discovery. In guided discovery, the student was given clues and prompts to direct him toward solving the problem. Steps were small, success was frequent, and the teacher was present to make sure that students did not stray too far from the path leading them to the appropriate goal. In problem solving, there are two important differences. First, the student is left on his own far more. This implies many guided discovery experiences that have preceded the problem-solving methodology. This closely resembles Gagné's learning hierarchy and internal conditions (see page 110). However, once the student has the necessary prerequisite experiences, the problem-solving methodology is appropriate.

The second major difference between problem solving and guided discovery is that problem solving offers the student many more choices, because the problems have many different solutions. The student is intimately involved with the problem, and his solution may differ from another student's solution, although one solution may not be better than the other.

Problems can be structured so that students *discover* things from simple facts to complex relationships, that is, there is an alternative to simply telling students what is a fact. For example, it is a fact that a wider base of support in the direction of movement produces greater stability. Students can be told this, but they also can be given problems through which they discover it.

Problem solving is especially appropriate and useful in examining concepts and strategies in which a number of variations are possible. Not all of the variations are of equal value, but perhaps no one variation is the final answer. This can be true about how to defend against a particular offense in basketball, how to move with a particular base of support from one line to another, and how to outmaneuver a player in soccer.

Again, it should be emphasized that the important educational goal of a problem-solving methodology is an independent thinker who can provide creative solutions to new problems. These tasks are primarily in the cognitive and affective domains, although they assuredly have correlates in the motor domain.

Do not be fooled by problem solving's deceptive simplicity. First, remember that it is preceded by experiences in guided discovery, which, like behavior shaping, require a sequence of steps gradually leading the learner to a final behavior product. Second, the creation of problems that are relevant and challenging is no easy task. The teacher must carefully consider the developmental level of the student in the motor, cognitive, and affective domains. The problems must not be beyond the reach of the student, nor should they produce an effect opposite to that intended by the teacher by

Table 7.4 Examples of questions used in a problem-solving approach to soccer

Purpose: To examine possible relationships between the body and the ball as decreed by the rules of soccer.

1. What are the parts of the upper body that can be used to move the ball from point A to point B?
2. Which parts of the lower body can accomplish similar results?
3. Which parts can move the ball from point A to point B, keeping the ball rolling on the ground?
4. Which parts can move the ball from point A to point B, getting the ball slightly off the ground?
5. Which parts can move the ball, getting the ball to fly above your own height?
6. Is there another part of the body that can accomplish what you did in 3, 4, and 5?
7. Are there still other alternatives?
8. Which of the above parts of the body moved the ball the farthest?
9. Which parts can move the ball in a straight line?
10. Which parts can move the ball along a curved line?

Source: Reprinted by permission from M. Mosston, *Teaching Physical Education,* p. 207. Columbus, Ohio: Charles E. Merrill Books, Inc., 1966.

being too simple and childish. Moreover, the problems must actually relate well to the subject matter, whether it be soccer, archery, swimming, or gymnastics. If you think this is an easy method to use, then you probably have not tried it yet. Once you do, you will find that it takes practice to use this method effectively.

Many educators have made a distinction between what might be termed *reception learning* and what we have described here as guided discovery and problem solving. In reception learning, the material is presented to the learner in a relatively complete form and his task is to *learn* the material that he has already seen, heard, or had explained in some other way. Guided discovery and problem solving emphasize that the learner discovers the solution primarily by himself, although the teacher does act as a guide. As has been mentioned, proponents of the *discovery* method of teaching claim that it produces educational outcomes beyond those achieved in methodologies relying primarily on reception techniques. You should be aware that reception learning *can* be very meaningful. A student who is taught the headstand may experience a tremendous thrill. The tennis player who learns how to hit a better backhand by being taught it may be able to play more competitively and gain all the intrinsic and extrinsic rewards that go with increased skill. In other words, reception methodologies are not inherently meaningless to the learner. Nor, on the other hand, are discovery methods inherently meaningful to the student. Discovery learning can be wasteful and boring, but it also can be exciting, challenging, and extremely meaningful. The problem is to apply the right method at the right time, and to apply it in a manner that achieves the ends for which it was developed.

Table 7.4 includes representative questions used in problem solving in soccer.

Movement exploration

The discussion of guided discovery and problem solving implied that they could be used to teach any content normally included in a physical education, health education, or recreation program. The proponents of these methods would certainly agree that the methods have broad applicability, and that basketball in the high school can be taught by problem solving just as well as stunts and tumbling in the elementary school.

The major use of guided discovery and problem-solving methods, however, has been in the elementary school, in programs described most often as *movement education.* The basic premise underlying movement education is that human movement is the heart of physical education, and that all sports, games, and dance activities are merely forms of human movement. The basic elements of movement are:

1. space
2. time
3. force
4. flow

Children can learn their movement capabilities by *exploring* these facets of movement through guided discovery and problem-solving techniques. As they become more accomplished in understanding their movement possibilities and capabilities, they develop "movement vocabulary."[12] They can then use this repertoire of movement capabilities to solve increasingly complex movement problems and to develop complex motor skills such as those found in sport and dance.

Guided discovery and problem solving are also used in a form of movement education most often referred to as *educational gymnastics.* Basically, educational gymnastics teaches gymnastics skills through guided discovery and problem solving with less emphasis placed on precise development of competitive gymnastics skills. Educational gymnastics and movement education rely heavily on the natural way in which children explore their environments. We all know how children love to climb trees, leap fences, crawl through tunnels, and tumble around a grassy yard. Movement education and

---

[12]N. Allenbaugh, "Learning about Movement," *NEA Journal,* March 1967.

educational gymnastics try to create environments that will encourage children to explore all of their movement capabilities and to learn their movement limitations and preferences. Proponents of these programs believe this is the best way to prepare a child for later skill development that is related more specifically to sport and dance.

Role playing

Role playing is a teaching method in which learners act out roles in simulated real-world situations. There are two primary uses for role playing as a teaching method:

1. the learner may act out a role for which he is training;
2. the learner may act out a role in order for him to learn something about a person who fulfills that role in the real world.

Role playing has been used for years in teacher preparation programs. Methods such as *microteaching* and *miniteaching* are often role-playing situations. College students act out the role of teachers as other college students (classmates in a methods course, for example) act out the role of younger students. Coaches have used simulated game conditions in practice to prepare their players for situations that will probably confront them during games. Football teams use a two-minute drill in which they simulate a situation in a game that has only two minutes left. The simulated situation allows the players to learn how to perform roles that they will need to perform when the situation actually occurs in a game. Basketball coaches have used simulated situations to practice a pressing defense or a stall, depending upon whether they want the practice to simulate their team's being slightly ahead or slightly behind toward the end of the game.

Role playing also enables students to experience roles that other people fulfill in the real world. This use of role playing is especially important in reaching goals in the cognitive and affective domains. Sportsmanship might be taught by having students act out a situation in which a crucial call by a referee changes the nature of a contest. Students might alternately play the role of referee, the beneficiary of the call, and the player, team, or coach adversely affected by the decision. By acting out the various roles, it is assumed that the student will come to some understanding of how "the other guy" feels when something crucial occurs.

The method used in most role-playing sessions is to set the situation carefully, have certain students act out the roles, and then have the group discuss what has occurred. The role players can explain why they behaved as they did, and other students might question them as to why they did not behave in some other manner. The resulting give-and-take among students helps them to understand the complexity of human behavior and perhaps come to some understanding of the positions and beliefs of others.

Role playing may be used to reach educational goals in areas as broad as sportsmanship and as specific as relations between a white coach and a black player. The role of the teacher is crucial for successful role-playing lessons. The method could obviously lend itself to lack of seriousness and irresponsibility. The situation must be carefully set and the members of the group must have some commitment to making the session work toward the desired ends.

Role playing has an advantage as a teaching method with a small group, usually defined as having between six and twelve members. If the group is cooperatively motivated, rather than internally competitive, evidence shows that productivity is very high and that members of the group tend to work together well in common pursuit of the group goal. If the group leader can engender such cooperation, can clearly establish the goal and the various roles to be played by the members of the group, then it is quite likely that the desired outcomes of understanding and empathy will be achieved.

Modeling

Modeling refers to a learning process in which one person (the model) does something and another person, watching the behavior, then attempts to reproduce the behavior in its entirety or in part. Modeling is used as a teaching method by most teachers and could be a part of all the teaching systems described in this chapter. When you demonstrate a tumbling stunt or an overhand volleyball serve, you are providing a *model* for your students. The implication is that the students will attempt to reproduce what they have seen you do. Verbal explanations also provide symbolic models for what to do or what not to do.

Despite the fact that all teachers use modeling, the full potential of this teaching method is seldom achieved, nor are its implications fully understood and appreciated. One of the more important factors about modeling is the degree to which its proper use can short-cut the learning process, in the sense that any particular behavior can be acquired much more quickly if proper modeling procedures are applied. This is dramatically demonstrated by the fact that we can learn things without ever actually doing them, that is, without ever making an actual response during the acquisition phase of learning. If, in a physical education class, a student is severely punished for asking a question without first raising his hand, it is quite likely that you will learn to raise your hand before asking a question even though you never actually made a response in learning that behavior. The student who was punished provided a model and you learned quickly from his behavior without ever making a response of your own. In psychology, this is called *no-trial learning.* The phenomenon of modeling is largely responsible for the human's enormous capability to learn many things and to learn them quickly. Without the benefit of modeling, it would take much longer to learn even the most simple skills.

Unfortunately, many teachers limit their use of modeling to the demonstration of skills and the occasional "making an example of a student," by punishing him before the class. The importance of modeling in motor-skill acquisition has been well documented and is obvious to all teachers who work within the motor domain. However, the potential use of modeling to teach other behaviors is too often overlooked. Some psychologists[13] believe that most social behavior is learned through modeling and that *personality* is best defined as the accumulations of those behavioral predispositions acquired through modeling.

Modeling's potential as a method for teaching appropriate social behavior is substantial: from teaching youngsters how to behave in an elementary playground environment to teaching high school athletes how to behave in terms of the many social behaviors associated with competitive athletics. The basic process of modeling is quite simple and follows the S-R-S formula that has been emphasized throughout this section. In a defined situation (two children sharing one piece of equipment), a student makes a response (one child allows the other to go first), and the response is reinforced (the teacher stops the class and praises the child for being courteous and cooperative). The rest of the class watches this interchange and this helps them to learn one of the ways in which they can be cooperative and courteous.

There is now ample evidence to show that children do learn by modeling. For example, a group of children who *watch* other children being rewarded for acting aggressively with toys will exhibit an increased tendency to act aggressively with toys themselves. Likewise, it is not too farfetched to suggest that the young football player who sees a teammate rewarded for acting aggressively on the football field might show an increased tendency toward behaving that way himself.

Two important points about using modeling as a teaching method warrant

[13] A., Bandura and R. Walter, *Social Learning and Personality Development.* New York: Holt, Rinehart and Winston, Inc., 1963.

A model of a high-jumping technique

emphasis. First, the student will tend to imitate the behavior of the model only along those dimensions with which he identifies. For example, a youngster may attempt to imitate the batting style of a baseball player without imitating any of his other behavior. Likewise, a student may attempt to reproduce a particular form demonstrated by a teacher even though he would not attempt to imitate any other behavior by the teacher. Second, the key to the effectiveness of modeling is found in the consequences of the model's behavior. If you demonstrate a skill and are unable to do it well, the student will be unlikely to attempt to reproduce your performance. In the 1968 Olympic Games at Mexico City, a young American high jumper, Dick Fosbury, won the gold medal with a new jumping style that has come to be known as the *fosbury flop*. In 1972, at Munich, many of the high jumpers used the *fosbury flop;* that is, they had modeled their high-jumping technique on Dick Fosbury's. The important point is that the modeling occurred because of the consequences associated with the model's behavior, that is, Fosbury won the gold medal. If he had gone out of the competition at 6 ft. 8 in., it is quite likely that no jumper would have been using the *fosbury flop* four years later at the Munich Olympics.

You probably have recognized that teaching through modeling severely restricts the behavior of teachers. You would be right to assume that students will model their behavior on yours to the degree that they identify with you and on the basis of the consequences of your behavior. If you are overweight, do not waste your time preaching physical fitness, because your weight problem is a visible consequence of your dubious commitment to physical fitness. If you are a coach and tend to lose your temper during games, arguing loudly with referees and hollering and yelling at your own players, do not waste your time preaching sportsmanship to your players, their parents, or the school officials.

Your behavior is a living example, and students will tend to model what you *do*, not what you *say*.

Other teaching methods

Other teaching methods, upon close examination, appear to be not separate systems but merely different models which incorporate in varying degrees the methods described in this chapter. When the implications of the traditional method, behavior shaping, behavior modification, contingency management, computer-assisted instruction, guided discovery, problem solving, role playing, and modeling are fully appreciated, then other models appear as packages utilizing these techniques to varying degrees. The following teaching methods and/or systems are briefly described because they do appear often in the professional literature.

Directive teaching

Directive teaching is analogous to what we have described in this chapter as the traditional teaching system in physical education. The term *directive* is used because of the central role played by the teacher in directing activity and managing the students. This has also been called *command* teaching.

Teaching by task

Teaching by task is analogous to using behavioral objectives as a primary instructional aid in teaching. The tasks are presented to the student and he progresses through them at his own rate, or at a rate determined by the teacher if the method is group oriented.

Team teaching

Team teaching means that (1) more than one teacher has instructional responsibilities or (2) two teachers are assigned to handle a certain class, sharing the responsibility. Perhaps they have differing abilities and this decides their varied contribution to the instructional situation. Regardless, team teaching would be possible in any of the teaching systems described here and could use any of the methods described.

Teaching by stations

Teaching by stations describes an organizational format rather than a teaching system. The class is divided into groups and each group practices at a station, which is usually one part of a large area such as a gymnasium. They practice for a certain length of time and then move on to the next station, so that the entire class rotates among the stations. The use of tasks or behavioral objectives at each station greatly increases the usefulness of this organizational procedure.

Reciprocal teaching

Reciprocal teaching describes a model in which students teach each other. It is similar to team teaching except the *team* is a group of students; they help each other by providing feedback to each other on progress. Advocates of this teaching system suggest that the interchange among students in this setting contributes to educational goals beyond those of the immediate development of skill and knowledge.

Summary

1. The selection and utilization of a teaching system is determined by educational and noneducational consequences at work in the learning environment.
2. The traditional model, while useful in its day, no longer represents an adequate teaching system.
3. Behavior shaping consists of reinforcing closer and closer approximations of a desired terminal behavior.
4. Behavior modification refers to changing the rate of occurrence of a class of behaviors.
5. Various methods for increasing or decreasing behavior rates are available for use in schools.
6. Behavior shaping and behavior modification can be used for motor, cognitive, or affective behaviors.
7. Contingency management systems use behavioral principles to form a total teaching system in which behaviors are clearly specified and clearly related to a reinforcement system.
8. Contingency systems may operate as task-reward, token, or contract formats.

9. Computer-assisted instruction may utilize a drill test, tutorial, dialogue, or simulation-diagnosis format.
10. Computers can also aid in diagnosis and prescription for counseling students and athletes.
11. Guided discovery and problem solving are systems that leave the solution to problems open-ended so that students may discover the answers on their own, thus developing cognitive and affective capabilities during the learning process.
12. Although guided discovery and problem solving are potentially usable with any subject matter, they have been most successful with movement-education programs.
13. Role playing can be used to practice for a role the student will play or to better understand a role that another person fulfills.
14. Modeling refers to a process where students imitate aspects of a model's behavior.

Questions

1. Is there a difference between a teaching method and a teaching system? Provide an example for each.
2. Criticize the traditional teaching model in view of the development and control of behavior theory.
3. Apply the basic principles of behavior modification to a specific situation.
4. What are the methods used to increase certain behavioral patterns? to decrease them?
5. What is contingency management?
6. Develop a contingency management plan for a specific activity and group of students.
7. Computer-assisted instructional programs have a very promising future. State some of the obstacles that one might encounter in an effort to make use of them.
8. Discuss Mosston's variables in developing and utilizing the guided discovery method of teaching.
9. Differentiate clearly the problem-solving and the guided-discovery methods.
10. Select a group of students and state your teaching strategy in using the two methods mentioned above.
11. Differentiate role playing and modeling. Offer examples.
12. What are the advantages and disadvantages of the team-teaching method?
13. Establish relationships between a teacher's personality, a teaching method, and a particular classroom environment.
14. When a physical education major graduates from college, do you think that he should have learned from his professors which method of teaching is the most effective? Why so?

8

ANATOMICAL AND PHYSIOLOGICAL FOUNDATIONS

Anatomical and physiological foundations underlie the study of exercise physiology, biomechanics, and growth and development. The science of the structure of organisms is *anatomy,* whereas the science of the function of organisms is *physiology.* Since function is a property of structure and all functions imply structure, it is appropriate to discuss these two areas of study together.

To understand the human body as a whole, professionals in health, physical education, and recreation must see the bodily systems as being closely interrelated. Each system forms a unit particularly adapted for the performance of some function. However, that function is dependent upon the cooperative activity of the other systems; for example, the skeleton does not support unless assisted by the muscular, nervous, and other systems.

The cell

The structural and physiological unit of the body is termed a *cell.* Although there are many types of cells that differ in size and shape, most of them are composed of a mass of protoplasm which consists of a nucleus, a nuclear membrane, cytoplasm, and a cell membrane. Protoplasm is the physical basis of life, and the nucleus consists of a specialized mass of protoplasm contained within a nuclear membrane. The nucleus functions:

1. to regulate the metabolic activities of the cell;
2. in cell growth and repair;
3. in cell reproduction.

Cytoplasm is that portion of the cell's protoplasm found outside the nucleus, but within the cell membrane. The cytoplasm is particularly concerned with such cellular functions as contraction, conduction, absorption, and secretions. Cells originate and increase in numbers through cell division. This is a process in which a parent cell divides and generates two daughter cells. It has been estimated that the human body contains 100,000,000,000,000 cells; that is, 100 million millions. Life processes are maintained by moving food, oxygen, hormones, salts, and so forth, into the cell, and by discharging water, carbon dioxide, products of secretion, waste materials, and so forth, from the cell.

Tissues

A tissue is a group of cells with intercellular material which is specific in amount and composition to that tissue. There are four types of tissues in the human body:

1. epithelial
2. connective
3. muscular
4. nervous

Essentially, the difference among the four types is based on the kinds of cells of which they are composed, the amount and compositions of intercellular material present, and the functions they perform. Epithelial tissue forms the covering of the outer surface of the body and of most internal organs, as well as the secreting aspects and ducts of glands and the sensory parts of sense organs. Connective tissue (for example, bone, cartilage, and tendon) forms the connecting and supporting structures of the body. Muscular tissue consists of a specialized group of cells whose function is to contract and exert the force employed for the bodily movements. Nervous tissue is composed of specialized groups of cells that function in the reception of stimuli, the conduction of nerve impulses, and the execution of responses to stimuli.

Organs and systems of the body

An organ (for example, kidney, heart) consists of tissues associated in performing some particular function for which it is especially adapted. A system is a special arrangement of organs closely related to one another and concerned with the same functions. The systems are discussed below.

Integumentary system

The integumentary system consists of the skin and its derivatives. The skin consists of the epidermis (outer layer) and dermis (inner layer). Its derivatives are made up of cutaneous, mammary, ceruminous glands, hair, hair follicles, and nails. The integument functions to:

1. protect underlying tissues;
2. prevent excessive tissue dehydration;
3. act as a reservoir for water and food;
4. serve as a temperature regulator;
5. help in the process of excretion via perspiration;
6. act as a sense organ for the cutaneous senses;
7. be the site of production of vitamin D.

Skeletal system

The components of the skeletal system are bones, cartilage, and ligaments, as shown in Figures 8.1 and 8.2. Bones make up the hard structure of the body, cartilage forms the supporting and connecting structures, and ligaments hold the bones together. The skeletal system consists of 206 bones and is divided into the axial and the appendicular skeletons. The axial skeleton has 80 bones and consists of the skull, vertebral column, and the thorax (sternum and ribs). The appendicular skeleton has 126 bones and contains the upper and lower extremities. The upper extremity consists of the pectoral girdle, and the arms, forearms, and hands; the lower extremity contains the pelvic girdle, the thighs, and the legs and feet. This system gives form to the human body. Its functions are to:

1. provide a structure for all the other systems;
2. provide connections for muscles, ligaments, and tendons;

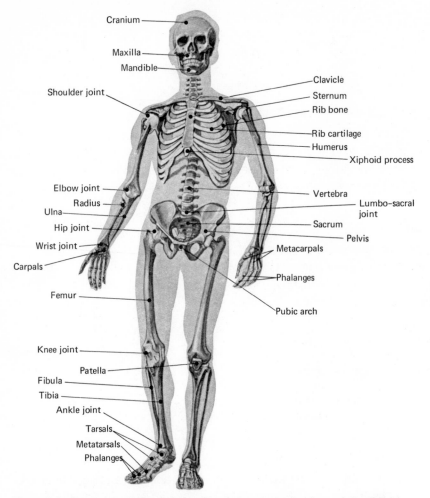

Figure 8.1   Front view of the skeleton. The ligaments are in place on the figure's right side, showing the manner in which they support and bind the bones together at the joints. Ligaments have been removed on the left side to show the bony structure of the joints. The shaded contour of the body shows the manner in which the skeleton supports the body and gives it form, and indicates the relative amount of soft tissues which overlie the bones.

Source: From *Principles of Modern Physical Education, Health, and Recreation,* by Wynn F. Updike and Perry B. Johnson. Copyright © 1970 by Holt, Rinehart and Winston, Inc. Reproduced by permission of Holt, Rinehart and Winston, Inc.

3. enclose and thereby protect vital organs;
4. act as the seat of manufacture of blood cells;
5. serve as a reservoir for calcium.

   A junction between two or more bones or between cartilage and bone is an *articulation.* The two main types of articulation are termed *synarthrosis* and

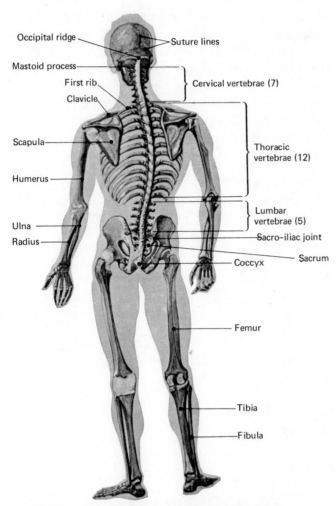

Occipital ridge — → Suture lines

Mastoid process —

First rib — ┐ Cervical vertebrae (7)

Clavicle ┘

Scapula — Thoracic vertebrae (12)

Humerus —

Lumbar vertebrae (5)

Ulna — Sacro-iliac joint

Radius —

Coccyx — Sacrum

Femur

Tibia

Fibula

Figure 8.2 Back view of the skeleton. The ligaments are in place on the figure's left side, while those on the right have been removed. This view of the skeleton reveals the sutures of the cranial bones, the scapulae with their broad surfaces for muscle attachment, and the sacroiliac joint with the ligaments which bind the sacrum and pelvic bones together. The ridges which are visible on many of the bone surfaces are for the attachment of muscles.

Source: From *Principles of Modern Physical Education, Health, and Recreation,* by Wynn F. Updike and Perry B. Johnson. Copyright © 1970 by Holt, Rinehart and Winston, Inc. Reproduced by permission of Holt, Rinehart and Winston, Inc.

diarthrosis. Synarthrosis is a joint that has a limited degree of movement or none at all, since it has a ligament, cartilage, or fibrous tissue between its components. Examples of this type of joint are the junction between two cranial bones, or the joint between bodies of vertebrae. *Diarthrosis* is a joint that has slight to great movement ranges, because its articular surfaces are covered with cartilage and separated by an articular cavity. Examples of this diarthrosis are the thumb (saddle joint), elbow (hinge joint), elbow-radius and ulna (pivot joint), wrist (ellipsoidal), hip (ball and socket joint), and sacroiliac (gliding joint).

In order to understand the diarthrodial articulation one must first be familiar with the planes (sagittal, frontal, transverse) and directional terms (anterior, posterior, lateral, medial) of the anatomical position. Diarthrodial articulations are described below and pictorially represented in Figure 8.3.

Flexion is movement in an anteroposterior plane, which results in a decrease in
the angle between the bones (for example, bending the arm at the elbow).
Extension is the opposite of flexion (for example, extending the arm at the
elbow).

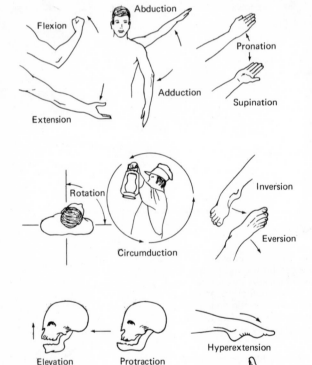

Figure 8.3   Types of joint movements

Source: Redrawn from Fig. 5-30 "Types of joint movements," by Janson (p. 85) in *Anatomy and Physiology*, Vol. I, by Edwin B. Steen and Ashley Montagu (Harper & Row, 1959)

Abduction is the movement of the part away from the median sagittal plane or the median sagittal plane of the part (for example, lateral upward movement of the arm).

Adduction is the opposite of abduction (for example, lateral downward movement of the arm).

Supination is turning the hand so that its palm is facing upward.

Pronation is the opposite of supination.

Circumduction occurs when the end of the limb nearest to the body remains fixed while the end farthest from the body moves in an arc (for example, swinging the arm in a circle).

Inversion occurs at the ankle joint when the sole of the foot is turned inward.

Eversion is the opposite of inversion.

Elevation occurs when a part is raised (for example, closing the jaw).

Depression is the opposite of elevation.

Hyperextension is the movement in which the part is extended beyond the straight line formed by normal extension (for example, extending the foot beyond the normal extension). *Plantar flexion* is extension of the foot. *Dorsiflexion* is the opposite of plantar flexion.

Rotation is movement in which a part turns on its longitudinal axis (for example, turning the head to the left or right at the joint between the atlas and axis).

Protraction is the forward movement of a part (for example, protrusion of the jaw).

Retraction is the opposite of protraction.

Muscular system

The muscular system is composed of the organs that contract and relax to produce movements of the entire body and its parts (see Figures 8.4 and 8.5). There are three types of muscle cells: smooth, striated, and cardiac. Smooth muscle is formed in such places as the wall of the digestive tract, walls of blood vessels, and the iris of the eye; its action is involuntary. Striated muscle tissue is found primarily in all the muscles that are attached to and move skeletal parts. The action of striated muscle tissue is largely voluntary. Cardiac muscle is found only in the heart, and its action is involuntary, automatic, and rhythmic.

There are four properties of muscle tissue that facilitate muscle functions:

1. contractility
2. extensibility
3. elasticity
4. irritability

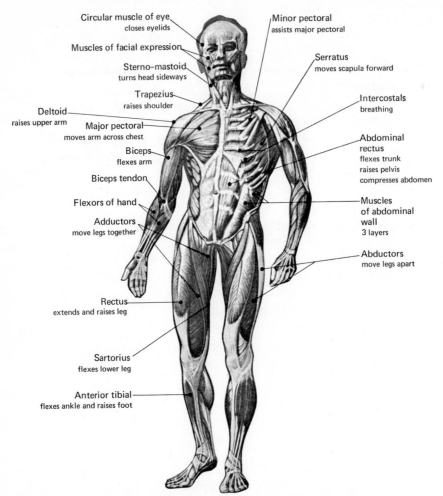

Circular muscle of eye
closes eyelids

Muscles of facial expression

Sterno-mastoid
turns head sideways

Trapezius
raises shoulder

Deltoid
raises upper arm

Major pectoral
moves arm across chest

Biceps
flexes arm

Biceps tendon

Flexors of hand

Adductors
move legs together

Rectus
extends and raises leg

Sartorius
flexes lower leg

Anterior tibial
flexes ankle and raises foot

Minor pectoral
assists major pectoral

Serratus
moves scapula forward

Intercostals
breathing

Abdominal
rectus
flexes trunk
raises pelvis
compresses abdomen

Muscles
of abdominal
wall
3 layers

Abductors
move legs apart

Figure 8.4   Front view of the skeletal muscles. The muscles are intact on the figure's right side. On the left side, some of the overlying muscles have been removed to show deeper muscles and parts of the skeleton to which they attach. The tendons attaching muscles to bones are visible in many areas. The sheath of the rectus muscle of the abdomen has been removed on the left side to show the division of this muscle into segments connected by areas of tendon. The slender cablelike tendons in the region of the wrist contrast with the broad, flat tendons in the region of the knee which are designed for more powerful muscles. Some of the larger and more familiar muscles are labeled in this figure. In the labeling, only the main action is described. Many muscles have other functions and, also, work differently in groups than they work singly.

Source: From *Principles of Modern Physical Education, Health, and Recreation,* by Wynn F. Updike and Perry B. Johnson. Copyright © 1970 by Holt, Rinehart and Winston, Inc. Reproduced by permission of Holt, Rinehart and Winston, Inc.

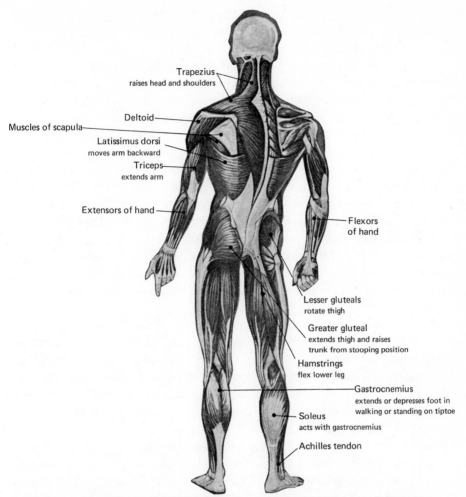

Trapezius
raises head and shoulders

Deltoid

Muscles of scapula

Latissimus dorsi
moves arm backward

Triceps
extends arm

Extensors of hand

Flexors
of hand

Lesser gluteals
rotate thigh

Greater gluteal
extends thigh and raises
trunk from stooping position

Hamstrings
flex lower leg

Gastrocnemius
extends or depresses foot in
walking or standing on tiptoe

Soleus
acts with gastrocnemius

Achilles tendon

Figure 8.5   Back view of the skeletal muscles. The muscles are intact on the figure's left side. Some of the overlying muscles have been removed on the right side. The attachments of muscles to the scapula are shown on the right side, as are the deeper muscle attachments to the pelvic bones and hip joint. The tendon of Achilles, extending upward from the heel, is shown in both lower legs. A divided muscle joining the tendon has been removed on the right leg to expose the full length of the Achilles tendon and the deeper muscle it also joins.

Source: From *Principles of Modern Physical Education, Health, and Recreation,* by Wynn F. Updike and Perry B. Johnson. Copyright © 1970 by Holt, Rinehart and Winston, Inc. Reproduced by permission of Holt, Rinehart and Winston, Inc.

Contractility is the capacity of muscle tissue to become shorter. Extensibility denotes that muscle tissue has the ability to stretch with the application of force. Elasticity is the property of muscle tissue that allows muscles to return to

197

their original size and shape after having been stretched. Irritability is the ability of muscle tissue to respond to a stimulus such as a nerve impulse.

When a striated muscle contracts, chemical, electrical, and thermal changes occur that result in modifying muscle length and tension. The energy used in contraction is the result of a process of chemical changes that do not directly require the presence of oxygen—hence, an anaerobic process. In excessive muscle exercise, the chemicals needed for the energy-producing process are soon exhausted and must be replenished. The energy used in replenishing the chemicals is the result of a resynthesis process in which oxygen is utilized and carbon dioxide and water are liberated—thus, an aerobic process. If excessive muscle exercise continues, an energy debt or oxygen debt results, since oxygen, which is not stored in the muscle, cannot be brought by the blood stream to the muscle fast enough to be used in the resynthesis process. Muscle fatigue, that is, the reduced capacity or inability to perform work, is the obvious consequence. Thus, typical exercise involves a combination of anaerobic and aerobic processes. If an oxygen debt results from excessive exercise it is usually paid off by the performer's continuing to breathe heavily after completing the exercise.

Types of striated muscle contraction are typically referred to as isometric, isotonic, concentric, or eccentric. The isometric type occurs when a muscle is overloaded and contracts, but does not shorten or lengthen. Isotonic contraction occurs when a muscle contracts to a load that is below the maximum, and the muscle shortens. The term concentric is synonymous with isotonic. An eccentric contraction occurs when a muscle is overloaded and tries to shorten during contraction, but is lengthened instead.

Pairing of muscle groups occurs about a joint to perform opposing action, for example, biceps-elbow flexion and triceps-elbow extension. To provide smooth efficient movement, opposing muscle groups must function cooperatively. When a signal from the nervous system commands contraction of the agonist (for example, biceps for elbow flexion), another signal must also reach the antagonist (for example, triceps for relaxation). This type of cooperative action is the result of a reflex and is referred to as *reciprocal innervation.*

Both striated and nonstriated muscles have tonus, or muscle tone. Muscle tone refers to slight state of contraction and depends on a regular stream of nerve impulses to the muscles. The maintenance of an upright posture as well as the preparation for movement depend upon muscle tonus. It is also well known that muscle tone varies with the individual's condition. For example, a person's muscle tone is usually lower when he is calm, relaxed, or in ill health than it is when he is highly emotional, physically active, and in good health.

Respiratory system

The respiratory system, shown in Figure 8.6, is composed of the lungs, bronchi, trachea, pharynx, larynx, and the nose. It functions to exchange gases between humans and their environment, that is, it takes in oxygen and releases

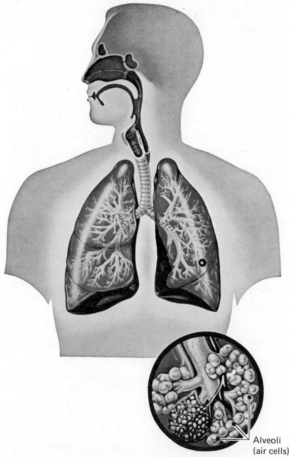

Alveoli
(air cells)

Figure 8.6   A diagrammatic view of the respiratory system. The nasal passages, pharynx, larynx, trachea, bronchi, and lungs are shown. The transparent lungs reveal the bronchial tree. A small part of the left lung, indicated by the circle, is magnified at the right to show a small bronchus and bronchioles ending in alveoli, surrounded by a capillary net between a pulmonary artery and a vein.

Source: From *Principles of Modern Physical Education, Health, and Recreation,* by Wynn F. Updike and Perry B. Johnson. Copyright © 1970 by Holt, Rinehart and Winston, Inc. Reproduced by permission of Holt, Rinehart and Winston, Inc.

carbon dioxide. The exchange of carbon dioxide from the blood to the air and oxygen from the air to the blood via the lungs is termed *external respiration.* The exchange of oxygen and carbon dioxide between the circulatory fluids (blood, lymph, tissue fluid) and the cells is referred to as *internal respiration.* The importance of respiration is that life processes depend largely on the release of energy from food. This energy simply cannot be released without a continuous supply of oxygen accompanied by the removal of carbon dioxide.

Circulatory system

The circulatory system consists of the blood vascular system, that is, the heart, blood and blood vessels, and the lymphatic vessels. Oxygenated blood circulates from the left ventricle of the heart through the aorta to the arteries (large vessels), to the capillaries (extremely small vessels) of each body part. It is here, between the capillaries and the cells, that oxygen, nutrients, and so forth, are exchanged with carbon dioxide, waste products, and so forth. From the capillaries the deoxygenated blood flows to the venuoles (extremely small vessels), to the veins (large vessels), to the right atrium, to the right ventricle, to the pulmonary artery, and to the lung capillaries. It is in the lung capillaries that carbon dioxide is exchanged for oxygen. The oxygenated blood now circulates through the pulmonary veins, to the left atrium, and back to the left ventricle. Meanwhile, the lymphatic system is moving lymph (clear, watery fluid) and tissue fluid from the body tissues back to the bloodstream. Thus, the circulatory system functions to supply essential nutrients and to eliminate cell secretions and excretions. The circulatory system exists for the action that occurs at the capillaries and helps maintain the constancy of fluids around and inside all cells, that is, *homeostasis.*

Nervous system

The nervous system is composed of the brain, spinal cord, ganglia, nerve fibers, and their motor terminals. The brain and spinal cord are illustrated in Figure 8.7. The structural unit is a specialized type of cell termed a *neuron.* A group of two or more neurons as a functioning unit constitute a *reflex arc.* Figure 8.8 displays a complex reflex action including many reflex arcs.

The nervous system may be divided structurally into integrated divisions referred to as the central and peripheral nervous systems. The central nervous system consists of the brain and the spinal cord; the peripheral system includes all the nerves (ganglia, nerve fibers, motor terminals) that are found outside the cranial cavity and the vertebral column. The nervous system may

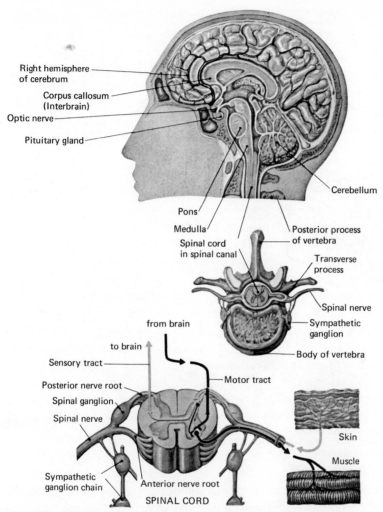

Right hemisphere of cerebrum

Corpus callosum (Interbrain)

Optic nerve

Pituitary gland

Cerebellum

Pons

Medulla

Spinal cord in spinal canal

Posterior process of vertebra

Transverse process

Spinal nerve

Sympathetic ganglion

Body of vertebra

from brain

to brain

Sensory tract

Posterior nerve root

Spinal ganglion

Spinal nerve

Motor tract

Skin

Muscle

Sympathetic ganglion chain

Anterior nerve root

SPINAL CORD

Figure 8.7   The brain and spinal cord. The figure shows the right cerebral hemisphere and lower brain structures in mid-line section. At the right is a single vertebra seen from above. Note the sectioned spinal cord with its membranes and the spinal nerves. The figure below shows the path of a spinal reflex, involving a sensory neuron, central or connecting neuron, and motor neuron. The sensory and motor tracts to and from the brain are shown.

Source: From *Principles of Modern Physical Education, Health, and Recreation,* by Wynn F. Updike and Perry B. Johnson. Copyright © 1970 by Holt, Rinehart and Winston, Inc. Reproduced by permission of Holt, Rinehart and Winston, Inc.

also be divided functionally into the autonomic and somatic systems, and both these systems have central as well as peripheral components. The autonomic system controls the actions of the heart, liver, lungs, stomach, intestines,

201

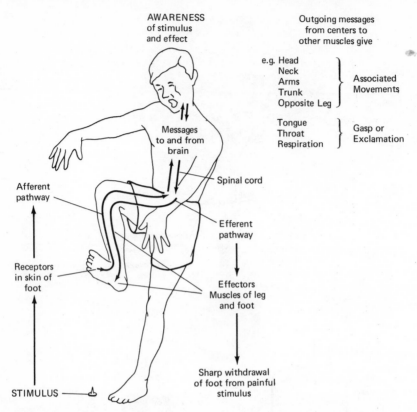

Figure 8.8   Reflex action demonstrating many reflex arcs.

Source: A. McNaught and R. Callander. *Illustrated Physiology.* Baltimore, Md.:
The Williams & Wilkins Company, 1963. (Fig. 2.11). Used by permission of
Churchill Livingston, Edinburgh.

kidneys, blood vessels, and endocrine glands without any conscious direction.
The somatic system controls voluntary actions, that is, actions that are
consciously directed.

The nervous system functions to provide sensory input, integration, and
output. Sense receptors provide input into the system. Receptors may be
classified as:

1. *exteroceptors*—located in the outer surface of the body, and stimulated by energy
   changes external to the body;
2. *interoceptors*—found in the linings of the digestive, respiratory, and circulatory
   systems, and stimulated by energy changes affecting them;
3. *proprioceptors*—located in between the inner and outer surfaces of the body in
   muscles, tendons, joints, and inner ear, and stimulated by energy changes internal
   to the body resulting from movement of these structures.

Stimulation from energy changes in the environment excites specialized receptor cells to emit nerve impulses. Specialized receptor cells are particularly sensitive to certain kinds of energy changes and are relatively insensitive to other ones. Each receptor cell has a threshold, a critical level below which energy changes are not capable of exciting the neuron. Special senses are typically categorized as visual (sight), auditory (hearing), olfactory (smell), gustatory (taste), and cutaneous (touch), kinesthesis (sense of movement), and proprioception (sense of movement, tensions, forces, pressures, balance). Once an impulse has occurred, it is sent into the central nervous system via afferent (input) channels. The brain correlates nerve impulses in the sensory centers and functions to coordinate impulses in the motor centers so that if action is needed, the appropriate command signal can be sent to the appropriate muscles (usually skeletal) or glands over efferent (output) channels.

Thus the nervous system functions to regulate and coordinate body activities in response to internal and external environmental conditions. This system is the basis for perception, memory, consciousness, intelligence, and higher cognitive processes such as reasoning and thinking. It also is the center of emotional responses as reflected in various arousal states.

Endocrine system

The endocrine system consists of organs that secrete hormones, that is, endocrine glands. These glands are the thyroid, parathyroids, pituitary body, adrenals, thymus, pancreas, duodenum, ovaries, and placenta. Endocrine glands are ductless and the hormones they secrete are organic chemical substances such as epinephrine. Hormones, carried by the blood and lymph, stimulate or inhibit the activity of cells, organs, and tissues. Thus, the regulation and correlation of body activities are accomplished to some extent by this system.

Digestive system

The digestive system comprises the organs that act on the food taken in so that it may be absorbed and provide nutrition for the body. Digestion begins in the mouth with the chewing and mixing of food with saliva containing enzymes. The passages and spaces from the mouth to the anus constitute the alimentary canal, in which digestible substances are absorbed and indigestible ones and waste are eliminated. Digestive glands (for example, the salivary glands, the pancreas, and the liver) secrete enzymes and other chemical substances that are necessary to the breakdown of food and its absorption into the blood.

Thus, the main functions are to receive, digest, and absorb food, and eliminate indigestible food and some waste.

Excretory system

The excretory system is composed of the urinary organs such as the kidneys, bladder, ureters, and urethra (excretory passages) and also the digestive and respiratory systems and the skin. Its main function is to eliminate the waste products that arise from cell activity.

Reproductive system

The reproductive system consists of the testes, seminal vesicles, penis, urethra, prostate, and bulbourethral glands in the male; the ovaries, uterine tubes, uterus, vagina, and vulva in the female. Obviously this system is concerned with the production of new individuals of the same species. However, it also exerts widespread effects on the entire life of the person through hormones produced by the sex glands. For example, these hormones can affect bodily development and behavior.

Summary

1. The nucleus functions (a) to regulate the metabolic activities of the cell; (b) in cell growth and repair; (c) in cell reproduction.
2. There are four types of tissues in the human body: (a) epithelial; (b) connective; (c) muscular; (d) nervous.
3. The integument functions (a) to protect underlying tissue; (b) to prevent excessive tissue dehydration; (c) to act as a reservoir for water and food; (d) to serve as a temperature regulator; (e) to help in the process of excretion via perspiration; (f) to act as a sense organ for the cutaneous senses; (g) to be the site of production of vitamin D.
4. The skeletal system consists of 206 bones; the axial skeleton has 80 bones and the appendicular skeleton has 126 bones. The skeletal system functions (a) to provide a structure for all the other systems; (b) to provide connections for muscles, ligaments, and tendons; (c) to enclose and thereby protect vital organs; (d) to act as the seat of manufacture of blood cells; (e) to serve as a reservoir for calcium.
5. There are three types of muscle cells: (a) smooth; (b) striated; (c) cardiac.

6. There are four properties of muscle tissue which facilitate muscle functions: (a) contractility; (b) extensibility; (c) elasticity; (d) irritability.
7. The respiratory system exchanges gases between humans and their environment; that is, it takes in oxygen and releases carbon dioxide.
8. The circulatory system supplies essential nutrients and eliminates cell secretions and excretions.
9. The nervous system regulates and coordinates body activities in response to internal and external environmental conditions.
10. The endocrine system consists of organs that secrete hormones.
11. The functions of the digestive system are to receive, digest, and absorb food and to eliminate indigestible food and some waste.
12. The excretory system's function is to eliminate the waste products that arise from cell activity.

Questions

1. What would be a good operational definition of anatomy? of physiology?
2. What are the functions of the nucleus?
3. Enumerate the four types of tissues in the human body.
4. What are the functions of the skin? the skeletal system?
5. Can you differentiate the movements that diarthrodial articulations are capable of performing?
6. Identify the following terms: isometric, isotonic, concentric, and eccentric.
7. What are the main organs in the respiratory and circulatory systems?
8. What are the divisions of the nervous system and their main functions?
9. Briefly compare the following systems: endocrine, digestive, excretory, and reproductive.
10. What is the value to the physical educator of learning the anatomical functions of the human body?

EXERCISE PHYSIOLOGY

Exercise physiology is basically concerned with the study of body functions when a performer engages in physical activity. Studies in exercise physiology have been greatly facilitated by the American College of Sports Medicine, a national organization established "to advance and disseminate knowledge dealing with the effect of sports and other motor activities on the health of human beings at various stages of life."[1] Knowledge generated from the study of exercise physiology provides a scientific basis for the study of the immediate and long-term (training) effects of exercise and physical fitness. In this chapter, we will discuss exercise physiology in three sections: (1) effects of exercise; (2) physical fitness; and (3) some factors affecting the physiology of human performance.

[1] "Medicine and Science in Sports," 4, *Journal of the American College of Sports Medicine,* Winter 1972.

Overview of some effects of exercise

The activity of striated muscle not only affects almost every other system of the body, but acts on the muscle as well. The effects of exercise are either immediate or long term, and are dependent upon intensity, duration, and type of exercise as well as the nature of the performer and his environment.

Immediate effects of exercise

After a person exercises, the following occur:

1. Increased rate and depth of breathing to meet the demands for more oxygen and for the removal of the increased carbon dioxide produced. When the oxygen consumed does not equal the oxygen required by the exercise, an "oxygen debt" occurs.
2. Increased rate of metabolism, since more food is used to supply energy for the activity and more waste products (for example, lactic acid, urine, carbon dioxide) are produced and must be removed.
3. Increased number of red blood cells to enlarge the oxygen-carrying capacity of the blood.
4. Increased cardiac output. Cardiac output equals heart rate multiplied by stroke volume. Stroke volume refers to the amount of blood ejected with each beat.
5. Increased heart rate and blood pressure. Blood pressure is the pressure the blood exerts against the walls of the vessels in which it is contained.
6. Increased dilation of the arteries supplying the muscle(s) being exercised. There are also an increased number of capillaries opened in active parts of the body. The vessels in the less active parts are more constricted.
7. Increased volume of the muscle(s) being exercised owing to the increase in blood flow.
8. Increased body temperature. Some of the heat produced is dissipated through the skin by sweating. If the amount of salt lost from sweating is great, exhaustion or heat cramps may result. Physical performance may be adversely affected when dehydration results in more than 2 percent loss of weight.
9. Decreased levels of cholesterol and fat in the blood.
10. Impairment of digestive processes by vigorous exercise.
11. Vigorous exercise results in a shortened blood-clotting time during and after exercise.
12. Blood circulation to the kidneys is impaired during exercise. This results in reduced glomerular filtration rates.

Long-term effects of exercise

If training programs are conducted so that intensity, duration, and type of exercise are properly related to the performer and his environment, the long-term or training effects of exercise can be beneficial. Some of the long-term effects of exercise are:

1. Increased muscle size (hypertrophy) due to the changes in the sarcoplasm of the individual muscle fibers and the increase in the amount of connective tissue between the fibers;
2. Increased muscle strength due to (a) an increase in the number of myofibrils and the size of muscle fibers resulting in an increase in the size of the muscle; (b) improved coordination; and (c) the improved neural functioning that brings about the contraction;
3. Increased muscular efficiency as a result of better coordination of all muscles involved, improvement of the circulatory and respiratory systems, improved movements at the joints, and the elimination of excess fat;
4. Increased number of capillaries resulting in increased muscular endurance and vascularization;
5. Increased size, strength, and efficiency of the heart results in a capability of greater cardiac output. There is also some evidence that training can increase cardiac muscle capillarization, which in turn enhances collateral circulation;
6. Increased work capacity at a lower heart-rate level owing to increased maximal oxygen intake (aerobic capacity) and increased ''oxygen debt'' tolerance (anaerobic capacity); further, less oxygen is needed to perform any given level of work;
7. Increased red blood-cell count, hemoglobin, and the total blood volume which results in increasing the oxygen-carrying capacity of the blood;
8. Decreased resting heart rate that results in reduced total work for the heart;
9. Decreased rate, but increased depth, of breathing at rest, which results in less work per minute for the inspiratory muscles;
10. Reduced body fat stores, provided that caloric intake is not consistently greater than caloric expenditure;
11. Reduced arterial blood pressures toward normalcy when these pressures were above normal prior to training.

Physical fitness

The American Alliance for Health, Physical Education, and Recreation (AAHPER) has listed the components of total fitness as follows:

1. optimum organic health consistent with heredity and the application of present health knowledge;
2. sufficient coordination, strength, and vitality to meet emergencies as well as the requirements of daily living;
3. attitudes, values, and skills which stimulate satisfactory participation in a full range of daily activities;
4. emotional stability to meet the tensions of modern life and an understanding of the value of physical activity in the reduction of stress;
5. social consciousness and adaptability with respect to the requirements of individual and group living;

6. sufficient knowledge and insight to make suitable decisions and arrive at feasible solutions to problems of fitness;
7. spiritual and moral qualities which contribute the fullest measure of living in a democratic society.[2]

   Physical fitness may be thought of as one aspect of total fitness and is the one with which physical educators are most concerned. However, the meaning of the term *physical fitness* is rather vague and its measurement is complicated by many factors, especially the performer's changing motivational states. Consequently, there is no universally accepted definition or measure of physical fitness. Nevertheless, we will use the conceptualization of H. A. deVries as a guide for discussing the nature and measurement of physical fitness. He thought of physical fitness as having two major components: motor fitness and physical working capacity (PWC). Motor fitness is concerned with measuring elements of physical performance, whereas PWC deals with evaluation of physiological function, that is, the capacity for transporting oxygen. Let us take a closer look at each of these components.

Motor fitness component

Motor fitness, one major component of physical fitness, consists of the elements of strength, endurance, speed, power and agility, flexibility, coordination, balance, and body control. Balance and body control will be treated indirectly throughout the discussion of the other elements. Many motor-fitness test batteries, such as the Army Air Force Physical Fitness Test, Indiana Motor Fitness Indices, California Physical Performance Test, and the AAHPER Youth Fitness Test Battery, were developed by physical educators to assess the elements of motor fitness. (For more detail concerning these tests the reader is referred to the typical tests and measurements books such as Clarke's[4])

Muscular strength Strength is the ability of the body or its parts to apply force. Strength involves a combination of three variables: "(a) the combined contractile forces of the muscles causing the movement (agonists); (b) the

[2] "Fitness for Youth," *Journal of Physical Education and Recreation,* September 1968.

[3] H. A. deVries, *Physiology of Exercise for Physical Education and Athletics.* 2d edition. Dubuque, Iowa: William C. Brown Company, Publishers, 1974.

[4] H. H. Clarke, *Application of Measurement to Health and Physical Education,* 4th ed. Englewood Cliffs, N.J.: Prentice-Hall, Inc., 1967.

ability to coordinate the agonist muscles with the antagonist, neutralizer and stabilizer muscles; and (c) the mechanical ratios of the lever (bone) arrangements involved."[5]   Strength may be developed at approximately the same rate with isotonic or isometric training methods or with some combination of them. However, the strength developed will be specific to the type of training method employed; its selection usually depends upon purpose, administrative feasibility, and personal preference.

Regardless of the method employed, the muscles should be overloaded and the load should be increased progressively. deVries[6] identifies some basic overload and progressive-resistance principles of strength training, presented below, that may serve as a guide for program development:

In isometric training:
1. Maximal contraction produces the fastest gains.
2. Duration of five seconds is optimal.
3. Higher end strength can be attained by increasing repetitions from one to between five and ten daily.
4. If contraction strength less than the maximum is used, it should be based on a maximum that is measured weekly.
5. Workouts four or five times per week appear to be optimal.

In isotonic training:
1. All contractions should be made through the full range of motion.
2. For the development of strength, a program based on two or three sets of four to ten repetitions each, using maximum resistance for the number of repetitions, seems to rest around experimental bases.
3. For the development of hypertrophy, the DeLorme Technique is most effective.
   first set: ten repetitions with ½ 10 RM.[7]
   second set: ten repetitions with ¾ 10 RM.
   third set: ten repetitions with full 10 RM.
4. Workouts should be scheduled no less than three and no more than four times weekly for optimal results.
5. The total exercise program should be scheduled so that no more than one workout per week approaches exhaustion.

Endurance Endurance has been defined as the ability to continue physical activity and resist fatigue. In physical education we are primarily concerned with

[5]C. R. Jensen and G. A. Fisher, *Scientific Basis of Athletic Conditioning.* Philadelphia: Lea & Febiger, 1972.

[6]deVries, *op. cit.,* p. 382.

[7]RM refers to repetition maximum, that is, 10 RM means using the maximum load that can be lifted successively ten times.

local muscular and cardiovascular endurance. Local muscular endurance depends upon the quality of the muscles involved, the extent of their capillary beds, and parts of the nervous system supplying them. It is generally agreed that increasing muscular strength also increases the endurance of those muscles—consequently, the overload and progressive-resistance principles for strength development of muscular endurance. However, if an individual wants to increase endurance without large gains in strength, then the training program should be modified so that a lighter load is used with as many as 20 to 30 RMs per set.

Cardiovascular endurance is considered to be the ability of the circulatory system to supply oxygen to the cells to sustain the oxidative energy demands of the body and to remove the waste materials of metabolism. Most physiologists agree that gas transport (especially oxygen) is the primary determinant of cardiovascular endurance. Gas transport depends on cardiac output, vascularization, and the oxygen-carrying capacity of the blood, that is, hemoglobin and the number of red blood cells per unit of blood. Thus, one reason for developing cardiovascular endurance is to improve the circulation to the muscles being exercised.

Training for cardiovascular endurance may be *aerobic* or *anaerobic*. The former involves conditioning the systems that supply oxygen to the cells, whereas the latter is concerned with the energy without the presence of oxygen. Aerobic endurance training usually consists either of exercising for long periods, as in jogging or cross-country skiing, or of a series of exercise bouts, with brief rest intervals between bouts. The latter is referred to as interval training and is believed to be the better of the two methods. To develop an optimal rate of aerobic endurance, interval training must consist of an adequate number of successive bouts of exercise, about three to five minutes in length separated by brief rest periods, that are intense enough to maintain the heart rate within ten beats of the performer's maximal rate. Anaerobic endurance training, on the other hand, usually consists of maximal effort with short (about one minute) exercise bouts of maximal effort with short rest periods between bouts. Anaerobic endurance usually results in increased heart strength, that is, a stronger contraction of the heart muscle.

Speed Speed refers to the rate at which a force can be applied. It may also be expressed in the formula:

$$\text{Speed} = \frac{\text{Distance traveled}}{\text{Time required to travel that distance}}$$

Speed of movement is specific to parts of the body involved, the type of skill being performed, and the direction of the movement. Even running speed can be thought of as being composed of two factors: rate of acceleration and maximal velocity. The former refers to how fast a performer can accelerate over approximately a twenty-yard range, whereas the latter is concerned with maintaining a maximum speed over distances greater than twenty yards. It is possible for a performer to have a fast rate of acceleration and a slow rate of maximal velocity, or for the opposite to be true. However, some gifted athletes possess both. It has been pointed out that:

1. Speed of muscle contraction can be increased a limited amount by training with repeated fast movements.
2. Speed of movement against resistance can be increased by increasing the ability to apply force (strength) against the resistance. This method is ineffective against light resistance, but it becomes progressively more effective as the resistance is increased.
3. Speed can be increased by improving the coordination of the various muscles involved in each movement and by improving the coordination of the various movements involved in the skill.
4. Speed can be increased by employing the optimum combination of angular velocity and length of the levers involved.[8]

Power and agility Power may be defined as the rate of performing work and is a function of strength and speed. It may also be expressed in a formula as:

$$Power = Strength \times Speed$$

where
1. strength refers to the ability to produce force;
2. speed refers to the rate at which the force can be applied.

Power can be developed by:

1. increasing speed with strength held constant;
2. increasing strength with speed held constant;
3. increasing both speed and strength.

Agility may be thought of as the ability to shift direction of the body and its parts quickly. It represents a combination of strength, speed of reacting and moving, power, and coordination. Agility can be increased by improving its component parts. However, we strongly believe that the most effective way to increase agility in a specific movement is to practice that pattern correctly and repetitiously at high speeds.

[8] Reproduced by permission from C. R. Jensen and G. A. Fisher, *Scientific Basis of Athletic Conditioning,* p. 119. Philadelphia: Lea & Febiger, 1972.

Flexibility Flexibility refers to the range of motions in one or more joints. Flexibility may be considered static, referring to a measure of the range of movement, or dynamic, referring to a measure of the resistance to movement produced by a joint. Flexibility depends upon the structure of the bone at the joint, the amount of mass surrounding the joint, and the capacity of ligaments, tendons, muscles, and skin that traverse the joint.

Flexibility can be improved by warm-up and exercises involving slow stretching of the antagonistic muscles followed by a conscious attempt to relax them for a few seconds. Slow stretching exercises appear to be more desirable than jerking, bobbing, or bouncing.

Coordination Coordination includes the skeletal, nervous, and muscular systems as well as the senses of sight, touch, and hearing. Also involved is the kinesthetic sense, that is, an individual's awareness of the position and the balance of the body at a given time.

There are two types of coordination, namely, multilimb and gross body. Multilimb coordination is the ability of an individual to coordinate simultaneous movements of two hands, two feet, or a combination of both hands and feet while operating a particular instrument. Gross-body coordination, more difficult to define, is generally the ability of an individual to coordinate movements of the whole body without expending a great deal of force or energy.

Some feel that there are other aspects of coordination, such as eye-foot coordination used in kicking a football or hand-eye coordination used in attempting to hit a pitched baseball with a bat. In general, coordination is the spatial and temporal timing of movements, resulting in more efficient movement, whether in driving an automobile, walking, writing, jogging, engaging in sports, or other activity.

The potential production of complex, coordinated movement is inherited, and is developed through practice. Development of coordination, however, is very specific to the particular activity. For example, strength, endurance, agility, reaction time, power, and speed are general athletic components that are necessary in football and equally so in other vigorous activities. On the other hand, passing, kicking, tackling, blocking, and centering are skills specific to football and not needed in other sports. Thus, in order to play football or golf well, an individual must develop and coordinate the specific skills of football or golf. Nor will he be successful in basketball until he learns to shoot, dribble, pass, and rebound. In summary, regardless of what other components an individual has, he will be unable to perform well in a particular activity until, through many hours of work and practice, he develops the coordinated skills specific to the particular activity.

Physical working capacity component

Another major component of physical fitness is an individual's PWC. PWC is the maximum level of work that a performer is capable of doing. Because PWC depends upon the performer's capacity to supply the working muscles with oxygen, it is sometimes referred to as aerobic capacity. PWC probably evaluates at least the following elements: (1) cardiovascular and respiratory function, (2) muscular strength, endurance, and efficiency, and (3) obesity.

The best method of measuring PWC is to have the performer engage in successive exercise bouts of increasing intensity, from three to six minutes in time, with adequate rest intervals between successive bouts. During each exercise bout, the oxygen consumption is measured. When the oxygen consumption does not rise with increased load, the performer has reached his maximum. This value is a measure of the performer's PWC or aerobic capacity.

However, this method is not appropriate for typical physical education settings since it requires laboratory facilities and cannot be used with large classes. Consequently, other methods of assessing PWC that are more applicable to physical education settings have been developed. Some of these methods are the PWC-170, Astrand Rhyming Nomogram, Cooper's Twelve-Minute Run-Walk Test, Harvard Step Test, and Progressive-Pulse Ratio Test. The Harvard Step Test is probably the most popular, since it can be used with large classes and does not require elaborate or expensive equipment. It requires only benches (20 inches high and 18 inches deep), a stopwatch for each observer, and a metronome.

The Harvard Step Test operates on the principle that the better the PWC of the performer, the greater the proportion of cardiac cost (total heart beats during exercise minus resting rate for the same duration) that is paid back during exercise, the smaller the recovery cardiac cost, and the lower the heart rate following exercise, that is, during recovery. Although this test is not as precise as the maximum oxygen-consumption method described above, it does provide a fairly accurate estimate of PWC. More detail concerning these types of tests can be found in several sources.[9]

Development of physical fitness

Many of the principles concerned with the development of physical fitness have already been discussed previously under the motor fitness heading and will not be treated again under this heading. However, we have not yet identified any principles that could help us design school physical education programs aimed at developing physical fitness.

[9]See *Suggested Readings* at end of text.

From a physiological-medical viewpoint, physical education in schools should:
1. train the oxygen transporting system (respiration and circulation);
2. generally train the locomotive organs (especially the muscles of the back and abdomen);
3. give instructions on how to lie, sit, stand, walk, lift, and carry;
4. give instruction in technique, tactics, and rules in games and sports in order to reduce or eliminate accidents (the events are eventually practiced in the students' leisure time);
5. provide physical and psychological recreation and variety;
6. arouse interest in regular physical activity after schooling has been finished.[10]

Some of the more popular programs on the market that are aimed at developing physical fitness include Youth Physical Fitness[11] and Adult Fitness: A Program for Men and Women,[12] both developed by the President's Council on Physical Fitness; Jogging,[13] a program developed by Bowerman and Harris; Royal Canadian Air Force 5BX Plan,[14] Kenneth Cooper's program The New Aerobics,[15] and Total Fitness in 30 Minutes a Week,[16] the program developed by Laurence Morehouse and Leonard Gross. Which program you select depends in part upon your present health status and the purpose for which you are trying to become physically fit. It is always advisable to begin with a complete medical examination in order to assess your present health status.

Some factors affecting the physiology of human performance

Three of the many factors that affect the physiology of human performance have been selected for discussion here.

[10]P. O. Astrand and K. Rodahl, *Textbook of Work Physiology.* New York: McGraw Hill, Inc. Copyright © 1967 by and used with permission of McGraw-Hill Book Company.

[11]President's Council on Physical Fitness, *Youth Physical Fitness.* Washington, D.C.: U.S. Government Printing Office, 1967.

[12]President's Council on Physical Fitness, *Adult Fitness: A Program for Men and Women.* Washington, D.C.: U.S. Government Printing Office, 1963.

[13]W. J. Bowerman and W. E. Harris, *Jogging.* New York: Grosset & Dunlap, Inc., 1967.

[14]Royal Canadian Air Force, *5BX Plan.* Ottawa: Queen's Printer and Controller of Stationery, 1961.

[15]K. H. Cooper, *The New Aerobics.* New York: Bantam Books, Inc., 1970.

[16]L. E. Morehouse and L. Gross, *Total Fitness in 30 Minutes a Week.* New York: Simon and Schuster, 1975.

Environment

The performer's body constantly strives for a balance between heat gained and heat lost. As noted earlier one immediate effect of exercise is an increase in body temperature due to the increases in metabolism demanded by the activity. Body heat may also be gained when the environmental temperature is above skin temperature. On the other hand, a large amount of body heat is lost by dissipation through the skin in sweating in environmental temperatures that are below skin temperature.

In a hot, dry environment the performer's ability to maintain thermal balance during activity is limited by increasing body temperature due not only to activity but also to the inability to dissipate the heat to the environment. In a cold environment the performer faces the problem of trying to select clothing appropriate to retaining the heat gained during warm-up and rest periods, and heat dissipation during activity periods.

Many times, athletes must perform at altitudes different from the one in which they trained, as, for example, in the 1968 Olympics at Mexico City. When successful performance depends upon aerobic energy (endurance-type activity) and is to be executed at 3000 feet or more above the training altitude, performance is impaired. However, recovery following performance can be facilitated by administering oxygen. The limitations placed on human performance by the types of environments described above can be reduced by acclimatization, that is, training in those environments prior to performing in them.

Warm-up

The physiological effects of warm-up are virtually the same as the immediate effects of exercise, discussed earlier. While research on warm-up is still somewhat inconclusive, the consensus is that if appropriate procedures are employed, warm-up can be beneficial to performance and can help prevent injury. Available evidence appears to justify the following warm-up procedures:

1. Warm-up should be appropriate for the performer and the sport activity involved.
2. Warm-ups should include some stretching and loosening exercises as well as movements related to or similar to the activity that is about to be performed.
3. Warm-up should be intense enough to raise body temperature and cause sweating, but not so intense as to approach the onset of fatigue.
4. Warm-up probably should begin to be reduced ten to fifteen minutes prior to performance and should terminate approximately five minutes before performance.

217

Ergogenic aids

Ergogenic aids are simply special aids such as drugs, "miracle" foods or drinks, oxygen, vitamin supplements, diet manipulation, and so forth, that are believed to improve performance. Some aids, like oxygen, can improve performance if administered during the exercise period. Further, a small improvement in recovery rate appears to occur when oxygen is given to the performer following exercise. Other aids, such as supplementing an adequate diet with vitamins, do not seem to be warranted. A disadvantage of using an ergogenic aid that seems to improve performance psychologically is that the performer may come to depend on it and use it as a "crutch." Obviously, at a critical moment when aid is not available, the performance may suffer. In summary, it is advised that ergogenic aids be used as no more than a supplement to sound training and conditioning and only when they do not constitute a hazard to the performer.

Summary

1. Exercise physiology is basically concerned with the study of body functions when the performer is engaged in physical activity.
2. De Vries defines physical fitness as a composite of at least two major components, and each major component is composed, in turn, of measurable elements of physical performance or physiological function. The major components include motor fitness and physical working capacity (PWC).
3. Motor fitness, one major component of physical fitness, consists of the elements of strength, endurance, speed, power and agility, flexibility, coordination, balance, and body control.
4. PWC is the maximum level of work that a performer is capable of doing. PWC depends upon the performer's capacity to supply the working muscles with oxygen and is sometimes referred to as aerobic capacity.
5. Among the many factors that affect the physiology of human performance are environment, warm-up, and ergogenic aids.

Questions

1. Do you see any difference between physiology and physiology of exercise? Explain.
2. What are some of the immediate and long-term effects of exercise?

3. Compare different definitions of physical fitness.
4. How do you define motor fitness? What are its components?
5. What are the principles involved in isotonic and isometric training? Give an example of your own.
6. Differentiate the following terms: muscular strength, organic strength, muscular endurance, and organic endurance.
7. A layman comes to you to have misconceptions straightened out about aerobics and anaerobics. Help this person.
8. Coordination is a term often talked about but misused in several ways. What is the truth about coordination?
9. How do you relate physical education programs, physical fitness, physiology of exercise, degenerative diseases, and habits?
10. What are some of the current misconceptions about warm-ups?
11. The use of drugs is a controversial issue in athletics today. What are some of the pros and cons?

10

BIOMECHANICS[1]

The biomechanics of human performance deals with the inherent relationship between the biological processes and function of the human organism and the physical laws associated with the environment within which it functions. It has been an area of study within the specialties of physical rehabilitation, aerospace science, industrial engineering, and medicine for many years. However, not until the mid–1960s did the term come to be associated with physical education in the United States. Before then, the term *kinesiology,* defined as the study of the science of movement, described the area within physical education which examined human movement on the basis of structural and applied anatomy and basic mechanical principles. In fact, even today some believe that the term kinesiology is more appropriate for the description of this subdiscipline. Therefore, you will find such courses as *kinesiology* and *applied*

[1]We wish to extend our appreciation to Professor Thomas P. Martin, State University College at Brockport, for writing the original draft of this chapter.

kinesiology in the curriculums of many physical education programs. However, the full meaning of the term kinesiology goes beyond the anatomical, physiological, and mechanical to include the psychological and sociological aspects of human movement. It follows that you could study the learning of physical skills (psychology of sport) or the cohesiveness of sport groups (sociology of sport) under the heading of kinesiology. Thus, it seems that the term biomechanics is the more descriptive and accurate title for the specialty within physical education which deals with the interrelationship between moving humans and the physical laws of their environment.

The First International Seminar on Biomechanics, held in Switzerland in 1967, initiated structured international communication and stimulated the rapid development of the biomechanics of sport. A second seminar followed in 1969 in Holland, a third in 1971 in Rome, and a fourth in 1973 at the Pennsylvania State University, at which the International Society of Biomechanics was founded. In addition, the First International Symposium on Biomechanics in swimming, waterpolo, and diving was held in Belgium, and the first U.S. meeting on biomechanics of sport was a Biomechanics Symposium at Indiana University in 1970. These symposia, along with the increased research on biomechanics of sport published in *Medicine and Science in Sports, Journal of Biomechanics, Kinesiology Review,* and the *Research Quarterly,* indicate a rapid development, a growing sophistication, and a pronounced interest of physical educators in the biomechanics of sport.

There is good reason for the rapid development of biomechanics in physical education. When you analyze a sport movement (as spectator, teacher, or coach) you draw on all your past experiences and analytic ability to interpret and evaluate the movement. Consider, for example, in the setting of a college football game, a female spectator in the stands, a former player watching on television, and a coach observing from the press box. A pass play is run unsuccessfully. Which of the three individuals mentioned would be best able to explain why the play was unsuccessful? Of course, the coach, not because of any superior intellectual ability, but because he has a tremendous amount of experience in performing, studying, and analyzing the play as a whole and the individual performances that form the basic units of the play. The more knowledge an individual has concerning the performance of a physical skill, the better he is prepared to analyze and suggest changes that will result in improved performance.

A knowledge of biomechanics can greatly aid the teacher and coach in understanding and improving sport skill. Why does a ball curve? Why should a shot putter remain in contact with the ground when the shot is released? Why does a diver spin faster in a tuck position than in a layout position? Why are swimming times slower in salt water? Why does a parachutist roll upon landing? The answers to these questions are directly related to, respectively, aerodynamics, Newton's law of reaction, conservation of angular momentum, hydrodynamics, and dissipation of force—that is, laws of physics. The answers and their application are one aspect of what is termed *qualitative analysis.*

Qualitative analysis

Qualitative analysis describes movement by analytical methods but without actual measurement. Putting aside such considerations as body type, strength, and endurance, qualitative analyses are presently based on championship performance. In other words, a teacher or coach draws on his descriptive and analytic ability to analyze championship performance as a model, and then attempts to transfer the derived knowledge to his performers. To accomplish this task he must have a solid foundation in anatomy, physiology, movement description, and the principles of physics.

Figure 10.1 presents the human body divided into eight segments and also shows the centers of articulation between segments. These segments can be classified as rigid (for example, arm and thigh), quasi-rigid (for example, forearm and leg), and flexible (for example, head and neck, trunk, hand, and foot). When muscles are stimulated to contract (electrical stimulus via the

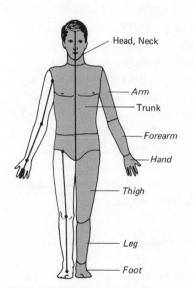

Segments in italics are appendicular

Figure 10.1   The segments of the human body.

Source: From David L. Kelley. *Kinesiology: Fundamentals of Motion Description* © 1971. Reprinted by permission of Prentice-Hall, Inc., Englewood Cliffs, New Jersey.

223

nervous system), they develop tension and exert a force at their attachments to generate or inhibit body-segment motion. In this way you are able to move your segments at their joint articulations and bring about coordinated purposeful movement. It follows that an understanding of a standard, logical, and precise classification of body-segment movement is essential for both description and analysis of movement. An excellent explanation of the current classification system is presented by D. L. Kelley.[2] If the movements of a particular skill are described, and you have a basic understanding of anatomy, you should be able to determine the major muscles that have operated to cause the segment movements. The importance of this knowledge is that it enables you to organize training programs that will result in increased strength, endurance, and flexibility in those regions of the body most important to the skill.

Center of gravity and physical principles

Sport skills are performed on the ground, in the air (supported or unsupported), and in water. The body as a whole and each body segment must function in accordance with the physical principles that control the movement of all objects. Every object, whether it be a car, bat, body, or body segment, has an imaginary point called its center of gravity. *The center of gravity* (CG) is defined as the weight center of an object and/or the point around which all parts of an object balance. For an individual in the standing position the CG is located in the pelvic region. Each body segment has a CG which can be considered to be located at a point that is a certain percentage of its length.[3] For example, the CG for a forearm segment is located 43 percent of its length from the elbow joint. The location of the whole body CG indicates the stability or lack of stability of any body position. If a straight line drawn from the CG to the ground (line of gravity) falls within the base of support, the individual is in a balanced position. Also, the lower the CG, the more stable the position. This is illustrated quite clearly in football, where the three- or four-point stance is much more stable than the upright position. A further advantage of using the CG as a reference point is that its path can represent the movement of the body as a whole. The critical factor in high jumping is the maximum height an individual can project his CG (body) above the ground. Thus, the concept of CG is basic to an understanding of the effect of physical principles on sport skill.

[2] D. L. Kelley, *Kinesiology: Fundamentals of Motion Description.* Englewood Cliffs, New Jersey: Prentice-Hall, Inc., 1971.

[3] W. T. Dempster, *Space Requirements for the Seated Operator,* WADC Technical Report 55159. Wright-Patterson Air Force Base, Ohio, 1955.

The following is a topical list of physical principles which can be directly applied to sport skill:

A. Motion
  1. Linear
     displacement
     velocity
     acceleration
  2. Angular
     displacement
     velocity
     acceleration
  3. Freely falling bodies
  4. Path of projectiles
     parabolic
     curvilinear

B. Force
  1. Weight and mass
  2. Newton's laws of motion
     law of inertia
     law of acceleration
     law of reaction
  3. Gravity
  4. Friction
  5. Centripetal
  6. Momentum
     transfer
     conservation
  7. Levers
  8. Moment of inertia

C. Work and Energy
  1. Work
  2. Power

3. Potential energy
4. Kinetic energy
5. Rotational energy

D. Aerodynamics
  1. Projection angle
  2. Flight velocity
  3. Spin
  4. Air resistance
     wind
     air density
     shape of projectile
     surface friction factor

E. Landing and Striking
  1. Angle of incidence
  2. Shape of striking surface
  3. Center of percussion
  4. Surface friction and resiliency
  5. Elasticity
  6. Rebound
  7. Dissipation of force

F. Hydrodynamics
  1. Buoyancy
  2. Surface area for propulsive force
  3. Bernoulli's law
  4. Water resistance
     waves
     eddies
     viscosity
     theoretical square law

This list is not all-inclusive, but does present many of the principles utilized in qualitative analysis. Although each of these principles could be discussed in relation to numerous sport skills, a brief example of one aspect of each heading will suffice for this overview of biomechanics.

Examples of physical principles applied to sports skills

Linear acceleration Acceleration is a change in velocity over some time interval. The faster a runner can reach top speed (accelerate) from the sprint start in track, the better will be his time for the race.

Transfer of momentum Momentum equals an object's mass (considered to be located at its CG) times its velocity. In executing a penalty kick in soccer, a few steps are taken to increase the momentum of the body, and then, as the nonkicking foot is planted, the momentum is transferred first to the thigh segment, then to the leg segment, then to the foot segment, and finally to the ball.

Power Power is the rate of doing work. Work is the product of a force and the distance over which it acts. Therefore, the more work done per time interval or the quicker a given amount of work is done, the greater the power. In football, the more powerful a block, the more likely its success. The power can be increased by increasing the performer's dynamic strength (ability to exert force per unit time) and/or by decreasing the amount of time required to make the movement.

Projection angle Theoretically, the ideal projection angle to achieve maximum distance is 45°, and to achieve maximum height, 90°. However, factors such as height of release above the ground, wind, shape of object, weight of object, and objective of the skill affect the ideal projection angle. In high jumping for objective maximum height, the performer must use a take-off angle of less than 90° to enable him to get over the bar. Cooper[4] states that the highest take-off angle he has recorded in championship performers was 78°, though a higher angle might be possible with improved technique.

Center of percussion Center of percussion, also known as the center of oscillation of a compound pendulum, is the point on an implement where impact with an object will result in minimal vibration and therefore efficient contact. In baseball and tennis, this area is called the "sweet spot" of the bat or racket. If a ball strikes a bat or racket at a point other than the center of percussion, the resulting vibrations are transferred to the hands and may even prove painful.

Bernoulli's law Bernoulli's law states that fluid pressure is reduced wherever the speed of flow is increased.

A swimmer swims more efficiently by moving a larger amount of water back more slowly than moving a smaller amount of water back more rapidly. The champion swimmers observed in this study accomplished this by applying Bernoulli's Principle. They moved their hands in elliptical patterns and changed the pitch of their hands so

---

[4]J. M. Cooper, "Kinesiology of High Jumping," in J. Wartenweiler, E. Jokl, and N. Hebbelinck, eds., *Biomechanics I.* Baltimore, Md.: University Park Press, 1968.

the flow of the water over the knuckle side of their hands was at a faster speed than that of the water on the palm side of the hand.[5]

It must be kept in mind that the foregoing examples represent only an indication of the value of the qualitative application of physical principles to sport skills.

Quantitative analysis

Quantitative analysis describes movement through biological and mechanical measurements. Quantitative analysis could be considered the scientific approach to biomechanics. Movement can be described quantitatively through the use of kinematic and/or kinetic methods. Kinematic methods describe movement in time and space by such measurements as linear and angular displacement, velocity, and acceleration. Kinetic methods describe the forces that motivate, control, or inhibit movement by such measurements as weight, power, momentum, energy, and moment of inertia. Whatever the method employed, an accurate record of the performance is critical for analysis.

Recall our example of an unsuccessful pass play in a football game, and assume the play took six seconds. How much information could the coach have recalled concerning the performance of the eleven players on his team?—very little: he was probably concentrating on only a few aspects, such as the pass pattern and defense. However, if films had been taken of the game, they could be run and rerun, in slow motion and with stop action, allowing all aspects of the play in question to be observed. Though this example is one of qualitative analysis, it also points up the importance of keeping an accurate record of performance that can be reanalyzed. In quantitative analysis, the records of performance must be not only accurate and reanalyzable, but also measurable. There are four basic modes of obtaining measurable records for quantitative analysis; cinematography, electromyography, electrogoniometry, and force platforms.

Cinematography

Cinematography, the production of motion pictures, is employed for both qualitative and quantitative analysis.[6] Many specific filming procedures are

[5] J. E. Counsilman, *The Application of Bernoulli's Principle to Human Propulsion in Water.* Bloomington, Indiana: Indiana University Publications, p. 7.

[6] A. W. Hubbard, "Photography," *Research Method,* 2d ed. Washington, D. C.: American Alliance for Health, Physical Education and Recreation, 1959, pp. 127–147.

necessary to obtain a measurable film record of a performance. Depending on the complexity and purpose of the study, either one (uniaxial), two (biaxial), or three (triaxial) stationary cameras are needed to record the performance. The camera(s) must be set up in such a way that the view(s) of the performance will contain all information necessary for analysis. In order to obtain a measurable film record, the subject-to-camera distance must be appropriate; horizontal, vertical, and scale references must be included in the photographic field; the camera speed (frames per second) must be appropriate; and a method for determining deviation must be established, in addition to normal quality photographic procedures. Finally, the segmental articulations (joint centers) should be clearly marked directly on the performer so that segmental movement can be measured. Considering these restrictions, it is understandable that of the very large amount of film taken at the 1972 summer Olympics in Munich, very little is of sufficient accuracy for quantitative analysis.

Once the films have been taken and processed, the next step is film analysis. Some type of viewing method or device must be used to extract data from the film. Typically the movement of segmental articulations is important and is recorded.

Figure 10.2 illustrates a stick figure diagram of the tennis serve. Note that the stick figure is constructed by connecting centers of segment articulations. By determining segment displacement for various time intervals one can calculate segment velocities and accelerations (kinematic analysis). If, in addition, segment weights, CG, and moment of inertia are known, the forces causing the movements can be calculated (kinetic analysis). Cinematography has been the most popular method of obtaining quantitative information on performance, and numerous investigations of various sport skills can be found in the literature.

Electromyography

Electromyography (EMG) is the graphic recording of the electrical impulses within a muscle or group of muscles.[7] Electrical stimuli via the nervous system bring about muscle contraction. EMG can determine the functions of individual muscles and groups of muscles, examine muscle coordination, study muscular fatigue, and investigate neuromuscular relaxation. EMG recordings are made by placing electrodes in (needle) or on (surface) the muscle(s) under study. Wires then connect the electrodes, which are sensitive to electrical change, to a graphic read-out device. Therefore, when electrical impulses cause a muscle to contract, their intensity will be recorded on graph paper to produce a

---

[7] J. V. Basmajian, "Electromyography Comes of Age," *Science,* 176, 1972, pp. 603–609.

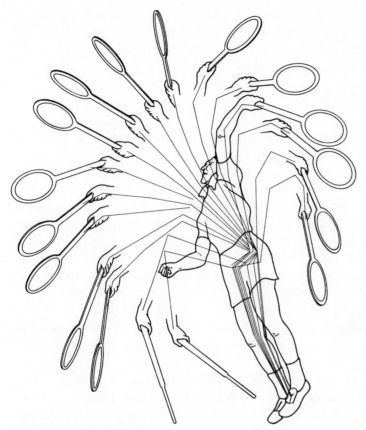

Figure 10.2   Tennis service

Source: From Stanley Plagenhoef, *Patterns of Human Motion: A Cinematographic Analysis* © 1971. Reprinted by permission of Prentice-Hall, Inc., Englewood Cliffs, New Jersey.

measurable record. EMG has been used in studies of walking, posture, throwing, golf, batting, and the shot put.

Electrogoniometry

Electrogoniometry is the electrical determination of joint angles (adrain). Electrogoniometers (elgons) consist of two moveable arms with a potentiometer (variable resistor) connected in the center. By placing the potentiometer over a joint (for example, the elbow) and strapping the arms of the elgon to the adjacent body segments (for example, arm and forearm), changes of joint angle will bring about electrical changes in the potentiometer which will be transmitted via wires to a graphic read-out device. In this way, changes in joint angle can be recorded for any movement between segments. Electrogoniometers have been used to investigate joint angle changes in walking, running, jumping, and swimming.

Force platforms

Force platforms determine forces exerted in various directions on some surface.[8] Strain gauges are attached to the surface in order to measure the downward, sideward, forward, and/or backward forces exerted by the subject. Electrical connections from the strain gauges to a graphic read-out device provide a timed record of the various forces produced during the performance. Force platforms have been used to study the sprint start, long jump, diving, and weight lifting.

These four methods of obtaining quantitative data have been presented separately for clarity. However, integration of methodologies can often prove far more informative than any single method. This being the case, a tremendous amount of data must be collected and analyzed. Computer technology, to assist in the collection and analysis of biomechanical data, is enabling researchers to investigate questions previously considered too complex and time-consuming for analysis.

In summary, biomechanics examines the relationship between moving humans and the physical laws of the environment. The objective of biomechanics is an understanding of the motivation, control, and integration of human movement. To this end teachers, coaches, and researchers employ qualitative and quantitative methods in order to describe, evaluate, and improve performance. Though biomechanics is presently primarily concerned with the *description* of performance, it is predicted that, with increased development of this area, biomechanicians will be *formulating* performance methodology based on sound biological and mechanical principles.

Summary

1. Biomechanics of human performance refers to the inherent relationship between the biological processes and function of the human organism and

[8] A. H. Payne, ''The Use of Force Platforms for the Study of Physical Activity,'' in J. Wartenweiler, E. Jokl, and M. Hebbelinck, eds., *Biomechanics I.* Baltimore, Md.: University Park Press, 1968.

the physical laws associated with the environment within which it functions.
2. The International Society of Biomechanics was founded in 1973.
3. Indiana University was the site of the first meeting (1970) on biomechanics of sport in this country.
4. Qualitative analysis describes movement using analytical methods but without actual measurement.
5. The center of gravity is the weight center of an object and/or the point around which all parts of an object balance. The lower the CG, the more stable the position.
6. Quantitative analysis describes movement by biological and mechanical measurement.
7. There are four basic modes of obtaining measurable records for quantitative analysis: cinematography, electromyography, electrogoniometry, and force platforms.
8. Cinematography, the production of motion pictures, is employed for both qualitative and quantitative analysis.
9. Electromyography (EMG) is the graphic recording of the electrical impulses within a muscle or group of muscles.
10. Electrogoniometry is the electrical determination of joint angles.
11. Force platforms determine forces exerted in various directions on some surface.

Questions

1. Does it make any difference if you use the term kinesiology for biomechanics?
2. What do you envision as the scope of the study of biomechanics?
3. What are some of the principles utilized in qualitative analysis?
4. Select one phase of a sport skill and apply the physical principle to it.
5. Describe a few applications for Bernoulli's law.
6. What distinction do you establish between kinematic and kinetic methods?
7. Give the respective characteristics of the four basic modes of obtaining measurable records for quantitative analysis.
8. What is the relationship between qualitative and quantitative analysis?

11

GROWTH AND DEVELOPMENT[1]

At what age can a child learn to ride a bike, ski, or tie his shoes? Most educators believe that an individual learns and performs best when he is ready. It can even be detrimental to a child to expect from him behavior of which he is not physically or emotionally capable at that particular age. Behavioral demands made on children at certain ages are often unreasonable, especially on the larger child. A child is *not* a miniature adult. Not only is his nervous system incompletely developed, but so also is his muscular development and bone growth. As professionals in health, physical education, and recreation, we have a complex and challenging task in determining when a child is best ready to learn a skill or develop a concept. Careful study of human growth and development is essential in determining a child's physiological, psychological, and sociological readiness for success in selected motor activities. Such study

[1]We wish to extend our appreciation to Professor Martilu Puthoff, Miss Linda Arena, and Miss Nanette Schnaible, State University College at Brockport, for their assistance in the development of this chapter.

233

informs us what motor behavior to expect and when to expect it. This in turn will tell us when to stimulate the child toward certain experiences and when certain experiences will be too advanced, thus causing failure and frustration.

Growth, development, and maturation

Growth, development, and maturation are three terms often interchanged throughout child development literature. Although these three aspects are closely interrelated in their influence on the aging human organism, they are not synonymous.

Growth

Growth is a quantitative change in body structure, such as an increase in physical size of bodily parts or of an organism as a whole. It generally refers to measurable physical and biological changes in the development of the individual. Since growth is quantitative in nature, it is generally visible and measurable anthropometrically, that is, by height, weight, and body proportions. Growth does not imply changes in characteristics or complexity of the organism that would be qualitative in nature.

Development

Development is a complex process of integration of the structures and functions of the body, and is the result of maturational and environmental influences combined. It includes not only quantitative structural changes (growth) but also the integration of structure and function of the body. Development also includes the variety of other bio-psycho-social attributes a child acquires as he grows up. Child development occurs in an orderly and coherent pattern, which results in new characteristics and abilities for that individual. Instructors must relate their teaching to these growth patterns for optimal productivity. Of particular importance to our profession are the sequences of motor development which are characteristic of most humans and which are somewhat predictable.

Since growth, development, and maturation are strongly interrelated, they will progress, to some degree, at the same rate in the normal child. Yet, to a certain extent they remain independent as they progress. "They are a broad highway along which every individual must travel. Each individual has his or her own unique heredity and nature . . . and will travel along that highway at his or her own rate of progress and will attain the size, shape, capacity, and developmental status which are uniquely his or her own at each stage of the life career."[2]

Maturation

Maturation is the development of inherent genetic characteristics through an ongoing process of physiological and anatomical change attributable to the passage of time rather than to practice or learning. Often considered as an unfolding of innate characteristics and abilities, maturation is very much genetically based. Although conditions in a child's environment may affect the age at which he reaches a certain maturation level, they do not affect the sequence of development. This ongoing differentiation of body structure and function forms the foundation for *readiness* in learning. Readiness refers to that time when the maximum sensory, physical, motivational, and psychological capacities are present. Physical readiness to learn tasks includes both neurological and muscular maturation. Hence, the effectiveness of teaching depends upon the development of various levels of maturation. Research shows that motor skill cannot be developed until a child's neuromuscular system is sufficiently ready. The ability to coordinate motor patterns into a highly skilled act is learned; it is not an automatic result of maturation. Maturation is what makes learning possible. A child will learn a motor task most effectively when prerequisite maturation has occurred. Until such time, practice has very little effect upon the success of acquiring skilled motor performance. Maturation levels are usually assessed through observation of children's behavior, chronological age and body-build formulas, the onset of sexual maturity, and most recently, skeletal maturity as it relates to long bone growth.

Heredity and environment

The genetic process

Researchers have unlocked many of the secrets regarding heredity and the genetic process. A real possibility exists that scientists will be able to direct the course of genetic action and deliberately select the best kinds of hereditary formations.

The keys to human developmental potential lie within the DNA and RNA molecules which make up the chromosomes found in the reproductive cell.

[2]L. K. Frank, "Genetic Psychology and Its Prospects," *American Journal of Ortho-Psychiatry,* 21, 1951, pp. 506–522.

Each human being possesses 23 unpaired chromosomes in the nucleus of an egg or sperm cell. During the process of fertilization, when an egg and sperm cell unite, the 46 combined chromosomes formed provide the genetic strains of body cells which will develop in the new offspring.

Hereditary differences result from the variations which arise within chromosomes and their genetic structures of DNA and RNA. They also result from the almost infinite combinative possibilities which arise when over 500 million sperm cells are set free during the process of fertilization. The genetic make-up within the DNA provides the developmental direction for the quality of responses that will result upon external stimulation from the environment.

The interaction of heredity and environment

The influence of heredity on the growth and development of children is greatly affected by environment. Genes do not determine one's traits; they merely provide the potential for developing a trait. Poor environmental conditions may limit the extent to which existing genetic potentiality can be developed. Although genes may establish the potential for structural development, it is the environment which influences the course and extent of that development.

Environment has a lesser influence on inherited physical traits, those which led humans to believe that they owed most to heredity. Genetic factors play the major role in such dominant trait characteristics as hair and eye color, facial appearance, body build, and bone structure, for example. Recessive traits such as sickle cell anemia, color blindness, or baldness are also definitely inherited. The final outcome of personality and achievement is not influenced so much by what one inherits as it is by the emotional and intellectual climate provided by the environment. The intellectual achievement of an average or below-average child can be greatly raised by the proper manipulation of environmental control.

Researchers have found that in the initial development of sensorimotor coordination, specific forms of contact with the environment are essential for the normal growth of spatial behavior. It has been proposed that humans possess different critical periods for various kinds of behavior. The environment must provide the proper learning opportunities during these developmental periods. It has also been found that during the early years of development, appropriate or inappropriate masculine and feminine patterns of movement and mannerisms may be imprinted on a child by adults.

Children as learners are not, however, merely passive recipients of heredity and of environmental influences. As a child grows, he will begin to shape his own environment through the process of selective attention, taking an active part in decisions regarding his optimal development. Thus, each learner evolves as a product of the interaction of a unique organism undergoing growth, development, and maturation with a unique physical and social environment. Teacher, curriculum, guidance, and expectation are extremely important influences on the final outcome of this learner product.

Phases of physical growth and motor development

Prenatal (conception to birth)

Prenatal development begins at conception. Fetal movements vary and are often related to maternal activity or condition. For example, fatigue and other emotional states tend to increase fetal activity. Research suggests that the duration and vigor of prenatal movements correlate positively with postnatal motor ability.

Infancy (birth to approximately 2 years)

Infancy is the period from birth to walking. During this period the rate of physical growth and motor development differs considerably among infants, primarily because each child is endowed with his own unique heredity characteristics. However, all infants tend to follow a predictable pattern of physical growth and motor development; these patterns have been identified as follows:

1. Growth tends to progress from head to foot, or in a *cephalocaudal direction.* Thus, the infant is able to gain control over the upper parts of his body before he can gain control over the lower parts.
2. Growth tends to progress from the center of the body toward the periphery, or in a *proximidistal direction.* As a result, the child is able to gain control over the medial parts of his body before he is able to gain control over peripheral parts.
3. Motor control tends to progress from *mass* to *specific.* Thus, the infant gains control over large movements before he gains control over smaller, more precise movements.

Factors (for example, curves, strength, extensors, balance) necessary for upright posture and walking are being developed during this phase. A child will eventually learn to walk after mastering the necessary intermediate steps of kicking, rolling, crawling, creeping, standing, and so forth. At this age the child is ambidextrous and has no hand preference.

Early childhood (approximately 2 to 6 years)

The early childhood period continues to be a time of rapid development in which a number of structural, muscular, and postural changes occur that are important influences in movement capacity. The body increases in length, reflected by both long bone and trunk growth. Girls tend to mature more rapidly than boys, as evidenced by their longer arms and legs, whereas boys tend to be heavier. During this period body build is related to motor proficiency. The child will be able to balance better owing to a smaller head and longer legs in proportion to body size. This also aids locomotor movements. Throwing skills will become more efficient due to the increased width in shoulders and the increased length of the arms. Around the fifth year, the rapid growth will decelerate until the prepubertal spurt.

During these years, the basic locomotor skills that were previously mastered are now extended into many locomotor patterns. The child is able to walk better because of the structural changes in the knee and increased strength of the legs. He is able to master such movements as running, hopping, jumping, galloping, skipping, and climbing. Even at this early age, sexual differences begin to emerge. Boys prefer to gallop, whereas girls like skipping. As hand skills are extended to include throwing and catching skills, children are able to learn to throw balls in numerous ways.

Early childhood contains the best years for developing basic movement patterns that, with refinement, are used later in complex motor skills such as those found in sport. The neuromotor system nears completion, and physical maturity starts to emerge. The child requires only experience to further enhance his capacities for movement. Hand preference is finally developed. During these years more complex acts such as cycling, swimming, and roller skating can be mastered if the child is given the opportunity.

Late childhood (approximately 6 to 12 years)

Structural changes continue through late childhood, and a regular increase in long bone growth occurs. The muscle quality of both sexes also undergoes modification with an increase in muscle density and power. Boys are stronger in the shoulder girdle and hip region, which will tend to make them better in tasks involving forceful and direct use of arms and legs. Myelination (sheathing of the nerve fibers) is also completed somewhere between the sixth and eighth years, allowing a variety of complex tasks to be mastered as the children reach this age range.

These late childhood years are very important, because now basic movement patterns can be refined. It is a period of perfection and stabilization of previously acquired skills and abilities rather than the emergence of new ones. Many specific motor skills are learned and the child becomes acquainted with the popular games and sports of his culture. A survey of changes in motor ability traits shows the changes are not as rapid as in the earlier years. Regular improvement occurs with age. Childrens' need for activity remains high and thus improvement should increase as a result of practice from frequent participation. Gross motor skills are improved and continue to improve throughout childhood. During this stage, boys begin to move ahead in tasks involving simple applications of force and power, such as throwing and jumping. However, at times girls catch up and pass boys, owing to hormonal changes. Girls tend to be superior in tasks involving agility and rhythm. It is likely however, that advancement by the girls in these two areas may be largely due to cultural pressure.

Adolescence (approximately 12 to 20 years)

Adolescence, the transitional stage between childhood and adulthood, is initiated by puberty. Growth is again rapid and consists primarily of body maturation and a beginning of a more adult body structure and function. The release of new genetic information in organizing cells is the fundamental cause of the growth spurt, triggered by the endocrine gland system. This hormonal change varies from individual to individual and thus can be seen at various ages. For girls, the average structural growth occurs between 11½ and 14 years, whereas in boys, it occurs from approximately 12½ to 15½ years.

During childhood, boys and girls are similar in their physical appearance except for the primary sex characteristics. Once puberty begins, differences emerge owing to growth of skeletal and muscular systems and growth related to secondary sex characteristics. For boys, the development of the testes, appearance of pubic hair, and a change in voice are the significant secondary sex characteristics. For girls, these characteristics are the development of breasts, the broadening of hips, and the onset of menstruation. Physical changes in adolescence reach their peak when sex glands receive structural maturity and begin to function. For girls, the average age is 12.5 years, whereas for boys it is 14.2 years. This entire process of sexual maturation requires about three years.

The greatest increase in strength also occurs with puberty, usually doubling between the ages of 12 and 16. Ossification and muscle development play considerable roles in the increase of strength. Muscle weight vastly increases. At age 8, approximately, only 27 percent of the body weight is muscle, whereas by age 16, 44 percent is muscle.

Muscle and bone development may cause problems if they do not proceed together. When cartilage is converted into bone at too fast a pace it often causes aches and pains. Bone development is consistent with the general rate of physical maturation, whereas the speed of muscular growth is influenced by the amount of physical exercise a person has. Poor muscle growth can be the cause of a lack of psychomotor coordination and clumsiness. There is also a close relationship between the nervous system and large muscle systems which, if not developed, may impair coordination.

During adolescence, the proper amounts of activity and diet are very important. Exercise is not only important to increase muscular development, but necessary to keep a proper level of fitness. Muscles not used will become flabby, weak, and smaller (atrophy). Studies show that the average high school student spends about two hours a week in group play or exercise. If this is true, it is no surprise that these students have difficulty in achieving high performances on physical fitness tests.

Adulthood and old age (approximately from 21 years on)

Following adolescent development is an interim of gradual increase in size and capacity, and then a leveling off in early adulthood, when almost no growth changes occur. Later adulthood is characterized by a gradual decline in physical abilities; giving up some responsibilities; and modification of family structure. Old age has been identified by some as beginning at about age 70. It is characterized by an increased decline in physical and cognitive powers; perhaps a restriction of social interaction; and an increased dependence upon others.

Sociopsychological development

Sociopsychological development is closely related to physical growth and development. Gaps or lags in physical development generally lead to immaturity in personality characteristics, whereas acceleration in physical development has been paired with greater maturity in social and emotional adjustment.

Body size and its compatibility with social and cultural expectations strongly influences a child's self-concept. An adolescent's individual growth pattern that deviates from the average can cause keen personal concern. The physical changes and sexual maturation sometimes accompanied by acne, breast development, awkwardness, disproportionate body parts, and so forth, all influence the emotional state of the individual. A marked psychological effect upon behavior can occur when an adolescent is unable to accept and adjust to bodily changes.

Teachers need to understand the reasons behind psychological problems that may arise during the spurts of students' individual growth patterns. They can greatly aid their students by establishing learning environments which lead to success, feelings of worth, and self-acceptance. Game experiences should especially contribute to skills in peer relationships. Choice in gym attire, elective options in coeducational classes, and individual exercise programs are examples of flexibility toward problems that learners face in adolescence.

Both cognitive and emotional development are extremely important in determining readiness for school. Young children start from scratch in their personality development and few old habits need to be broken. Contrary to widespread opinion, an individual's personality is not completely formed by age 5 or 6. Personality development is continuous to maturity, and perhaps beyond. Cognitive and subsequent emotional imprinting are not hard to make on a child's mind. As the child grows and behavior patterns become formal, it becomes more difficult and takes longer to alter personality factors. Consequently, it is so much easier for a child to start off with productive control of emotional behavior, rather than try to correct and change it later.

Social and emotional aspects

It has been said that social and emotional development are interdependent, and that all social interaction overlaps emotional interaction. In social development, experience becomes a much more important factor than physical development. Events that occur while growing, such as relationships with friends, peers, teachers, and employers, and conflicts and frustrations are all part of emotional development.

Researchers have found that early social interactions between young children greatly depend upon their ability to play. Young children use motor activity rather than language to express their emotions. As they grow, emotions give way to attitude development and self-control. A close bond is formed between social behavior and motor behavior. Older children find that cultural and social rules regarding physical activity greatly influence their behavior. The existing opinion that girls' physical performance peaks at age 15 is more than likely the result of a "culture curb." The concurrent opinion that boys peak at age 18 may well be due in part to the lack of opportunity for physical activity after graduation. Physical educators must keep in mind that physical activity can provide an important outlet for the release of muscular and emotional tension. Children not only enjoy physical activity, but they usually feel better afterward.

Whether attitudes are positively changed as a result of physical activity can only be conjectured.

Self-concept

Increasingly, some psychologists feel that self-concept, or the perceptions and judgments that one has of oneself, provides a major clue to understanding behavior. Self-concept may be one of the most important motivators of behavior.

The origins of an individual's self-concept appear to be learned. Self-concept is created by an individual's inference from that person's unique experiences. It is the way one sees oneself, one's body, and the way one moves in relation to the environment. The individual's perceptions of the feelings of others toward him or her strongly influence the self-image of that individual. Teachers can play a very important role in the development of this picture.

Self-concept influences and is influenced by a child's behavior. A child with a positive self-concept generally acts and learns in a positive way. A child with a negative self-concept often reacts in a negative way and fails to learn productively. A negative self-concept is developed through a lack of understanding of family, peers, and teachers. Teachers can help children to form a positive self-concept by recognizing the uniqueness of each student and capitalizing on special interests and abilities.

Researchers have found that a change in self-concept can lead to a change in overt behavior. But although self-attitude does continue to change throughout life, changes in self-concept are not made easily, particularly after the early stages of childhood.

Physical educators can both allow for and foster the growth of a positive self-concept in their students by utilizing self-testing activities, allowing for early exploration rather than mimic repetition of skill, providing learning experiences appropriate to the readiness of the child, and working toward an individualized curriculum.

Cognitive development

The cognitive process is one of humanity's greatest advantages over animal life. However, our ability to think and reason must be *developed.* Although all children are born with a certain mental capacity, unlocking that capacity depends heavily upon the kind and amount of exposure to various experiences in the environment. Poor socioeconomic status may not provide the proper intellectual stimulation needed for optimum development.

Children develop a mental picture of their world through their actions, imagery, language, and creative thought. Intelligence is dependent upon the process of perception for its development. It is through perception that a child interprets his environment. Defects in any of the sense organs can impair intellectual development in children.

Piaget's theory[3] of cognitive development categorizes four major stages of intellectual growth. It is important to realize that the ages that accompany these stages are approximations. The characteristics of these four stages are:

1. *Sensorimotor stage* (from birth to about 18 months).
   A. The use of movements and actions as intellectual expression.
   B. Memory begins to develop in regard to the child's physical actions.
   C. Children begin to recognize shapes and that objects are permanent.
   D. Through internalization of action, the child develops the ability to talk.
2. *Preoperational stage* (from 18 months to 7 years).
   A. The child learns to represent the world mentally by images, then symbols, and language concepts.
   B. Thinking and memory gradually develop through the internalization of action.
3. *Stage of concrete operations* (from 7 to 12 years).
   Children become able to interpret goals, rules, and a sequence of events.
4. *Stage of formal operations* (age 12 onward).
   A. Thought and imagination does not necessarily lead to overt action.
   B. Situations and problems can be analyzed and validly questioned.
   C. Problem-solving ability develops.

Intelligence develops rapidly during early childhood. Almost one-half a child's potential is said to be realized by age 10. Intellectual growth will continue through adulthood, provided that the environment allows for and stimulates such growth. Parents are important catalysts in the environment during early childhood. They greatly affect their child's development through enhancing or inhibiting early movement and through the degree of their verbal interaction.

As children reach a mental age of approximately 13 years, they are able to utilize formal operations in their thinking. Early learning should thus be geared for children who think in concrete terms. Children's prior experiences should be used in the introduction of new materials so that new learning has relevance to the child. The highest form of thinking takes place when students are presented with problems that have meaning for them and are partly based on their prior learning. Only then can children become creative.

Piaget has pointed out three categories of games that are directly related to the development of intellectual capacities in a child. They are:

[3]R. M. Beard, *An Outline of Piaget's Developmental Psychology for Students and Teachers.* New York: Basic Books, Inc., 1969.

1. practice games dealing with sensorimotor development;
2. symbolic games;
3. games with rules.

Recently, perceptual-motor learning tasks have been used to aid children overcome conceptual learning reading problems. Correcting delayed motor development patterns has improved a child's performance, and thus his capacity for intelligence development. Perceptual-Motor programs claim to enhance intellectual growth through the development of basic motor patterns needed as a foundation for future learning of specific skills. Success has also been achieved with games that teach verbal concepts at the elementary level.

Summary

1. Growth is a quantitative change in body structure, such as an increase in physical size of bodily parts or of an organism as a whole.
2. Development is a complex process of integration of the structures and functions of the body, and is the result of maturational and environmental influences combined.
3. Maturation is the development of inherent genetic characteristics through an ongoing process of physiological and anatomical change attributable to the passage of time rather than to practice or learning.
4. Readiness refers to that time when the maximum sensory, physical, motivational, and psychological capacities are present.
5. The influence of heredity on the growth and development of children is greatly affected by environment. Genes do not determine one's traits; they merely provide the potential for developing a trait.
6. Sociopsychological development is closely related to physical growth and development. Researchers have found that early social interactions among young children greatly depend upon their ability to play.
7. Piaget's theory of cognitive development categorizes four major stages of intellectual growth. These are: (a) sensorimotor stage (from birth to about 18 months); (b) preoperational stage (from 18 months to 7 years); (c) stage of concrete operations (from 7 to 12 years); (d) stage of formal operations (age 12 onward).

Questions

1. What are the interactions between growth, development, and maturation?
2. To what does one refer when one talks about readiness in learning?
3. In what ways do heredity and environment account for behavioral differences?
4. When one is dealing with children and adolescents, is there any practical value to inquiry about their background?
5. What is meant by critical periods? What is the implication of this concept?
6. What is the best period to develop movement patterns?
7. What are some of the late childhood characteristics in terms of motor skills?
8. If you notice that an adolescent lacks coordination, what are some pertinent questions to examine?
9. Why is it easier to develop and change behavior patterns in children than in adults? Support your answer with well-known theories.
10. Is there a clear relationship between self-concept and overt behavior?
11. How can you develop someone's postive self-concept?
12. Describe Piaget's theory of cognitive development.

12

PSYCHOLOGICAL DIMENSIONS

The science of psychology evolved from such disciplines as philosophy, physiology, and physics, with contributions from biology, astronomy, and mathematics. Psychology is a branch of science concerned with the description, explanation, and prediction of behavior.

Although psychologists differ about their perspective, there is consensus that psychology is concerned with the activities of living organisms, with an emphasis on understanding the individual as a total functioning unit. These activities may be investigated in part or as wholes, in behavior or in consciousness. Stated more simply, *the science of psychology* is the study of the responses of organisms to stimulation, or what are called psychological processes.

Psychology has contributed a vast body of scientific knowledge, some of which can be utilized in health, physical education, and recreation. Professionals in these areas usually seek knowledge that enables them to deal with (teach, coach) other humans. That is, they are typically interested in the psychological processes underlying human behavior—observable, goal-centered, purposeful, voluntary movement—in sport and physical activities such as dance, play, and exercise. Further, they should be acquainted with the factors that affect these psychological processes.

The International Society of Sport Psychology (ISSP) and the North American Society for the Psychology of Sport and Physical Activity (NASPSPA) are large-scale organized attempts to assist professionals in their quest for this knowledge. The psychology of sport and physical activity has emerged as a multidisciplinary area of specialization in the United States, whereas it is more a specialized subfield of psychology in Europe and the Soviet Union.

A professional who understands the psychological processes related to human-movement behavior is in a better position to deal with them than the one who does not understand such processes. Consequently, the purpose of this chapter is to provide you with an introduction to those psychological processes and factors relevant to physical education.

Sensing and perceiving

Any object or event with the potential to stimulate an organism is referred to as a stimulus. The senses receive information, but they are more than just receivers and transducers of energy. They seem to be systems for exploring, searching, and selecting surrounding energy.

To perceive, you must sense, but what does the term *sense* mean? Gibson[1] proposes two meanings of the term and makes a strong case for distinguishing between them. One meaning is sensitivity, the other is sensation. *Sensitivity* is defined as *the effects of stimulating the senses in general. Sensation* is defined as *the conscious impressions caused by certain selected variables stimulating the senses.* With this distinction in mind, Gibson argues that the senses and sensitivity are essential for sensation and perception. However, sensation is not a prerequisite for perception, even though at times it may contribute to perception.

When the senses are stimulated, that stimulation is relayed to the sensory cortex of the brain via the nervous system. The resulting sensitivity, with or without accompanying sensations but combined with memories, forms the basis for perception. The useful dimensions of sensitivity for perception are those which specify the external and internal environment and the performer's relation to those environments. Perception is a cognitive process by which stimulation is

[1] J. J. Gibson, "The useful dimensions of sensitivity," *American Psychologist,* 1963, Vol. 18, pp. 1–15.

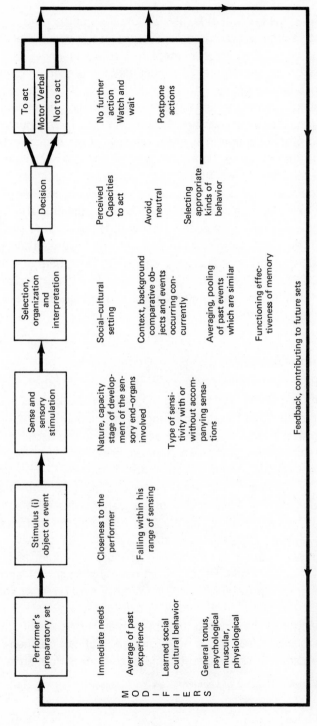

Figure 12.1   The perceptual process

Note: Modifiers are of three main types: developmental; those immediate to the event or object; those involving past experience and learning.

Source: Reproduced by permission from B. J. Cratty, *Movement Behavior and Motor Learning*, Figure 3.3. Philadelphia: Lea & Febiger.

structured so as to give meaning; that is, stimulation is organized and interpreted. To perceive is to know; it is an active process in which the perceiver participates completely. Thus, perception involves meaning, but sensitivity and sensation do not. Figure 12.1 illustrates the perceptual process, essentially based on Cratty's concept.

In physical education settings the perceptions of kinesthetic, proprioceptive, auditory, visual, and cutaneous sensitivities are probably the most significant. Both kinesthesis and proprioception involve the sensing of the speed, extent, and duration of bodily movement. Proprioception, however, also includes the sensing of muscular tensions, forces, pressures, and bodily orientation in space that might not include any movement. The auditory sense is concerned with hearing sounds (for example, game whistle, quarterback cadence). The visual sense involves attending to the movements of objects (for example, balls, opposing players). The cutaneous receptors are concerned with sensing touch (for example, an experienced baseball pitcher can place his fingers on seams of the ball the way he wants them, without the aid of vision). Decisions and judgments made by athletes, officials, and coaches in sport situations are very much the result of their perceptions.

Learning and motor learning

Because learning is difficult to define, many definitions exist, of which we have selected one. Hilgard and Bower state: "Learning is a process by which an activity originates or is changed through reacting to an encountered situation, provided that the characteristics of change in activity cannot be explained on the basis of native response tendencies, maturation, or temporary states of the organism (for example, fatigue, drugs, and so forth)."[2] Motor learning falls within the scope of this definition. The terms *motor* and *movement* are used interchangeably throughout this chapter. For motor learning, the term *activity* refers especially to behaviors involving observable, goal-centered, purposeful, voluntary bodily movement such as that found in sport, play, or game situations. Thus, the term learning is much more general than motor learning and encompasses it. Consequently, Hilgard and Bower's definition of learning also defines motor learning, provided that the term *movement-oriented activity* is included.

Evidence for learning must be inferred from performance (the act of executing or doing), because learning is not a process that can be seen directly. Of course, motor learning is also an inference from performance. One

[2]E. R. Hilgard and G. H. Bower, *Theories of Learning*. New York: Appleton-Century-Crofts, 1966, p. 2

may see rather permanent changes in performance brought about through practice, and infer that motor learning has occurred. However, it should be made clear that not all performance reflects true learning.

Traditional learning theories

Behaviorist theory: learning takes place through trial and error

Traditional theories may be classified as *behaviorist* or *cognitive.* Behaviorist, or connectionist, approaches, also termed stimulus-response or peripheral theories, essentially view learning as a connection between stimuli and responses. These connections have been called habits, stimulus-response (S-R) bonds, and conditioned responses. Behaviorist theory emphasizes observable responses, their eliciting stimuli, and the conditions of their reliable occurrence.

The principle of *contiguity,* the essence of connectionism, states that when a stimulus and a response are experienced together they tend to become associated and conditioning occurs. Conditioning is of two kinds: classical and operant. *Classical conditioning* involves the simultaneous presentation of two stimuli. One stimulus (unconditioned) normally elicits a particular response, whereas the other (conditioned) does not. With repeated presentation, the conditioned stimulus becomes effective for elicitation of the response. *Operant conditioning* involves the emitting of a response, from a repertoire of responses, via more or less random activity and without any prompting through presentation of a particular stimulus. The appropriate stimulus is present in the environment, however, and when the desired response occurs, it is reinforced. Repeating this procedure increases the probability that the desired response will occur when that same appropriate stimulus is presented. Operant conditioning techniques, developed by B. F. Skinner, have been recommended for use in physical education (see Selected Readings for sources). *Trial-and-error* learning occurs when the learner has to select the correct response from a large number of available responses in order to solve the problem. The stimulated learner may try a number of responses before eventually executing the correct one. With repeated practice, the occurrence of incorrect responses diminishes in favor of the correct response.

Thorndike firmly believed that learning took place through trial and error and based his well-known laws of learning on the principles of connectionist theory. His law of exercise, modified by subsequent research, led him to conclude that repetition with reinforcement strengthens the connection (bonds) between stimulus and response and, consequently, increases the probability that the same response to a given stimulus will recur. Research attacking his original law of effect has shown that an S-R connection appears to be strengthened when it is followed by or accompanied by reinforcement. Thorndyke's law of readiness emphasizes the importance of the performer's being set or prepared to learn. Readiness in this sense does not refer to reaching a particular maturational level, as we discussed in Chapter 11.

Cognitive theory: learning takes place through insight

Cognitive theory proposes that learning is fundamentally perceptual and individual, rather than behaviorist or mechanist. *Cognitions* (for example, perceptions, concepts, thoughts, and judgments) that the performer has concerning his environment, and the ways these cognitions influence his behavior, are primary concerns. The study of learning from a cognitive perspective involves the ways in which cognitions are modified by experience. For cognitive theorists, learning is not quite so mechanical as connectionists suggest. They believe that, rather than S-R connections or habits or bonds, it is cognitive structures that are learned. These cognitive structures, that is, facts or knowledges perceptually structured so as to correlate the relationships involved, result in an insight, a sudden solution to the problem. Learning takes place through this insight, not simply by trial and error. Cognitive theorists interpret trial-and-error behavior as purposeful searching or experimenting to gain the basic facts or knowledges necessary to insight.

Motor learning theory

These traditional learning theories as well as the newer neuropsychological, neurophysiological, mathematical, vigilance, information-processing, adaptive, and cybernetic theories have formed much of the basis for, and clearly manifest themselves in, the various theories of motor learning and skill acquisition. Except, however, for the pioneering efforts of a few researchers like Franklin Henry[3] to organize information theoretically, much material in motor learning has been a disjunctive collection of facts. Recently, some attempts[4] to synthesize and unify the vast number of motor learning facts have been based

---

[3]F. M. Henry and D. E. Rogers, "Increased response latency for complicated movements and a 'memory drum' theory of neuromotor reaction," *Research Quarterly,* 31, 1960, pp. 448–458.

[4]See Selected Readings at end of text.

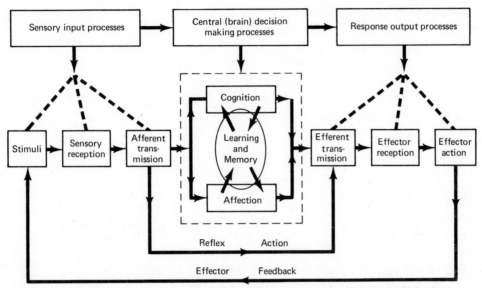

Figure 12.2   Model for the study of basic underlying processes of human motor behavior.

Source: R. W. Christina and L. G. Shaver. *Biological and Psychological Perspectives in the Study of Human Motor Behavior.* Dubuque, Iowa: Kendall/Hunt Publishing Company, 1972, p. 4. Reproduced by permission of publisher.

on a model or theoretical framework. Figure 12.2 illustrates Christina and Shaver's human-performance approach; Figure 12.3, Gentile's skill acquisition concept; Figure 12.4, Whiting's systems analysis idea; and Figure 12.5, Robb's information-processing notion. For a thorough explanation of these four models the reader is referred to the original sources.

An early attempt to organize material theoretically was made by the late Paul M. Fitts,[5] using essentially an information-processing approach to explain and

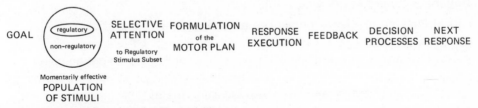

Figure 12.3   Initial stages of skill acquisition

Source: A. M. Gentile. "A working model of skill acquisition with application to teaching." *Quest,* 1972, Monograph XVII, p. 4.

[5]P. M. Fitts, "Skill Learning," in A. Melton, ed., *Categories of Human Learning.* New York: Academic Press, Inc., 1964. See also his chapter "Skill Training," in R. Glaser, ed., *Training Research and Education.* New York: John Wiley & Sons, Inc., 1962.

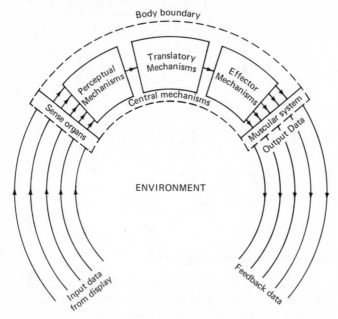

Figure 12.4   Systems analysis of perceptual-motor performance

Source: H. T. A. Whiting. *Acquiring Ball Skill*. London: G. Bell & Sons, Ltd., 1969, p. 5. Reproduced by permission of the author.

describe human behavior by comparing it to a computer's operational processes. We describe below Fitts' concept of the process of skill learning, placing feedback, whole versus part practice, massed versus distributed practice, and transfer of learning within his conceptual framework.

Cognitive phase: developing an image

Fitts divided the processes of learning a motor skill into three phases: (1) cognitive, (2) fixative, and (3) automatic. During the cognitive phase, instructions are important to the beginner who is attempting to get an idea or image of the response he has to execute. He also calls upon his prior learning experiences in trying to perceive and understand the movement sequence and distinguish the relevant from the irrelevant cues. In most cases, the learner will be unable to distinguish them and, consequently, the teacher must do it for him. The teacher must be careful at this point to present only the amount of relevant cue information to which he thinks the performer can attend. If too much information is presented, the beginner will not be able to deal with all of it and performance will suffer. This phase may take a few minutes or several hours.

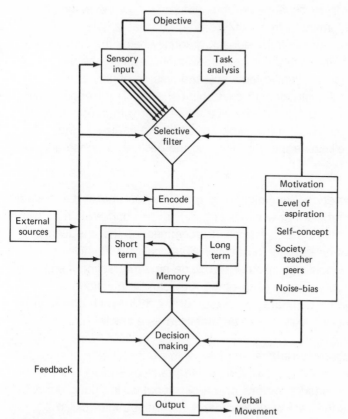

Figure 12.5   A working model of information processing and skill acquisition

Source: M. D. Robb. "Task analysis: a consideration for teachers of skills." *Research Quarterly,* 1972, 43, p. 369.

Fixation phase: practicing the response role of feedback

After developing an image of the desired response, the learner must practice the response in order to "fix" the movement sequence in the human system. It is during this fixation phase that the learner tries to reduce his errors through practice. Practice alone, however, is not sufficient—the practice must be meaningful with appropriate feedback. Feedback refers to information arising out of the performer's response. Feedback may be intrinsic (for example, proprioceptive, providing information about the feeling of the movement), arising as a natural consequence of the movement itself. Or it can be augmented (for example, a teacher's comment on a student's performance), originating externally to the performer from the teacher. During the early fixation phase, augmented feedback is very important. At this time the learner cannot use intrinsic feedback effectively because he does not know how the response would feel if it was performed correctly. More practice (that is, later fixation phase) accompanied by augmented feedback gradually helps the student to learn the feeling associated with the correct movement. At this time the performer can rely more on intrinsic feedback and less on augmented feedback provided by the instructor, to guide his behavior. The feedback may or may not be reinforcing, but it does provide the learner with information concerning the adequacy of his movement. Thus utilizing feedback, the performer attempts to eliminate the gap between the desired response and the response produced.

Whole versus part practice Frequently during the fixation phase, the teacher is confronted with the problem of whether to practice the sports skill as a *whole* or to break it down into its *parts.* It has been recommended that the teacher undertake *task analysis* on the skill in question. Task analysis identifies the important parts of the whole skill in order to decide how to practice them. If the parts appear to be independent of each other, they can be practiced separately. However, if the parts are organized so that their synchronization is crucial to success, then the skill should be practiced as a whole.

Massed versus distributed practice Another problem that the teacher must face during the fixation phase is how to distribute practice. Should practice trials be distributed over short durations or massed together in a long duration? In other words, what is the best work-rest ratio for learning motor skills? Research shows no optimal practice schedule for all skills, but a distributed form of practice is usually suggested. However, in order to determine the appropriate schedule of practice, each skill must be analyzed in relation to the performer's attitudes, capacities, and desires, as well as the environmental conditions under which the practice will occur.

Automatic phase: less cognitive control

Following a great deal of practice, sometimes over several years for complex skills, the learner eventually reaches the automatic phase. This final phase is characterized by ability to perform the response consistently with minimum error and little conscious effort. Response movements are more automatic, involving less processing and cognitive control. This automation of responses frees the performer to concentrate on other factors or aspects of a game. However, there are times when parts of the automated response itself develop error, for example, when a highly skilled golfer begins to slice the ball off the tee. Sometimes he can identify the error himself and "work it out" on the practice fairway; at other times he may have to rely on augmented feedback from a golf pro or motion pictures of his performance. In either case, he must first return to the cognitive phase to identify and understand his error. Only then can he move to the fixation phase to practice the proposed correction. Performance during this phase is usually at a low level until enough time and practice make the correction an integrated and automatic part of the complete swing.

Transfer of learning

Transfer of learning may be defined as the influence of prior practice and/or learning upon the learning and performance of new skills. That influence may improve (positive), be detrimental (negative), or have no effect on the learning and performance of a new skill.

To some extent Fitts saw the motor-learning process as a transfer of prior learnings to the new skill learning situation. Consequently, the effects of these prior learnings are manifested in all three of his learning phases.

Two major theories of transfer have been proposed. One, the *identical elements* theory, states that transfer from one task to another occurs only in closely related situations. In contrast, the *general principles* theory states that basic general principles as well as peripheral knowledge and skills can be transferred from one task to another. It posits that the performer applies the general idea to a new situation. Observation and research have demonstrated that transfer may occur according to either the identical elements theory or the general principles theory. Consequently, recent research has been concerned with establishing laws of transfer rather than proving either one of these theories.

Research in the transfer of motor-skill learning tends to support these principles:

1. The performer should practice the skill in the same form, speed, and so forth, and under the same or similar environmental conditions that obtain in the real situation;
2. The more similarity between skill elements, the greater the amount of positive transfer;
3. When negative transfer occurs, the two learning situations contain similar stimuli but require different responses;
4. Transfer is affected by the amount of practice on the prior skill, motivation, and the method of practice;
5. If transfer is to be optimized, it should be taught, for the learner must be aware of what is to be transferred.

Memory and motor skills

Numerous theories of memory have been proposed, among them the neuroanatomical, glial-cell, two-stage, three-stage, and biochemical. Memory is essential for learning, because one cannot learn without this process by which we store and retrieve information. It has three basic functions:

1. *Registration*—the selection of sensory information and its encoding (registration) in the nervous system;
2. *Retention*—the filing and storage of this encoded information in the brain;
3. *Retrieval*—the search through the filed and stored information in order to revive and use it.

Memory appears to originate at the sense organs where encoding occurs. The coded sensory information, in the form of nerve impulses, has been traced as far as the sensory cortex of the brain, but how that information is coded at higher levels of perception, thought, and imagination is still largely unknown. Research on the retention of motor skills appears to support these three general principles:

1. The greater the skill proficiency attained during initial learning, the more slowly the skill is forgotten.
2. A skill tends to be better retained when it has been overpracticed.
3. Those skills the performer perceives as meaningful to him are usually better retained than others.

The retention of learned motor skills is usually quite high; that is, motor skills are not easily forgotten. Once the individual has learned skills, he can perform them again at a reasonable level of proficiency even after long periods without practice. Typically, there is some loss of skill in that performance, but usually this can be overcome within a few practice sessions. Perhaps the reason motor skills are retained so well is that their movement patterns are so specific and are highly practiced and overlearned.

Motivation and motor activity

An optimal level of motivation is beneficial to motor learning and performance. Further, most teachers and coaches agree that to a large extent it is their responsibility to motivate the performance of students and athletes. To discharge that responsibility effectively, the physical educator should be familiar with the nature of motivation.

Needs, drives, and motives

Motivation may be defined as the drive to achieve some goal, an inner urge toward purposeful activity. How and why is behavior aroused? Why are specific behaviors expressed at a certain time? Why are particular goals selected? The answers to these questions lie in the study of motivation. Motivation is usually divided into two parts: physiological drives and social motives. A *drive* is a tendency to act in a certain way to satisfy a need. A *need* is a lack of an essential element. Thus, physiological or primary drives stem from bodily needs, and the individual is constantly developing new biological needs as he seeks to maintain a dynamic homeostasis, or physiological equilibrium. Social motives are more complicated than primary drives, and appear to arise from social sources, that is, interrelationships among people. Although the terms *motive* and *drive* have been used interchangeably, typically the former includes social urges as well as physiological drives. It is generally agreed that physiological drives are not learned, whereas social motives are.

Emotion and arousal

As emotions such as fear, anger, anxiety, joy, and love increase, so does arousal. Further, emotional reactions usually occur in high motivational states. All human behavior involved in learning and performing motor skills is motivated, and occurs in the presence of some level of arousal. Arousal prepares the performer for action; motives determine the particular behavior that is chosen. Arousal level refers to the intensity of neural activity evidenced by a performer at any given moment. Essentially, such systems and structures as the reticular formation, hypothalamus, limbic system, and adrenal medulla in the brain stem and midbrain influence the cortex and other brain centers to generate arousal. These structures interact with each other and with other bodily systems in regulating the level of arousal. When the level of arousal is too low or too high, learning and performance of motor skills is disrupted. There appears to be an optimal level of arousal that varies from performer to performer, depending upon the nature of the sport skill and the performer involved.

Oxendine suggests that a high level of arousal is optimal for sports skills involving large-muscle-movement activities based on strength, endurance, and speed, such as weight lifting or blocking and tackling in football. He recommends a lower level of arousal for more complex sports skills such as chipping and putting in golf or shooting a basketball free throw. His concept is represented in Table 12.1. However, successful performance also depends upon the skill level of the performer, the nature of the sports skill involved, and

Table 12.1   Optimum arousal level for some typical sports skills

Level of arousal	Sports skills
#5 (extremely excited)	football blocking and tackling performance on the Rogers PFI test running (220 yards to 440 yards) sit up, push up, or bent-arm hang test weight lifting
#4	running long jump running very short and long races shot-put swimming races wrestling and judo
#3	basketball skills boxing high jumping most gymnastic skills soccer skills
#2	baseball pitchers and batters fancy dives fencing football quarterback tennis
#1 (slight arousal)	archery and bowling basketball free throw field goal kicking golf putting and short irons skating figure 8's
0 (normal state)	

Source: J. B. Oxendine, "Emotional arousal for motor performance," *Quest,* 1970, Monograph XIII, p. 29.

the particular situation. Clearly, the physical educator's role is to help the performer learn to channel his arousal into goal-directed behavior that will maximize performance in sport.

Incentives and goals

Without strong motivation to learn or perform a skill at a high level, it is unlikely that a person will put forth the necessary effort to do so. Consequently, the physical educator must know how to motivate students, specifically how to manipulate incentives in order to develop and control motives. Incentives are environmental stimuli, usually grades, trophies, competition, praise, or threats employed to arouse and channel behavior toward a goal. Goals are objects or situations that the performer is seeking. The success of a particular incentive depends largely on the degree to which the performer perceives it as satisfying a need. For example, competition is usually an effective incentive if the performer perceives that he has a chance to win, less so if he perceives the opposite to be true.

Level of aspiration

The goal level a performer sets for himself has been termed level of aspiration, and it functions as an incentive to performance. In the teaching of motor skills, research appears to support the following principles:

1. To develop appreciation and enthusiasm for motor skills, we should allow the performer to experience a reasonable amount of success.
2. Setting specific goals that are high but attainable is a desirable method of improving individual performance.
3. Scheduling competitive contests so that success is attained regularly is desirable.

Personality and motor activity

Understanding *personality* is important to physical educators, because a student's behavior, which is unique, is very much interrelated with movement activities. Personality has been variously defined, but always with consensus that it is a product of heredity and environment and the sum total of all observable reactions. Guilford[6] describes personality as composed of a unique pattern of such traits as attitudes, interests, temperament, aptitudes, needs, physiology, and morphology. All individuals possess these traits but not to the same degree. Thus, these traits, differing in degree, interact to create a distinct personality.

Personality is measured indirectly by means of interviews, observations, ratings, projective tests, and psychological inventories. Psychological inventories, used most frequently in physical education, consist of questions or statements concerning feelings, attitudes, and interests. Some of the more popular inventories are the Minnesota Multiphasic Personality Inventory (MMPI), the Cattell 16 Personality Factor Test, the California Personality Test (CPT), the Edwards Personal Preference Schedule (EPPS), and the Athletic Motivational Inventory (AMI).

[6] J. P. Guilford, *Personality.* New York: McGraw-Hill, Inc., 1959.

Research on personality and motor activity appears to support the following generalizations:

1. Although it seems that particular activities attract certain personalities, it is not clear how the traits interact with each other to affect activity selection.
2. The influence of participation in athletic and physical education programs on personality development is largely undetermined.
3. Athletes, as a group, typically have personalities that differ from those of nonathletes;
4. A unique personality profile of the average athlete or the superior athlete has yet to be drawn. However, the personality traits identified with superior athletes appear to be similar to those found in high-achieving people.

It appears safe to conclude that more research, especially longitudinal type studies, on these generalizations is needed. Further, better personality tools and experimental techniques must be developed before the exact relationships and contributions of physical education to the growth and development of the individual's personality can be determined.

Specificity versus generality of motor abilities

Individuals differ greatly in their successful performance of motor skills, one cause being differences in motor abilities, the basis for skilled motor performance. Motor abilities are affected by learning and heredity, and signify the individual's present potential in a broad range of motor skills. A skill is usually thought of as a highly learned sequence of responses specifically related to particular tasks.

Studies conducted by Henry and his students[7] strongly support the view that motor abilities underlying successful performance in motor skills are more specific than general. According to specificity theory, abilities such as balance, strength, endurance, kinesthesis, coordination, and speed are specific to the sport skill being performed. For example, the body balance required for successful performance in gymnastics is somewhat different from that demanded in wrestling. The speed of response needed for the 100-yard dash is basically different from that required in playing basketball. Thus, success in a particular sport skill demands that the athlete develop the specific abilities required by that skill. Successful performance in one sport does not necessarily transfer to another sport.

[7] F. M. Henry, "Coordination and Motor Learning," *Proceedings of the College of Physical Education Association,* 59, 1956, pp. 68–75. See also his "Specificity vs. Generality in Learning Motor Skills," *Proceedings of the College of Physical Education Association,* 61, 1958, pp. 126–128.

However, if motor abilities are largely specific, then how does one explain individuals who appear to possess general motor ability—the "all-round athletes"? Henry[8] believes that such individuals are gifted with so many specific abilities that in this sense they have general motor ability. Thus, Henry understands general motor ability in an individual as a number of specific abilities. Singer[9] offers the explanation that certain other underlying factors are also operating in this situation. These factors are:

1. Experience and intensive practice in a wide range of motor skills will result in apparent ease in skill acquisition. The person who has benefited from a childhood enriched with experiences in basic-movement patterns and an assortment of activities will be more favored in motor-learning situations. These past experiences and the resultant skills serve as a foundation for the learning of new skills.
2. Genetics determine the limitations an individual faces in motor-skill attainment. Even as heredity determines potential intelligence levels, hair color, and body size, it creates the boundaries of motor development. It should be stressed here that research, especially on intelligence, points to the tremendous influence of the environment and life's experiences on an individual's achievements. As a further point, it should be realized that one has to go a long way before he reaches his maximum potential, whether in intellectual or in motor pursuits. Thus, it may be seen that although hereditary factors contribute to limit potential proficiency in motor acts, many of these factors can be overcome with the presence of the necessary drive and ambition.
3. Motivation is necessary for success. It is hypothesized that the athlete who has achieved success in one sport transfers his high motivation and perseverance to other motor-skill endeavors. The all-round athlete may very well be a highly motivated performer in general who possesses the necessary personality characteristics for varied motor accomplishments.
4. Related sports offer a greater probability of accomplishment for the athlete. Therefore, if an athlete is proficient in a number of sports, there is a good chance that basic skills common to all of them have been mastered.

Factors influencing motor-skill performance

Cratty[10] proposes that factors at three levels influence motor-skill performance, as shown in Figure 12.6. The basic qualities constituting the general supports of behavior are essentially those components of personality which form a basis for both intellectual and perceptual motor functioning. At the intermediate level,

[8] *Ibid.*, 1958.

[9] Reprinted by permission from R. N. Singer, *Motor Learning and Human Performance.* New York: Macmillan Publishing Co., Inc., 1975.

[10] B. J. Cratty, *Psychology and Physical Activity.* Englewood Cliffs, N.J.: Prentice-Hall, Inc., 1968.

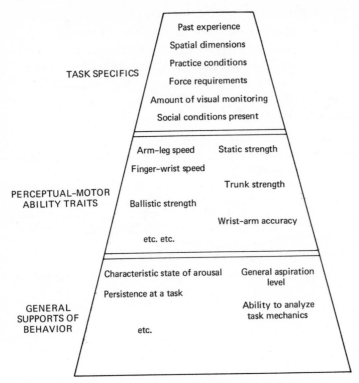

Figure 12.6 A three-factor theory of perceptual-motor behavior

Source: B. J. Cratty. "A three-level theory of perceptual-motor
behavior." *Quest,* 1966, Monograph VI, p. 6.

perceptual motor-ability traits affect performance in a number of motor-skill
tasks. At the final level, task specifics influence performance. Cratty states
that "these three-level factors are mutually dependent. For example, success in
the task itself feeds back into the basic level of behavior supports and raises
the individual's aspiration level. His aspiration level in turn encourages him to
participate more in the successful activity, and this participation contributes in
turn to the development of basic ability traits."[11]

Reaction time, movement time, and response time

Successful performance in many motor-skill activities partially depends upon
abilities involved in such acts as reacting quickly to signals. Reaction time (RT),

[11] *Ibid.,* p. 9.

movement time (MT), and response time are important measures of certain tasks in laboratory studies. RT is the duration of time from the onset of a signal to the initiation of a response. MT is time elapsed from the initiation of the response until its completion. Response time is the sum of reaction time plus movement time. RT is partially dependent upon the nature of the signal itself. RT is shorter (up to a point) (1) as the intensity of the signal increases; (2) to a visual signal than to an auditory one; (3) when it is followed by a simple rather than a complex movement. RT is also partially dependent upon the nature of the performer: age, sex, attention, motivation, anticipation, fatigue, and neuromotor make-up also affect RT.

MT is influenced similarly by some of the factors that affect RT. However, other factors, such as strength and practice, influence RT and MT differently. Strength does improve MT, but not RT. Practice improves MT considerably but, except for the first few trials, improves RT very little.

Finally, RT does not appear to be highly related to MT. Because they are independent of each other, one cannot be predicted from the other; thus they are more specific than general. That is, a performer who reacts quickly is not necessarily speedy in body movement and vice versa.

Summary

1. Any object or event with the potential to stimulate an organism may be referred to as a stimulus.
2. Sensitivity is defined as the effects of stimulating the senses in general.
3. Sensation is defined as the conscious impression caused by certain selected variables stimulating the senses.
4. Perception is a cognitive process by which stimulation is structured so as to give it meaning.
5. Hilgard and Bower define learning as a process by which an activity originates or is changed through reacting to an encountered situation, provided that the characteristics of change in activity cannot be explained on the basis of native response tendencies, maturation, or temporary states of the organism (for example, fatigue or drugs).
6. Motor learning falls within this definition of general learning. However, in motor learning, the term activity refers especially to behaviors involving observable, goal-centered, purposeful, voluntary bodily movement such as is found in sport, play, or game situations.
7. Trial-and-error learning occurs when the learner has to select the correct response from a large number of available responses in order to solve the problem.

265

8. Cognitive theory proposes that learning is fundamentally perceptual with emphasis on cognitive learning of stimuli and their meaning.
9. Fitts divided the processes of learning a motor skill into three phases: (a) cognitive; (b) fixative; and (c) automatic.
10. Transfer of learning may be defined as the influence of prior practice and/or learning upon the learning and performance of new skills.
11. Memory is the means by which we store information. It has three major functions: (a) registration—the selection of sensory information and its encoding (registration) in the nervous system; (b) retention—the filing and storage of this encoded information in the brain; (c) retrieval—the search through the filed-and-stored information in order to revive and use it.
12. Research on the retention of motor skills appears to support the following three general principles: (a) the greater the skill proficiency attained during initial learning, the more slowly the skill is forgotten; (b) a skill tends to be better retained when it has been overpracticed; (c) those skills the performer perceives as meaningful to him are usually better retained than others.
13. Research regarding the teaching of motor skills appears to support the following principles: (a) to develop appreciation and enthusiasm for motor skills we should allow the performer to experience a reasonable amount of success; (b) setting specific goals that are high but attainable is a desirable method of improving individual performance; (c) scheduling competitive contests so that success is attained regularly is desirable.
14. Motivation may be defined as the mechanism within humans that directs their behavior
15. A drive is a tendency to act in a certain way to satisfy a need.
16. A need is a lack of an essential element.
17. Incentives are environmental stimuli, usually grades, trophies, competition, praise, or threats which are employed to arouse and channel behavior toward a goal.
18. Goals are objects or situations which the performer is seeking.
19. Guilford describes personality as composed of a unique pattern of such traits as attitudes, interests, temperament, aptitudes, needs, physiology, and morphology.
20. Henry supports the theory that successful performance in one sport does not necessarily transfer to another sport.
21. Reaction time is the duration of time from the onset of a signal to the initiation of a response.
22. Movement time is time elapsed from the initation of the response until its completion.
23. Response time is the sum of reaction time plus movement time.

Questions

1. What is psychology concerned with?
2. What are the characteristics of the trial-and-error learning method?
3. Schematize Gentile's skill acquisition concept.
4. What were Fitts' ideas about the processes of learning a motor skill?
5. Whole versus part practice and massed versus distributed practice present problems that often challenge the teacher. State pertinent questions that will help reach a decision.
6. Select examples in which your performance is likely to be influenced either by the negative or by the positive transfer of learning.
7. What is the role of memory in learning?
8. State general principles applicable to the retention of motor skills.
9. Needs, drives, and motives are popular terms in the behavioral area. Are you familiar enough with these terms to define them?
10. Describe Oxendine's scheme about arousal and motor performance.
11. What role do environmental factors play in a person's level of aspiration?
12. How do you react to the statement that physical activity molds personality?
13. Describe some of the instruments more commonly used to measure personality.
14. Define specificity and generality of motor abilities. Apply the concept to a sport situation.
15. Reaction time, movement time, and response time are often used interchangeably. How do they differ? How do they interrelate?

13

SOCIOLOGICAL DIMENSIONS[1]

The terms *sociology, social psychology,* and the *sociology of sport* refer to
fields of knowledge that form the basis for the sociological dimensions of
health, physical education, and recreation. Consequently, it is important that we
understand the meanings of these three terms.

1. *Sociology* may be defined as a science concerned with the study of society, social
   institutions, and all human social relationships. Sociology attempts to isolate the
   underlying regularities of human social behavior; like all science, its primary function
   is to isolate and obtain the truth. Sociology as a science has no absolute truths that
   exist regardless of time, place, and circumstance. Scientific truth is always tentative
   and subject to reexamination and revision when new evidence becomes available.
2. *Social psychology,* the science evolved from the parent disciplines of sociology and
   psychology, is concerned with the study of an individual's behavior and experience
   within a social setting.

[1]We wish to extend our appreciation to Mr. Dan Gould and Professor Merrill Melnick, State
University College at Brockport, for their contributions to this chapter.

3. *Sociology of sport,* a new and expanding field, emerged during the last decade out of the work of Kenyon and Loy. A subdiscipline of sociology, it is concerned with applying the theories and methods of sociology to the environment of sport. Typically, this definition is extended beyond sport to include the social and sociopsychological dimensions of all physical and physical education activities.

The physical educator must keep in mind two important points about the scientific approach. First, scientific prediction is made about groups, not individuals. Second, the prediction can be fulfilled only under certain stated conditions. In other words, teachers and coaches should expect, not absolute predictions, but scientific information that can guide their decision making. They should be able to base their program less on trial-and-error technique and more on scientific knowledge.

The group as a social system

Group classifications

According to Loy[2] "a social system consists of a set of interacting individuals having a shared pattern of expectations and a common means of communication." Groups make up an important social system. Essentially, a group may be defined as two or more people engaged in social interaction. But all groups are not alike; sociologists and social psychologists have classified and defined several types of groups:

A *category* is a group of people who share a characteristic which describes them. An *aggregate* is a category of people who share the same time-space relationships. To illustrate: "all German physical educators" would constitute a category, while "all German physical educators at a 4 P.M. sports meeting" would compose an aggregate. Categories and aggregates are classifications; they differ from functional groups. A *functional group* is one whose members share a common goal and are involved in ongoing social interaction. The functional group is our main concern.

Types of group membership

Ascription and acquisition are the two basic ways by which an individual becomes a member of a group. By joining the softball team, one acquires a group membership. A person exercises a great amount of choice in becoming

[2]In R. N. Singer et al., *Physical Education: An Interdisciplinary Approach.* New York: Macmillan Publishing Co., Inc., 1972, p. 179.

a member of an acquired group. However, a person who becomes a member of an ascribed group has very little choice. For example, you are born into a family and thus become a member of an ascribed group; you have very little to say about your membership in that group. This is not to imply that it is undesirable to be a member of an ascribed group. For example, students may not care which intramural team they were originally assigned to, but as time passes, individuals may want to become members of other specific teams.

Of course the desire to be part of a group does not necessarily ensure membership in that group. Much depends on the group's boundaries and permeability.

Group boundaries

Permeability refers to how accessible a group is to an outsider desiring membership. Permeable groups are easily accessible to outsiders; impermeable groups set conditions to be met before membership can be obtained. To illustrate, varsity teams are impermeable: they usually set conditions for membership in the form of tryouts. However, intramural teams are permeable groups, because there are no qualifications for membership. People who are admitted into impermeable groups usually value their membership highly.

Types of groups

Primary and secondary groups Social relationships do not evolve to the same extent in primary and secondary groups. A primary group is characterized by face-to-face, intimate, personal relationships that are usually relaxed and informal. The social contacts of a secondary group are segmented and impersonal. Further, the personal attitudes of the group members are important. They may see a primary group as an end in itself, while they may see a secondary group as a means to an end, with certain goals set as group objectives. A primary group can also serve group objectives, but the personal human relationship is the most important and valued part of membership in that group. Thus, *primary groups are relationship-directed* and *secondary groups are goal-oriented.* Yet, to a certain extent all groups share some of the characteristics of primary and secondary groups. For example, a high school basketball team may start out as a secondary group with the objective of winning games, but as time passes some primary-group characteristics evolve. Players develop and value close friendships; they may even form cliques.

Primary- and secondary-group characteristics can be placed on a continuum, as shown in Figure 13.1. The two extreme points on the continuum represent

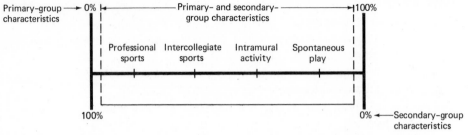

Figure 13.1 Continuum of group characteristics applied to selected physical activities

100 percent primary or 100 percent secondary characteristics. Such groups would probably never exist, since all groups have some primary and secondary characteristics. If this continuum is related to physical activity, one finds professional sports on the secondary end of the continuum, because the basic goal of professional teams is to win games. In contrast, the primary end of the continuum is made up of children's free-play groups and intramural activities, which are usually valued for the social relationships gained. Most groups probably fall into the middle part of the continuum, where they would exhibit both primary and secondary characteristics.

It is important to understand that functional groups are formed to attain goals, but goals vary with different groups. The fun of membership, social prestige, publicity, and monetary rewards are all benefits bestowed by the group. Probably group members have multiple motivations for maintaining their membership. Consequently, physical-activity groups cannot be labeled exclusively primary or secondary, since each situation is different. The coach or physical educator must learn what is important to the members of the group in order to structure the situation in terms of primary or secondary motivation.

Reference groups A reference group can have a psychological impact even on a nonmember of the group. The individual relating to a reference group actually uses it as a source of attitude, standard of conduct, and basis of judgment. For example, an adolescent might use an athletic team as a reference group by trying to copy what he thinks the role of that group is. Closely related to the reference group is the concept of the *role model,* an individual who is idolized and is used like the reference group. Professional athletes, teachers, and coaches are all used as role models by aspiring youngsters; it is of utmost importance that the models realize this and act accordingly.

Group norms

The group structure may be described as an organized pattern of rules and roles that create relationships within the group. The group members divide responsibilities and establish expectations, attitudes, and lines of communication. The rules of the group, which members are expected to follow, are called *group norms* and play a very important part in any group structure. Formal as well as informal norms exist in groups. Training rules can be considered formal group norms: they are stated expectations of the group members' behavior. During the interaction process, informal norms arise within the group, just as powerful as formal norms but seldom expressed. They evolve out of the group process and, in essence, are the unwritten rules of the group. For example, players may be aware of training violations (formal norm), but would never report a fellow-player for them because that would violate one of the informal group norms.

Roles

Role behavior or *role definitions* are the behavior patterns expected of an individual in a given social position or situation. Role definitions are learned, man-made, social, and constantly changing; they include attitudes, values, and learned behavior of the individual. Roles play an important part in forming an individual's self-definition; they can be created formally or may emerge informally. The elected president of an organization formally assumes the role of president, but the emergent opinion leader of a group informally assumes that role. An individual can not only play both formal and informal roles at different times, but can also maintain multiple roles simultaneously. For example, the professional athlete plays a particular role in public, and yet functions in an entirely different role at home as a father or a mother.

Anthropological studies have indicated that male and female roles are culturally determined. Society firmly differentiates sex roles. One thinks of a coach as a man, not a woman, because American society instills this view of sex roles into its members. Thus, a male entering adolescence is expected to exhibit masculine behavior via sports, whereas a girl is supposed to exhibit feminine behavior.

Group size

Groups differ from one another in many dimensions such as size, group communication, and cohesiveness. A group's increase in size can affect its performance as well as the performance of its individual members. In general, the larger the group, the more likely that frustrations will emerge, but this is not to say a large group is ineffective. A physical educator working with large groups to accomplish a difficult task might find it helpful to assign subgroups to find solutions for specific parts of the whole task.

The group process

The group process deals with the basic social processes which help a social system, including groups, survive. Leadership, communication, competition, cooperation, cohesiveness, and socialization are the essential components of the group process.

Leadership

Hollander[3] describes leadership as "a process which implies the existence of a particular influence relationship between two or more persons, though it usually refers to groups of more than two." In short, the leadership process implies influences among group members. The leadership process always involves a leader-follower relationship in which the leader influences the group and, in turn, the group influences the leader. One must think of leadership as a process made up of such important elements as the traits of the individual leader, the group's structure, the method of acquiring leadership within the group, the nature of the task, the group goals, and the past experience of the group. For descriptive purposes, we will isolate these elements and view them separately, but one must remember that they all interact dynamically to form the leadership process.

The relationship between certain personality traits and leadership has often been examined in the hope of isolating the important traits common to leaders. It is true that some evidence indicates that leaders are characterized by certain traits, but traits alone cannot account for a person's becoming a leader. Evidence generally indicates that leaders are slightly more intelligent than nonleaders, and are bigger, more assertive, and more talkative than other group members. Other traits considered have been height, self-confidence, extroversion, and dominance. Leaders frequently participate at a high rate in group interaction, usually in communication or initiation of actions.

[3] E. P. Hollander, *Principles and Methods of Social Psychology.* New York: Oxford University Press, 1971, p. 590.

Athletic prowess has been identified as a trait of leadership, and Cratty[4] summarizes that "athletic prowess as a criterion for leadership is dependent upon the nature of the task, age of the individual involved, and the presence of other forces and values within the social setting." For example, the little girl who at age 8 can run, jump, and throw better than most of her friends is identified as a leader of her peer group. However, this situation may totally reverse as she matures, if her peer group then places less emphasis on physical prowess as a criterion for a leader. Fiedler, one of the foremost authorities on leadership, states that it is of utmost importance to remember that "becoming a leader depends on personality only to a limited degree."[5] Almost any individual can become a leader at any time if the situation and circumstances are appropriate.

There are two basic ways to become a leader. Either one is appointed leader by an authority above the group, or one emerges as a leader from within a group. Formally structured groups tend to have appointed leaders; informally structured groups usually have emergent leaders. It is commonly assumed that a leader is also a popular group member, but this is not always true; much depends upon the situation.

Leaders also are of two basic types. Some fill the role of an emotional leader; others emerge within the group to play the role of the task leader. For example, one athlete might lead the team emotionally and get them "up" for the game, while another player leads the team on the field. It is also possible for one athlete to hold the roles of both emotional and task leader.

Types of leaders Fiedler identifies the two types of leaders found in groups as (1) task-oriented and (2) group-oriented.[6] The task-oriented leader can be described as an autocrat who takes all authority for making decisions. The group-oriented leader is characterized by a democratic, permissive, and equalitarian style, generally supervising the group rather than making all the decisions.

Both the task-oriented and group-oriented leader can be successful, depending upon the situation, and no evidence indicates the superiority of one type to the other. In short, different tasks require different types of leaders.

Fiedler further identifies three factors that classify group situations and affect the influence a leader has over the group:

[4]B. J. Cratty, *Social Dimensions of Physical Activity.* Englewood Cliffs, N.J.: Prentice-Hall, Inc., 1967, p. 56

[5]F. E. Fiedler, "Style of circumstance: the leadership enigma," *Psychology Today,* March 1969, p. 39.

[6]*Ibid.*

1. *Position and power of the leader.* This refers to the amount of authority and power a leader has within a group.
2. *Task structure.* In highly structured tasks a step-by-step progression can be made toward the goal; in unstructured tasks, this cannot occur.
3. *Leader-member personal relationships.* The leader-member relationship emerges as the most important factor in determining a leader's influence over a group.

Fiedler's research indicates that task-oriented leaders perform best in situations at extremes, that is, either when they have a great deal of power or when they have no influence over the group. Relationship-oriented leaders tend to perform best in mixed situations where they have a moderate influence over the group.

The physical educator, coach, and recreation director must realize that leaders are not born but that anyone can become a leader by carefully choosing the situations favorable to one's leadership style. Leadership is specific to the situation. Many feel that we can change leadership styles and, in fact, train leaders, but this is highly improbable. It would be much more useful to help a student recognize these situations in which they can become leaders than to try to change their leadership style, which is closely related to personality.

Spatial position Research on groups has shown that the spatial location of group members affects the group structure. Sociologists have found that the seating arrangements in discussions affect the line of communication within the group. One of the factors in leadership selection within a group is the spatial position of the group members. Thus, a person sitting at the end of a table is often selected as a leader by a group.

Grusky[7] found that the spatial position of people within a group or organization can affect the amount of interaction as well as the positions they hold. Baseball players who perform central independent tasks (infielders and catchers) are selected for managerial positions more often than players in noncentral positions (pitchers and outfielders). Some support also has been found for the hypothesis that players with a high rate of interactions are better liked and more often selected as captains by their teammates.

Communication networks

Communication plays a vital role in any group through lines or networks established to handle ongoing information. Communication becomes extremely

[7]O. Grusky, "The effects of formal structure on managerial recruitment," *Sociometry,* 26, 1963, pp. 343–345.

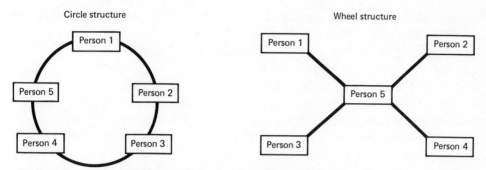

Figure 13.2 Two types of communication network structures. In the circle structure everyone is equally central and equally likely to be considered a leader. In the wheel structure everyone is not equally central; only Person 5 is central and is the leader.

important for any task requiring a group rather than an individual effort. Analyses of the structured communication networks of groups have been sought in an effort to determine which structures function best within groups. For example, both the wheel and the circle communication structures, shown in Figure 13.2, have been studied.

Circle networks of communication are found to be erratic, leaderless, unorganized, and active in communication. People perceive their membership within this network with great satisfaction. Wheel networks of communication are less active, are well organized, have a distinct leader, but are perceived as less satisfying by group members. Thus the wheel is highly organized, while the circle is informal and has no definite leader. The circle network is also able to adjust to new situations more quickly than the wheel can.

Certain group members hold central positions within networks of communications and they most probably will receive and send more information than the other group members. It is probable that an individual holding a central position will become a leader. The coach or physical educator who can single out these central figures in the communication networks will be able to transmit and receive information from the group much more effectively. Findings also indicated that persons in positions of centrality were more satisfied with membership than those in fringe positions. Members of the circle network held positions of equal centrality and, consequently, all perceived their membership as satisfying.

Competition and cooperation

Competition is a basic human quality which appears early in life. Two factors are necessary for competition: First, competitors must desire a common goal; second, they must feel capable of competing.

Many factors can affect competition, such as the traits of the competitors, the situation, cultural conditions, and the task. Experiments have shown that children can be taught to compete or cooperate. For example, highly competitive cultures will usually foster many competitive games in order to train the young for competition. Thus, a person from a highly competitive background will probably perceive more situations as competitive than would a person from a different background. Moreover, many factors can also affect an individual's competitive behavior, for example, experience, needs, skills, attitudes, status, and socioeconomic level.

The desire to obtain a reward that would be unobtainable without the help of others often leads to cooperation within a group. The basketball player has to compete with the other members of the team in order to break into the starting line-up, but at the same time he must also cooperate with his teammates so as to attain a goal (for example, winning the game). Cooperation also provides the cooperator with other valuable outcomes. For example, the individual who cooperates is rewarded by close social relationships with his teammates. Generally, groups whose members are evaluated on the basis of a common score tend to show a greater degree of cooperation. This cooperation increases as group members recognize their interdependence.

There is an ongoing battle in physical education on the question of competition versus cooperation. Many feel that competition is not good for children and adolescents, while others feel it is a valuable experience. Although evidence is insufficient, it seems reasonable to assume that an optimal balance of competitive and cooperative experiences should exist in physical education and athletic environments.

Cohesiveness and group effectiveness

Cohesiveness can be described as the cement that holds a group or team together, a feeling of unity. Cohesiveness increases within a group whose members have similar attitudes and conform to its norms. Many believe that a highly cohesive team is the most effective in competition, but experimental findings to date conflict. Basically, these findings imply that a coach may develop a cohesive team which is not necessarily effective. Much depends on the specific situation.

Group socialization

Socialization is the process by which one inherits the culture of one's society, learning its norms, roles, values, and expectations. Socialization, a dynamic process beginning in childhood and continuing throughout one's adult life, fits an individual into society.

Socialization agents, those organizations carrying out the socialization process, include the family, school, peer group, and mass media. The process of socialization takes place in both formal and informal ways. Schools, for example, are a primary agent of formal, conscious socialization, while the family, peer group, and mass media are agents of informal socialization. Socialization in schools is more formal; however, students also learn interaction skills from associating with their peers at school. Societal values are also learned through socialization. American society values achievement, and its members learn achievement through the process of socialization. From childhood and through adult life, they are rewarded for achievement, reinforcing this cultural value within them. Yet, it must be remembered that although people are generally socialized in the same manner, no two individuals ever have the same socializing experience.

It is generally agreed that sport, athletics, and physical education are all agents of socialization in that many of the interaction skills, values, and attitudes learned in these situations transfer to nonathletic situations. For example, children who learn how to compete in socially accepted ways in athletic situations may more easily learn how they are expected to behave when competing in other social settings. Many have described how sport acts as a vehicle for learning positive societal expectations, values, and norms. But it is important that the physical educator realize that deviant behavior is learned, just as conforming behavior is. For example, the athlete who falls under the influence of an unethical coach may learn deviant behaviors, such as cheating to win, and may transfer this to a nonathletic situation.

Games as a socializing force

Play is considered a cultural universal in that it appears in all societies. Compared to play, games are not universal, although they still exist in many societies. Play and games are often used in society to prepare children for adult life. Children can develop self-identity as well as establish roles and identities of others through play and games. Games have been commonly classified into three basic areas:

1. *Games of physical skill.* The outcome of games of physical skill is determined solely by motor ability.
2. *Games of strategy.* The outcome of games of strategy is dependent upon the rational choice of the participants.
3. *Games of chance.* The outcome of games of chance is uncontrolled and determined completely by chance.

These classifications may also be combined as follows:

1. *Games of physical skill and strategy.* The outcome of games of this nature depends upon both motor ability and strategy. An example of this type of game is football.
2. *Games of physical skill, strategy, and chance.* The outcome of games of this nature depends upon motor ability, strategy, and chance. An example of this type of game is the child's game of ''steal the bacon.''

Sociologists and social psychologists have studied the relationships between games and child-training practices both across and within societies. Generally the findings indicate the following:

1. Games of strategy are related to obedience training, psychological discipline, and complex social systems. Within our own society, games of strategy are usually played by high-status rather than low-status groups.
2. Games of chance are associated with routine tasks, responsibility training, and belief in the supernatural. Lower-status groups usually prefer games of chance more than do upper-status groups. Women usually engage in this type of game more than men. Possibly women and lower-status groups engage in this type of game more often because society usually assigns them routine tasks.
3. Games of physical skill are usually associated with achievement training and mastery over one's environment. Upper-status groups play this type of game more often than lower-status groups. Men are also more likely to play this type of game than women. Western society is often labeled an achieving society, and one cannot help but notice its abundance of games of physical skill. Men, traditionally the breadwinners, find they are offered more opportunities in childhood to engage in this type of game within our society.

What is of utmost importance for the physical educator and recreationist to grasp is that play and games offer much more than simple motor efficiency and coordination to the performer. One must recognize the values of play and games in preparing children for adult social life.

Ethnic-group contact in sport and physical education

Many coaches and physical educators feel that contact between different ethnic groups in sport situations reduces tension and prejudice. Very little research deals with contact between ethnic groups in athletic and physical education settings. Most studies have considered only the contact between group variables while neglecting other important variables. From the pertinent sociological, sociopsychological, and physical education literature, eight theoretical propositions have been derived for the purpose of helping the practitioner better understand this complex situation. These eight propositions are:

1. *Ethnic-group contact appears to reduce tension and prejudice if the participants are engaged in truly intimate relationships.* Mere physical proximity of members of different ethnic groups does not necessarily lead to a reduction of prejudice. It seems that reduction of prejudice occurs where truly intimate relationships develop, because becoming friendly with the member of an out-group (a different ethnic group) makes a person more amenable to information that favors tolerance. In short, just having students of different ethnic groups in the same class will not necessarily lead to reduction of prejudice.

2. *Reduction of prejudice is likely to occur more often if the group is striving to attain or overcome some superordinate goal(s).* Reduction of prejudice is facilitated by the group's effort to achieve goals that cannot be obtained by one individual alone.

3. *Depending upon the outcome of the shared-coping situation, prejudice may be increased or decreased. If the outcome is successful, reduction of prejudice is more likely than if the outcome is failure.* When racially mixed groups work on projects whose outcome is successful, prejudice is likely to be reduced in such groups. It must be remembered that teams and projects are not always successful, and then one group will blame the other for the failure. In such cases it is unlikely that racial attitudes will change for the better. If an athletic team is unsuccessful in that it is not winning, the coach may try to establish other team goals that can be accomplished.

4. *Equal-status contact situations are likely to reduce prejudice more often than unequal-status contact situations.* Generally it has been found that individuals are more likely to change their attitude in a positive way toward another racial group when they become acquainted with equal-status or upper-status members of that group.

5. *The personalities of athletes or students play a vital role in their racial attitude.* Certain personality types do not seem to be influenced by interracial contact. Even if the situation is structurally conducive to a positive interracial experience, attitudes may or may not change depending upon the individual's personality.

6. *If other factors are held constant, the younger the participant in the contact situation, the more likely he is to develop a favorable attitude toward the other racial group.* If interracial contact situations are positive, the younger the children involved, the higher the probability of positive attitude change. It appears that early childhood experiences are very important in forming racial attitudes, and they could very easily occur in sport situations.

7. *The racial attitude of the coach and/or teacher can affect the attitudes of the members of the class or team.* This involves the concept of role models that we discussed earlier in this chapter. American society requires by law that children have a formal education. Consequently, children spend much of their early life under the influence of a teacher and/or coach who will in turn have some effect on their development. The teacher acts as an example for the children. Much of the informal education of children comes through their teachers carefree remarks and general way of acting. Teachers and coaches may not realize it, but they influence children through their facial expressions or even by their tone of voice. If the coach or teacher fosters an attitude of racial prejudice, it is highly probable that the students or athletes will be directly or indirectly affected by it.

8. *Institutional support may facilitate or inhibit the reduction of prejudice of the*

participants. Institutional norms of a company, family, school, team, or any organization have a profound effect upon the people who participate in that situation. If the institution fosters racist norms, it will probably reinforce this type of norm within the group.

It is important to realize that interracial contact is a highly complex area of study, and mere proximity, per se, does not always reduce prejudice. So many variables are involved in ethnic-group-contact situations that the solutions are largely specific to the problem in each situation. However, it is hoped that the above propositions can at least function as guides for professionals in health, physical education, and recreation.

Social facilitation

Coaches and physical educators have always displayed an interest in the effects an audience has upon students' learning and performance. Social facilitation, the theory that deals with the audience effect, examines the influence that the mere presence of others has on individual behavior. Essentially the theory indicates that the presence of an audience will facilitate the emission of a dominant response. Zajonc,[8] the originator of the theory, found that the mere presence of others is a source of arousal which increases the chance of the dominant response's occurring. He also made an important distinction between learning and performance: When one is learning, the dominant response is an incorrect one, but when one is performing an already learned task, the dominant response is a correct one. Thus, an audience will inhibit learning because the performer has not yet learned any single correct response to the task but, instead, has a wide range of incorrect responses that are dominant. Later, after the performer has learned a single correct response to a task, the presence of an audience should enhance performance by facilitating the emission of this learned dominant response.

Social facilitation theory has frequently been supported by tests in areas ranging from verbal learning to complex motor tasks, and involving passive audiences. A passive audience usually observes the performer but never emits any verbal or facial behavior. Although little research has been carried out on the audience effect in natural settings, it is still advisable for the physical educator and coach to follow the reasoning of this theory, from which it appears that the best skill-learning environment contains no audience. After a

[8]R. B. Zajonc, "Social facilitation," *Science,* 749, 1965, pp. 269–274.

skill has already been learned, on the other hand, it appears that the presence of an audience facilitates performance.

Social psychologists and physical educators have attempted to determine if social facilitation affects all age groups in the same manner. Missiuro[9] found that children from the age of six on exhibited an improvement in performance when observed by an audience, but children of a younger age failed to exhibit this improvement. This tends to support the opinions of many educators that children develop and increase social awareness at the age of six and above.

Another way of classifying an audience is by the term *coaction*. Coaction occurs when two or more people perform the same task but do not directly interact with each other. As with social facilitation, coaction is a complex process involving many variables. It can generally be stated that the effects of coaction are similar to the effects of a passive audience in that coaction enhances performance and impairs learning. Individuals have been able to endure more electric shock in coacting situations than when alone. Triplett,[10] informally observing cyclists, noticed that those who raced against the clock recorded slower times than those who raced with other cyclists pacing them. Later, he observed that paced performers recorded slower times than performers in actual competition. Triplett empirically tested and confirmed his findings in one of the first sociopsychological experiments.

In some instances it has been found that learning was enhanced by the presence of coactors, and this finding is contradictory to the social facilitation theory. However, in these instances the coactors who were learning received informational cues about what was correct and incorrect by observing their fellow coactors. Performance is generally more correct in coaction than when a person performs in isolation, exceptions appearing in problem solving and judgment tasks.

The verbal-remarks audience is still another way of classifying an audience. The verbal remarks may be designed to encourage or discourage the performer. The research on this topic is very sparse and much needs to be done. Nevertheless, it might be hypothesized that regardless of the kind of remarks, this type of stimulation causes arousal in the performer, and such arousal may lead to the emission of dominant responses. However, if the performer realizes that disparaging remarks are coming from individuals whom he considers friends, his performance may be adversely influenced.

[9]W. Missiuro, "The Development of Reflex Activity in Children," in E. Jokl and E. Simon, eds., *International Research in Sport and Physical Education.* Springfield, Ill.: Charles C Thomas, Publisher, 1964.

[10]N. Triplett, "The dynamogenic factors in pacemaking competition," *American Journal of Psychology,* 9, 1898, pp. 507–539.

Summary

1. Sociology may be defined as a science concerned with the study of society, social institutions, and all human social relationships.
2. Social psychology, the science evolved from the parent disciplines of sociology and psychology, is concerned with the study of an individual's behavior and experience within a social setting.
3. Sociology of sport is a subdiscipline of sociology concerned with applying the theories and methods of sociology to the environment of sport.
4. A functional group is one whose members share a common goal and are involved in ongoing social interaction.
5. Permeable groups are easily accessible to outsiders; impermeable groups set conditions to be met before membership can be obtained.
6. A primary group is characterized by face-to-face, intimate, personal relationships.
7. The social contacts of a secondary group are segmented and impersonal.
8. Hollander describes leadership as a process that implies the existence of a particular influence relationship between two or more persons, though it usually refers to groups of more than two.
9. Fiedler identifies the two types of leaders of groups as (a) task-oriented and (b) group-oriented.
10. Fiedler identifies three factors that classify group situations and affect the influence a leader has over the group. These are (a) position and power of the leader; (b) task structure; (c) leader-member personal relationships.
11. It is generally agreed that sport, athletics, and physical education are all agents of socialization in that many of the interaction skills, values, and attitudes learned in these situations transfer to nonathletic situations.
12. The complexity of ethnic-group contact situations indicates that solutions to problems are largely specific to each situation.
13. The theory of social facilitation as proposed by Zajonc indicates that the presence of an audience will facilitate the emission of a dominant response.
14. Coaction occurs when two or more people perform the same task but do not directly interact with each other. Triplett confirmed that the effects of coaction are similar to the effects of a passive audience in that coaction enhances performance and impairs learning.

Questions

1. Compare sociology, social psychology, and sociology of sport.
2. What are the two basic ways a person becomes a member of a group?

3. What are the characteristics of a primary, a secondary, and a functional group?
4. Give examples of role expectations regarding sport.
5. Define and differentiate leadership, communication, competition, cooperation, cohesiveness, and socialization. Provide examples.
6. What are some leadership determinants?
7. What are Fiedler's ideas about leadership?
8. What is the significance, if any, of the spatial location of the members of a group listening to a lecture in a gymnasium?
9. Why is competition involving young children and adolescents a controversial question? What are the pros and cons?
10. What is the relationship between cohesiveness and group effectiveness?
11. What do research studies indicate concerning sport as a socializing agent? concerning its transferability to nonathletic environments?
12. Would it be a good idea to encourage ethnic or racial group contact in sports?
13. Zajonc is the originator of a theory. What is it? What is the most common shortcoming of research studies in this area?
14. In what ways is coaction similar to and different from social facilitation?

14

MEASUREMENT AND EVALUATION

If progress in achieving objectives is to be effectively determined, professionals in health, physical education, and recreation must be competent in the measurement and evaluation process. More specifically, they should at least be familiar with:

1. the nature and role of measurement and evaluation;
2. the purposes of measurement and evaluation;
3. test selection and construction;
4. test administration.

Nature and role of measurement and evaluation

Evaluation is the art or skill of judgment scientifically applied according to some preestablished standards, a process representing one essential phase of the larger process of education. For example, physical educators may establish values and select the type of product they think society needs. The term *product* refers to the student changed, modified, or adjusted as a result of experience. To fashion that product, they develop *goals* to guide them in a specific direction. Goals of the distant future are referred to as *aims;* more immediate goals are termed *objectives.* Objectives are exact, explicit statements of the steps in the process of achieving an aim. The objectives for physical education set forth by the American Alliance for Health, Physical Education, and Recreation can serve as an example. These objectives are:

1. organic development involving strength, power, physical fitness, cardiovascular endurance;
2. neuromuscular development involving coordination, motor ability, sport, and movement skills;
3. personal-social development involving attitudes, sportsmanship, leadership, social grace, ideals, and democratic behavior;
4. interpretive development involving knowledges, strategies, and understandings.

Once the product and goals are determined, objectives may be formulated and a program scientifically planned to produce the product. The program may be seen as procedures of implementation (personnel, facilities, equipment, methods, and materials), that is, a means to an end. In the next phase, the process of evaluation, the instructor makes judgments about how effectively the objectives were met, how efficient the program, and how good the product. In this phase tests and measurements are applied to the program and the product to provide a basis for evaluation.

A *test* is a measurement tool that requires a response from the student being assessed. Typically, it consists of a set of questions, problems, or exercises for determining a student's knowledge, abilities, aptitude, or qualifications. *Measurement* is a technique of evaluation in which numbers are assigned to objects or individuals to indicate differences in the degree to which each possesses the property being assessed. *Evaluation* places value on those numbers, determining their meaning and significance within the whole structure of objectives. Evaluation may be subjective (qualitative) or objective (quantitative). Whether applied to the program and/or the product, it requires data and measurement techniques.

On the basis of evaluation results, objectives are appraised and restated, the program or parts of it are replanned, and measurement techniques are applied again, followed by further evaluation. Thus, evaluation is a dynamic, continuous process, which represents one important phase of the larger process of physical education. It is a means to an end and not an end in itself.

Purposes of measurement and evaluation

Evaluation's most important role in physical education is the measurement of student status and progress; to accomplish this it is necessary to know about the product (student) and the program. The acquisition of this knowledge depends to some extent upon measurement; consequently, we need to measure the product and the process. Measures are supposed to assess status and thereby identify progress. Measures of the product may be used for purposes of grading, classification (or the grouping of pupils for educational purposes), guidance and counseling, student motivation, and research. Measures of the program such as assessment of facilities, equipment, activities, methods and materials, supervision, administrative devices, personnel, as well as the teacher may be used for purposes of evaluating objectives and replanning the program.

Some of the purposes of measurement in the evaluation process just discussed, as well as others, are more specifically stated as follows:

1. motivate students when there appears to be a leveling off of interest in the instruction. Tests also help the teacher to end the unit of instruction with a high level of interest;
2. help the teacher assess students' performances.
3. help students evaluate their own knowledge and/or skills in various physical activities;
4. enable the teacher to measure improvement objectively by testing before and after the unit of instruction;
5. assist the teacher in pinpointing the limitations as well as the strong points in a program;
6. aid the teacher in evaluating different methods of instruction;
7. provide a means for determining the better performances within a group and for gaining insight into the potential ability of others;
8. provide a basis for the classification of players and teams for practice and competition;
9. diagnose needs in relation to body mechanics, fitness, and motor skills;
10. help establish age, sex, and grade-level norms for use within a school or school district as well as for comparison with national norms;
11. determine status and changes in status brought about by physical education for public relations purposes;
12. collect data for research;
13. help determine the relative values of sports activities in meeting desired objectives;
14. determine the needs of individuals within the program and the extent to which educational objectives have been accomplished;
15. enable teachers to evaluate their own teaching effectiveness.[1]

[1] "The heed for measurement in the Evaluation Process," reprinted by permission from *Practical Measurements for Evaluation in Physical Education,* 2d ed., 1974, by Barry L. Johnson and Jack K. Nelson, Burgess Publishing Company (Minneapolis, Minnesota); pp 3–4.

Test selection and construction

Among the many different kinds of tests available are tests of motor fitness, physical fitness, general motor ability, motor skill, knowledge, attitude, personality, and social efficiency. Test selection should be made on the basis of the objectives being sought as well as some predetermined standards. *Standards* refer to the degree of attainment using criteria of quality or quantity. *Criteria* are standards by which a test or a quality may be judged or evaluated. Standards for test selection may be classified as either technical or practical.

Technical standards for test selection

1. *Validity.* The validity of a test refers to the degree to which it measures what it purports to measure. In other words, to what extent did the test do the job for which it was intended? The validity of a test is usually ascertained by comparing the new test with some previously established independent criterion or standard.
2. *Reliability.* The reliability of a test refers to the degree to which it is dependable and consistent. A test is considered to be reliable if similar results are obtained when it is readministered by the same instructor to the same students under like conditions. The reliability of a test is determined by correlating measures of the same test with each other. A test must be reliable in order to be valid. However, a test can be reliable without being valid.
3. *Objectivity.* The objectivity of a test is a measure of worth of the scores obtained. A test is considered to be objective if similar results are obtained when it is readministered by different instructors to the same students under like conditions. That is, its administration differentiates the objectivity of a test from its reliability. Objectivity is concerned with the clarity of the directions for administering and scoring the test.
4. *Correlation coefficient.* The statistic used for reporting test validity, reliability, and objectivity is a correlation coefficient. It is a measure of the degree to which two scores are related. The coefficient is computed mathematically and ranges from -1.00 to 0 to $+1.00$. When selecting a test, an instructor should consider the magnitude of the coefficients as well as the criteria employed to determine the coefficients. Some arbitrary standards which may be used as a guide for interpreting correlation coefficients are shown in Table 14.1.
5. *Norms.* A norm is a scale that allows the instructor to convert raw scores to scores that can be compared and interpreted. Norms are usually based on some larger population than is being tested. Tests accompanied by norms can be more effectively evaluated and selected by the instructor.

Practical standards for test selection

When selecting a test the instructor should consider:

1. ease of administering the test;
2. cost involved;

Table 14.1   Arbitrary standards for interpreting correlation coefficients of tests

Correlation coefficients	Reliability and objectivity	Validity
.90–.99	Very good to excellent. More than satisfactory for individual and group measurement.	Excellent. Seldom obtained but more than satisfactory for individual and group measurement.
.80–.89	Good. Satisfactory for individual and group measurement.	Very good. More than satisfactory for individual and group measurement.
.70–.79	Fair. Unsatisfactory for individual measurement, but satisfactory for group measurement.	Good. Usually unsatisfactory for individual measurement, but satisfactory for group measurement.
.69 and below	Poor. Satisfactory only for some group measurement.	Poor. Satisfactory only for some group measurement. Generally, below .59 the test is not useful for either individual or group measurement.

3. time required;
4. space needed;
5. equipment required;
6. number of testers needed;
7. amount of training required by the testers;
8. ease and objectivity of scoring;
9. utility of the test results;
10. its challenging and meaningful properties.

Procedure in test selection

The procedure in selecting a test is contained in the following seven steps:

1. Establish the purpose for which the test is needed by specifically identifying what is to be measured.
2. Determine if the test meets specific needs by identifying its original purpose and examining its content.
3. Decide whether the test is compatible with the program's characteristics, such as philosophy, location, facilities, and the nature of the pupils.
4. Determine if the test's validity, reliability, objectivity, and norms are appropriate to the testing purpose and situation.
5. Establish the administrative feasibility of the test. Considerations include

administering and scoring the test, cost, adaptability of the test to needs and to the program.
6. Identify the teaching utility of the test. Qualities of the test should be able to be used for instructional purposes.
7. Select the test considered the best of those available.

Steps in test construction

When available tests do not seem appropriate to the instructor's purpose, the instructor must construct his own. The steps in constructing a performance test differ somewhat from those for a written test. Steps for both tests are presented here to introduce you to test construction. These steps are.

Steps in constructing a performance test

1. Determine purpose of test.
2. Analyze ability to be measured.
3. Determine criteria for test-item selection.
4. Select experimental items.
5. Select criterion measure(s).
6. Construct record form(s) and directions for administering and scoring items and criterion measure(s).
7. Obtain equipment and facilities necessary.
8. Conduct a pilot study in item administration.
9. Revise items, forms, and directions.
10. Select sample of subjects.
11. Administer experimental test items and criterion measure(s).
12. Score test items and criterion measure(s).
13. Analyze test and criterion measure(s).
14. Combine items and obtain multiple correlation with criterion.
15. Compute regression equations or sum T-scores.
16. Compute norms.
17. Make up test manual.

Steps in constructing a written test

1. Determine purpose of test.
2. Establish curricular validity for areas and items.
3. Set up table of specifications.
4. Set up criteria for good test items.
5. Construct test items.
6. Construct preliminary test.
7. Set up scoring device or key.
8. Set up format and directions for test and scoring device.
9. Conduct pilot study in administration of test.
10. Revise test directions and scoring device in light of pilot study.
11. Select sample of subjects to be tested.
12. Administer preliminary test.

13. Analyze preliminary results—difficulty and discrimination of items.
14. Revise test in light of test results.
15. Select sample of subjects to be tested.
16. Administer final test results.
17. Analyze final test.
18. Revise final test in light of analysis.
19. Set up norms.
20. Make up test manual.[2]

Test administration

An obvious competency in the evaluation process required of the instructor is test administration. This competency can be broken down into three general areas: (1) advance preparations; (2) responsibilities during testing; and (3) responsibilities after testing.

Advance preparation

First, the test(s) must be selected or constructed. The instructor should know the test thoroughly and be well prepared to deliver the instructions in a standardized manner. Any scoring forms that the test requires should be designed and prepared. Methods of recording the scores must also be determined. Further, the instructor should arrange for equipment, facilities, and testing area to be in order and ready. All organization and administration procedures must be planned. It is also advisable to tell the students the purpose of the test and the way the test results will be used, in order to encourage a positive attitude of the students and to motivate them.

Responsibilities during testing

It is always appropriate to make a last-minute check before beginning, to ensure that everything is in order. If the test is a physical performance test, a short warm-up is certainly desirable. Next, a demonstration and the standardized instructions of the physical performance or written test item should be given; here the students should have an opportunity to ask questions. Following the questions, the test is administered. During this period the instructor must be certain that the conditions are conducive to performing the test.

[2] Reprinted from *Research Methods in Health, Physical Education, and Recreation*, 2d ed., 1973, with permission of the American Alliance for Health, Physical Education and Recreation, 1201 Sixteenth Street, N.W., Washington, D.C. 20036.

Responsibilities after testing

One of the first responsibilities after testing is collecting the test scores or measures. These original measures, referred to as raw scores, are sometimes used essentially as they are. For example, raw performance scores for boys ten years old may be used immediately with the norms on the physical fitness testing score sheet shown in Table 14.2. However, in some situations raw scores must be converted to percentile or standard scores. These two types of scores may be defined as follows:

Percentile A score in a distribution below which falls the percent of cases indicated by the given percentile. For example, the 10th percentile denotes the score below which 10 percent of the scores fall.
Standard score A general term referring to different transformed scores (for example, *T*-score, *Z*-score), in terms of which raw scores may be expressed for purposes of comparability and ease of interpretation.

Converting raw scores to percentile or standard scores typically takes place through the use of norms presented as scoring tables. Table 14.3 shows percentile scores, and Table 14.4 *T*-score norms. However, in some situations instructors must prepare their own norms. In either case, they should have some knowledge of elementary statistics to analyze the test results. Further, ability to use a calculator or even a computer can certainly reduce the labor of statistical computation.

Once raw scores have been collected, and converted if necessary, they may be compared with norms and interpreted. The meaning of these test results should be passed on to students and parents, administrators, or other interested individuals. The instructor must not stop at this point; he should use the results and follow them up. Test measures serve the purpose when they are applied to meet the needs of the students (product) or to improve the program.

Summary

1. Evaluation is the art or skill of judgment scientifically applied according to some preestablished standards.
2. A test is a measurement tool that requires a response from the student being assessed.
3. Measurement is a technique of evaluation in which numbers are assigned to objects or individuals to indicate differences in the degree to which each possesses the property being assessed.
4. Evaluation's most important role in physical education is to measure student

Table 14.2 Sample physical fitness testing score sheet
(For boys 10 years of age)

Pupil_____ School_____ Teacher_____

1st test—Circle scores in *red*. 2nd test—Circle scores in *green*. 3rd test—Circle scores in *blue*. Connect circled scores after each test to show physical fitness profile.

	Sit-ups	Pull-ups	Broad jump	50-yard dash	Shuttle run	Softball throw	600 yards
Excellent	60	6	5'6"	7.6	10.3	122'	2:15
	58	5	5'5"	7.7	10.4	121'	2:17
					10.5	119'	2:18
	56		5'4"	7.8	10.6	117'	2:20
					10.7	115'	2:22
	54		5'3"	7.9	10.8	113'	2:24
Good		4			10.9	111'	2:26
	52		5'2"	8.0	11.0	109'	2.28
					11.1	107'	
	50		5'1"			105'	
	48	3	5'0"	8.1	11.2	103'	2:30
	46		4'11"	8.2	11.3	102'	2:32
	44				11.4	100'	2:34
	42			8.3	11.5	98'	2:36
	40		4'10"		11.6	96'	2:38
Satisfactory	38	2		8.4	11.7	94'	2:40
	36		4'9"		11.8	92'	2:42
	34			8.5	11.9		2:44
	32						2:45
	30		4'8"	8.6			
	29		4'7"	8.7	12.0	90'	2:47
	28						2:49
	27		4'6"	8.8	12.1	88'	2:51
	26						2:53
Poor	25	1	4'5"	8.9	12.2	86'	2:55
	24						2:57
	23					84'	
	22		4'4"	9.0	12.3	82'	2:58

Note: This score sheet will serve one boy for all three tests during the school year.

Source: Youth Physical Fitness; President's Council on Youth Fitness, Washington, D.C.: U.S. Government Printing Office, July 1961, p. 55.

Table 14.3   Percentile scores for college men

Percen-tile	Pull-up	Sit-up	Shuttle run	Standing broad jump	50-yard dash	Softball throw	600-yard run-walk
100th	20	100	8.3	9' 6"	5.5	315	1:12
95th	12	99	9.0	8' 5"	6.1	239	1:35
90th	10	97	9.1	8' 2"	6.2	226	1:38
85th	10	79	9.1	7'11"	6.3	217	1:40
80th	9	68	9.2	7'10"	6.4	211	1:42
75th	8	61	9.4	7' 8"	6.5	206	1:44
70th	8	58	9.5	7' 7"	6.5	200	1:45
65th	7	52	9.5	7' 6"	6.6	196	1:47
60th	7	51	9.6	7' 5"	6.6	192	1:49
55th	6	50	9.6	7' 4"	6.7	188	1:50
50th	6	47	9.7	7' 3"	6.8	184	1:52
45th	5	44	9.8	7' 1"	6.8	180	1:53
40th	5	41	9.9	7' 0"	6.9	176	1:55
35th	4	38	10.0	6'11"	7.0	171	1:57
30th	4	36	10.0	6'10"	7.0	166	1:59
25th	3	34	10.1	6' 9"	7.1	161	2:01
20th	3	31	10.2	6' 7"	7.1	156	2:05
15th	2	29	10.4	6' 5"	7.2	150	2:00
10th	1	26	10.6	6' 2"	7.5	140	2:15
5th	0	22	11.1	5'10"	7.7	125	2:25
0	0	0	13.9	4' 2"	9.1	55	3:43

Source: Reprinted from *AAHPER Youth Fitness Test Manual,* Revised Edition, 1965, with permission of the American Alliance for Health, Physical Education, and Recreation, 1201 Sixteenth Street, N. W., Washington, D.C. 20036.

status and progress; to accomplish this it is necessary to know about the product (student) and the program.

5. Measures of the product may be used for purposes of grading, classification, guidance and counseling, motivation, and research.
6. Criteria are standards by which a test or a quality may be judged or evaluated.
7. Technical standards for test selection include: (a) validity, (b) reliability, (c) objectivity, and (d) norms.
8. Percentile refers to a score in a distribution below which falls the percent of cases indicated by the given percentile.
9. Standard score is a general term referring to different transformed scores (for example, *T*-score, *Z*-score), in terms of which raw scores may be expressed for purposes of comparability and ease of interpretation.

Table 14.4 *T-score norms for squat jumps*

	College men							
	T-scores	*Raw* scores		**T-scores**	*Raw* scores		**T-scores**	*Raw* scores
	100 — 95			66 — 68			32 — 34	
	99			65 — 67			31 — 33	
	98 — 94			64 — 66			30 — 32	
	97		Good	63 — 65			29 — 31	
	96 — 93			62 — 64			28 — 30	
	95			61 — 63			27 — 29	
	94 — 92			60 — 62			26 — 28	
	93 —			59 — 61			25 — 27	
	92 — 91			58 — 60			24 — 26	
	91			57 — 59			23 — 25	
	90 — 90			56 — 58			22 — 24	
	89			55 — 57			21 — 23	
Excellent	88 — 89			54 — 56			20 — 22	
	87			53 — 55			19 — 21	
	86 — 88			52 — 54			18 — 20	
	85 — 87			51 — 53			17 — 19	
	84 — 86			50 — 52			16 — 18	
	83 — 85			49 — 51			15 — 17	
	82 — 84			48 — 50	Very		14 — 16	
	81 — 83			47 — 49	Poor		13 — 15	
	80 — 82			46 — 48			12 — 14	
	79 — 81			45 — 47			11 — 13	
	78 — 80			44 — 46			10 — 12	
	77 — 79			43 — 45			9 — 11	
	76 — 78			42 — 44			8 — 10	
	75 — 77			41 — 43			7 — 9	
	74 — 76			40 — 42			6 — 8	
	73 — 75			39 — 41			5 — 7	
Poor	72 — 74			38 — 40			4 — 6	
	71 — 73			37 — 39			3 — 5	
	70 — 72			36 — 38			2 — 4	
	69 — 71			35 — 37			1 — 3	
	68 — 70			34 — 36				
	67 — 69			33 — 35				

Source: Reproduced from *FM 21-20,* 8 October 1957, by permission of the Department of the Army.

Questions

1. Do you consider the evaluation process to be essential or a waste of time in a school setting? Support your answer.
2. Differentiate evaluation, test, and measurement. Give an example of each.
3. Define goals, aims, and objectives. Select a specific area and apply your definitions.
4. If you have stated precise performance objectives, do you still have to worry about evaluation?
5. What are some of the factors that have kept most physical educators away from the necessity of evaluating?
6. Identify the criteria used to judge or evaluate a test.
7. What elements should you consider before selecting a test?
8. Compare the steps in constructing a performance test with those in preparing a written test.
9. Do you see any value to a pretesting period? Why is it advisable?
10. How much time should be devoted to evaluation in your physical education program?

15

RESEARCH

Research plays an important role in health, physical education, and recreation by producing scientific knowledge to form the basis of these professions. All the scientific knowledge we have discussed up to now has been the result of research. Since research apparently is so crucial to these professions, let us find out more about its nature and function as well as some of the different methods employed to achieve that function.

The aim and method of science

The fundamental and ultimate aim of science is *theory,* which we may define as "a systematically related set of statements, including some lawlike generalizations, that is empirically testable."[1] It is a systematic interpretation of

[1] R. S. Rudner, *Philosophy of Social Science.* Englewood Cliffs, N.J.: Prentice-Hall, Inc., 1966, p. 10.

an area of knowledge that can be subjected to testing which relies on experience and observation. If a theory withstands the rigor of systematic, controlled, empirical, and critical investigation, it is considered to be confirmed. It may eventually be regarded as a law, which is a particularly well-verified theory. The purpose of theory is to explain and predict phenomena. It has been proposed that if we can explain phenomena successfully, we have understanding to some extent, and if we can predict phenomena, we have control to some degree. If this proposal is acceptable, then the purposes of theory are explanation, understanding, prediction, and control. Further, since the ultimate aim of science is theory, the purposes of science are the same as those of theory.

The method employed to achieve the ultimate aim of science is termed *research.* It may be seen as a diligent inquiry into or examination of solutions to our problems. More formally defined, "scientific research is systematic, controlled, empirical, and critical investigation of hypothetical propositions about presumed relations among natural phenomena."[2] Scientific research is a means to an end. It provides us with facts, the basic information that can lead us to knowledge, that is, the solutions, answers, and truths we seek. Research can verify theory, the ultimate aim of science.

The method of scientific research

Scientific research is considered to be the modern method of acquiring knowledge. A systematic and refined way of thinking, it employs special tools, instruments, and procedures. The scientific method provides us with a more adequate solution of a problem than would an ordinary, unsystematic means, such as common sense. Methods of scientific research differ in their specific applications to solving problems in different fields of knowledge. However, characteristics of all scientific research investigations are:

1. *Observation.* The collection of data that eventually verify the degree of truth of facts. Data are recorded results of observations, and facts are symbolic propositions that are usually stated verbally.
2. *Classification.* The grouping, arranging, and averaging of these data and facts.
3. *Verification.* Replication of the conditions of the investigation until there is little doubt of the uniformity of the result.
4. *Generalization.* The formulation of this uniformity into principle or law.

[2] F. N. Kerlinger, *Foundations of Behavioral Research: Educational and Psychological Inquiry,* Second Edition. New York: Holt, Rinehart and Winston, Inc., 1973, p. 11.

When engaged in scientific research, the scientist employs both deductive and inductive thinking. In other words, he becomes involved in reflective thinking. John Dewey analyzed the stages of reflective thinking in solving a problem. More recently, these stages were described as steps by Van Dalen. These steps are presented in successive order below, although they do not always occur that way in practice:

1. *A felt difficulty.* Man encounters some obstacle, experience, or problem that puzzles him. (a) He lacks the means to get to the end desired; (b) he has difficulty in identifying the character of an object; (c) he cannot explain an unexpected event.
2. *Location and definition of the difficulty.* Man makes observations—gathers facts—that enable him to define his difficulty more precisely.
3. *Suggested solutions of the problem hypotheses.* From his preliminary study of the facts, man makes intelligent guesses about possible solutions of the problem. The conjectural statements—generalizations he offers to explain the facts that are causing the difficulty—are called *hypotheses.*
4. *Deductively reasoning out the consequences of the suggested solutions.* Man deductively reasons that if each hypothesis is true, certain consequences should follow.
5. *Testing the hypotheses by action.* Man tests each hypothesis by searching for observable evidence that will confirm whether or not the consequences that should follow actually occur. By this process, he finds out which hypothesis is in harmony with observable facts and thus offers the most reliable answer to his problem.[3]

The problem and review of literature

A problem may be regarded as a question that needs to be answered. It is the first hurdle that confronts the researcher. Although numerous problems in health, physical education, and recreation need to be solved, the inexperienced researcher usually has difficulty in locating one. Perhaps the most appropriate way to begin is to select a person considered an expert in the field of knowledge of interest to you. That person, usually a faculty member, can offer you guidance by suggesting problem areas or controversial issues that need to be researched. Another approach to locating a problem consists of reviewing and analyzing the literature (completed research) in a field of knowledge of interest to you. In some situations, discussing this literature with fellow students results in finding a problem with which you can deal. Also, it is recommended that the researcher become familiar with professional groups that facilitate

[3] From *Understanding Educational Research: An Introduction* by D. B. Van Dalen. Copyright © 1962 by McGraw-Hill Book Company. Used with permission of McGraw-Hill Book Company.

specific kinds of research. The Research Council of the American Alliance for Health, Physical Education and Recreation, the President's Council on Physical Fitness and Sports, the International Society of Sports Psychology, and the American College of Sports Medicine are just a few organizations that can offer guidance in locating a problem to be researched.

Having located a problem, the researcher must then determine its appropriateness and feasibility by considering the questions listed below. If the researcher's answers to these questions are positive, there is little doubt of the problem's appropriateness:

1. Is the problem of interest to you?
2. Is it possible to collect data appropriate to the solution of the problem?
3. Are techniques, instruments, and other facilities available for the solution of the problem?
4. Is the research feasible, especially in terms of time and cost?
5. Do you have adequate professional preparation and experience to analyze the data and interpret the results?
6. Will the solution to the problem make a significant contribution to the field of knowledge and/or to the profession?

Once the problem has been selected, thorough review of the literature is necessary before the data are collected. A number of tasks confront the researcher after a problem has been selected. Some of these tasks are:

1. defining and determining the problem;
2. being certain that the problem has not been researched before or study of it is not currently in progress;
3. understanding and justifying the techniques, instruments, and procedures required to solve the problem;
4. knowing how to interpret the results in order to solve the problem;
5. understanding the significance of the solution to the problem.

A thorough knowledge of the literature will help the researcher accomplish these tasks. There is no easy way to survey the literature. It requires long hours of study, a great deal of note taking, and perserverance. The search should be conducted systematically. A working bibliography should be established, card systems for recording important and relevant information should be maintained, references should be classified, literature should be skimmed and abstracted, and the resulting notes should be recorded.

Library sources to assist the researcher's survey of the literature include microcards, periodicals, indexes and abstracts, and computer retrieval systems. A few examples of these sources are:

1. *Microcard.* Many sources such as master's and doctoral theses and out-of-print publications are also being placed on microcard. *The Health, Physical Education and Recreation Microcard Bulletin,* Vols. I and II, of the University of Oregon, provides a complete listing of these references on microcard.
2. *Periodicals. Research Quarterly, Journal of Physical Education and Recreation, Physical Educator, Journal of Motor Behavior, Journal of Sports, Medicine and Physical Fitness, International Journal of Health Education, Journal of Health and Human Behavior, Quarterly Bulletin of American Recreational Society, Journal of School Health, Perceptual and Motor Skills, Recreation, International Journal of Sport Psychology, Journal of Biomechanics, Kinesiology Review,* and *Today's Health* provide excellent references for the researcher.
3. *Indexes and abstracts.* Dissertation abstracts, microfilm abstracts, nutrition abstracts and reviews, *Psychological Abstracts, Social Science Abstracts, Research Quarterly* indexes, index to the Literature of Leisure, recreation, parks, and other recreational sources, synthesis of research in selected areas of health instruction, *Completed Research in Health, Physical Education, and Recreation, Education Index,* and *Quarterly Cumulative Index Medicus* are valuable resources.
4. *Computer retrieval systems.* There are computer systems designed to disseminate information or references to you. Since the computer does the searching, these systems save the researcher a great deal of time. Most of these systems require you to complete an application and pay a fee for their services. Some of these systems are: *Datrix*—University Microfilms, Xerox Corporation, Ann Arbor, Michigan; *Medlars Search Request*—National Library of Medicine, Medlars Management Section, 8600 Rockville Pike, Bethesda, Maryland; *ERIC*—U.S. Office of Education, 400 Maryland Avenue, S.W., Washington, D.C.

Basic and applied research

Although there is no fine line of distinction, methods of scientific research generally may be classified as basic or applied. *Basic research* seeks to increase the amounts of scientific knowledge common to all, whereas *applied research* aims to determine the most appropriate ways of employing this knowledge in practical settings. The immediate concern of basic research is to increase humanity's understanding of itself and its environment. Of course, this understanding can in turn mediate the discovery of solutions to practical problems. In contrast, the immediate concern of applied research is not so much with increasing basic understanding as with solutions to practical problems. In either case, new scientific knowledge can be produced from applied research as well as basic research. Most research in health, physical education, and recreation is applied research. However, with the emergence of an academic discipline, there probably will be an increasing trend toward basic research.

Descriptive research

Descriptive research attempts to determine the current status of phenomena, identify relationships and trends among phenomena, and examine existing conditions, practices, and attitudes. Among the numerous types of descriptive studies are:

1. *Surveys* usually employ questionnaire, interview, or normative instruments for identifying present status and/or making comparisons.
2. *Case studies* aim to explore the complex variables that determine the distinctness of a social unit, that is, an individual, family, group, social institution, or community.
3. *Correlational studies* attempt to establish the extent to which two factors are related.
4. *Growth, development, and trend studies* try to ascertain current status and interrelationships as well as changes that occur as a function of time.

The steps involved in descriptive research usually include:

1. defining the problem to be solved, that is, the questions to be answered;
2. extensively reviewing the related literature;
3. stating the hypotheses or the solutions to the problem;
4. elaborating on all procedures;
5. stating the assumptions underlying the above hypotheses and procedures;
6. selecting or constructing techniques and instruments for data collection;
7. determining categories for classifying data;
8. validating techniques and instruments used for data collection;
9. making observations that are clearly discriminating and objective;
10. describing, analyzing, and interpreting the findings so as to produce significant theoretical generalizations that will advance scientific knowledge.

Historical research

Historical research is concerned with searching for the truth about the past. It attempts to discover and present reliable knowledge about the past that will endure the test of critical evaluation.

On the basis of knowledge of past problems, historical method makes generalizations that can help us anticipate similar problems and take precautions for the future.

All scholars are interested in historical research to learn truths about the past that are related to their specific fields of knowledge. Once a problem to be researched has been identified, historical research techniques are needed to review the past literature on that problem. Thus, even researchers who do not deal with historical problems employ historical research techniques.

In general, the steps involved in historical research include:

1. Defining the problem to be solved, that is, questions to be answered about the past.
2. Collecting primary and secondary source material. *Primary sources* are original materials such as remains or relics, and documents or traditions, and are the basic materials of historical research. *Secondary sources* are writings or oral testimony, such as encyclopedias and textbooks, informing us about original sources. Classification of source materials depends upon the problem being researched and how the materials are used. A particular source material may be classified as primary in one situation but secondary in another.
3. Criticizing source materials externally and internally. External criticism questions the authenticity of the material as a piece of evidence. Once this is established, internal criticism determines the meaning and dependability of the information within the material.
4. Stating hypotheses. Hypotheses are solutions to the problem, answers to questions about the past that attempt to explain the past.
5. Interpreting and reporting findings that explain the past; these may include some generalizations concerning the present and the future.

Philosophical research

Philosophical research is concerned with the facts and principles of reality and of human nature and conduct. To a large extent it is subjective, aiming to solve problems through critical and reflective thinking. Although scientists employ philosophical techniques in their research, they are concerned mainly with discovering more exact ways to describe objects and occurrences that are observed and experienced. Philosophers, on the other hand, seek primarily to determine the meaning and value of the scientist's discoveries in relation to the whole universe. Logical induction and deduction are the essential methods, and analysis and synthesis the tools, of philosophical research. These methods and tools are applied to the facts that are available.

Clarke and Clarke outline the steps in philosophical research as follows:

1. Identify the problem area; the problem is defined and delimited to manageable proportions.
2. Collect available facts related to the problem.
3. Synthesize and analyze the facts, working them into patterns that identify relationships among them.
4. From these patterns, derive general principles that describe the relationships inherent in the principles.
5. State these principles in the form of hypotheses or tentative assumptions.
6. Test the hypotheses for acceptance, rejection, or modification.[4]

[4] David H. Clarke and H. Harrison Clarke, *Research Processes in Physical Education, Recreation, and Health.* © 1970. Reprinted by permission of Prentice-Hall, Inc., Englewood Cliffs, New Jersey.

Experimental research

Experimental research deals with designing and employing an experiment to determine how and why a particular event or condition occurs. The design of an experiment employs controlled observation. An *experiment* is a designed situation which assesses the influences of one or more independent variables on one or more dependent variables. A *variable* is a factor or condition that is able to change. *Independent variables* are those manipulated by the experimenter to make a prediction. *Dependent variables* are factors or conditions about which predictions are made. If an experiment is properly controlled, it can be concluded without doubt that the changes in the independent variable caused the changes in the dependent variable.

Perhaps an overview of the steps in experimental research will provide a further understanding of what the method involves.

1. Define the problem to be solved, based on a thorough review of the literature.
2. State hypotheses and deduce their consequences. It is the consequences that are directly tested in the experiment. If the deduced consequences are observed in the controlled experiment, it is concluded that the hypotheses have been supported.
3. Contrive an experimental design that depicts all the elements, conditions, and relations of the consequences. This may include (a) selecting a random sample of persons to represent a certain population; (b) randomly assigning these persons to treatment groups; (c) identifying independent and dependent variables; (d) determining independent variable manipulations; (e) controlling extraneous variables; (f) selecting or constructing and validating techniques and instruments to measure the effects of the independent variable on the dependent variable; (g) conducting a preliminary study in order to perfect procedures, instruments, and design; (h) establish the time, place, and duration of the experiment.
4. State assumptions underlying the above hypotheses and experimental design as well as the limitations of the experiment.
5. Conduct the experiment, that is, observe and collect the raw data.
6. Analyze the raw data in such a way that it will produce an unbiased evaluation of the effects of the independent variable on the dependent variable.
7. Apply an appropriate statistical test of significance to determine the credibility of the results of this experimental research.
8. Interpret the results so as to produce significant theoretical generalizations that will advance scientific knowledge.

Most experimental research in physical education has been conducted in laboratory settings. These settings may be specially equipped rooms with precise measuring instruments or other sites such as a gymnasium, a swimming pool, or an athletic field. Control of variables and precision of measurement are the two main advantages of laboratory situations. Experimental research in such fields of knowledge as exercise physiology, kinesiology or biomechanics, motor learning, psychology of sport, sociology of sport, and growth and development typically is conducted in laboratory settings. Historical and philosophical studies, and some descriptive research, especially surveys and questionnaires, are usually conducted in nonlaboratory settings.

Summary

1. Theory may be defined as a systematically related set of statements, including some lawlike generalizations, that is empirically testable.
2. The purposes of theory are explanation, understanding, prediction, and control.
3. The method employed to achieve the ultimate aim of science is termed research.
4. Scientific research is the systematic, controlled, empirical, and critical investigation of hypothetical propositions about presumed relations among natural phenomena.
5. The method of scientific research is a systematic and refined way of thinking that employs special tools, instruments, and procedures.
6. Characteristic of all scientific research investigations are (a) observation; (b) classification; (c) verification; and (d) generalization.
7. Basic research seeks to increase the amount of scientific knowledge common to all.
8. Applied research aims at determining the most appropriate ways of employing knowledge in practical settings. Most research in health, physical education, and recreation is applied research.
9. Descriptive research attempts to determine the current status of phenomena, identify relationships and trends among phenomena, and examine existing conditions, practices, and attitudes.
10. Historical research is concerned with searching for the truth about the past.
11. Philosophical research is concerned with the facts and principles of reality and of human nature and conduct.
12. Experimental research deals with designing and employing an experiment to determine how and why a particular event or condition occurs. An experiment is a designed situation which assesses the influences of one or more independent variables on one or more dependent variables.

Questions

1. What are the relationships among science, theory, law, and phenomena?
2. What is research?
3. What are the characteristics of a scientific research investigation?

4. What is the purpose of a review of the literature?
5. What steps are involved in locating a problem? Are there any set ways to narrow a problem down?
6. Is it really important that the solution of the contemplated problem be of immediate significance to the field of knowledge or to the profession?
7. What are some of the tools a library possesses to aid researchers?
8. What is the difference between applied research and basic research?
9. Compare the different approaches of descriptive, historical, philosophical, and experimental research.
10. Find a problem that you might wish to investigate. Determine the independent and the dependent variables.
11. What phase of an experimental research seems the most complicated? Give your reasons.

16

PROFESSIONAL RECREATION SERVICE

During its early development, recreation had been a field of professional service closely related to physical education. However, in the past two decades it has acquired a distinct identity, in terms of specialized preparation, functional roles, and professional status.

Recreation is most commonly regarded as an *activity*—what people do for pleasure or relaxation in their leisure. Some authorities argue that recreation should be defined as *experience*—what happens to participants when they engage in such activities. Recreation is also a *professional service* provided by community agencies, and a *social institution* that is an important area of government responsibility and a key element in the national economy.

Recreation defined

Here, we will define recreation as follows:

Recreation consists of activities or experiences of leisure time, usually chosen voluntarily because of the satisfaction or pleasure participants derive from them or

Municipal swimming pool in St. Petersburg, Florida

because participants perceive certain personal or social goals as potential outcomes of recreation.

Recreation provided as part of organized community or voluntary agency services must meet socially acceptable standards and achieve constructive goals for the participants and for society at large. The activities commonly found in recreation programs range widely from sports and games, outdoor pursuits, hobbies, social activities, arts and crafts, travel, entertainment, the performing arts, reading, to volunteer leadership. It should be understood that recreation may consist of a single act or experience, involving the participant in only superficial ways, or may be a deep-rooted interest carried on through a lifetime of absorbing commitment.

Personal goals of recreation

The personal outcomes of recreational participation fall under the following major headings: physical, social, emotional, creative, and intellectual.

Physical

Physical play is extremely important in the developmental process of children and youth. Most elementary school physical education programs provide only a few hours of activity each week. Young children, therefore, must find additional release for their energies, as well as the opportunity to develop fitness and to improve their motor skills, in recreational activities. In adulthood, appropriate recreation activities maintain the fitness level of participants and counteract the tendency toward obesity and inactivity that threatens the health of many middle-aged and older persons. Most community or voluntary recreation agencies offer a wide variety of team and dual sports, dance, and exercise or other conditioning programs.

Social

At every stage of life, recreation provides a channel for healthy social development and constructive group involvement. In after-school, evening, or summer recreation programs, children and youth take part in social clubs, teams, drama groups, orchestras, and similar peer-group activities. Inevitably, they learn to relate to others, live by the rules, adopt the values of the group or contribute to its success. Children thus are helped significantly in the process of socialization.

Emotional

Leading medical authorities attest to the contribution that recreational participation makes to mental health. William Menninger, the psychiatrist, wrote:

Mentally healthy people participate in some form of volitional activity to supplement their required daily work. . . . Their satisfaction from these activities meets deep-seated psychological demands, quite beyond the superficial rationalization of enjoyment. . . . There is considerable scientific evidence that the healthy personality is one who not only plays, but who takes his play seriously.[1]

The specific value of recreation for emotional health is twofold:

1. It provides a medium through which individuals may relate to others in healthy ways and find supportive group acceptance.
2. It offers an outlet for self-expression and personal creativity, as well as a useful channel for discharging hostility or aggression, or meeting other important psychosocial needs.

[1]William C. Menninger, "Recreation and mental health," *Recreation,* November 1948, p. 343.

311

Creative

Recreation provides a means of developing one's individuality and personal creativity. Art, music, theater, or dance—as well as creative cookery, travel, or hobbies—make it possible to discover and affirm one's own life style in an increasingly depersonalized world.

Intellectual

Although recreation may have a restricted meaning for many, it actually encompasses a host of cognitive or learning activities. These include reading, writing, group discussions, scientific or mathematical hobbies, and other involvements that promote awareness of the environment or contribute to the formal educational process.

In addition to its value for the individual's personal development, recreation has important goals related to community needs. Today, it is generally accepted that government on the local level has a responsibility for providing facilities and programs that meet the needs of the public for enjoyable, inexpensive, and constructive recreational opportunities.

Objectives of community recreation

Recreation offered by community agencies, such as municipal recreation and park departments, or voluntary organizations, has the following goals:

1. to enrich the over-all *quality of life* by providing constructive, creative, and socially desirable recreational opportunities for people of all ages, races, religions, and socioeconomic backgrounds;
2. to contribute to the *physical health, social development,* and *emotional well-being* of participants, and to extend the formal educational experience offered by the schools;
3. to preserve and improve the *physical environment* by developing a network of natural areas and green spaces in the community, and by providing leadership in the total effort to protect land and water resources;
4. to enrich the *social integration* of the community by encouraging neighborhood residents of different social or ethnic backgrounds to work and plan together, to meet shared, recreational needs;
5. to assist in *reducing* or *preventing antisocial behavior among youth,* by offering constructive and attractive recreational activities in group settings that promote desirable social values and contact with favorable adult models;
6. to provide leisure opportunities for *groups with special needs* in the community, who are unable to meet their recreational needs independently, such as the mentally retarded or the physically disabled;

7. to provide *inner-city* or other economically disadvantaged areas with vocational counseling or training, youth employment, tutorial, drug-abuse, or similar special services to supplement the work of other social agencies;
8. to support the *economic well-being and stability* of the community by providing facilities and programs that make it an attractive place in which to live, thus keeping up real estate values and encouraging industrial or residential development.

To understand how these goals have arisen and are being realized today, it is helpful to examine the development and present structure of professional recreation service.

Historical overview of recreation

Throughout history, humans have always enjoyed varied forms of play. As far back as the pre-Christian or early Greek and Roman eras, they took part in sports and games, theater, music, dance, the arts, hunting and fishing, and a host of other pursuits. Generally, both the opportunity to play (in terms of free time, money, and social approval) and the forms of play were dependent on social class. During the Renaissance, for example, the nobility had the leisure as well as the wealth to engage in varied recreational pursuits. On the other hand, peasants and artisans had much less opportunity nor were they permitted by law to enjoy many of the forms of play, such as hunting, reserved for the nobility.

Attitudes toward play and leisure have varied throughout history. For example, classical Greece believed that leisure was the ideal state of being and that play helped greatly in molding character. Plato wrote:

Our children from their earliest years must take part in all the more lawful forms of play, for if they are not surrounded with such an atmosphere they can never grow up to be well-conducted and virtuous citizens./Education should begin with the right direction of children's sports. The plays of childhood have a great deal to do with the maintenance or nonmaintenance of laws.[2]

During the Protestant Reformation, many forms of play were condemned by the new churches. In colonial America, the Puritans of New England sharply restricted sports, games, dance, music, and theater. The Protestant "work ethic" became a dominant value and influenced Americans for centuries in the way they regarded recreation.

With the beginning of the Industrial Revolution in Europe and America, the

[2]Plato, *The Republic*. Cambridge, Mass.: Harvard University Press, 1953, p. 335;/*The Laws*. Cambridge, Mass.: Harvard University Press, 1961, p. 23.

amount of available free time declined sharply; industrial and agricultural laborers worked an average of almost 70 hours a week, with few holidays during the year. The work week peaked during the mid-nineteenth century and then declined steadily, as a consequence of increased mechanization, child labor laws, and labor union contracts. As leisure spread, the American public began to enjoy a great variety of pastimes. Both amateur and professional sports gained new popularity. Cultural activities and entertainment, hobbies and travel, all became widely enjoyed.

In the latter decades of the nineteenth century, the development of the recreation movement in the United States was fostered by several factors:

1. the establishment of national, state, and municipal parks throughout the country;
2. the founding of settlement houses and similar community centers in the rapidly growing cities, chiefly to serve immigrant families and aid in their Americanization;
3. the spread of major youth organizations, which provided extensive programs of sports, games, and other forms of social recreation;
4. the establishment of networks of publicly sponsored playgrounds throughout the country.

Some examples of this development are:

founding of the Young Men's Christian Association (YMCA) (1854);
development of Central Park in New York City, the first major park in an American city (1857);
acquisition of Yellowstone, the first National Park in the United States (1872);
establishment of the Boston Sand Garden, the first public playground for young children, under voluntary auspices (1885);
establishment of first county park system in Essex County, New Jersey (1895);
opening of school buildings as community evening-recreation centers in New York City (1898);
appropriation of $5 million to establish ten neighborhood parks in Chicago (1903);
founding of Playground Association of America, Boys' Clubs of America, and Young Women's Christian Association (1906);
founding of Boy Scouts of America, American Camping Association, and Camp Fire Girls (1910).

The key factor in this period was the establishment of playgrounds in cities and towns of the nation. At first these were sponsored by groups of public-spirited citizens, but, before long, responsibility for them was assumed by municipal government or public school systems. Their chief purpose was to provide sports, games, and other constructive forms of recreation for slum children, in order to keep them out of such tempting settings as saloons, dance halls, pool parlors, or bowling alleys, which frequently led to prostitution or other forms of delinquent activity.

In 1900, 12 cities were reported to be providing recreation through public funds. The number grew rapidly. In 1920, there were 465 such cities, and twice as many ten years later. There was a particularly rapid growth of park and other recreation facilities during the 1920s. Butler wrote: "Playgrounds, golf courses, swimming pools, bathing beaches, picnic areas, and game fields were constructed in unprecedented numbers. Municipal park acreage, especially during the latter half of the decade, expanded more than in any other period of equal length."[3]

During the Depression of the 1930s, the federal government spent millions of dollars to develop public recreation and park facilities through varied work-relief programs, and employed over 45,000 recreation leaders to provide badly needed recreation activities throughout the nation. Following World War II, as millions of soldiers left the armed forces and Americans moved en masse into suburban housing developments, public recreation accelerated greatly. By the mid-1960s, over 3000 cities and towns throughout the United States had established public recreation and park departments. Instead of programs designed to serve children and youth with a limited number of activities chiefly during vacation periods, these departments now offered to all ages, on a year-round basis, a full range of activities, including physical, cultural, and social programs.

The recreation movement today

The four major types of sponsors of organized recreation services in the United States today are (1) public (governmental) agencies, (2) voluntary (nonprofit) community organizations, (3) private (closed membership) organizations, and (4) commercial (profit-making) organizations. We will examine these in turn.

Public agencies

On every level of government, hundreds of agencies and departments deal with recreation as an important responsibility.

Federal Among federal agencies, for example, the National Park Service and National Forest Service offer outdoor recreation opportunities for millions of vacationing Americans each year. The Bureau of Land Management and Bureau of Indian Affairs operate similar facilities. The Bureau of Outdoor

[3]George D. Butler, *Introduction to Community Recreation.* New York: McGraw-Hill, Inc., 1967, p. 89.

Recreation helps to coordinate such programs, provides subsidies for state and local open-space acquisition, and plans for meeting the nation's outdoor recreation needs.

The Department of Health, Education, and Welfare supports many programs that include recreation, especially for children, youth, and the aging, or the mentally and physically disabled. The Department of Defense provides a network of recreation facilities and programs in each of the armed forces; and numerous other federal agencies, such as the Department of Housing and Urban Development, or other federal departments concerned with the socially disadvantaged, support recreation-related programs and the development of facilities in the nation's cities.

State   Each of the 50 states provides extensive outdoor recreation opportunities for vacationers, including parks for camping and hiking; lakes, reservoirs, and beachfront areas for boating, fishing, and other water sports. State governments also operate many recreation programs directly, in hospitals, youth homes, or special schools, homes for the aged, and penal or correctional institutions.

Through enabling legislation, states influence the development of local recreation and park programs. State funds are combined with federal funds to assist many municipalities in obtaining open space and developing recreation and park facilities. State colleges and universities frequently offer professional training in recreation service and, finally, most states offer financial assistance to local programs, particularly for youth and the aged.

Local government   The major governmental responsibility for providing recreation programs is assumed by local government (county, city, township, village) agencies. Most commonly today, a unified recreation and park department builds, maintains, and staffs playgrounds, parks, athletic fields, and community centers, and operates a diversified recreation program to meet community needs. Such departments are supported primarily through public tax funds, although they may also rely on special grants, gifts, fees, and charges to participants, or income from concessionaires. A summary of the growth of such agencies after World War II is found in Table 16.1.

The functions of local government in recreation and parks include (1) operating facilities, (2) providing programs under leadership, and (3) coordinating and assisting other community organizations, such as voluntary agencies or service clubs, that provide recreation programs.

Table 16.1   Growth of local recreation and park agencies

	1950	1965
Total number of park and recreation agencies reported	2,277	3,152
Personnel: Total full- and part-time paid leadership	58,029	119,515
Personnel: Full-time year-round	6,784	19,208
Total acreage in parks and recreation areas	644,000	1,496,378
Total expenditures (in millions)	$269	$905

Source: Recreation and Park Yearbook, 1966. Washington, D.C.: National Recreation and Park Association, 1967, pp. 41, 44–58.

Voluntary agencies

These agencies include thousands of nongovernmental, nonprofit organizations throughout the nation that have recreation as a significant responsibility. Among the most important are youth-serving organizations, such as Boy Scouts of America, Girl Scouts of the United States of America, Children's Aid Society, Police Athletic League, Boys' Clubs of America, and Camp Fire Girls. Voluntary recreation agencies also are part of religious-affiliated groups, such as the YMCA and YWCA, the YMHA and YWHA, the Catholic Youth Organization, or other denominational youth fellowship groups.

Some voluntary agencies specialize in meeting the needs of the urban poor, for example, settlement houses or antipoverty agencies composed largely of neighborhood residents. Others, usually structured as national federations with local chapters, serve the physically and mentally disabled, including the blind, the orthopedically disabled, the mentally retarded, and those with cerebral palsy and other major disabilities. Still other voluntary organizations have been formed to promote participation within particular fields of recreation, such as sports, hobbies, or cultural activities.

Private organizations

Private organizations sponsoring recreation are country clubs, golf or tennis clubs, or other athletic and social organizations which usually operate their own facilities with a restricted membership. Such groups are numerous; for example, in the early 1960s there were 3300 country clubs in the United States. Such organizations may be privately owned and operated on a money-making basis, but also may be cooperatively owned by their members, with elected boards and officers and paid managers and staff who operate facilities or provide leadership.

Typically, such private organizations serve the upper socioeconomic classes, although increasing numbers of cooperative swimming pools and other recreational facilities have been created in middle-income housing developments. In addition, many industries provide extensive recreation opportunities for their employees.

Commercial recreation

Commercially organized play accounts for the bulk of recreational activity in the United States today. It includes all the leisure services, products, or facilities offered to the general public on a profit-making basis.

Bowling alleys, skating rinks, ski centers, cruise ships, night clubs and taverns, movie houses, and hundreds of other enterprises charge fees for admission, instruction, rental of equipment, or use of areas. Those charges, added to what Americans spend for equipment for leisure purposes, such as television, radio, or hi-fi sets; golf clubs, tennis rackets, skis, snowmobiles, and power boats, total over $125 billion a year. This huge sum makes recreation one of the key industries in the national economy. Tourists visiting the national parks alone spend over $6 billion each year.

Professionalism in recreation service

It is chiefly within public and voluntary agencies that recreation is regarded as a professional area of service. In such agencies, emphasis is placed on hiring professionally qualified leaders, supervisors, and administrators.

In the mid-1960s, there were approximately 65,000 full-time, year-round, and 178,000 seasonal or part-time, recreation and park employees in American city or county recreation departments.[4] Adding the recreation workers in state, federal, and voluntary agencies, and allowing for growth since then, it is probable that between 150,000 and 200,000 persons are employed on a full-time, year-round basis in the field of recreation. Hundreds of thousands are employed in such leisure-related fields as the manufacturing of sports equipment or the operation of travel facilities; however, they are not considered recreation professionals.

Exactly what is a profession? Several criteria are usually used to determine the professional status of various occupations, including:

[4]*Recreation and Park Yearbook, 1966.* Washington, D.C.: National Recreation and Park Association, 1967, pp. 41, 44–58.

1. public awareness and acceptance;
2. specialized higher education;
3. the existence of a body of research and knowledge;
4. standards of selection or admission to professional practice;
5. professional organizations;
6. a professional code of ethics; and
7. a significant occupational contribution to public well-being.

On all of these counts, recreation has rapidly been gaining acceptance as a profession in the United States. Historically, however, people from many diverse backgrounds, such as health and physical education, social work, landscape architecture, civil engineering, or business administration, have entered the recreation field. Consequently, many people still do *not* see the recreation professional as a person with specialized training and qualifications. Often, they have only a superficial understanding of the work performed, partly because of the very diverse roles played by recreation workers. Sessoms wrote:

We would like to be all things to all people: entertainers, promoters, counselors, psychiatrist aides, and social analysts. . . . I am afraid the public sees us either as ex-athletes, or gregarious fun-and-game leaders wearing short pants, knee socks, and an Alpine hat, calling for all to join in.[5]

This misunderstanding is being corrected by the rapid growth of specialized programs of higher education in recreation and in park leadership and administration throughout the United States. Such curricula were introduced in the 1930s and today are offered in about 300 colleges and universities, including approximately 50 community colleges.

Higher education

At the undergraduate level, emphasis is on preparing leaders, supervisors, and administrators for three types of settings:

1. general recreation-program supervision, in public or voluntary agencies;
2. positions in unified recreation and parks departments, with responsibility both for programs and for facilities;
3. positions with a major responsibility for the development, maintenance, and management of outdoor recreation areas and facilities.

[5]H. Douglas Sessoms, "A Critical Look at the Recreation Movement," *Recreation for the Ill and Handicapped.* Washington, D.C.: National Association of Recreation Therapists, July 1965, pp. 11, 14.

319

At the graduate level, a number of specialized options are frequently provided in college recreation curricula. These include the following:

1. program supervision and administration in public and voluntary agencies;
2. over-all recreation and park administration in municipal, county, and state agencies;
3. recreation-resource management, usually for county, state, or federal agencies that operate extensive outdoor facilities and areas;
4. therapeutic recreation supervision and administration;
5. camping administration, with emphasis on nature activities or outdoor education programs;
6. college union administration.

Whereas during the 1950s and early 1960s only about 500 persons a year received degrees in recreation and parks administration, today several thousand receive such degrees each year. In addition to expanded higher education in the field, an effective group of professional organizations have been developed to promote recreation throughout the United States.

Professional organizations

The major professional organization in the field of recreation and parks today is the National Recreation and Park Association. This body was formed in 1965 through a merger of several organizations, including the National Recreation Association, the American Recreation Society, the American Institute of Park Executives, and the National Conference on State Parks. Within a year or two, other groups, such as the National Association of Recreation Therapists, merged with it.

NRPA, as it is commonly known, has the following major functions:

1. It sponsors annual conferences, district meetings, and institutes that stimulate professional efforts and lay support of the recreation movement.
2. It publishes numerous periodicals, management handbooks, and research reports to upgrade professional performance in recreation and parks.
3. It sponsors or stimulates research, independently or in cooperation with governmental agencies.
4. It serves as a major spokesman for recreation and leisure needs, and promotes or supports legislative and other governmental action with respect to recreation and open space.
5. It is instrumental in defining standards for recreation and park facilities, services, and personnel.
6. It offers field services to thousands of agencies, governmental bodies, or other institutions throughout the United States and abroad.

The specialized interests of members of NRPA are served by affiliation with separate branches of its professional division. For example, municipal or county recreation and park administrators normally belong to the American Park and Recreation Society; college professors, to the Society for Park and Recreation Educators; and those working with the disabled, to the National Therapeutic Recreation Society.

Other national organizations also play an important role in recreation in the United States. For example, the American Alliance for Health, Physical Education, and Recreation (AAPHER) effectively promotes the role of schools and colleges in sponsoring or cosponsoring recreation programs, in making facilities available to other community agencies, and in providing education for leisure. AAPHER actively supports outdoor education and camping, lifetime sports, aquatics, and dance—all important elements in many recreation programs. Like NRPA, it sponsors research in the field and publishes numerous reports on recreation and leisure. Also active are the American Camping Association, the Association of College Unions—International, the National Association of Social Workers, the National Industrial Recreation Association, the Society of State Directors of Health, Physical Education and Recreation, and the Athletic Institute.

Personnel practices in recreation and parks

Employment in public and voluntary recreation agencies today is normally categorized on three levels of responsibility: administrative, supervisory, and leadership.

Administrative positions

The title of the highest executive positions in recreation and park agencies is superintendent, commissioner, director, or general manager. In extremely large cities, deputy administrators or major division heads are also executive employees. Where professional standards prevail, such positions require college degrees or in some cases graduate degrees, specialization in the field, as well as a minimum of several years of professional experience in recreation, supervision and administration. However, it is fairly common for top administrators in city government to be political appointees, rather than civil servants. Many superintendents or commissioners of recreation and parks in American cities, therefore, have less specialized background in the field than do their subordinates.

Recreation and park administrators have the following typical responsibilities:

1. planning, organizing, and carrying out a total program of recreation and park services within a community;
2. recruiting, hiring, training, supervising, and evaluating staff members on various levels;
3. preparing, presenting, and carrying out annual budgets for their department, usually in cooperation with other fiscal officers or departments;
4. planning, acquiring, designing, building, and maintaining a network of recreation and park facilities;
5. working closely with an elected or appointed board, commission, or advisory body, and maintaining good working relationships with other municipal or governmental officials;
6. carrying on an effective public relations program to involve the community in planning and policy making.

Recreation and park administrators work closely with municipal specialists in each area of responsibility. For example, they would have the assistance of landscape architects, civil engineers, and other specialists, in designing parks, playgrounds, or other outdoor recreation facilities. In very large city or county departments, deputy administrators or divisional or department heads assume responsibility for personnel management or budget development. In smaller agencies, the executives themselves are likely to be directly responsible for such functions.

Supervisory positions

The secondary line of management responsibility in recreation and park departments is also at the professional level and normally requires college training and previous experience. Supervisors are generally assigned two major types of responsibilities: area supervision and program supervision.

The area supervisor customarily is in charge of a large district or geographical area of the city or county in which he is employed. Typically, in a city of 50,000 to 100,000 population, there might be three or four such areas. Within each district, the supervisor represents the chief administrative officer, who has a major responsibility for personnel management, developing and carrying on programs, making budget requests, supervising the expenditure of funds, overseeing the maintenance of facilities and equipment, and carrying on public relations activities. Within each of these functions, supervisors may make many routine decisions on their own, but refer major decisions or matters of policy to the department head. The title of supervisor is also sometimes given to the individual in charge of a large community center, sports complex, or other special facility, such as a nature museum, a stadium, or a major park.

Program supervisors are usually assigned department-wide responsibility for the activities of a special program area or special population. They would coordinate activities throughout the city in such special areas as arts and crafts, performing arts, aquatics, girls' and women's sports, programs for the physically and mentally disabled, golden age clubs, or similar areas. This might involve planning schedules and special events, teaching some classes themselves, providing clinics in leadership training for others, assisting in the development of facilities, or whatever else is required to make the program area successful.

Leadership positions

Recreation leaders are directly responsible for actually providing programs and guiding participants of all ages in a variety of recreation activities. Although some leadership positions are held today by college-trained personnel, the bulk of them in many community recreation agencies are held by part-time or seasonal workers.

In some settings, paraprofessionals without college training are employed to direct activities and work with groups. In others, heavy reliance is placed on graduates of two-year community colleges. In still others, most activities are led by part-time employees, including school teachers, college students, or others with special skills, who work in recreation positions during the late afternoon or evening and are paid by the session or on an hourly basis.

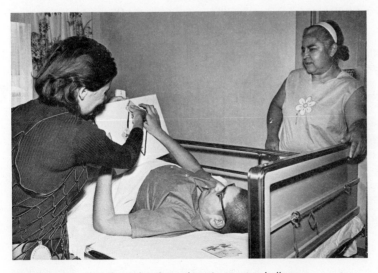

Hospital recreation therapist shows how to score a ballgame

Many municipal recreation departments categorize leaders by status and responsibility. Thus, *Leader I* may be a high-school graduate, who acts as a recreation aide under supervision. *Leader II* may hold a two-year degree, and be responsible for direct leadership in a small playground or a community center program. *Leader III* may need a college degree to be in charge of a larger playground, community center, or other recreation facility. Other settings may similarly differentiate levels of leadership: a hospital recreation department, for example, might have *Recreation Therapist I, II,* and *III.*

Subprofessional positions

Subprofessional positions, a fourth level of employment in recreation and parks departments, are usually recreation *attendants, aides, interns,* or *assistants.* They may have specific responsibilities for equipment, transportation, or other areas of leadership, or may simply assist in the conduct of recreation programs. Many urban recreation departments have established such positions in recent years and, through work-study programs, enable subprofessionals to continue college study and move up to professional levels of employment.

Employment standards

As indicated earlier, many persons with varied backgrounds have been employed in recreation in the past and continue to hold key positions today. There are three basic reasons for this:

1. Recreational participation is so widespread in our society that individuals with advanced skills in sports and games or the arts have often found jobs as recreation leaders.
2. The comparatively few graduates of college programs in recreation and parks did not fill the need, leading to the employment of persons trained in other fields.
3. Employment standards in public or voluntary agencies have been loosely defined and administered.

Today, the screening of applicants for positions in recreation and park departments is usually through (1) civil service procedures, (2) certification, or (3) registration.

Civil service represents the most common method of screening and categorizing public employees in the United States today. In the majority of federal, state, or local recreation and park departments, including recreation services in hospitals, correctional institutions, and the armed forces, civil service defines educational or experience-based job requirements. In addition, it customarily also prepares and administers examinations to screen applicants for entry-level positions or for promotion.

Through certification, an individual who meets the requirements for professional employment in a given field is examined and approved, usually by an appropriate state agency. However, unlike the situation in law, medicine, teaching, or health-related fields such as physical therapy or occupational therapy, formal certification in recreation has thus far been established in only two states.

Registration identifies qualified applicants within professional fields through national or state professional societies. Such organizations' personnel codes and voluntary registration procedures serve as the basis for awarding registration for professional employment on specified levels of responsibility. A considerable number of state societies have developed such procedures for employment in recreation and parks.

Recreation programs

At the heart of all professional recreation service is the need to develop interesting, varied, and constructive leisure opportunities to serve the public at large. This responsibility, the "program" function, comprises three major categories.

Provision of facilities

Recreation and park departments must provide a broad network of parks, playgrounds, and other facilities for unsupervised and unstructured public use. This can range from casual family enjoyment of picnic grounds to areas requiring a permit or a schedule, as for public ballfields, golf courses, or tennis courts.

Provision of organized programs

Local public recreation and park departments provide a variety of organized or structured program opportunities. These include vacation day camps; sports clinics and leagues organized by the department itself; instruction or special interest groups in music, dance, drama, arts and crafts, or other hobbies; senior center programs and other types of social clubs; special events, and similar activities under direct leadership.

Coordination of community programs

Municipal or county recreation and park departments also have a broad responsibility for promoting and assisting recreation on a community-wide basis. They help to publicize the need for effective recreation programs and meaningful planning to meet leisure needs. They work with other organizations that offer recreation programs, lending equipment or providing skilled leadership, conducting training clinics, consulting on program development or facilities design, and coordinating schedules.

Categories of program activities

The major program activities sponsored by community recreation agencies fall under the following headings: active sports and games, aquatics, outdoor recreation, arts and crafts, performing arts, hobbies, services for the disabled, mental and linguistic activities, social programs, special events, trips and outings, and service activities. In general, whether in a playground, a community center building, an after-school center, or other facility, these are the primary activities provided.

Active sports and games Recreation departments sponsor clinics or instructional classes, tournaments and league play, coaching or officiating courses, displays or field days, and free play in many sports and games. The activities themselves include *individual* or *dual sports,* such as golf, tennis, or fencing; *team sports* like volleyball, basketball, baseball, football, soccer, hockey, or track and field; *combatives* like boxing, wrestling, judo, and karate; *conditioning* or individual-skill activities like gymnastics, physical fitness classes, or stunts and tumbling; *lead-up games* like dodge ball, longball, kickball, or tag games, and relays; and *equipment games* for indoor or outdoor play, such as croquet, darts, billiards, horseshoes, shuffleboard, chess, or checkers.

Aquatics Although water-based recreation might be regarded both as a form of sport or as an outdoor recreation activity, it is of such major interest that it is often administered as a separate program division. It includes swimming, diving, fishing, life-saving and water-safety instruction, and sailboat classes and competition. Aquatic activities may provide instruction in basic or advanced skills, leadership training, competition, or informal participation.

Outdoor recreation Outdoor recreation activities are those which emphasize the natural environment. Among the most popular are camping, fishing, gardening, hiking, hunting, ice skating, mountaineering, nature projects, outdoor cooking, skiing, and target shooting.

Arts and crafts A wide range of activities suitable for all age groups. Some are primarily creative or aesthetic, like drawing, watercolor or oil painting, or sculpture. Others, such as furniture refinishing, metalcraft, or weaving, are geared to utilitarian purposes. Frequently, such crafts as ceramics, jewelry making, or leatherwork both create useful objects and involve a high degree of artistic creativity. Arts and crafts activities may range from the simplest projects,

Fishing contest in a municipal park

like finger painting for very young children, to highly advanced skills for adult artists and craftsmen.

Art fair sponsored by a recreation department

Performing arts Music, drama, and dance have become increasingly popular forms of involvement. *Music* may include informal folk singing, rhythm bands, or rock-and-roll groups, or extend to ambitious choral, operatic, band, or orchestral programs. *Drama* involves simple charades, puppetry, or dramatic games for young children, and may go as far as full-fledged, theater-production organizations for teenagers and adults. *Dance* frequently includes modern dance and ballet, as well as the more social forms of dance, like ballroom, folk, and square dancing. For younger children, children's rhythms and creative dance are usually stressed. In each of these forms of activity, recreation departments may provide both instruction and the opportunity to perform before audiences.

Hobbies In community centers, youth or adult clubs, or on summer playgrounds, hobbies may be presented, either for individuals or special-interest groups. For example, collectors may swap coins, stamps, autographs, or other interesting items. Hobbies also include construction activities, such as building model airplanes, boats, cars, kites, railroads, or antique furniture, or restoring and collecting automobiles. Frequently, recreation departments sponsor hobby shows to encourage such interests.

Services for the disabled Most community recreation and park departments as well as many voluntary agencies recognize the need to provide programs for the mentally or physically disabled. These are the mentally retarded, discharged psychiatric patients, or those receiving day care while living in the community, the orthopedically disabled, the blind, the deaf, confined aged persons, and those with other disabilities such as cerebral palsy or muscular dystrophy. When possible, recreation administrators seek to involve disabled persons in ongoing activities with the able-bodied, removing any physical or architectural barriers to participation (such as steps making it difficult for a person in a wheelchair to enter a community center). When this is not feasible, many departments sponsor special group activities for disabled persons.

Mental and linguistic activities Cultural or intellectual activities, such as book clubs, discussions of current events, creative writing classes or clinics, or, on a simpler level, mental games, quizzes, puzzles, and paper and pencil games are also promoted. In institutions such as Veterans Administration hospitals, patients are involved in publishing newspapers or magazines, or operating hospital radio programs. In schools and colleges, extracurricular clubs may include science, mathematics, and other cultural and intellectual interests.

Social programs Community recreation departments often sponsor social clubs or organizations that serve special segments of the population, such as teenagers, families, adult couples, unmarried persons, and the aging. Typically, most public recreation and park departments sponsor or assist golden age clubs or senior centers, in which aging persons may find friendship, creative interests, and the opportunity for continuing social involvement.

Special events Community centers and playgrounds often schedule such special events as parties, dances, family get-togethers, barbecues and potluck suppers, talent shows or exhibitions. In addition, they may plan and organize community-wide celebrations on Christmas, Halloween, and the Fourth of July, or commemorations of local or state historical events. Such celebrations usually involve band concerts, firework displays, parades, and pageants, which attract

329

large audiences and stimulate community awareness and cohesion. Customarily, recreation and park departments work closely with civic groups and service clubs in organizing such special events.

Trips and outings Most summer playground programs schedule weekly trips and outings to nearby lakes, beaches, state parks, historic sites, and museums. In some cases, recreation directors may even plan charter flights for teenagers and adults on a more expensive and elaborate basis; some communities have sponsored vacation trips to Hawaii or foreign countries. An increasing number of municipal recreation and park departments now operate summer and year-round camps at a distance from their communities, scheduling outings of residents to these camps.

Service activities An important component of the program of many community recreation departments is providing residents an opportunity to volunteer for public service activities. This may include working with children in community centers or playgrounds, managing or coaching sports teams, providing instruction in special classes, or working in Big Brother or tutorial programs. Frequently, residents work with the homebound in institutions, or with other groups of disabled persons with special recreation needs. Transportation, for example, is an important problem in such programs, and requires considerable volunteer assistance. While such service activities are a means of solving staffing problems for recreation departments, they also should be regarded as meeting the leisure needs of residents in a constructive and personally enriching way.

In general, public recreation and park departments tend to offer a high proportion of free-play activities, large-group events, sports participation, and outdoor recreation. In contrast, voluntary agencies like Boys' Clubs or YMCA's usually sponsor more club activities, small-group programs, and organized indoor activities under direct leadership.

Principles for the organization of recreation programs

The actual programming of recreation activities and events is carried on in a variety of ways. Activities are usually seasonal, geared to climatic factors that compel indoor or outdoor programming. The activities selected should reflect the needs and interests of participants as determined through surveys, suggestions made to the staff, neighborhood councils or community advisory groups, and similar means. They may also reflect current practices and trends in the recreation field; the recreation administrator and his staff should be alert to new interests and innovative programs in other communities.

Some guidelines for the development of community recreation programs are:

1. Community recreation should serve all citizens, without discrimination based on age, sex, race, religion, or socioeconomic class.
2. Community recreation should meet the significant needs and interests of participants, and make a constructive contribution to societal well-being.
3. Community recreation should include a wide range of activities, providing diversity, balance, and the opportunity to participate at varied levels of skill.
4. Special groups in the community, such as the mentally or physically disabled, should be served by community recreation programs.
5. Recreation programs should be flexibly scheduled throughout the week, season, or year, to permit maximum participation at all times.
6. Recreation programs should make the fullest possible use of all community resources, including, by cooperative arrangement, facilities owned by private, voluntary, commercial, or other public agencies (such as schools or colleges).
7. Recreation programs should be administered and supervised by qualified professionals, although direct leadership may be provided by part-time, seasonal, subprofessional, or volunteer workers.
8. Recreation programs should be meaningfully interpreted to the community at large, through newspapers, posters, radio or television, and meetings, open houses, or tours. Whenever possible, community representatives should play a positive role in planning programs.

Although all groups should be served by public recreation and park departments, this does not mean that they are all to be involved in exactly comparable programs. For example, a well-to-do suburban community whose residents, for the most part, own their own homes with extensive properties and private recreation resources, has little need for picnic areas or neighborhood playgrounds. Instead, the public recreation and park department might concentrate on offering such facilities as golf courses, tennis courts, marinas, sportsmen's centers, or such activities as arts and crafts workshops, and performing arts groups.

In contrast, recreation departments in disadvantaged urban areas would stress basic recreation facilities and programs, as well as purposeful, socially oriented activities. These might include projects stressing vocational orientation and job opportunities for teenagers and young adults, preschool and day care programs, drug or health counseling, family activities, and similar programs intended to promote the social well-being and group cohesion of community residents. Because of their close contact with urban youth and the appeal they hold for them through their sports and other programs, recreation and park departments are often in the best position of all city agencies to provide socially oriented activities of this type.

Similarly, many local recreation departments have taken major responsibility for sponsoring antipollution or environmental protection projects, such as cleanup or recycling campaigns or area restoration programs. In many communities, recreation administrators are able to undertake such efforts because:

1. They have a major responsibility for the protection of the natural environment, since they must maintain many city-owned open spaces.
2. They possess the men, machines, and technical expertness to carry on ecology-related projects.
3. They have already established good working relationships with community service clubs or youth organizations.

Thus, in addition to program activities that are clearly play-oriented, recreation and park departments often assume other responsibilities that make a significant contribution to community life.

Program development in other settings

In industrial, military, or therapeutic recreation agencies, somewhat different sets of goals may prevail. For example, the goals of recreational therapy in a psychiatric hospital would encompass the following:

1. To help psychiatric patients become involved in real situations and to relate effectively to others.
2. To improve the self-concept of patients, by giving them the opportunity to interact with others, thus gaining a sense of accomplishment and success.
3. To provide emotional release and the opportunity to express hostility, aggression, or other bottled-up drives in socially acceptable ways.
4. To provide information useful for diagnosis of the patient's needs and to contribute to the over-all treatment process.
5. To help patients become aware of their leisure needs (typically, many mentally ill persons have extremely limited recreational interests and resources) and to provide them with skills that will be useful in community life, after discharge from the hospital.

Recreation activities in psychiatric hospitals should not simply stress the enjoyment of leisure time, but should also place emphasis on strengthening the self-concepts of patients, compelling them to come to grips with real situations, gaining group acceptance, and building ties to community groups and activities, as part of the total rehabilitative effort. Similarly, in such institutions as special schools for the mentally retarded, recreation programs should make a strong effort to help residents who are "community candidates" (those who have the potential for independent or semi-independent living in the community) gain the social skills that will help them avoid isolation and live happily away from the institution.

Recreation and park facilities

As indicated earlier, one of the major responsibilities of public recreation and park departments is to acquire, construct, and maintain a network of facilities and areas for recreational participation. These normally include the following:

tot-lots (small playgrounds for preschool children)
larger playgrounds for elementary school-age children
small neighborhood parks (vest-pocket parks)
larger community parks
aquatic facilities (pools, beaches, lakes, ponds)
community center buildings
sports complexes (ballfields, tennis courts, handball courts, or tracks)
golf courses

Vest-pocket park in downtown Detroit

marinas and other boating facilities
nature centers or natural science museums, which may be used for
    conservation-oriented programs
sportsmen's centers, for target shooting, archery, and similar activities
arts and crafts centers and workshops
centers for the performing arts
stadiums and civic auditoriums
reservations, or large outdoor areas kept in a primarily natural state

Customarily, smaller communities are limited to the operation of such basic facilities as small parks, playgrounds, community centers, pools, or limited athletic areas. Larger communities, as well as township, county, or park and recreation districts, are likely to provide major facilities, such as large parks, stadiums, or centers for more specialized activities, to meet the needs of larger and more diverse population groups.

The acquisition and planning of recreation facilities are usually based on standards developed in recent decades by the National Recreation and Park Association and its predecessors or by other national bodies concerned with municipal government.

Standards for areas and facilities

The most widely applied standard for recreation and park development has been the recommendation, supported by the International City Managers Association and similar organizations, that each city should have at least 10 acres of permanent, publicly owned, open space for every 1000 residents. This standard has been modified on practical grounds by the American Society of Planning Officials, which recommended 10 acres for each 2000 residents in cities of over 500,000, and 10 acres for each 3000 in cities of over 1 million.

Recent recommendations have taken into account the availability of open space provided by other levels of government. For example, in 1965 the National Recreation and Park Association urged local governments to provide 10 acres for each 1000 residents, and adjacent county or state park agencies to provide 15 acres for each 1000 residents, within one hour's travel time from the local area. Other facilities-planning standards have been based on a percentage of land area devoted to recreation and parks, and recommend that 10 percent of a community's total area should be so utilized. Still another formula, the ''service radius'' concept, recommends that playgrounds be available between one-quarter and one-half mile, athletic playfields between one-half and one mile, and large parks, between one and three miles distance from all community residents.

Finally, the need for specific types of facilities has been defined in terms of population numbers. Typical recommendations were:

Facility	To serve recommended population
Neighborhood playgrounds	1 acre per 800 population
Baseball diamonds	1 per 6000 population
Tennis courts	1 per 2000 population
Golf courses (18 hole)	1 per 25,000 population
Field houses	1 per 15,000 population
Community centers	1 per 25,000 population

In addition, professional organizations have developed precise standards for each type of facility as to the number of persons to be served at a given time, the appropriate age levels of participants, the size of the facility, and the types of equipment or structures that should be provided. Typically, the following guidelines have been developed for *neighborhood playgrounds:*

1. They should primarily serve children and youth between the ages of 6 and 15, with limited opportunities for older youth and adults.
2. They should range in size from about 4.5 to about 7.5 acres, and should be located within a one-quarter-mile radius of each home in heavily crowded neighborhoods, and a one-half-mile radius of each home in less dense areas.
3. They should include the following equipment: play apparatus (slides, swings, and so forth), a wading pool, a shaded quiet area with benches and a sandbox, multiple-use games areas, a small building with storage space, lavatories, an office for the playground director, and sometimes an indoor room that can be used for activities.

Today, it is recognized that such uniform standards or guidelines are not applicable to all communities. Space standards, for example, are somewhat arbitrary and do not take into account the needs and capabilities of individual communities, in terms of population density and growth projections, available public funds, and the mobility of residents. Thus, they serve only as general guidelines for recreation and park planning. Similarly, the standardized, "boiler-plate" designs formerly used in planning recreation facilities are no longer widely accepted. Playgrounds, in particular, have moved away from standardized designs; a number of leading architects have developed unusual designs for "adventure" or "creative" playgrounds that stress exploratory learning and varied forms of self-motivated play.

In the development of new types of recreation facilities, technology has played a major role. For example, year-round ice-skating rinks, swimming pools under removable bubbles (air-supported structures), artificial toboggan slides or ski slopes, and swimming pools with artificial surf are being constructed by increasing numbers of local recreation and park departments. In addition to acquiring properties and designing facilities, the construction and maintenance processes are major concerns of recreation and park professionals (see Suggested Readings for further material).

Fiscal support of community recreation

The basic sources of funding for community recreation and park facilities and programs are taxes, bond issues, fees and charges, income from concessions, government grants, and other gifts or bequests.

It has been estimated that over 90 percent of the annual budget of municipal and county recreation and park departments is derived from local tax revenues. Taxes fall into four categories: general, special, millage, and special assessment. *General taxes* are paid into the public treasury, and consist chiefly of real estate taxes; they support all public services, such as police, schools, sanitation, and highways. *Special taxes* are often used in special park districts, and may be imposed on liquor sales, amusement admissions, or motorboat sales; in some cases, they are directly assigned to the support of public recreation programs. *Millage taxes* represent an extremely low tax (usually expressed in mills) on real estate, which is assigned to the support of recreation and parks. In some states, such as California, millage taxes are authorized by the state education code to support school recreation, or other community service programs. Finally, *special assessment taxes* may be levied on residents within a particular district or locality, to support construction of recreation programs or facilities serving that area of the city.

Bond issues are commonly used to support major capital programs of recreation and park facility development. Typically, substantial bond issues are floated to acquire large properties for the development of major parks, stadiums, golf courses, or other large-scale facilities. They represent a form of deferred payment, in which the cost of acquiring and developing properties is paid over a period of time from general tax revenues, or the specific income derived from the use of facilities by the public.

Fees and charges are a growing means of supporting public recreation and park programs. Particularly in well-to-do communities and suburban areas, substantial fees are charged for admission to recreation areas, use of equipment or property, licenses and permits, or special services, such as course instruction charges or entry fees in league competitions. There has been considerable resistance to the expansion of fees and charges in public recreation, since it is a form of double taxation and tends to exclude economically disadvantaged residents. Nevertheless, many recreation administrators have come to rely increasingly on such revenue sources. Income from concessions—refreshment services, operation of amusement areas, riding stables, or similar facilities in public parks, golf "pro" shops, and similar businesses—is also a rapidly growing source of funding for recreation and park departments.

Government grants have provided considerable financial assistance for public recreation and park programs in recent years. The federal government has spent hundreds of millions of dollars to subsidize state and local acquisition of open space and park properties, through the Land and Water Conservation fund. Other federal agencies, such as the Office of Economic Opportunity, the Department of Housing and Urban Development, and the Labor and Agriculture Departments, have given special grants to assist urban recreation programs particularly for disadvantaged populations.

Finally, a number of foundations and large business concerns have given special grants to assist recreation departments in sponsoring special events, programs that serve the disabled, or other experimental projects. As an example, the Joseph P. Kennedy, Jr., Foundation has assisted many recreation departments in initiating sports and fitness programs for mentally retarded children and youth.

Voluntary community organizations, such as the Boys' Clubs of America or the Young Men's and Young Women's Christian Associations, usually have a different pattern of budgetary support. Since they are not granted tax funds to support their annual budgets, they rely heavily on membership charges, fees from classes and program activities, and fund-raising drives, including grants from Community Chest funds and contributions from private donors, to support their programs.

Recreation leadership

At the heart of all successful community recreation programs is the leader. Although administrators, supervisors, and other high-level personnel are essential to the smooth operation of recreation and park departments, it is obviously the leader who is responsible for the day-by-day conduct of recreation programs. Certain qualities may be identified as crucial to the success of recreation leaders.

Leaders must like people, get along well with them, and be able to elicit their best efforts.

They should have a great amount of patience, a good sense of humor, and the ability to meet and communicate with people on various levels of society.

They should have the skills needed to present activities, such as games, sports, arts and crafts, music, and drama, or to direct assistant leaders in such areas.

They should have a clear vision of the importance of recreation in the lives of those they serve, and in promoting community well-being.

They should possess initiative and imagination, and be innovative in interesting participants and involving them in programs.

It is important to recognize that the effective recreation leader is more than a teacher of activities. In working with children or youth, leaders may serve as teachers, and also as counselors, role-models, disciplinarians, spokesmen, and as a channel to adult authorities within the community. When they work with groups of other professionals in planning programs or with residents in developing recreation projects, they should be skilled in group dynamics and sensitive to the needs and reactions of others.

Some suggest that leaders should play a strongly authoritarian role, if others are to follow and trust them. On the other hand, some argue that the leader should play a highly permissive or nondirective role, encouraging members of the group to develop their own ideas and leadership skills.

Persuasive research in the field of group leadership has revealed, however, that effective leaders tend not to be *dictatorial* (authoritarian) or *laissez-faire* (permissive). Instead, they are *democratic;* they encourage group members to grow in responsible behavior, to learn democratic values, to develop their own ideas, and take responsibility for group activities. Instead of playing a passive role, the leader offers advice, gives assistance, helps group members share in decision making, and resolves conflicts.

Leadership functions

Obviously, the specific functions of recreation leaders vary according to the setting in which they are employed. For example, summer playground leaders must:

1. Get to know children as individuals, and develop constructive relationships with them.
2. Organize total programs of varied activity to meet the needs and interests of varied age groups.
3. Teach games, arts and crafts, sports, music, or similar activities, and provide supervision for self-directed activities.
4. Oversee the use and condition of facilities and equipment, and lend equipment for individual or group participation.

5. Maintain safety on the playground by enforcing safety rules and eliminating various types of hazards.
6. Maintain appropriate behavior on the playground, including a sense of regard for the well-being of others, and prevent undesirable forms of play, such as gambling, vandalism, or rowdyism.
7. Organize special events, trips and outings, or culminating activities, to keep interest in the program high.
8. Keep accurate records of attendance and participation, and prepare reports as required by supervisors.
9. Develop sound relations with parents and other community residents, and carry out an effective public relations program to promote interest in the playground.
10. Cooperate with other members of the recreation department and with representatives of other municipal agencies, such as policemen, youth workers, or school administrators.

On the other hand, the leader in a *golden age club,* which serves retired men and women in the community, might have a somewhat different set of responsibilities:

1. Plan and carry out a total program of daily activities, such as arts and crafts, quiet games, hobbies, music and dancing, group discussions, and refreshment.
2. Plan and organize special events, such as trips and outings, monthly parties, guest speakers and entertainment, and similar programs.
3. Develop publicity materials and news releases, and visit neighborhood churches, housing projects, and other organizations, in order to recruit additional members for the club.
4. Recruit and work with volunteers who assist in the program, screen and train them, supervise their work, and coordinate their total contribution.
5. Plan transportation services, with the help of volunteers or service clubs, to help senior citizens get to the center or other needed agencies and services.
6. Work with community groups in fund-raising projects, such as theater parties, bazaars, cake sales, and raffles, to provide financial support for the center.

Thus, in different kinds of situations, recreation leaders are faced with varied kinds of responsibilities. The most successful leaders are generally those who are imaginative, forceful, and vigorous. At the same time, they must be sensitive to those they serve and to their coworkers. It has been said that the most effective leaders are not those who seek the "spotlight," but rather those who are "enablers," helping others achieve their fullest potential.

Supervisory process in leadership

A key element in all community recreation programs is supervision. Since so many persons employed in this field are part-time, seasonal, or volunteer workers with little specific training in recreation, it is essential that they be given consistent, helpful guidance by qualified professionals. This personnel guidance includes (1) orientation of new workers; (2) in-service training; and (3) on-the-job supervision.

Orientation

When new workers are employed in a recreation agency, either public or voluntary, they should be carefully introduced to the agency, its goals, its operational procedures, and their own responsibilities.

As an initial step, new employees might be given a tour of the department, to view different facilities, meet unit supervisors or division chiefs, and observe programs in action. They should be given a detailed manual of policies and guidelines outlining departmental objectives, rules, and procedures. They should also be carefully briefed on their job responsibilities, particularly those related to control and discipline, handling of funds, and accident-prevention and first aid.

In-service education

As staff members function over a period of time, they should receive regular in-service training designed to improve their skills and make the over-all program more effective. Such staff development efforts may take the following forms:

Recreation leaders train in jazz dancing

1. *Preseason workshops.* In many recreation and park departments, particularly those in large cities or major county or township programs, it is customary to provide two- or three-day special training workshops at the beginning of the summer playground program or before other seasonal programs get under way. These frequently include orientation, scheduling procedures, analysis of common problems, guidelines for safety, and activity demonstrations.
2. *Special clinics in activity skills.* To upgrade the leadership skills of all staff members, some departments regularly sponsor clinics or workshops in such skills as sports coaching, officiating, folk and square dancing, nature activities, or arts and crafts. Customarily, these are intensive one-day or half-day sessions, directed by specialists in the areas concerned. During the course of a year, several such workshops might be sponsored by a single department, thus ensuring that staff workers are regularly upgraded in leadership skills.
3. *In-service courses.* Other departments sponsor weekly courses to deal with practical aspects of the leader's work, including such areas as facilities, maintenance, or first aid and safety, or with broader concerns such as community relations or methods of working with youth gangs.
4. *Team approaches.* A final approach to in-service training consists of organizing personnel teams who develop special projects or constitute task forces for problem solving. Such experiences are extremely helpful in motivating workers to improve their programs and in giving them a sense of involvement in departmental decision making.

In each of these types of in-service education, employee participation may be voluntary or required, usually depending on whether or not the sessions are held during working hours. Often, attendance and performance in training sessions may be made the basis for personnel ratings that go into employee folders.

On-the-job supervision

Generally, recreation supervisors have a continuing responsibility for working closely with recreation leaders, assisting and advising them, making sure that they are putting forward their best efforts, helping them solve problems, and evaluating them for promotion, job transfer, or, when necessary, disciplinary action or job termination.

In the past, supervision was thought of as threatening and autocratic. Supervisors were regarded as foremen or overseers, who rewarded or punished in order to ensure maximum worker productivity. Today, in line with enlightened personnel policies based on sound human relations that prevail in many business concerns or public agencies, supervisors are encouraged to play much more understanding and sympathetic roles.

Challenge of recreation leadership

College students who are considering possible specialization in recreation should recognize that this field is extremely diversified. Depending on the particular situation, the recreation leader may be working with children, youth, adults, or aging persons. Participants may be healthy and function effectively in most respects, or may suffer from a degree of physical, mental, or social disability. The leader's task is usually not just to coach sports, teach games, or direct other activities. As he advances to supervisory or administrative levels of responsibility, it is his job to direct other individuals, to assist in the planning, design, and maintenance of facilities, to work with community groups to develop their interest and support, to cooperate closely with those in other departments or disciplines, and to carry on a variety of other functions.

Rarely routine or boring, the job of the recreation leader demands great physical and emotional output, as well as long hours or irregular schedules. However, recreation leadership can also be extremely rewarding for the person who is innovative, likes to work with people, and has a vision of the importance of recreation as a vital force in modern life.

The school's role in recreation

Our final concern is the appropriate role of the schools in recreation, and the specific relationship between recreation and physical education.

Historically, the public school was one of the first sponsors of organized community recreation programs, in the form of after-school and summer-vacation programs. During the early decades of the 1900s, a substantial number of municipal recreation programs throughout the United States were conducted by public school administrators. Many teachers took courses in play leadership and playground organization, and it was widely assumed that recreation sponsorship was an appropriate task of the public schools. Those in favor of this arrangement offered the following arguments.

Arguments for school sponsorship of recreation

1. Recreation is closely linked to education, and play can be used to promote and enrich many academic areas of study. A well-known English educator, L. P. Jacks, wrote, "The education which is not also recreation is a maimed, incomplete, half-done thing. The recreation which is not education has no re-creative value."[6]

[6]Lawrence Pearsall Jacks, *Education through Recreation.* New York: Harper & Row, Publishers, 1932, p. 2.

As a consequence, particularly during the so-called "progressive" era of American education, playlike activities were stressed in elementary school education, and recreation programs were seen as a legitimate responsibility of education.

2. Schools possess major networks of facilities, including gymnasiums, meeting rooms, swimming pools, and music and art rooms. These resources should be used to their fullest throughout the year; it would be financially wasteful for each community to build a second set of facilities for recreational use.

3. Teachers are well equipped by training for work with children and youth, and have many useful recreation-leadership skills.

4. The schools have the prestige and community status needed to support recreation as a vital community service and to give it stability and financial support as part of a total framework of youth service.

5. Finally, the "community school" concept, introduced in the 1920s and 1930s, stressed that the school should play a significant role in community life by providing a base for important community-improvement or social-action programs. Recreation was viewed as one such area of social concern.

Many of the same points were argued in reverse. Those who opposed the school's playing a role in recreation sponsorship offered the following arguments.

Arguments against school sponsorship of recreation

1. Although they have certain purposes in common, education and recreation are distinctly separate disciplines, each with its own set of objectives and methods. The primary responsibility of the schools is education, not recreation.

2. While schools possess many facilities useful for recreation, these tend to be used exclusively for regular classes during the day, and therefore are not available until late afternoon for groups, such as the aging or the disabled, with daytime program needs. Further, school districts do not operate other types of resources, such as large parks, golf courses, or marinas, that are essential for well-rounded recreation programs.

3. Although teachers are knowledgeable about child development and may have certain recreation-leadership skills, they tend not to be recreation-oriented, and to lack both training in recreation and a respect for recreation as a major professional objective.

4. In the late 1950s and 1960s, many school systems, under considerable financial pressure when their budgets were voted down, tended to cut the nonacademic areas of their programs. Thus, it was argued, recreation would be best served as a separate, independent agency in municipal government.

5. The "community school" approach, although it included recreation as an important element, has been accepted and supported only in a few states and cities. Schools tend to be somewhat cut off from other community agencies, and school administrators do not cooperate as fully as recreation directors must in team efforts to meet community needs.

As recreation and park departments gained fuller support in American towns and cities, and as recreation became a more specialized professional area of service, public schools tended to give up the recreation-sponsorship function. In the early 1960s a high proportion of the school systems that continued to sponsor recreation concentrated on serving children and youth in after-school and summer-vacation programs. Although some cities, such as Los Angeles and Milwaukee, offered diversified recreation programs serving all ages throughout the year, many others provided only limited activities. They tended to assign recreation responsibilities to teachers who accepted them on a part-time basis and who lacked training and special interest in the field.

As a consequence, in recent years fewer and fewer school systems have been the community agency chiefly responsible for recreation. However, it is clear that schools should continue to carry out certain major responsibilities in recreation and leisure. These include the following:

1. partial sponsorship of recreation programs;
2. cosponsorship of recreation;
3. cooperation with other community agencies;
4. education for leisure.

Partial sponsorship In a number of cities throughout the United States, public school systems continue to sponsor recreation programs, operating side by side with municipal recreation and park departments that offer other services. For example, schools may concentrate on providing activities for children and youth in such areas as music, art, dance, dramatics, or sports. They may also assume responsibility for adult-education activities that include leisure interests and skills. On the other hand, municipal recreation departments tend to offer a wide range of outdoor recreation activities, making use of their special facilities. If school administrators wish to undertake such responsibilities, it is essential that they support them adequately by hiring well-trained staff members, assigning sufficient funds, and making available, or constructing, facilities to meet the needs of varied groups during the school day as well as at other appropriate times.

Cosponsorship of recreation In some communities, school boards have contracted with municipal recreation and park departments to provide jointly sponsored recreation programs. Such agreements usually specify the amount of money to be provided annually by each department as well as the specific areas of program responsibility. There may also be contractual arrangements for the reciprocal use of facilities, interchange of staff members, and shared maintenance of indoor and outdoor facilities at different times of the year. In an increasing number of cities, agreements have been reached for constructing new park-school complexes or other special facilities that are used to their maximum for both educational and recreational purposes by school and community agencies throughout the year.

Cooperation in use of facilities In most cities of the United States where school districts do not operate recreation programs directly, their facilities should be made available for use by public recreation departments. This should be done by contract which may also provide for use of public recreation and park facilities by the schools. Rental fees, arrangements for security, maintenance, insurance liability, and similar matters should be specified. It is also helpful to involve school personnel as leaders or supervisors in such programs, in order to avoid the friction that may occur when one agency is using another's facilities.

Education for leisure As early as 1918, the National Education Association published a report, "Cardinal Principles of Secondary Education," which included the following:

Aside from the immediate discharge of these specific duties (home membership, vocation, and citizenship), every individual should have a margin of time for the cultivation of personal and social interests. This leisure, if worthily used, will recreate his powers and enlarge and enrich life. . . . In view of these considerations, education for the worthy use of leisure is of increasing importance as an objective.[7]

The report stressed the need for schools to provide creative and absorbing involvement in music, art, drama, and social activities that would lead to the constructive use of leisure. During the following decades, several major policy statements of the Educational Policies Commission of the National Education Association and the American Association of School Administrators reaffirmed this basic responsibility. Since the school's task is to equip students for total living and since leisure is an increasingly important part of the lives of all Americans, the school curriculum should emphasize education for leisure. Through both classroom learning and cocurricular activities, schools should enrich students' knowledge, attitudes, skills, and behavior with respect to leisure.

In fact, however, few school systems have given priority to this goal. A 1967 report of the National Education Association indicated that school teachers regarded education for leisure as the educational objective least effectively

[7]Bureau of Education Bulletin 35, *Cardinal Principles of Secondary Education*. Washington, D.C.: Department of the Interior, 1918, p. 10

attained.[8] Within this context, it is important to recognize that physical education is the school discipline with the most obvious potential for leisure education. By teaching basic skills in sports, games, aquatics, and dance, physical educators can help students develop life-time interests in leisure enjoyment and good health. Intramural and interscholastic competition, outdoor education and school camping programs, outing clubs and similar projects—many of which are the logical responsibility of physical educators—enrich this educational function.

Relationship between recreation and physical education

Exactly what is the relationship between these two fields today? In the past, we have noted, many physical educators assumed a responsibility for recreation programs, and recreation was widely regarded as an offshoot of physical education. Today, recreation and physical education continue to share a number of major responsibilities and characteristics. We will examine these with respect to objectives, program elements, those served, training and professional affiliation, and employment opportunities.

Objectives

Obviously both recreation and physical education share a concern for helping students or program participants reach their fullest potential for physical, social, emotional, and intellectual growth, and well-being. However, physical education is, for most students, a required educational experience that prepares them for the future, while recreation attracts students to a full range of voluntary activities to be enjoyed in the present.

Program elements

Physical education deals primarily with the medium of movement in games, sports, dance, aquatics, and gymnastics. While recreation programs also emphasize such activities, they include many creative, social, or intellectual experiences involving little physical activity.

[8] National Education Association Research Division, ''A New Look at the Seven Cardinal Principles of Education,'' *NEA,* January 1967, pp. 53–54.

Those served

Physical education serves chiefly children, youth, and young adults, in school and college settings. In contrast, recreation involves participants of all ages, chiefly in nonschool settings. With the exception of a limited number of programs of adapted or corrective physical education, physical educators serve chiefly those of normal health and function. Recreation agencies, however, serve many individuals and groups with mental and physical disabilities, often with specifically rehabilitative goals.

Training and professional affiliation

Professional education tends to link physical educators and recreation professionals through college and university departments or divisions of health, physical education, and recreation. However, recreation programs are becoming increasingly independent in their course requirements, objectives, and faculty. Moreover, college recreation curricula, which stress park administration, have been established either independently or within departments of land management, conservation, or landscape architecture. Physical educators customarily take a substantial number of courses in the physical sciences, including anatomy, kinesiology, physiology, and motor learning, while recreation students are encouraged to study social and behavioral sciences, business or public administration, and areas of activity leadership.

With respect to affiliation, physical educators normally join the American Alliance for Health, Physical Education, and Recreation, while recreation professionals usually become members of the National Recreation and Park Association.

Employment opportunities

The bulk of physical educators are employed in schools and colleges, only a limited number finding positions in community agencies, such as Young Men's and Young Women's Christian Associations, as directors of departments of physical activity. The bulk of recreation professionals hold positions in public recreation and park departments, where they are part of the civil service, rehabilitation institutions such as hospitals, schools for the retarded, nursing homes, or voluntary organizations in the community.

Thus, despite their shared past, recreation professionals and physical educators today function in separate areas of public service; however, it is essential that they continue to work together. In fact, many physical educators who enjoy teaching and leading sports activities, dance, and outdoor recreation activities still assume part-time duties in recreation programs or make recreation a full-time career choice.

In most communities, recreation administrators and physical educators should work closely together to provide sequential experiences for those served. Physical education programs should be planned with a clear understanding of the follow-up opportunities in community recreation programs. Tournaments, workshops, clinics, courses, and a variety of other projects may be cooperatively planned by physical educators and recreation personnel. Often, recreation departments sponsor sports courses and events that are staffed by skilled sports specialists.

Finally, adequate community recreation programs need the full cooperation of the schools. Hjelte wrote:

No single agency can be expected to administer all of the public parks and recreation facilities in the metropolitan city. . . . The provision of neighborhood playgrounds cannot be complete according to any reasonable standard in any large metropolitan city unless the school grounds complement the municipal park and recreation centers. Parks and recreation centers will always be fewer than schools within a city.[9]

Beyond the shared use of school and community facilities, it is obvious that provisions for the fullest and most creative use of leisure require the involvement of both recreation professionals and appropriate school personnel—particularly physical educators. In this common effort, both fields are united.

Summary

1. Recreation is most commonly regarded as a form of activity—what people do for pleasure or relaxation in their leisure.
2. Recreation consists of activities or experiences carried on in leisure time, usually chosen voluntarily because of the satisfaction or pleasure participants derive from them, or because they perceive certain personal or social goals as potential outcomes of recreation.
3. Personal outcomes of recreational participation fall under these major

[9] George Hjelte, "Leisure and the Schools" in John L. Hutchinson, ed., *Yearbook of the American Alliance for Health, Physical Education, and Recreation.* Washington, D.C.: AAHPER, 1961, pp. 182–183.

headings: (a) physical; (b) social; (c) emotional; (d) creative; (e) intellectual.

4. In the latter decades of the nineteenth century, several major factors fostered the recreation movement in the United States. These included (a) founding of the Young Men's Christian Association (1854); (b) development of Central Park in New York City (1857); (c) acquisition of Yellowstone, the first national park in the United States (1872); (d) establishment of the Boston Sand Garden, the first public playground for young children (1885); (e) establishment of the first county park in Essex County, New Jersey (1895); (f) use of school buildings as community evening-recreation centers in New York City (1898); (g) appropriation of $5 million to establish ten neighborhood parks in Chicago (1903); (h) founding of Playground Association of America, Boys' Clubs of America, and Young Women's Christian Association (1906); (i) founding of Boy Scouts of America, American Camping Association, and Camp Fire Girls (1910).

5. The four major types of sponsors of organized recreation services in the United States are (a) public agencies; (b) voluntary community organizations; (c) private organizations; (d) commercial organizations.

6. The functions of local government in recreation and parks include (a) operating facilities; (b) providing programs under leadership; (c) coordinating and assisting other community organizations.

7. Commercial recreation accounts for the bulk of recreational participation in the United States. Over $125 billion is spent each year on recreation and equipment.

8. The major professional organization in the field of recreation and parks today is the National Recreation and Park Association.

9. The major categories of program activities sponsored by community recreation agencies are: active sports and games, aquatics, outdoor recreation, arts and crafts, performing arts, hobbies, services for the disabled, mental and linguistic activities, social programs, special events, trips and outings, and service activities.

10. The basic sources of funding for community recreation and park facilities and programs are taxes, bond issues, fees and charges, income from concessions, government grants, and other gifts.

11. The heart of all successful community recreation programs is the leader.

12. Recreation and physical education continue to share a number of major responsibilities and characteristics. These may be examined with respect to objectives, program elements, those served, training and professional affiliation, and employment opportunities. However, recreation professionals and physical educators today operate in separate areas of public service.

Questions

1. Interview a recreator and a physical educator. Compare their interpretations of the term *recreation.*
2. Describe the personal outcomes of recreational participation.
3. What are the goals and objectives of community recreation?
4. What agencies in your community provide recreation services? What are their functions (governmental, voluntary, commercial, private)?
5. Discuss the criteria of a profession in relation to recreation.
6. Describe the three levels of responsibility within public and voluntary recreation agencies.
7. Discuss recreation as a major employer of people, those both with and without formal preparation for park and recreation work.
8. Into what basic groups would you classify recreation activities?
9. What are the specific principles underlying the development of community recreation programs?
10. Discuss the recreational needs of patients with varying illnesses. Why should they be provided with recreation services?
11. List and describe the basic sources of funding for community recreation and park facilities.
12. What is the meaning of recreation leadership? Explain briefly three theories of leadership and support one of them.
13. What forms of in-service training help staff development?
14. Should the schools administer the community recreation program? What are the pros and cons?
15. Distinguish between physical education and recreation in reference to objectives, program elements, population served, professional affiliation, and employment opportunities.

17

HEALTH EDUCATION

Having come this far in your education, can you now answer the question, "What is the single most important purpose of physical education? What does it really seek to accomplish?"

A simple way to find the answer is to look at the name of the department responsible for the courses, Health and Physical Education. Can the most important purpose of physical education be to maintain health?

Of course, other purposes or objectives of physical education are elaborated upon elsewhere, but here our emphasis is on health. We need to consider the relationship of health to general, as well as to physical, education.

Health education and physical education

While physicians such as Hitchcock, Sargent, and Wood were influencing the health of students through physical education, others were concerned about health problems and conditions from other vantage points.

For his essays on aspects of school health and particularly for the "Essay on the Construction of Schoolhouses," written in 1829, William A. Alcott has been called the "father of health education."[1] Health books written by physicians were used as school texts in the early 1800s.

In 1850, Lemuel Shattuck wrote the *Report of the Sanitary Commission of Massachusetts* urging that "the science of physiology be taught in the schools. . . . Everything connected with wealth, happiness and long life depends upon health. . . ."[2] He recommended this be implemented as soon as persons capable of teaching this subject were found. In that same year, a program to prepare classroom teachers of physiology and hygiene was initiated, a result of Horace Mann's efforts to make these subjects compulsory in the public schools.

In 1866, California required that "Instruction shall be given in all grades of schools, and in all classes, during the entire school course in . . . the laws of health; and due attention shall be given to such exercises for pupils as may be conducive to health and vigor of body, as well as mind."[3] Ohio followed in 1892, and North Dakota in 1899.

Other significant forces and events influenced school health instruction and programs. Charles Dickens' novels, exposing the cruel and unhealthy conditions to which children (and adults) were subjected early in the Industrial Revolution, generated social reforms. The advances of medical science, particularly the discoveries of Jenner, Koch, and Pasteur, were instrumental in the control of major diseases. The fight against tuberculosis led by the National Tuberculosis Association was conducted in "open-air schools." Just before the turn of the century, a committee of the National Education Association declared the need for courses in school sanitation and hygiene in schools and universities. It also recommended more training on the subject be given to public school teachers. Boards of Education concerned themselves with, and the American Medical Association published standards for, school buildings. The U.S. government, which had previously issued reports on health and education as well as hygiene in the schools, early in the 1900s initiated programs in child health and school health. "Health instruction" (not yet so identified) was promoted by the Women's Christian Temperance Union in the late 1800s. This organization was credited with influencing 38 states to require the teaching of physiology and

[1] In Richard K. Means, ed., *A History of Health Education in the United States.* Philadelphia: Lea & Febiger, 1962, p. 32.

[2] *Ibid.,* pp. 43–44.

[3] D. B. Van Dalen and B. L. Bennett, *A World History of Physical Education,* 2d ed. Englewood Cliffs, N.J.: Prentice Hall, Inc., 1971, p. 403.

hygiene, with emphasis on its particular concern—the evils of tobacco, alcohol, and narcotics.

This review of some highlights of the history of health and physical education demonstrates the close association between hygiene (health education) and physical education. The early physical training and hygiene programs to promote health were conducted by physical educators. Today physical educators are still expected to "teach health." Indeed, most state teaching certificates for physical education are issued in the name of "health and physical education"; so also are the teacher-training curricula.

Early in this century it was noted that physical education, which was created as a health measure, "failed to keep up with and apply the important contributions of the medical sciences, and thus failed to serve adequately the health needs of our schools."[4] Even today, requiring the gym teacher or coach to teach a class in health (on rainy days) usually results in a negative educational experience. It is not sufficiently understood that modern physical education is an important subject requiring the dedication of a full-time physical education teacher. Health education has a similar requirement.

Physical educators and coaches continuously contribute to the health of children and youth through their concern with medical examinations of students and athletes; nutrition and weight control; misuse and abuse of drugs; immunizations against certain communicable diseases; proper uses of safe equipment; use of mouthguards to prevent dental injury; appropriate matching of opponents by size and maturity; emotional health and self-esteem of students. The American Alliance for Health, Physical Education, and Recreation, the Joint Committee on School Health Problems of the National Education Association, and the American Medical Association sponsor professional conferences, conventions, and publications directed to the improvement of teachers' and coaches' competence in promoting and protecting the health of students and athletes.[5]

In 1960, the American Medical Association resolved that:

Whereas, The medical profession has helped to pioneer physical education in our schools and colleges and thereafter has encouraged and supported sound programs in this field;

---

[4] Means, p. 72.

[5] AAHPER, *Nutrition for Athletes,* 1971; K. S. Clarke, ed., *Drugs and the Coach,* 1972; and C. P. Yost, ed., *Sports Safety,* 1971, all published by AAHPER, Washington, D.C. See also, Robert Kaplan, ed., *Answers to Health Questions in Physical Education,* 1970, and C. C. Wilson and E. A. Wilson, eds., *Healthful School Environment,* 1969, especially chap. 12, both published by the Joint Committee of the NEA and the AMA, Washington, D.C. See also, Committee on Medical Aspects of Sprots, *Tips on Athletic Training—I through XI.* Chicago: American Medical Association.

Whereas, There is increasing evidence that proper exercise is a significant factor in the maintenance of health and the prevention of degenerative disease; and

Whereas, Advancing automation has reduced the amount of physical activity in daily living, although the need for exercise to foster proper development of our young people remains constant; and

Whereas, There is a growing need for the development of physical skills that can be applied throughout life in the constructive and wholesome use of leisure time; and

Whereas, In an age of mounting tensions, enjoyable physical activity can be helpful in the relief of stress and strain, and consequently in preserving mental health; therefore be it

Resolved, That the American Medical Association through its various divisions and departments and its constituent and component medical societies do everything feasible to encourage effective instruction in physical education for all students in our schools and colleges."[6]

Health

"It is health which is real wealth and not pieces of gold and silver."   M. Gandhi

In modern times, society seems to be more conscious of health than ever before, perhaps because now we can do more to improve it. Physical educators are acutely conscious of the deterioration of health through the loss of physical fitness in a mechanized society, where physical activity is required less and less. On the other hand, they are aware of their need to contribute to the healthful use of growing leisure and recreational time.

But is health primarily a physical matter of muscular development, endurance, and skill? What is health? There are as many definitions of health as there are individuals trying to define it.

We cannot readily say, "I am healthy since I ran a four-minute mile, but I'm despondent and considering suicide because I can run it faster." To visualize the wholeness, interdependence, and interrelatedness of all the elements of health, look at Figure 17.1. Imagine each of the circles as a separate disc, all mounted on a common axis. If we spin them rapidly, the signs blur and then blend into one image.

Expanding our concept of health is the idea that degrees of health are associated with our ability to function in our environment. One comprehensive definition subscribing to this dynamic interpretation states that health is "a quality of life involving dynamic interaction and interdependence among the individual's physical well-being, his mental and emotional reactions, and the

[6] American Medical Association, "Resolutions on School and College Health and Physical Education," *Journal of Health, Physical Education, and Recreation, 31* (October 1960), p. 18.

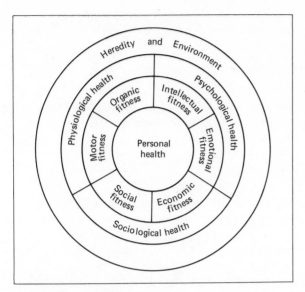

Figure 17.1   A wheel of health

Source: With permission from Robert Kaplan,
"Teaching Problem-Solving with Television to
College Freshmen in Health Education."
Unpublished Ph.D. dissertation, The Ohio State
University, 1962, p. 154.

social complex in which he exists."[7] This is related to an earlier definition by
Oberteuffer: "Health can be defined as the condition of the organism which
measures the degree to which its aggregate powers are able to function."[8]
Oberteuffer may well have been influenced by his colleague Jesse Feiring
Williams, who said, "Health is not mass, but function."

These definitions reflect the thinking of those who have worked in physical
education for many decades; who believe that health is a "quality of life that
enables the individual to live most and serve best."[9] They also see physical
education as a means of attaining higher levels of health. Physical fitness, for
example, is related to health by many physical educators:

Fitness is that state which characterizes the degree to which the person is able to
function. Fitness is an individual matter. It implies the ability of each person to live most

[7]School Health Education Study, *Health Education: A Conceptual Approach to Curriculum Design.*
St. Paul, Minn.: 3M Education Press, 1967, p. 10.

[8]Delbert Oberteuffer and Mary K. Beyrer, *School Health Education,* 4th ed. New York: Harper &
Row, Publishers, 1966, p. 14.

[9]J. F. Williams, *The Administration of Health and Physical Education,* Philadelphia: W. B. Saunders
Co., 1934, p. 17.

effectively within the potentialities. Ability to function depends upon the physical, mental, emotional, social, and spiritual components of fitness, all of which are related to each other and are mutually interdependent.[10]

How much like "health" this sounds. But health, like physical fitness, which is a part of it, is a means to an end and not an end in itself. We seek health to enable us to function at our highest levels of ability in our *total* environment, of which the gymnasium, swimming pool, and playing field are a part.

The school health program

Physical educators, who might have wished otherwise, could not easily avoid being health teachers or instructors in physiology and hygiene, as they were called in 1894. At that time, a city supervisor of physical education in the schools stated:

Quite as important as the exercises, is instruction in physiology and the hygienic care of the body. In my own work a course of physiology is studied by all grades during the school year. The subject is presented in as practical a form as can be done in the classroom. Charts are used, and in many cases the actual tissue. The pupils not only have an intelligent appreciation of the subject, but in many cases the teaching has produced practical results outside of the school by changes in dress, food and mode of life. This part of the work aiming, as it does, to develop the body into a sound and perfect instrument, is the first and most important duty in physical training.[11]

At about the same time and pace as instruction in hygiene was developing, school health services were beginning. The early concept of hygiene and sanitation and the control of communicable disease required that ill children be seen by a physician, known as a "medical visitor" or "medical inspector." Later, school nurses were employed to assist physicians and to provide more continuous services. Some larger school systems also employed full-time school physicians and dentists. Laws were passed requiring medical examinations of students and periodic inspections of schools.

The almost simultaneous evolution of health instruction, school health services, and healthful school environment (a very early concern of educators and physicians for sanitation in school buildings) established the basic framework of the school health program. Figure 17.2 presents the school health program and its components.

[10] The Basic Physical Education Committee, *Physical Education: Basic Concepts for College Students,* 2d ed. Dubuque, Iowa: William C. Brown Company, Publishers, 1968, p. 38

[11] N. D. Kimberlin, "Physical Training and the Public Schools," in Means, ed., *A History of Health Education,* p. 57.

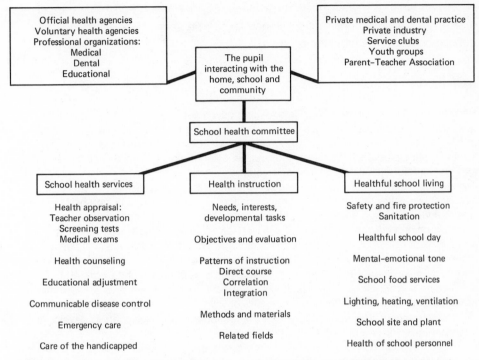

Figure 17.2 The school health program to promote and maintain the health of pupils and teachers

Terminology

Because names are misused or no longer have the same meaning, or because we want to attach more prestige to them, new names arise. *Physical training,* for example, became *physical education,* and is now being reconsidered to denote *movement education.* Shattuck's 1850 report suggested that *sanitary science* would teach people the causes, removal, and prevention of disease, and how to increase the vital force and avoid premature decay. Later, hygiene was called *applied physiology.*

The term *hygiene* had fallen into disrepute about the time of World War I because it had come to represent an ineffective, factual presentation of health when health habits (behaviors) were believed to be more significant and effective in promoting health. The Director of the Child Health Organization of America, Sally Jean Lucas, is credited with proposing the newly accepted, broader term *health education* in 1918.[12]

More recently, the term *health science instruction* has replaced *health*

[12]Means, *A History of Health Education,* p. 149.

education when it means *health instruction. School health education* means more than classroom instruction alone. As can be seen in the following definitions, some ambiguities exist.

Definition of Health Education[13]

Health education. A process with intellectual, psychological, and social dimensions relating to activities that increase the abilities of people to make informed decisions affecting their personal, family, and community well-being. This process, based on scientific principles, facilitates learning and behavioral change in both health personnel and consumers, including children and youth.

Community health education. That health education process utilizing intergroup relationships, value patterns, and communication resources in a specific social system.

Health education program. A planned and organized series of health education activities or procedures implemented with: (1) an educational specialist assigned primary responsibility; (2) a budget; (3) an integrated set of objectives sufficiently detailed to allow evaluation; and (4) administrative support.

Healthful environment. The promotion, maintenance, and utilization of safe and wholesome surroundings, organization of day-by-day experiences, and planned learning procedures to favorably influence emotional, physical, and social health.

Health information. The communication of facts about health designed to develop the cognitive base for health action.

Health instruction. The process of providing a sequence of planned and spontaneously originated learning opportunities comprising the organized aspects of health education in the school or community.

Health science. Health science has many connotations. It is used to describe a broad complex of disciplines concerned with the observation and classification of facts, concepts, generalizations, principles, and laws pertaining to the life process of growing and developing, interacting, and decision making. It also includes facilities such as a health science center encompassing professional schools for health personnel and health services for students and others.

In addition, it is used to refer to a college or university department offering health science instruction and professional preparation of health personnel. Health science education as a process may be defined synonymously with health education.

Public (community) health educator. An individual with professional preparation in public health and education, including training in the application of selected content from relevant social and behavioral sciences used to influence individual and group learning, mobilization of community health action, and the planning, implementation, and evaluation of health programs.

---

[13] Joint Committee on Health Education Terminology. "Tentative Draft—Report of the Committee," unpublished, November 1972. The committee comprised representatives of the American Association for Health, Physical Education, and Recreation; the American School Health Association; both the Public Health Section and the School Health Section of the American Public Health Association; the Society of Public Health Educators; the Academy of Pediatrics; and the American College Health Association.

School health education. That health education process associated with health activities planned and conducted under the supervision of school personnel with involvement of appropriate community health personnel and utilization of appropriate community resources.

School health education curriculum (also *school health education program*). All the health opportunities affecting learning and behavior of children and youth in the total school curriculum. These health experiences are gained in both school and community settings as the individual interacts with his environment, including other students, school personnel, parents, and community members.

School health education curriculum guides (including instructional guides or teaching-learning guides). The plans or framework for the curriculum. The plans are developed and implemented cooperatively by health personnel, teachers, administrators, students, parents, and community representatives, preferably under the leadership of a qualified health educator.

School health educator. A person with professional preparation in health education or health science who is qualified for certification as a health teacher and for participation in the development, improvement, and coordination of school and community health education programs.

School health program. The composite of procedures and activities designed to protect and promote the well-being of students and school personnel. These procedures and activities include those organized in school health services, providing a healthful environment, and health education.

School health services. That part of the school health program provided by physicians, nurses, dentists, health educators, and other allied health personnel, social workers, teachers, and others to appraise, protect, and promote the health of students and school personnel. Such procedures are designed to (1) appraise the health status of pupils and school personnel; (2) counsel pupils, teachers, parents, and others for the purpose of helping pupils obtain health care, and for arranging school programs in keeping with their needs; (3) help prevent and control communicable disease; (4) provide emergency care for injury or sudden illness; (5) promote and provide optimum sanitary conditions and safe facilities; (6) protect and promote the health of school personnel; and (7) provide concurrent learning opportunities that are conducive to the maintenance and promotion of individual and community health.

In 1938, the Educational Policies Commission of the NEA characterized the educated person as one who: ". . . understands the basic facts concerning health and disease; . . . protects his own health and that of his dependents; and, . . . works to protect the health of the community"[14]. This relationship was recognized and further elaborated by the EPC in 1961:

The central purpose of education is to develop rational powers of the individual or his capacities to think and reason. . . . Basic to this development is physical health since

[14]Educational Policies Commission, *The Purposes of Education in American Democracy.* Washington, D.C.: National Education Association, 1938: see also, Joint Committee, *Health Education.* Washington, D.C.: National Education Association, 1961, pp. 2–3.

disease, defects, or disability may interfere with learning. Mental health is also of profound importance; with it the pupil may have the desire and respect for learning that promotes optimum mental performance; without it the likelihood of such development is drastically reduced if not rendered impossible. . . . Health, for example, depends upon a reasoned awareness of the value of physical and mental fitness and the means by which these may be maintained. . . . Making intelligent decisions relating to the individual and community health requires the exercise of one's rational reasoning powers and an understanding of the scientific factors involved.[15]

Rational thinking, health, physical and mental fitness: these are the mutual and interdependent goals of health and education. To what extent can the physical educator assist in the attainment of these goals?

Health instruction

Health instruction as part of the school health program (see Figure 17.2) has received great attention as well as misunderstanding in recent years. Real or imagined increased rates of venereal disease, illegitimacy, abortion, divorce, homosexual acts, drug abuse, cancer, especially lung cancer due to smoking, heart attacks, and obesity have been frequently ascribed to the absence of health education or the incompetence of those teaching it.[16] In 1960, the American Medical Association stressed the importance of and need for health instruction in the schools and colleges in the following resolution:

Whereas, the rapid advances in medicine can be fully utilized only when the people are properly informed about them, motivated to use them wisely, and willing to accept personal responsibility for health; and

Whereas, health instruction programs in schools and colleges offer a unique opportunity for the teaching of the necessary health concepts and principles to all of our people during their formative years; and

Whereas, the American Medical Association through its Joint Committee on Health Problems in Education with the National Education Association, its Department of Health Education, and other departments and councils has stimulated and supported such teaching; and

Whereas, good health significantly assists the individual to achieve his optimum contribution to community and national welfare; and

Whereas, in the current reevaluation of school and college programs, it is important to give careful consideration to instruction in the science of healthful living in the curriculum; therefore, be it

[15]Educational Policies Commission, *The Central Purpose of American Education.* Washington, D.C.: National Education Association, 1961.

[16]Committee on Public Health, "Health Education: Its Present Status," *Bulletin of the New York Academy of Medicine.* New York: The Academy. *41* (November 1965), pp. 1172–1188. See also "New Emphasis Sought on Illness Prevention," *American Medical News,* April 3, 1972, p. 10, and "Survey Shows Public Deficient in Health Education," *American Medical News,* January 17, 1972, p. 19.

Resolved, that the American Medical Association reaffirm its longstanding and fundamental belief that health education should be an integral and basic part of school and college curriculum and that state and local medical societies be encouraged to work with the appropriate health and education officials and agencies in their communities to achieve this end."[17]

Health instruction, like all good educational practices, takes a variety of forms. Certainly it differs from physical education; even though they share some goals and objectives, they also have distinct ones. For example, encouraging the wearing of a mouthpiece to prevent dental injury is common to physical education and health education, but emphasized more by the former. Drug abuse would be emphasized more by health education. Skill in making a foul shot in basketball is unique to physical education, while skill in breast self-examination for potential cancer is unique to health education.

Planning the schools' curricula requires that administrators and teachers consider a variety of possibilities for presenting subject matter, providing learning opportunities or activities, facilitating learning, and encouraging independent learning. Curriculum planning can be framed around four deceptively simple questions:

What educational purposes should the schools seek to attain?
  What educational experiences can be provided that are likely to attain these purposes?
  How can the educational experiences be effectively organized?
  How can we determine whether these purposes are being attained?"[18]

These questions can never be finally answered, but they must be repeatedly asked. Good teachers should not become so set in their way of teaching that they neglect to reexamine their purposes. Administrators, often under pressure from parents and Boards of Education, may find it difficult to experiment readily with new and different ways of organizing the curriculum. The controversy over and change in school programs in recent years are related to a new look at purpose and result, or objective and evaluation. This ferment can be seen in the following statement on establishing priorities for the school:

Some people question the school's concern for the social development of the child and for his physical and mental health. They say, in effect: "These responsibilities belong to the home and the church. When the school tries to take them on, it usurps the prerogatives of other institutions and abdicates its own major responsibility, the intellectual development of young people."

[17] American Medical Association, p. 18.

[18] Ralph W. Tyler, *Basic Principles of Curriculum and Instruction.* Chicago: University of Chicago Press, 1950.

Others reply: "There is a difference between what ought to be and what is. The physical and mental health needs of many children are not being met by the family or any other agency. If a student has difficulties with health or with emotional adjustment, the school can make little progress in encouraging his intellectual development until these problems are solved—through the school if no other institution accepts responsibility." On this particular debate, most educators believe that health services are a shared responsibility of the schools. However, the content of health instruction belongs in the school curriculum because such knowledge is necessary, is most efficiently learned in school, and no other public agency provides such instruction.[19]

To illustrate the scope and concern of health instruction we will review some curriculum guidelines. Early in the 1960s, the privately funded School Health Education Study (SHES) examined the status of health instruction in the schools.[20] To assist in overcoming deficiencies in health instruction, SHES developed a curriculum guide based upon ten concepts that are considered to be the "major organizing elements of the curriculum," and show the scope of health instruction.

First, health is defined as "a quality of life involving dynamic interaction and interdependence among the individual's physical well-being, his mental and emotional reactions, and the social complex in which he exists."

From this are derived three key concepts or "processes of life underlying health and serving as the unifying threads of the curriculum. They characterize a process in the life cycle that is typical of *every* individual, regardless of sex, occupation, economic level, or social status:

Growing and developing: a dynamic life process by which the individual is in some ways like all other individuals, in some ways like some other individuals, and in some ways like no other individual.

Interacting: an ongoing process in which the individual is affected by and in turn affects certain biological, social, psychological, economic, cultural, and physical forces in the environment.

Decision making: a process unique to man of consciously deciding to take or not take an action, or of choosing one alternative rather than another.[21]

These three key concepts illuminate the over-all concept of health and form a framework for health education. Their dynamic interrelationship can be illustrated by the following application to the use, nonuse, or misuse of alcoholic beverages:

[19] National Education Association, *Schools for the 60's: A Report of the NEA Project on Instruction.* New York: McGraw-Hill, Inc., 1963, pp. 30–31.

[20] Elena M. Sliepcevich, *School Health Education Study: Summary Report.* Washington, D.C.: SHES, 1964.

[21] School Health Education Study. *op. cit.*

In the *growing and developing* process that is living, the individual, during childhood, comes in contact with—*interacts* with—the phenomenon of alcoholic beverages—or, more specifically, with people who use them. At some point in the life of each individual, probably in the mid-teens, *interaction* leads to the necessity of making a *decision* about use of or continued nonuse of alcoholic beverages. If the *decision* is to try drinking, then other *interactions* take place—with the beverage itself, with others who drink, with those who do not, with society and the adult world and, in some way, with the individual's own self-concept and conscience. *Growing and developing* continues, of course, with this new element included.

If one's reactions—physical, emotional, and social—to the beverage are basically more pleasant than painful, the individual may continue *growing and developing* as one who uses alcoholic beverages. If the balance becomes more painful than pleasant, the "tester" may *decide* to go back to abstinence. If the *decision* is to maintain abstinence, when drinking is a possibility, then still other *interactions* take place.

In New York State, a law, passed in 1967, requires health instruction in the elementary, junior, and senior high schools. Immediate provisions were made to develop a comprehensive course of study; to initiate a program to improve teacher preparation; and to strengthen the certification requirements of health education teachers. The curriculum outline, developed around five main content areas, is shown in Figure 17.3.

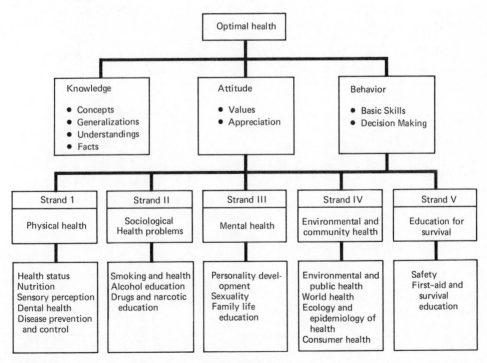

Figure 17.3 New York State health curriculum plan

Table 17.1 Drug use and misuse

Major concept	Primary level	Intermediate level
I When used properly, drugs are beneficial to mankind.	Grade-level concept: Medicines are helpful for maintaining health. Objective: Tells how medicines may be beneficial. Content: (1) prevent infection; (2) relieve pain; (3) control coughs; (4) ease upset stomach. Objective: Discusses why medicine should be taken under supervision of parent as prescribed or recommended by a physician or a dentist. Content: (1) the correct drug for illness; (2) proper dosage; (3) proper frequency of use.	Grade-level concept: Drugs with different properties are prescribed for medical use. Objective: Gives examples of different forms in which common medicines may be taken. Content: (1) pill—aspirin; (2) injection—penicillin; (3) liquid—cough medicine; (4) capsule—antihistamine. Objective: Tells difference between prescription and nonprescription drugs. Content: (1) prescription drugs are prescribed by a doctor or a dentist; (2) nonprescription drugs are sold over the counter; (3) more rigid controls are needed for the manufacture and sale of prescription drugs; (4) prescription drugs are generally more potent; (5) nonprescription drugs are intended usually for minor ailments of short duration.
II Many factors influence the misuse of drugs.	Grade-level concept: A variety of conditions contribute to the misuse of medicines. Objective: Discusses conditions under which a person might take the wrong medicine. Content: (1) not reading the label; (2) taking medicines in the dark; (3) accepting substances from strangers; (4) using another person's medicine; (5) taking more than the prescribed dose; (6) taking medicine from an unlabeled bottle.	Grade-level concept: Misuse of drugs often starts early in life. Objective: Explains why misuse of drugs often starts early in life. Content: (1) being motivated by curiosity; (2) imitating adults; (3) using accidentally; (4) being influenced by other users; (5) acting on a dare; (6) experimenting. Objective: Summarizes examples of the misuse of drugs. Content: (1) uses medicines prescribed for another person; (2) takes more than the

III Tobacco is harmful; and alcohol and other drugs, if misused, are harmful to the individual and to society.	Grade-level concept: Some substances that are commonly used can be harmful if misused. Objective: Identifies substances that can be harmful if misused. Content: (1) cola drinks; (2) tea and coffee; (3) alcohol; (4) medicines (aspirin, vitamins, diet pills, antibiotics, antihistamine).	prescribed or recommended amount; (3) does not follow a prescribed or recommended time schedule; (4) uses nonprescription drugs indiscriminately; (5) takes drugs for "kicks." Grade-level concept: Individuals react differently to the chemicals contained in tobacco, alcohol, and other drugs. Objective: Cites individual differences that cause people to react differently to drugs. Content: (1) bodily size; (2) sensitivity; (3) metabolism. Objective: Describes individual reaction to drugs. Content: (1) may become psychologically dependent; (2) may become physiologically dependent; (3) may have drug reaction-sensitivity; (4) may lose control of behavior.
IV The individual and society need to accept responsibility for preventing the misuse of tobacco, alcohol, and other drugs.	Grade-level concept: Each person must treat medicine and other substances with respect. Objective: Cites ways in which the individual shows his respect for drugs. Content: (1) uses only when necessary; (2) takes only in recommended amounts and at recommended times; (3) takes only under supervision.	Grade-level concept: Personal goals and practices established early in life can help one to avoid the misuse of drugs. Objective: Discusses the values of personal goals and practices in avoiding the misuse of drugs. Content: (1) self-respect; (2) respect for one's body; (3) healthy standards of behavior; (4) sound personal decisions.

Note: Objectives and content are intended as examples only.
Source: California State Department of Education, 1970.

California, as do many states, requires education about narcotics, alcohol, first aid, and safety. The state's guide for health instruction, constructed around concepts, is shown in Table 17.1.

An instructional guide for the Los Angeles schools is based upon seven units, as shown in Table 17.2.

In Washington, D.C., the curriculum for kindergarten through twelfth grade is titled "Health and Family Living." Emphasis is on family health, with specific concern for the problems of illegitimacy and unwed mothers among older teenagers, and venereal diseases; these problems are discussed with children ten years old and older.

The scope of health instruction is exemplified by the variety of nation-wide school curricula. For the most part, providing instruction in health is seen as a *preventive* aspect of the health program, the primary phase of preventive medicine. (Though various kinds of health instruction are necessary in therapeutic and rehabilitation programs, these are usually the responsibility of other health professionals.)

Teaching health today differs from the methods of the past. Traditional health instruction was concerned with inspecting fingernails and other aspects of grooming to establish primary behavioral goals; memorizing the systems of the body, the bones, and the organs; and showing horrifying films or reading gruesome stories (the "blood, bones, and guts" approach) to frighten students into "healthful" behavior. Nowadays health educators are aware that memorizing facts alone is not enough; they emphasize behavior.

The objectives of health education include three areas:

1. cognition—thinking, problem solving, and calculating;
2. effect—emotion, feeling, and attitudes;
3. action—behavior, doing, and manipulating.

Table 17.2 Los Angeles seven units of health instruction

Junior high	Senior high
Unit I Introduction to Health Science	Orientation to Health Needs
II Growing and Maturing	Guidelines for Improved Nutrition
III Achieving Personal Health	Transitions to Maturity
IV Food for Growth and Health	Narcotics, Alcohol, Tobacco and Other Harmful Substances
V Addicting, Habit Forming and Other Dangerous Substances	Progress in Public Health
VI Progress in Community Health	Consumer Health Protection
VII First Aid and Safety	Essentials of First Aid

Each of these aspects of learning and behavior is dependent upon the others.

New techniques and approaches to health instruction tend to replace telling, ordering, and commanding with guiding, counseling, and facilitating. The older, one-way communication resulted in passive and obedient students who recited on command and were tested later. The newer, two-way (or more) communication calls for teacher and student(s) to interact, and allows continuous evaluation. These conditions give more opportunity for openness, individuality, freedom of choice, and democratic procedures. (Of course, if strict discipline is the most important goal, it will not work very well, if at all.)

Methods in health instruction are, therefore, more varied. (Any good teacher uses a variety of methods.) Among these methods are:

Audio-visual	Oral reports
Brainstorming	Panel discussion
Buzz sessions	Problem solving
Case studies	Projects
Checklists	Question-answer
Committee projects	Readings
Creative activities	Recitation
Critical incident techniques	Reporting
Debates	Role playing
Demonstrations	Self-testing
Drills	Skits
Field-trips	Small group discussion
Forums	Sociodrama
Games (trust, simulation)	Surveys
Group discussion	Symposium
Guest speakers	Television
Health inventories	Term papers
Inquiry	Tests
Interviews	Textbooks
Laboratory experiments	Values clarification
Lectures	Workbooks
Library research	Workshops

Newer methods or techniques in health instruction are often variations of older ones. The current emphasis on changing behavior (as opposed to memorizing facts and statistics) requires teachers to be more knowledgeable about:

1. behavior modification;
2. inquiry;
3. value clarification.

To individualize instruction and allow for more independent study by students, teachers need to utilize:

1. behavioral objectives;
2. computer-assisted instruction;
3. learning packages.

Perhaps most important of all, teachers must know that they teach people—young people, mostly—their subjects or topics. Thus teachers are learning more about:

1. developmental tasks;
2. self-defeating and self-destructive behaviors; -
3. encounter, awareness, and sensitivity.

Physical educators, as we noted earlier, are often required to "teach health." The schedule may call for alternating physical education in the gymnasium with health education in the classroom, or six weeks of physical education to be followed by six weeks of health education, or, a full semester of "health" and physical education and coaching a team. How will they manage? What will they do? Will the girls still be separated from the boys? Will they be able to discuss sex education? drugs? venereal diseases?

Another vital aspect is the *correlation* of health education with other subjects in the curriculum. Some administrators believe that health instruction does not require a *specific* course because the teachers of science, home economics, social studies, as well as physical education teachers, are all providing health instruction. Unfortunately, this is often disorganized and inadequate health education in which many topics are overlooked, duplicated, and poorly taught.

A *physical-health-education teacher* could be the one to make correlation work. He or she could coordinate the curriculum and help keep other teachers well informed and up to date on health information and communication techniques. In-service training programs could be offered to the staff. Schoolwide health programs could be organized by the physical education teacher who is truly prepared in health education.

When the curriculum is *integrated,* the physical-health-education teacher is one of a team of teachers, expert in a particular field, developing themes, projects, and problems in the subject. A curriculum so patterned could be exciting for both students and teachers, but is rarely offered. This is not only because the teaching is more difficult, but because we are all accustomed to separate courses with identifiable credits and grades. We need teachers who are open to experiment and change and, most of all, who like young people.

School health services

All teachers, but particularly physical-health-education teachers, have a direct concern for the school health services. Perhaps physical education teachers *correlate* best with this component of the school health program

Health appraisal is a continuous process to prevent or detect illness and injury. Who can observe better than the physical education teacher the health of students from day to day? Supervising students during gymnasium activities, in the swimming pool, the locker rooms, and the showers gives the teacher an excellent opportunity to observe changes, for better or worse, in students' health.

Height, weight, and fitness tests are screening devices for assigning students to appropriate activities or noting conditions that should be referred to a physician. Physical educators need to know the signs and symptoms of possible heart and lung deficiencies that preclude vigorous activities. They need to know how to adjust their programs according to the recommendations of a student's physician.

Physical educators should be able to interpret students' medical records containing physicians' and nurses' recommendations. Periodic medical examination for all students is a helpful practice, but even more significant is the annual medical examination for student athletes. The physical education coach contributes to the health and well-being of his students by his knowledge and recognition of the importance of such matters. Further, he must be able to work with the team physician and/or the school physician to promote the health and safety of the student athletes. Communicable diseases must be guarded against. Students in physical education may be susceptible to athlete's foot, a fungus infection of the skin; impetigo, a bacterial infection of the skin; and herpes, a viral infection of the skin.

When a student returns to school after an illness, the physical education teacher will need to consider how he can be safely exercised and conditioned to help restore his health. Here again, the physician's instructions must be properly interpreted and followed.

The physical educator is often relied upon for his knowledge and competence in first-aid or emergency treatment. (Often the first-aid course is given in physical education.) The various activities conducted by the physical educator require a better than average acquaintance with first-aid techniques.

Finally, the physical education teacher is often the one person who contributes most significantly to the health of the temporarily or permanently handicapped. In addition to designing, planning, and administering healthful activities for these students, the physical education teacher is often their counselor, friend, and source of encouragement. Again, he or she must work closely with the students' physicians and parents.

Directly and indirectly the teacher is involved in school health services. Where there is no regular school nurse, physician, or health education specialist, the professional nearest to health problems is the physical education teacher.

Healthful school environment

Figure 17.2 presented under the heading Healthful School Living several items that deserve elaboration.

Prevention of illness and injury is a basic responsibility of a teacher. The environment, the school, can make it easy or difficult to maintain health and safety. Maintaining clean and properly chlorinated swimming-pool water may be a custodian's job but the physical education teacher or swimming coach is often responsible for supervising the condition of the pool. This includes checking on temperatures, condition of the tile, diving boards, safety equipment, and practices and procedures in classes, practice sessions, and swimming meets. Showers must operate properly and shower and locker rooms must be kept clean lest they transmit infection. In the gymnasium, tumbling and wrestling mats, as well as protective wall mats, must be maintained to prevent accidents and must be cleaned regularly to avoid skin infections.

The physical education coach usually orders equipment and supplies. Only the safest and most reliable gymnastics apparatus, football uniforms, wearing apparel, playing equipment, and protective equipment should be purchased.

When schools launder their own uniforms and towels, then, too, hygienic standards must be maintained. A proper system for collecting, storing, and distributing laundered items on a regular schedule should be established and supervised.

On the playing fields and playgrounds the physical educator-coach needs to supervise the safe condition of the surfaces and apparatus. Holes, loose gravel, cracked and irregular blacktop, mud, and grass clumps could be hazardous. The apparatus, from teeter-boards and swings to blocking sleds and pole-vault pits, needs constant evaluation.

The physical educator who does not intend to teach health education nevertheless has important professional responsibilities for the health of students, as well as important ethical and moral responsibilities.

Qualifications and career possibilities

Teachers generally and health educators especially need to consider the personal characteristics that seem to contribute to a successful career.

Do you like and get along well with most people? Are you flexible and adaptable? Do people feel free to approach and talk to you? Do you have a sense of humor and a pleasant personality? Are you patient? Do you have good judgment and common sense? Are you enthusiastic and energetic? Are you in good general health? How well do you communicate? Can you express yourself well? Can you speak, write, and create novel ways to communicate clearly and logically? Are you scholarly? Do you have intellectual curiosity? Is your work accurate and does it reflect current authoritative sources? Are you interested in and suited for studies in the behavioral sciences and the biological sciences?

Health education seeks to bridge the gap between science-technology and behavior, the cultural lag. Scientific discoveries and new knowledge, if applied, can prevent, reduce, and cure illnesses at a greater rate than is being realized. Humanity can be liberated from superstition and disease and enabled to live a longer life of greater quality. Health educators can interpret scientific knowledge for the layman. They can help people think critically and rationally, make decisions, and choose intelligent healthful behaviors. Perhaps the greatest role of the health educator is in helping people understand their health needs and showing them ways to meet those needs.

In preparing to become a health educator, a person has two broad career fields to consider: school health education and community health education. Both have a common core of study requirements and necessary competencies. Courses in English, writing, journalism, speech, and communications are basic to communication skills. The basic sciences would include biology, chemistry, anatomy, physiology, and microbiology (bacteriology). Human growth and development, psychology, and sociology are essential to understanding human behavior, motivation, and behavioral change.

Teachers will have had education courses necessary to understand and work with school children. Their experience would include observation and field study in schools as well as student teaching. Meeting their colleges' requirements and their states' teacher-certification requirements, they would graduate with a bachelor's degree with a major or minor in health education. As the professional standards of teaching improve, more physical educators are taking a full minor or even a double major in health education. The "health and physical education" major seems to have started a rapid decline.

A sample of the courses taken by a health education major—after general courses—would include:

Biology	First aid
Chemistry (or physics)	Education (theory and practice)
Anatomy	Education (student teaching)
Physiology	Education (testing)
Microbiology	Education (exceptional children)
Nutrition	Personal health
Psychology (educational)	Community health
Psychology (adolescent)	Safety education
Psychology (mental health)	Human sexuality
Sociology (general)	Drug education
Sociology (social issues)	Environmental health
Sociology (family)	Critical health issues
Communications (speech)	Methods in health
Communications (A-V aids or TV)	School health services
Education (foundations)	School health programs

Community health educators are sometimes former school health educators. However, undergraduates who seek careers in voluntary health organizations (American Cancer Society, American Lung Association, Epilepsy Foundation, Planned Parenthood, and the like) or in governmental agencies (city and state departments of health, family services, World Health Organization, and the like) find they need field experiences in the community and with the agencies in which they seek to work. Many health educators have school and community training.

Community or public health educators were formerly trained only in government-supported schools where they earned an MPH (Master of Public Health) degree. Currently several universities provide approved programs. The undergraduate program in community health education, although not accredited by the American Public Health Association, is nevertheless a growing field with many career opportunities.

Many health educators go on to obtain a master's degree to improve their competencies, to qualify for supervisory or administrative positions, and to earn more money. (Public school teachers' starting salaries average $8500 a year.) Those interested in teaching at the college or university level and in research and writing continue their studies to earn a doctorate. (Starting salaries at universities range from about $10,000 for an instructor to $18,000–$25,000 for a full professor, on the average. Teaching contracts are based on a nine-month or twelve-month schedule, which, of course, affects real income.

School health coordinator is another health education career. Though for budgetary reasons, few schools presently hire these health program specialists, several states have recognized the need for these professionals. New York, Ohio, and Texas, for example, have made recommendations for their employment.

In small schools, the health coordinator teaches and coordinates the various activities of the school health program. In larger schools, the duties of the coordinator require full-time attention.

The responsibilities of the coordinator include: working with the principal, faculty, public health agency, and medical and dental societies to plan and provide health services; acting as the interpreter and information officer for the school health program to the schools and to the community; serving as chairman or executive officer of the school health council or committee, which is concerned with developing and improving the school health program and coordinating school and community efforts to resolve critical health problems.

Interest in school health coordinators was recently stimulated by training plans of the New York State Department of Health Education. An experimental program at New York University was designed to train school administrative personnel in health education, and health educators in administration. Thus, school health coordinators would be prepared while they earned a master's degree.

What then does a health educator do? In schools, he or she teaches personal and community health, marriage and family life, first aid and safety, and, when qualified, a biology or general science course. The health educator works cooperatively with physicians, nurses, and parents, and counsels students on health problems.

The health educator also helps organize a school health council or committee and serves on it. Further, he or she participates in community health activities, perhaps working with the community health agencies as a member of a committee or even of the board of directors.

A community health educator's activities include working with local governmental and community leaders to solve health problems; working with planning agencies to coordinate efforts to provide preventive and therapeutic services in a comprehensive health program; and helping to educate the community through public presentations, newspaper articles, radio and television programs, and meeting with individuals who seek assistance.

The health educator in a voluntary health agency focuses interest on a specific health problem, such as heart disease, lung disease, or cancer, and engages in activities similar to those of the community health educator. This health educator also writes pamphlets and news releases, develops and staffs exhibits, encourages fund raising, and provides guidance to individuals who need health services.

Health education attempts to narrow the gap between scientific knowledge and what people can do with that knowledge to benefit their health. The health educator is an interpreter who translates technical laboratory research into understandable information for students and the public. He is a communicator, persuader, discussion leader, moderator, program developer, human-relations leader, and evaluator, to name a few roles he must perform. It is an exciting career.

Summary

1. Historically, physical education programs emphasized physical ability, strength, vigor, and health.
2. William A. Alcott has been called the father of health education.
3. Factors that helped initiate health classes in schools and colleges are (a) the Shattuck report in 1850 urged that physiology be taught in the schools; (b) in 1866, California required that instruction in the laws of health be given in all grades in schools; (c) just before the turn of the century, a committee of the National Education Association urged courses in school sanitation and hygiene in schools and colleges; (d) the Women's Christian Temperance Union was credited with influencing 38 states to require the teaching of physiology and hygiene, with emphasis on the evils of tobacco, alcohol, and narcotics.
4. Health is defined as "a quality of life involving dynamic interaction and interdependence among the individual's physical well-being, his mental and emotional reactions, and the social complex in which he exists."
5. Oberteuffer similarly defined health as "the condition of the organism that measures the degree to which its aggregate powers are able to function."
6. Physical fitness and health are closely related. Fitness is the degree to which the individual is able to function most effectively. Ability to function depends upon the physical, mental, emotional, social, and spiritual components of fitness, all interdependent.
7. Health education, a process with intellectual, psychological, and social dimensions, increases the abilities of people to make informed decisions affecting their personal, family, and community well-being.
8. School health education consists of health activities planned and conducted under the supervision of school personnel, with involvement of appropriate community health personnel and utilization of appropriate community resources.

9. The three key concepts of the School Health Education Study (SHES) are (a) growing and developing; (b) interacting; (c) decision making.
10. The objectives of health education include three areas: (a) cognition—thinking, problem-solving, and calculating; (b) effect—emotion, feeling, and attitudes; (c) action—behavior, doing, and manipulating.
11. Numerous opportunities to integrate health with other subjects exist within the school curriculum.
12. Health appraisal is a continuous process to prevent or detect illness and injury.
13. The physical education teacher is often the most significant contributor to the program of school health services.
14. A health educator could work in either school health education or community health education.
15. Health education attempts to narrow the gap between scientific knowledge and what people can do with that knowledge to benefit their health. The health educator is an interpreter, one who translates technical laboratory research into understandable information for students and the public and provides assistance in the decision-making process.

Questions

1. Name a few early leaders who favored physical activity to develop and maintain health.
2. Mention forces that had a deciding effect upon the development of the health concept.
3. Do you see any implications for health and physical education in the resolution adopted by the American Medical Association in 1960?
4. Why should the president of a country be concerned about the health of its citizens?
5. Health means many things to many people. What is your own understanding of the health concept?
6. Reconstitute the history of the term *health*.
7. What terminology describes the various activities of health education?
8. In what way do physical education and health education differ? Do they share common goals?
9. List contemporary problems that should be studied through health instruction.
10. Do you consider the professional preparation of physical educators acceptable for teaching health? Support your answer and propose alternatives if appropriate.
11. Discuss the health curriculum plan adopted by New York State in 1967.
12. Prevention is a fairly new concept in school heath programs. In what ways do the new trends differ from traditional health programs?

13. Who are the various health specialists to whom a student is subjected? Should there be any communication among these specialists?
14. What things do you deem essential for a physical health educator to evaluate?
15. Is there any difference in the professional preparation of a school health educator and a community heath educator?
16. What kind of future do you forecast for health educators?

18

SCHOOL AND COLLEGE PROGRAMS OF PHYSICAL EDUCATION

Except for a few outstanding programs throughout the country, the general criticism of physical education programs and leadership made in the following article cannot be denied by most physical educators. Although the criticism applies to programs of the 1950s, much evidence indicates that many of our programs still contain the shortcomings indicated.

When I was six, a next-door neighbor gave me my first candy bar, and I fattened immediately in a home where food was love. It is hardly surprising that when I first entered physical education courses in the eighth grade my coaches were markedly unimpressed or that thereafter I compensated by working harder at books, where I was more successful. Although I did learn to take jokes about my size and experienced the "bigness" of being able to laugh at myself (the standard fat man's reward), at 35, I am furious to recall how readily and completely my instructors defaulted in their responsibilities to me. Some remedies I have learned in my thirties persuade me that it is not inevitable that the system will continue to fail other fat boys.

My personal remedies for physical ineptitudes have a firm base in ideas. Four years ago I weighed 265 pounds. Only my analyst needs to know how much I consequently hated myself. In six months I took off 105 pounds and initiated a regular jogging and exercising schedule that has gradually, very gradually, led to increased self-confidence. Yet my physical education teachers in secondary school and college never showed the least interest in my physical problems, never sat down and initiated the simplest diagnosis of my physical needs, never tempted me into the personal discoveries that I had to wait more than a decade to make for myself.

Instead, my physical educators offered two alternatives. Either I could enter the fierce competitive sports that predominate in our culture and therein make and accept the highest mark I could achieve; or I could opt for the less competitive intramurals, modeled after the big boys' games, and accept my role as a physically incompetent human being, sitting on the sidelines to cheer for a chosen team of professionals. These limited alternatives were repeatedly justified as teaching me how it is out in the "real world," in "the game of life," allegedly divided between the participators and the watchers.

Now, as I jog in midwinter dawn, all muffled with socks over my hands, making tracks with the rabbits in Carolina dew, I am not competing with anyone, unless I whimsically imagine Father Time having to add another lead to my book. I am celebrating me, this morning, this pair of worn-out tennis shoes, the tingle in my cheeks, the space being cleared in my stomach for my simple breakfast when I get back. . . .

I was very articulate at fourteen—fat but articulate—and I believe that a sympathetic, interested coach could have shared this type of insight, this type of reality, with me, and perhaps thereby he could have teased me into the discoveries I had to make many years later. But the coach would have had to love kids like me more than he loved winning if he had hoped to participate in my physical education. I had no such coach.

Perhaps an athletic friend could have shared insights into my physical needs and suggested alternative fulfillments. I certainly had many athletic friends, because I sought avidly to compensate for my physical failures by liking and being liked by athletes. Unfortunately, these friends were all schooled in the competitive rules of keeping trade secrets and of enjoying and hoarding compliments. Human sharing had not been a part of their education.

I recall how at 32 I tentatively jogged around a block for the first time, how the fierce hurt in my gut was less bothersome than the fear that I would not make it. I had to learn to love myself for making it, and for making it again the next day, rather than to participate with my hecklers and being laughed at by the coach, who kept me that much longer a prisoner in my role as the jovial class clown.

I became a water boy and trainer, winning the school's award for most unselfish service. Is not the role familiar? I even served two summers as a camp counselor. I could not walk to first base without puffing, but I could call a kid "out" with a tongue of forked lightning. I had been taught well.

My physical educators were signally unimaginative. We played only the few sports that had always been played in our area. Further, they maintained a rigid separation between *sports* and *play*. Football, baseball, basketball, and track were *sports*. Fishing, hiking, boating, and jogging were *play*. Golf was *play* until you had a team that won five trophies; then you developed the cool rhetoric of *sport*.

I remember going on a boy scout trip in the Talledega National Forest in Alabama for a week. My anticipation was immense. I liked the woods. I liked walking. I liked the sky, trees, rocks, ferns. . . . We were to walk only about five or ten miles a day through a wilderness, camping out around an authentic chuck wagon that would move in advance during the day. The trip itself, however, was a nightmare for me. The coach/scoutmaster led at a frantic pace, because he wanted to get each lap done with and, as he said, he wanted "to make men" out of us. The major activity was to race ahead so as to enjoy breathers while waiting to heckle us slower folk when we caught up. When we came to a clearing overlooking the vast chasms of blue-green shimmer, the biggest breach of the unwritten code would have been to stop to look for ten minutes. The trip was to get somewhere (nobody quite knew why or where), not to be somewhere.

For a long time I treasured illusions that my experiences with physical miseducation resulted merely from my provincial isolation, that real professionals elsewhere had surely identified and rectified these ills. But as I have moved from south to west to east, even to England, I have found very few real physical educators. Almost no one is interested in educating individuals to discover their own physical resources and to integrate them with all other personal experiences. Almost everyone is interested in developing ever better professionals to provide vicarious entertainment for a physically inept society.[1]

Fortunately, some rather radical changes are taking place in many programs of our schools and colleges. The 1970s may very well be the decade of the most positive changes in the short history of physical education. We intend in this chapter to identify certain problems facing physical education, intramural, and athletic programs, but, more important, to present guidelines for the improvement of existing programs.

Historical aspects

Physical education has undergone numerous changes since the German and Swedish gymnastic movements of the mid-nineteenth century. In the early part of the twentieth century, physical education departments became more numerous in colleges and universities, and sports, team games, and recreation became an important part of our American culture. World War I revealed that a shockingly high percentage of our young male population was physically unfit for military service. This stimulated legislatures to try to improve quickly the physical proficiency of students in schools and colleges. Several states enacted legislation requiring students to undertake calisthenics, marching exercises, and running to improve their strength, endurance, and general appearance.

[1] Louie Crew, "The Physical Miseducation of a Former Fat Boy," Copyright 1973 by Saturday Review Co. First appeared in *Saturday Review,* February 1973, pp. 11, 16, 17. Used with permission.

Although the laws were concerned with male students, separate programs for female students had similar objectives.

This program was short-lived primarily because of the limited appeal of these activities. Very few people enjoy "punishing" their bodies with calisthenics just to improve their conditioning. Many physical educators experienced these exercises, but they were striving to perform more effectively in baseball, football, basketball, tennis, swimming, and track and field.

The conflict in physical education between sports and physical training has gone on for many years. Physical fitness movements sprang up during World War II, the Korean War, and the war in Vietnam. In support of the President's Council on Physical Fitness, President John F. Kennedy said:

Identify the physically underdeveloped pupil and work with him to improve his physical capacity.

Provide a minimum of fifteen minutes of vigorous activity each day for all pupils.

Use valid fitness tests to determine pupils' physical abilities and evaluate their progress.[2]

Although few questioned the emphasis on fitness in physical education, no one itemized the long-range benefits of a physical instructional program. Sports programs were dominated by team activities, with limited instruction in carry-over sports such as swimming, tennis, and badminton. In 1965, the Lifetime Sports Foundation was established to help promote sports that could be enjoyed by people throughout their lifetime. Some educators felt that the intention of the Foundation, supported by private enterprises, was to increase the commercial sale of sports equipment rather than to offer sound instructional programs to students. However, in that same year the American Alliance for Health, Physical Education, and Recreation established the Lifetime Sports Education Project to coordinate efforts with the Foundation. As a result, almost every college physical education program today offers instruction in archery, badminton, bowling, golf, and tennis, the sports most emphasized by the Lifetime Sports Foundation. As programs for lifetime sports succeed in the colleges, the high schools are beginning to inaugurate similar programs.

The physical miseducation of the fat boy is one of the unfortunate educational experiences that many have encountered. If changes continue in the direction that they appear to be going, boys and girls, regardless of size and general motor ability, should have the opportunity for successful experiences in physical education.

[2] *President's Council Manual,* Chapter 16.

Changes in college basic instruction (service) programs

Mountaineering, orienteering, rock climbing, snow skiing, ski touring, water skiing, judo, karate, aikido, hathayoga, kayaking, canoeing, sailing, river boating, trap shooting, skeet shooting, riflery, aerobics, jogging, cycling, scuba diving, surfing, deep-sea fishing, angling, skydiving, horseback riding, international-style ballroom dance, formation ballroom dance, ice skating, ice hockey, roller skating, and field archery classes appear quite frequently in college programs throughout the country. Why are these classes gaining in popularity? Are these classes really physical education? Before answering these questions, we might identify a few of the lesser known activities.

Mountaineering combines hiking, climbing, living, surviving, enjoying, and protecting mountainous terrain. It may include rock climbing, snow and ice climbing, expedition planning, camping, map and compass instruction, knot tying and rope handling, first aid, survival, glacier travel, rescue techniques, and the ecological awareness of the environment. *Rock climbing* may be included in

Orienteering

a comprehensive mountaineering course or taught separately. Classes devoted specifically to rock climbing emphasize the basic skills and techniques of grappling, peak ascents, climbing, rope work, and emergency evacuation procedures. Safety, judgment, care, and use of equipment are integral parts of these courses. *Orienteering,* a relatively old Scandinavian sport but fairly new to the United States, is basically a form of running that challenges the runner to find his route around the course using only a topographic map and a compass. The winner of a race navigates the designed course in the least amount of time.

Judo, karate, and aikido constitute the Oriental martial arts. These sports, also relatively new to this country, were brought back by the GI's stationed in Korea and Japan during World War II. *Judo,* a two-person sport, is a method of bare-handed fighting. An Olympic sport, judo is divided into two main techniques: the throw (from a standing position), and grappling (on the mat). A well-executed throw is awarded one point and the match is over; grappling techniques are used only after an imperfect throw. *Karate,* although still primarily a defensive art, has in the past 25 years developed into an injury-free competitive sport that resembles a composite of boxing and *savate,* French feet fighting. Unlike judo, karate is not a body contact sport. The blows and kicks executed in a karate match are pulled back before touching the opponent. Karate has been called the ultimate in self-defense, because it develops such keen reflexes that the practitioner can effectively defend himself against multiple assailants; yet he is able to spar vigorously with fellow students without

Judo

Karate

protective equipment and in complete safety. *Board breaking* is only one small aspect of advanced karate training, not associated with the competitive sport. *Aikido,* relatively unknown to this country, is not a sport but a jujitsu-like style of painless self-defense. Aikido combines wrist twists, turns, and dodging techniques to subdue an opponent without causing injury. An aikidoist is graceful to watch, often dodging and twirling away from five or six attackers at once. American students have dubbed aikido "the honorable art of getting the hell out of the way."[3]

Self-defense classes, especially designed for women, provide them a weaponless defense against attack. These courses have attempted to combine skills from judo, karate, wrestling, and boxing. By learning the basic skills of self-defense, a woman can develop confidence and poise, and will be better able to cope with the problems that may arise in modern living.[4]

Hathayoga is a type of yoga combining physical and mental well-being. The yoga exercises are applied to the anatomy and the internal functions of the human body, and aim to obtain maximum benefits with minimum movement and minimum expenditure of energy. Deep breathing and relaxation are emphasized with different exercises. The advocates of hathayoga equate the results with what are supposed to be the characteristics of youth: flexibility, grace, relaxation, ability to sleep restfully, vitality, endurance, maintenance of proper circulation, strength of vital organs and glands, firmness and strength of

[3]Kim Daeshik, *Judo.* Dubuque, Iowa: William C. Brown Company, Publishers, 1969, pp. 4–8.

[4]Donald I. Gustuson and Lind Masaki, *Self-Defense for Women.* Boston: Allyn and Bacon, Inc., 1970, pp. ix, 1.

muscles, smooth skin, normal weight, quick recovery, alertness, and clarity of mind. Since these are highly desirable characteristics, it is quite natural that any system professing to develop them would be eagerly welcomed. Hathayoga does not promise to prolong life; it promises only to forestall the appearance of aging, which is identified particularly with loss of flexibility.[5]

Running rapids in kayaks, canoes, and inflated rafts is a thrilling recreational and competitive sport. Courses in *river boating, kayaking,* and *canoeing* combine the skills of boat handling, boating safety, respect for fast-moving water, basic ecology, and, in many cases, studies in geology, anthropology, and history.

Collegiate *trap* and *skeet shooting* took a giant step forward when, in 1969, 50 shooters representing some 20 colleges participated in the first annual National Intercollegiate Trap and Skeet Tournament at the University of Iowa's claybirding facilities. In four years, the number of shooters participating in collegiate trap and skeet shooting nearly quadrupled. Trap and skeet shooting are two sports in which the object is to shoot at and hit a moving target (clay pigeon) with a shotgun.

Aerobics, made famous by Dr. Kenneth Cooper, is a scientific program of exercise aimed at over-all fitness and health, with a unique point system for measuring health progress. Physiologically, aerobic power is the rate of oxygen consumption during exercise. Aerobic exercises, therefore, are primarily directed to the development and maintenance of the cardiovascular and pulmonary systems to withstand the stresses of modern living. The unique

Skeet shooting

[5] Allan J. Ryan, "Yoga on Fitness," *JOPER,* February 1971, p. 26.

Aerobics

feature of the aerobics program designed by Dr. Cooper is the scope of activities to attain the same objective: running, swimming, cycling, walking, stationary running, handball, squash, and basketball.[6]

Scuba diving offers the thrill of exploring and discovering the underwater

Scuba diving

[6]Kenneth Cooper, *Aerobics.* New York: M. Evans and Co., 1968, cover page.

world, with the diver carrying his or her own air supply. Oceans, bays, lakes, and rivers are the liquid wilderness that attracts thousands of people to this sport. Courses in scuba diving include underwater physiology, techniques and skills necessary to dive safely, and an understanding of proper equipment and the "rules of the game." Instructors say, "you may only get one mistake in scuba diving, so learn the sport properly before you pursue the activity on your own."

What is unique about these classes

As you may recall from high school, the success that you enjoyed in participating and competing frequently depended upon your ability to run fast, utilize your strength and power, and throw and catch a ball, the normal skills of American physical education. The Youth Fitness Test of the American Alliance for Health, Physical Education, and Recreation typifies what we expect young Americans to exemplify. Of the seven test items, five attempt to measure speed (fifty-yard dash and agility run), strength and power (pull-up and standing broad jump), and throwing ability (softball throw). The remaining two test items attempt to measure endurance.

The unique feature about the new physical education activities we discussed above is the absence of balls. In these sports, nothing is thrown and, consequently, nothing is caught. Nor is speed necessary to achieve some degree of success in most of these activities. Of course, people who react slowly are not likely to be superior to those possessing a high degree of speed and agility, but many of these sports eliminate speed completely. Strength and power, assets in almost every physical endeavor, are not critical to enjoyment of these sports.

Why these classes are gaining in popularity with college students

"Doing your own thing" expresses the feeling of many young people attending colleges and universities. It is impossible to interpret this phrase as it applies to each individual, but it seems to connote a degree of individuality. This may be illustrated by the lack of conformity of college students in dress style. In most colleges, dress codes are being eliminated, giving students their choice of clothes and hair lengths, and responsibility for their over-all appearance. The decline in sorority and fraternity membership in many colleges indicates that students do not feel the need for group endeavors and associations. With the increased emphasis on individuality, many college students understandably find the individual activities of physical education appealing.

Also appealing to college students is their exposure to a new and different experience. For most, mountaineering, orienteering, rock climbing, scuba diving, sailing, trap shooting, and so forth were not in their high school physical education programs. The excitement and adventure of these new activities can be enjoyed without a prerequisite level of motor skills. Students begin at approximately the same level. No one is penalized for past physical education experiences or for lack of them. This is especially important to the "fat" boy or girl, the uncoordinated, and those with little interest in sports who have had very bitter, unsuccessful, almost cruel exposures to physical education. These activities may help overcome the hatred toward physical education that is deeply imbedded in some students.

Americans enjoy more affluence and leisure time than ever before. Many college students desire to be part of that affluent society that has not only the leisure but also the money to participate in leisure pursuits. To most Americans, the very word *leisure* inspires thoughts of enjoying the great outdoors. During vacation periods, thousands of people seek to relax and participate in their favorite activities. Many of these activities require a knowledge of safety precautions as well as skill and technique to perform them. Most learn these by trial and error and, for some, this is a most unfortunate and costly way to learn a sport. For example, the following skiing account, based on an experience of the author, illustrates the lack of judgment of young adults.

It was a beautiful day at Brighton, Utah. The sun was shining brightly and a new layer of soft, fluffy snow blanketed the mountains. The skiers arrived quite early in the morning in order to get a full day of skiing. Putting on their boots, coats, hats, and mittens they began discussing the enjoyment of skiing with four college students, learning that one of the two girls, Jane, had never been skiing before and had borrowed equipment. She was looking forward to an enjoyable experience skiing with her friends who were "veterans" on the slopes. Remembering the first few agonizing days of learners, the skiers wished her good luck and a safe experience.

As they moved to the lift ticket-line, it was obvious that Jane's friends had no intention of placing Jane in a beginner's class available for a fee at the ski slope. Instead, she purchased a regular day pass and headed for the chair lift. Since her friends were good skiers, they progressed to the lift serving intermediate runs. The skiers anticipated that Jane would be lying in the path that leads away from the chair lift at the top of the mountain. And so she was. Fortunately, as they slipped off the lift at the top, they were able to avoid her and prevent a pileup.

Throughout the morning as the skiers went down the different runs, they would invariably see Jane lying in a snow bank laughing and enjoying herself while her friends were trying to help her back to her feet. Approximately one hour from the time Jane began her first run, she arrived at the bottom of the slope. An average skier is capable of making the run in ten minutes, skiing at a leisurely pace. Jane was eager to try it again. At that time, the skiers told Jane she deserved a courage award just for attempting to come down that mountain her first day on skis. Unfortunately, Jane's next trip was not so enjoyable. She had fallen after losing control of her skies and had fractured her leg.

This incident illustrates several things, but here it indicates the necessity for proper instruction in some attractive leisure pursuits that involve a degree of risk. A broken leg or a broken arm can heal; but hundreds of lives are lost unnecessarily each year in accidents resulting from poor judgment. Most college students recognize the need for instructional programs in appealing leisure activities as a part of their educational opportunities. They are also aware that the cost of private instruction is much greater than college class instruction.

Competition is not being eliminated completely in these new sports but many of them are enjoyed primarily for the merits of participation, not to determine a winner and a loser. This element appeals to many college students, especially those who have had limited opportunities to be a part of "winning" in sports. One newspaper reporter commented when covering a riot in a large city, "fighting is as American as cherry pie." Similarly with "competition" in sports. College students and all young people have been trying to communicate to older generations that fighting may not be the best nor the only way to solve national and international disputes. At the same time, many have also challenged the competitive, materialistic drive of their elders, indicating that a more sensitive awareness of each other may be more important to our future than is the cherished democratic ideal of private enterprise. For years, physical educators and coaches have proudly claimed that competition in the gymnasium and on the athletic field is the best training for facing the "real" world. In evaluating those who have experienced competitive physical education and athletics, it is difficult to generalize about what effect any specific school experience has had on their total development. Perhaps athletics and physical education competition is not necessarily good for everyone. Equally, it would be erroneous to say that no one should be exposed to competition in the gym or on the field. Each student has different needs. Some need competition daily in order to develop their utmost potential, while others are not motivated by competition but may suffer some very critical setbacks. Recognizing the individuality of young adults, college basic instructional programs of physical education are responsible for providing some expressive means for all students. Very few subjects in any curriculum have the opportunity to serve some need of all students better than does physical education. However, in order to fulfill this goal a range of opportunities must be available to students.

Many of the student racial problems on college campuses in the past several years have centered around the monocultured curricula presented to all students regardless of their ethnic background, race, or nationality. Physical education programs shared their guilt: all students were expected to learn the cultural patterns and the sports of the white middle-class American. Fortunately, many colleges and universities have recognized that students with different customs, language, clothing, and patterns of living should have opportunities to preserve and share that culture. Physical education programs with activities specific to other cultures not only provide a program for foreign students, but give the student of one country and culture an opportunity to learn the sports of other countries and cultures. With the increased number of foreign students seeking advanced degrees in this country, this provision is critical to all areas of education.

Are these classes really physical education?

Physical educators have asked, what constitutes a physical education activity? Thompson has referred to *cycling* as an informal activity.[7] Traditionally, physical education is distinguished from other activity programs by contributing to the education of the students through big-muscle activity. However, the interpretations of physical education have become broader and more inclusive. Neilson has described activities in physical education as *movement arts*.[8] Huelster has discussed human movement as the total and patterned response of the human organism to its natural and social environment. She relates physical education to the purposeful performance of generic and refined motor patterns in play and worklike form; highly specific skills in gamelike forms; and movements expressive of ideas, sentiments, attitudes in dancelike forms.[9] The American Alliance for Health, Physical Education, and Recreation has stated that physical education is concerned with why humans move, how they move, and the physiological, sociological, and psychological consequences of the movement patterns that comprise their movement repertoire.[10]

One reason the question has risen is the real or imaginary distinction between recreation programs and physical education programs. The Society of State Directors of Health, Physical Education, and Recreation has distinguished

[7] John C. Thompson, *Physical Education for the 1970's.* Englewood Cliffs, N.J.: Prentice-Hall, Inc., 1971, p. 44.

[8] N. P. Neilson, "Supporting Reaction to Position Paper: Should We Drop the Designation Physical Education in Favor of a Different Name?" The Academy Papers No. 6, *Quality of Life through Human Movement,* September 1972, p. 5.

[9] Laura J. Huelster, "Supporting Reaction to Position Paper: Should We Drop the Designation Physical Education in Favor of a Different Name?" The Academy Papers No. 6, *Quality of Life through Human Movement,* September 1972, p. 5.

[10] AAHPER, *Guide to Excellence for Physical Education in Colleges and Universities.* Washington, D.C.: National Education Association Publications, 1970, p. 2.

between school programs of physical education and those of recreation by describing the basic context of each. The Society suggests that high school programs of physical education emphasize lifetime sports and carry-over activities, as well as the involvement, knowledge, and understanding necessary to provide insight and motivation for a lifetime of vigorous physical activity. In recreation, the Society has recommended that the school curriculum offer many opportunities for developing attitudes, understanding, knowledge, and skills that will lead to the wise use of off-the-job hours.[11]

To interpret these two general statements of belief as entirely separate and distinct would be erroneous. Yet, recreation specialists and physical educators have debated at length whether such activities as surfing, skiing, kayaking, sailing, trap shooting, angling, river boating, and cycling should be in physical education instructional programs or recreation programs. It may not be long before these problems are resolved, for recreation and physical education appear to be moving in a similar direction. Recreation, which has been primarily devoted to leadership study and organization, now includes some basic skill instruction in many programs. Camping and outdoor education programs have been designed for the recreation major student and indeed have enrolled many university students. These classes have included the basic skills of outdoor living, camping, and recreational sports as well as leadership experiences. At the same time, physical education programs include more and more classes in leisure activities.

If this pattern continues, separate programs of recreation and physical education in colleges and universities might tend to merge their classes and experiences. Where separate departments exist, a merger of faculty, programs, and efforts might be introduced, as in Ohio State University.

Class scheduling and organization

Changes in education have been slow and, in many cases, quite difficult. To initiate new ideas and new programs takes time in any educational institution. However, one of the most difficult changes has been modifying the time schedule of classes. College classes are designed to meet for one hour, several times a week, depending upon the subject matter. This is still the pattern in most universities and colleges.

Trump,[12] in his work on staff utilization, has recommended that time blocks

---

[11] The Society of State Directors of Health, Physical Education, and Recreation, *A Statement of Basic Beliefs*, 1972, pp. 9, 15.

[12] J. Lloyd Trump, *New Directions to Quality Education*. Washington, D.C.: National Association of Secondary-School Principals, 1962, p. 7.

and class schedules should vary with each subject; education should not be ruled by the ringing of bells.

However slowly, several colleges are adopting calendars and schedules that permit a degree of flexibility in students' schedules. One of the calendars meeting with approval is the 4–1–4 academic schedule. This consists of 2 four-month semesters with a one-month interim for intensive study programs, workshops, travel, and other innovative learning experiences.

In physical education this 4–1–4 calendar has fostered numerous innovative schedule changes. Many initial programs for the one-month interim consisted of a series of concentrated instructional workshops devoted to golf, tennis, archery, and bowling. A few colleges arranged for skiing trips in Europe or in the mountains of the United States; such trips were popular because the interim month was usually January and the ski slopes were in perfect condition.

Since these concentrated learning experiences have been successful in terms of: (1) students' capacity to learn the motor skills; (2) efficient use of faculty time and abilities; (3) effective use of facilities; and (4) increasing student interest in participation, more physical education programs have attempted to utilize vacation periods, weekends, and holidays for scheduling physical education classes.

No longer are two periods a week for a quarter or a semester the magic time schedule for a physical education class. Stockton, in his study of class scheduling, found no significant differences in students' performance of basketball skills regardless of the scheduling of instructional class time.[13]

Accompanying these rather drastic schedule changes has been the realization that physical education is concerned with far more than body fitness or conditioning. It was also recognized that two or three hours a week in physical education were not going to contribute, to any great extent, to conditioning a student who did not participate in any leisure time activity. As a result, physical education has concentrated more and more on the lifetime, carry-over, or leisure-time activities. These three terms are synonyms for those class activities that we have discussed earlier.

Coeducational classes

Can girls compete favorably against boys in sports? This question, asked since physical education activities were introduced into school programs, is usually answered *no.* However, it is well known that some girls can perform much

---

[13] Gerald Stockton, *The Relationship of Four Time Schedules to the Development of Selected Basketball Skills,* unpublished doctoral dissertation, University of Utah, June 1970, p. 61.

better than some boys. Nevertheless, differences in speed, strength, endurance, and body structure have been major arguments in keeping boys' and girls' classes separate.

There have been many successful attempts to integrate boys' and girls' classes in such individual and dual activities as tennis, badminton, golf, archery, bowling, swimming, and dance. In most programs, these classes are only a portion of the total offered. Classes in basketball, volleyball, softball, soccer, speedball, lacrosse, weight training, handball, gymnastics, wrestling, and posture have remained segregated, many for obvious reasons. However, as college physical education programs change to include the numerous noncompetitive, nonball, lifetime activities, the demand for coeducational classes is peaking. This increased interest can be attributed to several specific reasons in many classes. First, many leisure-time classes focus on participation rather than competition, creating a more social and relaxed climate that many young people welcome in their busy college schedules. Second, the limited emphasis on the neuromuscular skills of speed, strength, throwing, and catching gives girls virtually the same opportunities for achievement as boys. Third, the girls' attractive wearing apparel makes coeducational classes more enticing. For many years, the gym clothes designed for girls were loose-fitting-bloomer outfits in which even your favorite actress would finish last in a beauty contest. Supplying fashions to women and men in skiing, golf, and tennis is probably as big a business as supplying them the sporting equipment. Also, in mountaineering, horseback riding, rock climbing, cycling, trap shooting, skeet shooting, angling, and river boating, no special uniform or wearing apparel is required for participation.

The trend toward elective programs

Historically, curricula of colleges and universities were so limited that all students took almost every class. As curricula have expanded and specialization has developed, required classes are a much smaller portion of a student's program. Some colleges do not require any course of all students, but most still require English and physical education. Physical education is being given careful scrutiny on many college campuses, and even English has become elective in some schools. Among the arguments against requiring a course in physical education for all are:

1. Every student should be given free choice in his or her college education. No class should be required of every student.
2. Students assert that physical education offerings do not seem relevant to their needs.

3. University faculty have frequently condemned physical education service classes for their lack of "a body of knowledge," contending that they should not even be a part of the educational offerings, much less required of all students.

Among colleges and universities, response to the attacks on requiring physical education courses has varied. Most have fought diligently to retain the requirement under the present structure and organization. Others have made some radical changes in their programs, in an attempt to meet the demands of students, while still maintaining the requirement. A few colleges have abolished the requirement, forcing physical education into the "open market" to compete for student enrollment, like most other departments.

The "foundations course" concept of physical education can be traced back to the first programs of physical education in this country. It was revived, however, to meet the criticisms about the lack of academic substance in physical education. Physical educators introduced courses in the scientific foundations of the human organism and its functions, as at Michigan State University, the University of Illinois, and the University of Toledo. These programs attempted to move from the more traditional curricula of sport skills to programs combining some motor-skill instruction with studies of the physiological, psychological, and sociological outcomes of physical education activities.

The aims of the foundations course of physical activity at the University of Illinois were[14]:

1. To develop an understanding of the role of physical education within our society.
2. To acquaint the individual with the human organism in relation to physical activity.
3. To acquaint the individual with some effects of physical activity on the growth and development of the human organism.
4. To develop an adequate understanding of fatigue, relaxation, rest, sleep, diet, and aging as these factors relate to health and well-being throughout life.
5. To conduct a testing program that includes classifying each student's physique and evaluation aspects of his organic and motor fitness.
6. To provide a progressive conditioning program in which the student is exposed to several selected methods of training.
7. To provide counseling and guidance in the selection of activities gauged to meet immediate and future needs, emphasizing the values and limitation of various types of physical activity.
8. To acquaint the student with special services offered within the university environment by the College of Physical Education.
9. To make known facilities and methods from which a personal program can be designed and implemented.

[14] King McCristal, "The Foundations Concept in Physical Education," *NCPEAM Proceedings*, December 27–29, 1965, p. 56.

10. To inform the student of reliable sources of information concerning the effects of exercise on his personal health.

The University of Toledo[15] has taken a problem-solving approach to the foundations course concept. Based on two hours of lecture and discussion, with two hours of laboratory activities, the Toledo program for all freshmen includes:

Lecture and discussion (coed):
  Introduction: mental fixation; physical and mental take-it-easyism in the United States
  Understanding the heart; the ECG
  Cardiopulmonary resuscitation and other important emergency procedures
  Cardiovascular pathology
  How to have a coronary
  Cardiovascular benefits of regular exercise
  Metabolism and work capacity
  Diet, exercise, and weight control
  The muscle myth
  Smoking, performance, and health
  Human sexuality
Laboratory activities (some coed sections):
  ECG for each student; follow-up analysis of ECG's and discussion
  Film: "The Pulse of Life"
  Practice cardiopulmonary resuscitation using "Rususa Anns"
  Cardiovascular experiment
  Fitness testing
  Planning a cardiovascular fitness program; introduction to jogging
  Measurement of percent body fat; diet-activity recall
  Experiments with physiological effects of smoking
  Planning and conducting a personalized fitness program

A second-semester course emphasized the psychological, sociological, and mental-health aspects of physical exercise. Laboratory experiences included participation in swimming, fencing, badminton, handball, and conditioning. Students have expressed their approval of this approach to the study of physical education.

Oxendine[16] conducted two studies of physical education basic instruction programs in four-year colleges, in 1967–1968 and again in 1971–1972. In the four-year interval, he found that 10 to 15 percent fewer institutions required physical education. However, this still left 74 percent of the colleges requiring

[15] Perry B. Johnson, "The Toledo Approach after Six Years: Is It Working?" *NCPEAM Proceedings,* December 27–30, 1969, pp. 149, 150.

[16] Joseph B. Oxendine, "Status of General Instruction Program of Physical Education in Four Year Colleges and Universities—1971–1972," *JOPER,* March 1972, p. 27.

physical education. Chase[17] supported these findings with a similar study involving a smaller sample in which he reported that 71 percent of the schools required physical education.

Other findings from Oxendine's study revealed that:

1. There had been a slight shift from the two-year requirement to the one-year requirement.
2. Lifetime sports continued to grow in popularity while team sports showed a decrease.
3. Coeducational courses were increasing; in fact, most physical education courses were coeducational.
4. Institutions with elective physical education courses expressed satisfaction with improved programs and students' attitudes.[18]

Colleges and universities that have initiated elective physical education programs have observed several significant changes. These include:

1. A slight decrease in enrollment for the first year or two, then enrollment surpassing any previous figures by about the third year. Some even reported an immediate increase in enrollment. Enrollment is important to most programs because a reduction frequently means a reduction in faculty.
2. The program becomes more student-centered. Student input and student involvement in decision making tend to accompany an elective program. As one director stated to the faculty, "Remember we are here to serve the students, without them we are without a job."
3. The scope of the program broadens to include many more lifetime activities, appealing to more students.
4. Part-time specialists teach classes in sailing, scuba diving, kayaking, rock climbing, and horseback riding. They are experts in their field and provide excellent instruction. The National College Physical Education Association for Men supported the employment of part-time specialists in the following resolution at its annual convention of 1973[19]:

Whereas the scope of basic instruction programs has broadened beyond the teaching competencies of many physical education faculties, and for this reason the NCPEAM supports the use of highly skilled specialists when necessary and practical to meet the instructional competencies of expanded programs, therefore be it resolved that the NCPEAM recommends the careful selection and supervision of specialists by appropriate administrative personnel, and encourages their development as teachers.

5. Advertising and promotion of the total program become very important to its success. Media, demonstrations, displays, bulletin boards, and student

---

[17] David D. Chase, *NCPEAM Proceedings,* January 1972, p. 11.

[18] Oxendine, *JOPER,* p. 111.

[19] NCPEAM Business Meeting Minutes, January 1973.

intercommunication are ways to advertise successfully.

6. With the loss of a captive audience, quality instruction becomes very important to the success of each faculty member's classes and to the total program.

7. Grading procedures vary with institutions but the pass/fail and credit/no credit grading systems seem to complement the elective program of physical education.

8. Since many lifetime activities are conducted off campus, the additional student enrollment does not place any burden upon the teaching facilities at the college or university. In addition, the institution does not have to be concerned with building and maintaining some of the very expensive physical education facilities.

Noting the trend toward elective physical education, the NCPEAM also resolved:

Whereas the trend in higher education is toward the elimination of specific requirements and

Whereas the NCPEAM supports the principle of freedom of choice and selection of college experiences, and

Whereas society, of which the college and university campus is a significant segment, supports basic instruction programs of physical education which are developed with individual needs, interests, and goals in mind.

Therefore be it resolved that basic instruction of physical education at the college level be on an elective basis.[20]

Whether physical education remains a required subject or becomes an elective, the major concern of physical education is to make programs relevant, meaningful, and attractive. The strongest argument for an elective program may be that through it improvements in physical education will take place more rapidly. As mentioned earlier, changes take place in education at a relatively slow rate. But do not be too surprised if most physical education service programs in colleges and universities are elective by 1980.

Secondary school physical education programs

In fairness to those dedicated secondary school physical educators desperately trying to improve their programs, we should examine some of the major problems confronting physical education in secondary schools. Fortunately, some have already been resolved in many secondary schools, which gives us good reason to believe that the future of physical education is very bright. Nevertheless, several schools must resolve many problems to give students successful physical education experiences.

[20] NCPEAM Business Meeting Minutes, January 1973.

Problems confronting physical education

Among the critical problems confronting secondary school physical education programs are:

1. money
2. large classes
3. range of age and ability levels
4. schedule
5. facilities
6. equipment
7. competencies of faculty

Money Money means program. Without an adequate amount of money available, it is most difficult to conduct a physical education program that will meet the needs of all students. Money determines the size of faculty employed and the quality and quantity of supplies and equipment. Money dictates, to a large degree, the types of activities that compose a program. The few very good physical education programs with only limited funds are the exceptions. An adequate budget is certainly a key factor to the success of any program.

Large classes A student teacher of physical education once asked, "What would you do with a physical education class of 76 eleventh-grade boys?" The immediate response was, "See the school principal."

It almost appears as if in some schools the administrator determined class size by the square feet of floor space available. An English teacher may have 30 students in an average-sized classroom. Since the physical education facility is two or three times as large as an English classroom, the administrator calculates, the enrollment in physical education should be 60 or more students. How innovative can we expect physical education teachers to be in a class of 76 students?

Range of age and ability levels Compare the physiological development of a seventh-grade boy with that of a ninth-grader. There is only a two-year difference in their ages, but a tremendous difference in their development and athletic ability. Yet, some schools will assign seventh-grade and ninth-grade students to the same physical education class. Combining the problem of large classes with the problem of a wide range of abilities makes effective teaching extremely difficult.

Schedule As long as physical education classes are "locked in" to traditional scheduling, programs will be limited to short-term exposures on the school property. In physical education classes, approximately 10 minutes of each period is occupied with undressing and dressing prior to the activity time, and another 10 or 15 minutes with undressing, showering, and dressing at the conclusion of the activity. Actual participation time is thus usually limited to 25 or 30 minutes.

Facilities The oldest, smallest, and most isolated secondary school building in the country probably has a gymnasium within its walls. At each end of that gymnasium hangs a basket and a backboard. These are the predominant physical education facilities in most high schools.

   During the 1950s and 1960s, educators recognized that it was more profitable to combine small education units (schools) into one larger unit. In many areas of the country this meant combining two, three, or more small high schools into one large school. This arrangement was more economical to operate and provided all students with a much broader curriculum. The abandoned schoolhouses were converted to junior high schools or, in some instances, to elementary schools. What has been the effect of the consolidation movement on physical education?

   The new, large, modern structure, consolidating two, three, or more schools, included a bright and significantly larger gymnasium. Instead of one basket and one backboard at each end of the gymnasium, frequently baskets were suspended along the sides of the gym in order to permit more than one basketball game at one time. Occasionally, a folding or sliding curtain was installed to provide two separate teaching stations, one for boys and one for girls. The greatest advantage of the larger gymnasium was the added seating capacity for competitive basketball games. The physical education programs had traded several small gymnasiums for a large gymnasium, resulting in a net loss of one or two teaching stations to accommodate the combined enrollments. It was obvious that the physical education facility was overcrowded before the first basketball hit the floor. In some schools the only lines painted on the floor of the new gymnasium were those outlining a basketball court. Is there any reason to be amazed at the type of physical education program that prevails in our secondary schools?

Equipment What pieces of equipment will provide the most physical education activity for the money expended? This seems to be the major criterion for purchasing equipment for physical education programs. It should surprise no one to find that, as a consequence, softball, touch football, soccer, basketball, volleyball, and track are the major activities in secondary school physical education programs for boys and girls.

Competencies of the faculty The scope of most programs is directly related to the over-all competencies of the faculty. It is very possible to find a program of activities devoid of gymnastics, even when several pieces of apparatus are collecting dust in a storage room. Because no faculty member is competent to teach the activity, the equipment for it is never used, and students lose the opportunity of becoming acquainted with that specific sport. Even where class sizes permit, many programs limit individual sports because of limited teaching competencies of the faculty. In most schools, it is fair to say, the ability of the instructor determines the quality of the program. On the other hand, it is unfair to criticize competent instructors who are hampered by the problems we have been discussing.

Guidelines for secondary school physical education

The American Alliance for Health, Physical Education, and Recreation has provided a set of guidelines for secondary school programs:

1. The instructional program has as its foundation a common core of learning experiences for all students. This core of experiences must be supplemented in ways that serve the divergent needs of all students—the gifted, the average, the slow learner, and the physically handicapped. It must be geared to the developmental needs of each pupil.
2. The program should provide for a reasonable balance in those activities commonly grouped as team and individual sports, aquatics, gymnastics, self-testing activities, dance, and rhythms.
3. Sequential progression in the specific skills and movement patterns involved in the activities included in the above grouping is essential.
4. There should be opportunity for elective learning experiences within the required program.
5. The acquisition of knowledge and understandings related to the development and function of the human body, and to the mechanical principles of human movement is necessary.
6. Learning experiences (physical activities) should be designed to foster creativity and self-direction and to encourage vigorous activity that includes emphasis on safety procedures.
7. Physical fitness—agility, balance, endurance, flexibility, and strength—should be developed.
8. Experiences that reinforce the development of behaviors, attitudes, appreciations, and understandings required for effective human relationships are important.
9. Special opportunities should be offered for those students who find it difficult and

uncomfortable to adjust to the regular program because of physical, social, or emotional problems.
10. The program should present basic skills that can be employed in a comprehensive intramural, interscholastic, and recreational program for all girls and boys.[21]

Innovative ideas in high school programs

Timberlane Regional High School in Plaistow, New Hampshire, has initiated an independent study option to upperclassmen to satisfy their physical education requirement. Students are given the option to (1) explore new activities; (2) improve their performance and understanding of activities to which they have been exposed. Students must have a genuine interest in the activity; they may participate as a group or individually, depending on the activity; they may utilize community recreational resources and their staffs. Each week the students meet with a faculty advisor to evaluate their progress in terms of their own capabilities and goals established. The Timberlane independent study option has provided students the opportunity to direct their learning experiences and develop responsibility.[22]

Ridgewood High School in Norridge, Illinois, also offers an independent study program in which juniors and seniors may select six areas from the following: adaptive activities, apparatus, archery, badminton, baseball, basketball, bowling, camping skills, cheerleading, exercise program, fencing, first aid, football, golf, indoor recreation, judo, modern dance, outdoor recreation, personal defense, pom pom, soccer, softball, tennis, therapy, track and field, trampoline, tumbling, volleyball, weight training, wrestling, and yoga.[23]

Each student selects an area for study, designs the unit, and establishes goals and objectives. Working with a team of instructors, the student completes the project and is evaluated by a written and a skill test. The physical education department feels that this approach will contribute to a carry-over of physical education after graduation and that the experience will become part of the students' lives.[24]

Eagle Grove High School in Eagle Grove, Iowa, and Framingham North High

---

[21] AAHPER, *Guidelines for Secondary School Physical Education,* Washington, D.C.: American Association for Health, Physical Education, and Recreation, 1970, p. 5.

[22] Carolyn Stanhope, "Independent Study Option," *JOPER,* September 1971, p. 24.

[23] Gregory M. Sadowski, "Flexible Modular Scheduling Allows for Student Choice of Independent Study Units," *JOPER,* September 1971, p. 25.

[24] *Ibid.*

School in Framingham, Massachusetts, have given girls' physical education classes the opportunity to work independently on individually determined goals in gymnastics. Once the goals were determined, each girl was given the opportunity to reach her goals by the end of the unit, utilizing all available resources.[25]

One type of elective curriculum is working successfully at Stevenson High School in Livonia, Michigan. In an attempt to provide students the opportunities for some choice in their physical education program, each day a student may select from two activities being offered.[26]

The extended school year plan in operation in the Dade County Public Schools in Miami, Florida, may be the best solution to numerous problems facing many areas of education, especially physical education. The calendar year is divided into 5 nine-week sessions, called *quins.* Students attend any four quins throughout the year; they may attend all five sessions if they desire.[27]

This scheduling arrangement appeals strongly to physical educators because it permits classes out of doors during the summer months. Except in a few sections of the United States, inclement weather limits outdoor physical education to three or four months of the school year. Just think what an additional three-month period of outdoor activities could do for a physical education program.[28]

The Dade County program of physical education has identified 70 different activities for health and physical education. Among them are touch football, girls' football, track and field, combatives, lacrosse, water polo, sports appreciation, bowling, fencing, outdoor life (including hunting, fishing, and hiking), horseback riding, sailing, and water skiing.[29]

Ft. Pierce Central High School in Ft. Pierce, Florida, has experimented with "contracting" physical education, permitting all seniors and some juniors to pursue units of study of their own choice. This not only provides meaningful and relevant experiences, but also reduces the size of classes for the remaining students taking physical education. Copies of contracts are kept with materials

---

[25] Patricia Geadelmann, "Self-directed Learning," *JOPER,* September 1971, pp. 25, 26. Also Sandra Mathieson and Doris Mathieson, "Goal-centered, Individualized Learning," *JOPER,* September 1971, pp. 26, 27.

[26] Lois J. McDonald, "An Elective Curriculum," *JOPER,* September 1971, p. 28.

[27] Hy Rothstein and Robert F. Adams, "Quinmester Extended School Year Plan," *JOPER,* September 1971, p. 30.

[28] *Ibid.*

[29] *Ibid.*

to aid the student in completing the contract. When a contract is completed, the work is evaluated and a new contract is made.[30]

Omaha public schools have designed a new learning model for physical education that allows each student to regulate or control his own learning, in the following way:

1. an assessment of the student's educational status;
2. individually prescribed (phy-pak) program;
3. self-directed learning experiences;
4. self-appraisal;
5. peer assessment;
6. teacher evaluation.

Individual learning units have been developed for boys and girls in archery, body mechanics, basketball, badminton, gymnastics, softball, soccer, rope skipping, track and field, volleyball, physical conditioning, tennis, golf, swimming, diving, square and round dance, flagball, wrestling, weight training, and modern dance.[31]

In conjunction with Florida State University, an ambitious program of curriculum development was undertaken by the Duval County schools in the Jacksonville, Florida, area. Cellular components in selected areas of study were developed, allowing a student to progress on a pathway concept that stresses performance, performance-academic, or developmental growth. Opportunities for individual strategies and processes are provided in each pathway with clear and predetermined terminal performance objectives. This process has increased cooperation between public schools and universities in the area. Public school personnel are becoming involved in college methods and theory classes, and a mutual respect has resulted.[32]

Taking advantage of the wintry setting, the sports of broomball, curling, and skating are popular physical education activities at P. J. Jacobs High School in Stevens Point, Wisconsin. In Anchorage, Alaska, broomball, ice hockey, figure skating, speed skating, and cross-country skiing are integral parts of the physical education programs. Equipment such as skis and poles are purchased through Army surplus, and a community drive for discarded skates has proved successful.[33]

---

[30] Barbara Fast, "Contracting," JOPER, September 1971, pp. 31, 32.

[31] Robert D. Shrader, "Individualized Approach to Learning," JOPER, September 1970, pp. 33–36.

[32] Barbara A. Landers and James W. Ragans, "Revitalizing a County-wide Program," JOHPER, September 1971, pp. 38, 39.

[33] Lin M. Hinderman et al., "Winterizing Physical Education," JOPER, November–December 1971, p. 38.

Silverton High School in Silverton, Colorado, provides an elective physical education program for juniors and seniors completely planned by the students themselves. Being located in the mountains of southwest Colorado, the students turned to their surroundings for meaningful activities. They developed a course including new and challenging units in Alpine and Nordic skiing, backpacking, orienteering, and mountaineering, along with the standard activities of soccer, softball, volleyball, badminton, and first aid. Classes are conducted three days a week on the school premises; most activity, however, occurs after school and on weekends. The course provides a cross-country ski tour in the high country and a backpacking expedition to the isolated Havasupai Indian Reservation eleven miles into the Grand Canyon. The additional expenditures are handled in many ways. The home economics department provides instruction for cooking rice, keeping food costs low; a shop class makes hunting bows for an archery class; local merchants give discounts on fishing rods; and the ski patrol swap operation is an inexpensive source of equipment. Physical education extends far beyond the gymnasium and the playing field in Silverton.[34]

With the increase of innovative, relevant program ideas in physical education at the secondary level, student interest will continue to improve, and school administrators will recognize very quickly that meaningful experiences are available to more and more students. Parents become involved and interested. When that point is reached, resolving some of the critical problems confronting physical education programs in secondary schools is possible.

Elementary school physical education programs

The physical miseducation of the fat boy, with which we opened this discussion of physical education programs, concerns high school and college and makes no reference to elementary school. That, undoubtedly, is because physical education was not a part of the elementary school program at the time he attended. Very few instructional programs of physical education existed in elementary schools in the 1940s. The obvious question is, would the fat boy have been inept in movement activities, overweight, and the jovial class-clown if he had been exposed to a quality elementary school physical education program in his childhood?

The developmental tasks accomplished in childhood may very well determine the degree of success an individual will enjoy in adolescence and adult life. Therefore, learning to move effectively and efficiently during the elementary

[34] George Pastor, "Student-Designed," *JOPER,* September 1971, pp. 30, 31.

years may be very important to one's later participation in and enjoyment of sports and recreational pursuits. It is an unfortunate fact that movement patterns missed during childhood years cannot be made up in adolescence. A well-planned, comprehensive, instructional physical education program taught by professional personnel may be more important to elementary-age children than to any other age group. In fact, some school districts are even attempting to incorporate instructional activity programs for preschool-age children. Preschool and elementary school physical education need more research, but the limited evidence seems to indicate that properly conducted movement experiences may contribute to the success of children in other school subjects.

Elementary school physical education ranges from the recess period with only limited supervision to the planned program of instruction under the direction of a professional specialist, prepared to teach physical education at the elementary level. Most elementary schools place the responsibility for physical education on the nonspecialist in physical education primarily because the budget does not permit the employment of a specialist. Some school systems have employed a "specialist" in a supervisory role, assisting classroom teachers through workshops, demonstrations, instructional outlines, and individual conferences. These supervisors may be responsible for several schools within one system. This process has been an effective step in moving to the full-time specialist. There is no way of predicting the budgetary priorities of school boards. However, as more elementary physical education programs reveal the results of their efforts, it may not be long before physical education, under the direction of a specialist, will be an integral part of every elementary school program.

The emergence of elementary school physical education programs has occasioned many different approaches and programs, together with a new vocabulary. Basic movement, fundamental movement, movement education, movement exploration, motor perception, skill development, games of low organization, lead-up games, and rhythmic activities are some of the most frequently used terms associated with elementary school programs. These terms are defined below.

Basic movement and fundamental movement These terms, used synonymously in most programs, refer to the elements of locomotor, nonlocomotor, and manipulative movements. Locomotor movements, moving from one place to another, include running, skipping, jumping, and hopping. Nonlocomotor movements, such as bending, twisting, and stretching, are performed in a stationary position. Manipulative movements, such as throwing, striking, and kicking, give momentum to an object.

Movement education Movement education is a comprehensive approach to develop efficient and effective motor movements in children. It recognizes that the development of specific sports, dance, and tumbling skills must be built on basic movement concepts.

Movement exploration This term describes a method of instruction in the movement-education approach, providing children with the opportunity to explore methods of solving problems presented by the teacher, at their own rate and in their own way.

Motor perception This term describes the awareness of one's own body and its potential for movement. Motor perception activities are more specifically prescribed for children with learning disabilities.

Skill development Skill development occurs through the more challenging, combined movements needed to perform specific sports, rhythmic, and gymnastic tasks.

Games of low organization Games and activities requiring a lower performance level of locomotor, nonlocomotor, and manipulative movements are frequently referred to as games of low organization.

Lead-up games Lead-up games and activities utilize some of the necessary movement tasks that are preparatory to performing specific sports skills.

Rhythmic activities This term refers to movements performed to a rhythmic "beat." Although dance is the most common rhythmic activity in most programs, numerous other activities can be performed to music or to a rhythmic pattern.

AAHPER guidelines

The American Alliance for Health, Physical Education, and Recreation has described the essential qualities of an instructional program of physical education in the elementary schools. The Association believes:[35]

[35] AAHPER, *Essentials of a Quality Elementary School Physical Education Program.* Washington, D.C.: National Education Association, 1970, pp. 9, 10.

1. A well-conceived and well-executed program of physical education will contribute to the development of self-directed, self-reliant, and fully functioning individuals capable of living happy, productive lives in a democratic society.
2. A comprehensive physical education program for all children has as its foundation a common core of learning experiences. This common core of learning is concerned with efficient body management in a variety of movement situations. It serves the divergent needs of all pupils—the gifted, the slow learner, the handicapped, the culturally deprived, and the average—and is geared to the developmental needs of each child.
3. The program must be planned and conducted to provide each child with maximal opportunities for involvement in situations calling for mental, motor, and emotional responses that will result in optimal and desirable modifications in behavior: skills, knowledges, and attitudes.
4. A variety of learning experiences should be planned and carried out to emphasize the development of basic concepts, values, and behavior associated with the ultimate goal for the physically educated person.
5. Curricular content should be so organized that levels of learning in attitudes, understandings, and skills are recognized and can take place in a sequential and developmental arrangement.
6. The instructional program should be designed to: (1) encourage vigorous physical activity and attainment of physical fitness; (2) develop motor skills; (3) foster creativity; (4) emphasize safety; (5) motivate expression and communication; (6) promote self-understanding and acceptance; and (7) stimulate social development. It should include such experiences as basic movement, dance, games, practice in sport skills, stunts, and tumbling work with large and small apparatus. When possible, the program should include aquatics. Each must be so structured that it is interrelated with the others, permitting children to generalize from one learning experience to the next.
7. To deal effectively with the whole child, many styles of teaching must be brought to bear on the learning situation. These include both teacher-directed and self-directed learning. If learning is to be personalized and concerned with the cognitive and affective domains, problem-solving as a teaching strategy becomes vital.
8. To foster the development of generalizations and key concepts, a range of instructional aids as well as teaching styles must be employed. Innovative use of audio-visual materials, large- and small-group instruction, individual help, and interdisciplinary approaches must all be considered.
9. Opportunity should be provided for participation in organized intramurals and such extramural programs as play days and sports days. These should be designed to serve the purpose of the class-instruction phase of the program.

Innovative physical education activities

Movement education in elementary school physical education can be applied to any specific objective. To illustrate, let us assume a class of third-grade students and a specific objective of having them explore some of the basic motor movements. The following directions would apply:

Teaching Techniques:
A. *Class organization*—Students informally spaced throughout the activity area.
B. *Signal*—At the sound of a drum, children are to stop, look, and listen.
C. *Directions for activity*—Who can . . . , or Show me . . . , or See if you can. . . .
    1. Walk any place throughout the room.
    2. Walk from one place to another, taking as few steps as possible.
    3. Walk quickly, but quietly.
    4. Change directions on the signal while walking.
    5. Walk angrily.
    6. Walk cheerfully.
    7. Change from a high position to a low position.
    8. Change from a high position to a low position while walking.
    9. Keep your hands low while walking in a high position.
    10. Keep your hands high while walking in a low position.
    11. Walk in a circle.
    12. Balance on one part of your body.
    13. Balance on two parts of your body.
    14. Balance on one part of your body in a low position.
    15. Balance on two parts of your body in a low position.
    16. See if you can make a bridge with your body.
    17. Make your body as long as possible.
    18. Make your body as wide as possible.
    19. Make your body as short as possible.
    20. Run heavily, changing directions on the signal.
    21. Run lightly, changing directions on the signal.
    22. See if you can tell me what helps you start fast.
    23. See if you can tell me what helps you stop fast.
    24. Make your body into a circle.
    25. Walk, changing directions on the signal.
    26. Find a spot—move in a circle about the spot.
    27. Leave the ground with one foot and return on the same foot.
    28. Leave the ground with one foot and return on the same foot four times in a row without losing your balance.
    29. Hop forward, then backward, on the signal.
    30. Hop in a circle.

Parachutes have become vital equipment in many elementary school programs. They are inexpensive and useful in numerous ways. Students enjoy the parachute activities and derive numerous developmental benefits. Among the activities are: static exercises, trailing the parachute, under-the-parachute activities, and game activities.

Tires and hoops are also inexpensive and lend themselves to spontaneous activity. Their use can be very strenuous or less demanding.

Parachute play

Intramural sports programs

United States society is extremely interested in resolving many of the social and environmental problems confronting it. Young people are activists, not wanting their nation to crumble through such weaknesses as;

1. sedentary way of life;
2. willingness to be contaminated with the disease of "spectatoritis";
3. acceptance, as a fact, that our bodies are secondary to our vocations;
4. unpreparedness for leisure.

Fortunately, the change in values is not too late. People of all ages are swept up in the "participation movement." It is not uncommon to see husband and wife jogging down the street or a group of middle-aged cyclists. In many communities, special streets are reserved for bicycles only. Hiking and backpacking, traditionally reserved for boy scouts, now are crowding the wilderness country with enthusiasts. What does this mean to intramurals?

As Anderson[36] stated, the "golden age of intramural sports" could be just around the corner. For years, intramurals have been the forgotten program of

[36] Don R. Anderson, "Intramural Sports in a Changing Society," *JOPER,* November–December 1971, p. 67.

physical education and athletic departments. Physical education was required of most students, and athletics possessed the glamour to attract every student who could qualify. Nowadays, physical education programs are undergoing drastic changes, as we have seen, and the position of athletics is uncertain at this point.

Intramural sports programs have been hampered by limited (1) budgets, (2) facilities, and (3) personnel. These problems are being resolved in many schools and colleges, often through student demands. Students' representation on budget allocation committees, especially where student fees support most of the program, has given many intramural budgets substantial increases because of the numbers of students participating. High school principals are employing physical educators to devote their after-school efforts to intramural programs instead of coaching interscholastic teams. In many schools and colleges, facilities are being shared more equally among the classes, intramurals, and athletic teams. Ease of transportation for high school students has extended utilization of school facilities for intramurals and athletics into the evening hours. For intramural programs to capitalize fully on the interest expressed, many programs must continue to broaden their scope and improve opportunities for participation.

Changes in college intramural programs

The University of Iowa[37] offers a *guys and gals* program in eight competitive sports. In the first year, 32 teams reported for flag football, 15 teams for softball, 27 teams for volleyball, 16 teams for basketball, and 44 participants for a swimming relay meet, along with coed competition in tennis, badminton, and paddleball. Brigham Young University has initiated a similar program with overwhelming success. A few rule changes are necessary in some of the team sports, especially where the official rules for boys and girls are different. The University of Utah has added coed inner-tube water polo to the existing program of coed tennis, volleyball, golf, and softball.

College and university programs have expanded their competitive offerings for boys and girls to include such activities as horseshoes, water polo, weight lifting, judo, karate, fencing, archery, paddleball, handball, golf, tennis, skiing, cross-country skiing, orienteering, table tennis, trap shooting, skeet shooting, riflery, cycling, ice hockey, lacrosse, and team handball. The more traditional

---

[37]Delbert Gehrke, "Guys and Gals Intramurals," *JOPER,* January 1972, p. 75.

Coed intramural volleyball

activities of flag football, basketball, soccer, volleyball, swimming, track and field, wrestling, and softball still constitute most of the sports. Johnson[38] has indicated that approximately 14 percent of the colleges and universities offer gymnastics as an intramural sport.

The sports-club movement Perhaps the most dramatic change in intramural programs in most colleges and universities is the sports-club movement developed from two different sources. First, a group of students, seeking participation in a designated activity beyond the basic instructional level but finding no existing organization, forms a *club* under the direction of the intramural department, in which it participates as an organized group. The club may engage in competition with other clubs in the area or just offer its members the sheer pleasure of participation. Clubs in this category may include:

1. sailing
2. skiing
3. ski touring

[38] Marvin Johnson, "Intramural Gymnastics, Why Not?" *JOPER,* November–December 1972, pp. 69, 70.

 4. water skiing
 5. skydiving
 6. rugby
 7. fencing
 8. judo
 9. karate
10. ballroom dance
11. cycling
12. rodeo
13. bowling
14. trap and skeet shooting
15. rifle
16. mountain climbing
17. backpacking
18. snowmobiling
19. motorcross

The second source is the athletic department that states to a group of eager soccer enthusiasts, ''We are sorry that we cannot include soccer in our athletic program; we are not budgeted for the sport; we do not have anyone who is capable of coaching soccer; and we have no facility to conduct the sport. ''Why don't you go to the intramural office and request to be instated as a soccer club?'' In this category of clubs, we frequently find:

1. lacrosse
2. rugby
3. team handball
4. fencing
5. volleyball
6. skiing

The sports clubs are by no means free of problems. For example:

 1. Where do they belong in institutional administration?
 2. Who supervises or manages them?
 3. What policies and regulations govern them?
 4. How are facilities scheduled and maintained for them?
 5. Who schedules their practices and events?
 6. How are they financed?
 7. Who controls them?
 8. What eligibility standards are established?
 9. Who composes the membership?
10. How are the participants insured?
11. How are transportation and travel arrangements handled?
12. How are injuries cared for and who assumes the responsibility?
13. Who supplies and maintains the equipment?
14. How are medical exams handled?

Rugby club

Each institution is faced with these problems as the sports-club movement prospers. There is little doubt that the interest is great; the primary question is, what responsibilities rest with the universities?

Intramurals in the secondary and elementary schools

Secondary school intramural programs, rather limited to date, are being strengthened by the employment of personnel to teach physical education and conduct intramurals. As specialists figure more in elementary schools, intramural activities will expand there also.

Of seven Highland, Indiana, elementary schools five have elementary specialists. Their programs for fifth- and sixth-grade boys and girls include softball, volleyball, newcomb, wrestling, floor hockey, tumbling, square dance, basketball, and track. The highlight of their intramurals is the track program, for over 600 students, held two afternoons a week in April, usually with boys and girls alternating days. The track program is followed by an all-school track meet, and the total program is climaxed by an all-city meet, which has attracted some 500 spectators. In addition, exhibition races are a special event during varsity track meets at Highland High School.[39]

[39] Larry Yazel, "An Elementary Intramural Track Program," *JOPER,* April 1972, p. 63.

Elementary grade intramural track

Interschool athletic programs

Of all the programs offered by schools and colleges, none have received so much praise and criticism as athletic programs. Generally, Americans seem to be more interested and better informed about sports than about any other institution or vocation. This intense concern is clearly a natural outgrowth of the country's development as a nation. The spirit behind the *Declaration of Independence,* the Protestant "work ethic," our competitive free-enterprise system, and our affluent life-style have clearly nurtured the American sports scene.

The limelight on athletics is constantly reinforced by prolific newspaper, television, and radio coverage, as well as by an endless stream of magazines specializing in sports news. That athletics play a major role in American society is incontestable.

For the average American, *athletics* means organized, competitive sports, with the natural outcome of winning or losing equated with success and failure. Athletic fields and arenas have been acclaimed by many as legitimate laboratories for preparing young people for the "real world," the democratic society of free enterprise. The association of the outcomes of competitive sports with business was credited to William G. Sumner, a Yale University professor. As Walter Camp, the legendary football coach at Yale University from 1880 to

413

1910, was urging his players to struggle for victory on the gridiron, Professor Sumner was urging Yale students to struggle for wealth and power in America's market place.[40]

Camp's competitive spirit was illustrated by his statement: "When you lose a match against a man in your own class . . . shake hands with him, do not excuse your defeat, do not forget it, and do not let it happen again if there is any way to prepare yourself better for the next match." In Camp's philosophy of sport there was little room for sheer enjoyment, because winning was the overriding concern. He regarded football not merely as a game but as a spectacle. He was thrilled by the huge crowds, thus giving tacit support to one of the sources that has made professionalism unavoidable.[41]

The famed slogan, "Winning isn't everything, it's the only thing," expressed the same dynamic force that was prevalent during Walter Camp's tenure as coach of the Yale University "Bulldogs." Bill Musselman, the youthful basketball coach at Minnesota, has been quoted as saying, "Defeat is worse than death because you have to live with defeat."[42] The pressures of winning are felt at all levels of competitive sports from the professionals down to the "little leaguers."

Athletics have prospered in schools and colleges because they offer the individual participant the chance to develop self-dignity, self-worth, the ability to think for oneself, appreciation for other people's assistance, cooperation, a faith in humanity, teamwork, an understanding of the words sacrifice, self-discipline, humbleness, and respect for authority. Because these factors are so difficult to measure, the yardstick most often used to determine a successful athletic organization is the win-loss record. Winning is basic to all athletic programs—no one teaches losing. At a small college, where athletics were voluntary with no recruiting budget or scholarships, a coach made the statement, "In my program winning is not the most important thing, I will only insist on excellence." That coach was relieved of his head coaching responsibilities after two losing seasons.

Although athletics affect a lot of people, directly and indirectly, within an educational institution, the coach and the players are in the most vulnerable positions. They can profit most and be hurt most.

The coach fits very neatly into a cycle that determines, for the most part, his or her present position. Figure 18.1 illustrates the coaching cycle. There are

[40] Allen L. Sack, "Yale 29—Harvard 4: The Professionalization of College Football," *Quest,* January 1973, p. 32, citing H. Powel, *Walter Camp,* Boston: Little, Brown & Co., 1926, p. 112.

[41] *Ibid.,* p. 32.

[42] *Sports Illustrated,* February 7, 1972, p. 19.

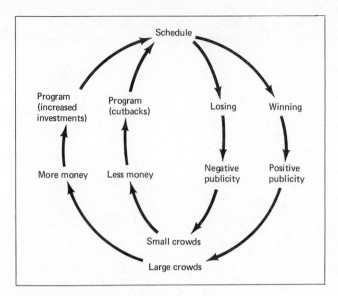

Figure 18.1   Coaching cycle

basically two pathways in the described cycle with only one variable—the schedule—remaining constant. For most coaches, the schedule determines which pathway will be taken. However, the program is extremely critical: coaching, recruiting, administration, and finances. Without some degree of equality in programs with scheduled opponents, the chances of moving into the winning cycle are minimal. The number of cycles that a coach can make on the loser's pathway depends upon many factors. Some of these factors might include:

1. tenure in the position;
2. contribution made to the participants and to the total program;
3. the sport;
4. the level of competition;
5. conditions surrounding the job;
6. the objectives of the program;
7. the internal and external pressures of winning.

Athletics have emerged so far and have grown so large in some educational institutions that the athlete has become secondary to the sport, the team, and the program. The administrative control of athletics has been removed, in some instances, from the office of athletics to an athletic committee representing students, faculty, administrators, alumni, players, and coaches. Yet, these educational competitive experiences were originally designed for the participant.

What is the impact of these internal and external forces on the individual athlete? If any concern remains for the participant, then this question must be dealt with. One approach to the relationship of these forces is illustrated in Figure 18.2. In this model, the forces exerting pressure on the athlete are:

1. the coach;
2. the athletic administration;
3. the institutional administration;
4. the student body;
5. society.

Each sport has one person, the "head" coach, responsible for the performance of the players. Traditionally, the coach has been dominant, with great influence on the participants. In this model, the assistant coaches are included in the force labeled "coach."

The athletic administration is responsible for the organization and administration of athletics. In colleges, the athletic administration might include a faculty athletic committee, an athletic director, an assistant athletic director, and a business manager. In high schools, the administration might range from a faculty manager of athletics to an organization similar to many colleges. In junior high and elementary school programs, any separate athletic administration is unlikely; the coaches would assume any duties of athletic administration.

The principal, superintendent, and board of education would constitute the institutional administration of most high schools and junior high schools. There are numerous structures of administration at colleges and universities, but the most common organization includes the president, his cabinet of vice

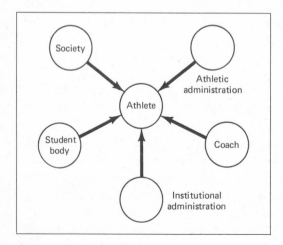

Figure 18.2 Conceptual model of an athlete

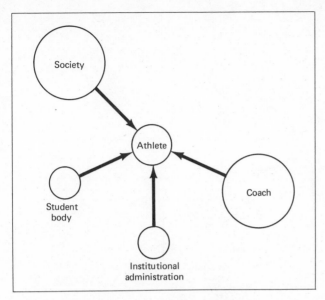

Figure 18.3   Conceptual model of a seventh-grade
athlete

presidents, deans, and a board of directors (trustees). The students enrolled in
the school or college constitute the force labeled the ''student body.''

The external force of the ''society'' in this model includes alumni, fans, and
mass media. This is a very forceful pressure group because it includes
newspapers, television, radio, and magazines.

In Figure 18.2, each force is represented by the same sized circle to show
that each pressure group actually exerts an equal force on the athlete. Usually,
more pressure is exerted by one or more groups at different times; this model
shows only the different forces affecting the athlete. Figure 18.3 represents a
model of a seventh-grade basketball player. The force of the athletic
administration is deleted, because none exists in schools at this level. Student
body and institutional administration are diminished, indicating limited student
body interest and pressure on this athlete. Also, the principal and district
administrators are not placing undue pressure on the athlete to perform as a
basketball player in this school. Society is composed primarily of parents in this
model. Although parental pressures will vary, their presence, excitement,
interest, and remarks place a great deal of force on their children to perform
successfully.

The model in Figure 18.4 illustrates the forces on the quarterback of a
national championship football team. How does society affect the individual

417

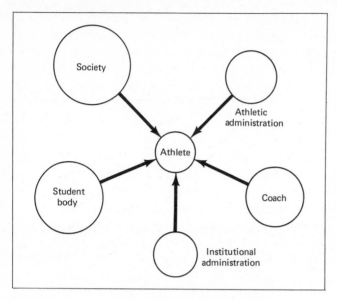

Figure 18.4   Conceptual model of a football athlete

development of this young man? What relative influence does his coach have on him? How does he envision the sensitivity of his fellow man? What degree of self-confidence does he possess? Can he make decisions without outside pressures affecting him?

In this model, the quarterback is under a great deal of pressure from all forces, especially society and the student body, those forces outside the institutional organization. The coach is extremely important but may not be as influential as society or the student body. For example, the pressures of the press on the quarterback to excel in a championship contest may be much greater than those imposed by his coach. Coaches recognize limitations within which a young athlete must perform. Sports writers only record performance, regardless of circumstances. You're either a winner or a loser, according to the post-game sport's report. In this case, the quarterback is definitely a winner and the reinforcement that he receives from society and the student body would contribute immensely to his self-concept, self-worth, and many of the individual benefits of athletics. Students in many universities are the most emotional fans and their force is felt by every performer. The athletic and institutional administrations are keenly interested in outcomes of athletic competition but their forces more frequently act on the coach than on the athlete.

How would the forces of Figure 18.4 affect a forward of a high school basketball team that had lost twenty consecutive games? What would be his self-concept? What would be his opinion of his fellows? Would sacrifice have the same meaning to him as to the quarterback of a national championship team? How would he evaluate his experiences in competitive athletics, based upon this season?

Figure 18.5 is the model of a golfer at a university that had won the national golf championship. The forces affecting his participation, development, and general concept of athletics are vastly different from those affecting the quarterback at the same university. Would a winning or a losing season have any major effect upon his self-dignity, self-worth, ability to think for himself, and faith in humanity? How would he rate his athletic participation with other educational university experiences? Would the fact that golf is classified as a nonspectator sport have any effect upon his benefits as a participant?

These conceptual models of athletes illustrate the tremendous differences that exist in athletics within our schools and colleges. To express our thoughts intelligently about athletics, their benefits, their problems, their relationship to physical education, and their place in the educational institutions, we must identify:

1. the type of institution;
2. the level of emphasis of the program;
3. the program budget;
4. the specific sports.

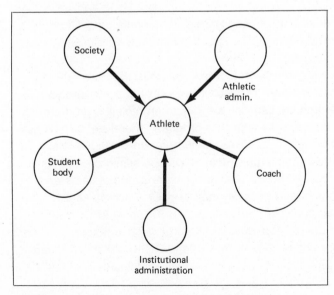

Figure 18.5 Conceptual model of a college athlete

Many of us have been guilty of generalizing in our criticisms of athletics. The following statements are typical of the general indictments against athletics: "Athletics are professional and their purpose is entertainment." "They have no education benefits." "They only exist for institutional publicity." "The players are exploited puppets." "Athletics are just a big business." Supporting these statements are isolated quotations that newspapers feature, such as the following, ascribed to Coach Al McGuire, basketball coach of nationally ranked Marquette University: "We are in the entertainment business, and in order to compete with the professionals for the leisure dollar, we must put on a good show."[43]

These critical statements are all most unfortunate because they tend to indict the entire profession of amateur athletics. Yet, a careful evaluation of all athletic programs in our schools and colleges, including all sports, athletes, and coaches, would reveal that a very high percentage of our athletes are reaping the benefits of competitive sports. This is why athletics will always remain with us.

Intercollegiate athletic programs: problems and direction

In order to identify specific problems, discuss alternative solutions, and relate to the changes in athletics, it is necessary that athletics in schools and colleges be further subdivided. The National Collegiate Athletic Association, the governing body for intercollegiate sports for men, divides college and university athletic programs into three classifications to provide national competition at three distinct levels. The classifications are based on student enrollment, program emphasis, and schedule.

The conceptual model of the athlete in Figures 18.4 and 18.5 illustrates the tremendous differences that can exist between the football and golf programs at the same university. It is extremely difficult to evaluate an athletics program without reference to a specific sport within that program. Therefore, we will use two common terms of our sports' vocabulary, *semiprofessional* and *amateur,* to identify different sports within athletic programs. A college semiprofessional sport would be a *sport that included 80 percent or more of the athletes on NCAA full scholarships.* This does not mean that the NCAA scholarship regulation constitutes professionalism, but merely that it distinguishes the predominately scholarship sports. The present NCAA athletic scholarship includes the costs of room, board, tuition, books, and $15 a month for laundry expenses. All sports with less than 80 percent of their participants on "full"

[43] John Mooney, *Salt Lake Tribune,* April 2, 1973.

scholarship would be classified as *amateur.* This subdivision would be applicable to the three NCAA classifications. To help further distinguish between semiprofessional and amateur sports, it might be proper to assume that the semiprofessional sports lean more toward the *business-entertainment* objective as opposed to the *student-educational* objective, the original purpose of amateur sports. This subdivision should help us place in perspective sports in our educational institutions of higher learning. For example, a major criticism levied against athletic programs has been the numerous scholarships needed for them to operate competitively.

If the subdivision into semiprofessional and amateur college sports were accepted, then the philosophical dichotomy that now exists in collegiate athletics might begin to be dissolved. The semiprofessional sports could continue to operate under the NCAA and the amateur sports could resume their original role as a part of physical education with a new national association in control. Olson[44] proposed that athletics return to the umbrella of physical education and that national controls be reorganized as an arm of the American Alliance for Health, Physical Education, and Recreation.

Semiprofessional college sports Some educators, coaches, alumni, and administrators would not accept the semiprofessional college sports concept because of its threat to amateur athletics. Perhaps terms like *big-time* college sports, or *entertainment-oriented* college sports might be more acceptable, but that is not the real issue. The purpose of the division is to allocate both benefits and problems to their proper sources. To state that athletics is one of the strongest unifying forces still on college campuses and imply that a fencing meet would accomplish this unification is unrealistic. Such an accomplishment can be more properly claimed by an athletic program if the sport is football or basketball.

The semiprofessional sports in colleges and universities contribute tremendously to the total structure and offering of an institution. These benefits could be:

1. a unifying force;
2. entertainment;
3. publicity;
4. income;
5. an operation that employs several people;
6. a laboratory of experiences for the athletes.

[44] Edward Olson, "Intercollegiate Athletics, Is There No Way To Live With It?" *NCPEAM Proceedings,* January 1973, pp. 19–22.

This listing is not in rank order because each benefit might be evaluated differently by each university. The publicity given the finals of the 1973 NCAA basketball championships was far more important to Memphis State University than it was to the University of California, Los Angeles. Every basketball fan in the country is familiar with UCLA's basketball dynasty. The benefit that Memphis State University received from being in the finals of the basketball tournament is impossible to measure.

According to T. Marshall Hahn, president of Virginia Institute of Technology, winning the National Invitational Basketball Tournament resulted in thousands of dollars being pledged to the college treasury. He also expected that because of the championship, alumni, corporations, and the Virginia General Assembly would look more favorably upon the school.[45]

To the athlete, the benefits of athletic competition can be innumerable. The opportunities to develop self-confidence, self-esteem, self-discipline, and self-dignity are ever present. Loyalty, cooperation, sacrifice, and competitiveness are characteristics that athletes may obtain from one of the best laboratories for learning. A small percentage of performers become professionals and continue athletic competition as a vocation. Many, because their athletic accomplishments have given them public exposure, are offered lucrative positions.

College and university semiprofessional sports are by no means free of problems, such as:

1. finances;
2. coaching personnel;
3. conference and national controls;
4. exploitation of athletes;
5. eligibility;
6. professional leagues;
7. public relations and promotion;
8. impact of experiences on athletes.

Is the total educational development of a student who participates in a university semiprofessional sport affected thereby? Would the outcomes received by the semiprofessional athlete differ noticeably from those presently received by athletes in many major universities' sports programs? Would the open identification of the semiprofessional be harmful or helpful to the athlete, coaches, student body, athletics administrators, and institutional administrators? Answers to these questions may be the key to acceptance of the university semiprofessional sports concept.

[45] Robert Creamer, "Scoreboard," *Sports Illustrated,* April 16, 1973, p. 21.

Some universities already separate the revenue-producing sports from the remainder of the athletics program, usually by placing football and basketball in a separate department or division. The problems of university athletics appear to be bringing about major organizational changes. The details must be worked out by the leaders of athletics, the coaches, athletics directors, faculty athletics committees, conference commissioners, and national executive personnel.

Amateur college sports All college and university sports are amateur, that is, they are educational and student-oriented. The college or university amateur sports program, in this subdivision, would have some of the same benefits and problems found in semiprofessional sports. The differences would be in budget, external pressure groups, and purpose. An amateur sport would be included in a total athletics program to provide the opportunities for interested and qualified college or university students. The intensity of competition and the athletes' need to win would be no different in an amateur than in a semiprofessional sport. However, the external forces of student-body reaction and society would be much less in most sports, although there might be exceptions in some specific sports from one year to the next.

Sports classified as amateur would not be expected to produce an income; their program would be justified by the educational opportunities afforded the

College amateur tennis

participants. Financial support for these sports would be a part of the budget of the institution, either as part of the physical education budget or identified separately. Amateur sports would have the same general objectives as physical education, the basic difference being the ability of the participants. In many colleges and universities, faculty members would undertake coaching responsibilities and physical education teaching assignments.

Intercollegiate athletics for women Interschool athletics for women have been a part of collegiate programs for many years. Until the establishment of the Commission on Intercollegiate Athletics for Women (CIAW) in 1967, most intercollegiate sports contests were in the form of "play days." These events attracted teams representing several colleges to one campus for one or two days of competition in a sport, organized as a tournament. Winning appeared to be secondary to the opportunities for participation and socialization. Many colleges referred to these events as *extramurals,* meaning competition outside their college. In fact, this is still the label for the program of interschool athletics for women in many colleges.

The CIAW, a part of the Division of Girls' and Women's Sports (DGWS) of the American Alliance for Health, Physical Education, and Recreation (AAHPER) was organized to:

1. encourage organization of colleges and universities and/or organizations of women physical educators to govern intercollegiate competition for women at the local, state, or regional level;
2. hold DGWS national championships as the need for them becomes apparent;
3. sanction closed intercollegiate events in which at least five colleges or universities are participating.[46]

The work of this Commission, combined with the movement to provide women equal opportunities in the total society, stimulated the expansion of intercollegiate athletics programs for women. This growth was so rapid that the Commission was replaced by the Association of Intercollegiate Athletics for Women (AIAW) in 1971–1972, which is presently the national governing body for intercollegiate sports for women. Its purposes are to:

1. foster broad programs of women's intercollegiate athletics which are consistent with the education objective of member schools;
2. assist member schools to extend and enrich their programs of intercollegiate athletics for women;

[46] Martha Adams and Doris Soladay, eds., *AIAW Handbook.* Washington, D.C.: American Alliance for Health, Physical Education, and Recreation, 1972–1973, p. 5.

3. stimulate the development of quality leadership among persons responsible for women's intercollegiate athletic programs;
4. encourage excellence in performance of participants in women's intercollegiate athletics.[47]

"At this early stage in the development of women's sports, very few women athletes are recruited. However, as team championships begin to replace the objectives of participation and individual satisfaction, recruiting and subsidizing athletes will undoubtedly accompany this change in emphasis."[48]

Intercollegiate athletics for women are present on most college campuses in one form or another. Where separate programs for women are not available as yet, women are competing for positions on the college teams, which formerly consisted entirely of men. This integration has created a few problems, the major one being that conference regulations have not accounted for team representation by women. However, combined representation on intercollegiate teams is limited, since most colleges and universities have developed specific programs for women.

As the intercollegiate sports programs for women develop, it is apparent that DGWS is striving desperately to avoid the pitfalls of exploitation and commercialism that have plagued men's programs. The DGWS statement on scholarship follows:

The Division of Girls' and Women's Sports reaffirms its concern that the provision of scholarships or other financial assistance specifically designated for athletes may create a potential for abuses that could prove detrimental to the development of quality programs of athletics. Specifically, the DGWS deplores the evils of pressure recruiting and performer exploitation which frequently accompany the administration of financial aid for athletes.

The DGWS is concerned that many collegiate athletic programs as currently administered do not make available to female students benefits equivalent in nature or extent to those made available to male students. While a curtailment of programs of financial aid to female students involved in athletics does eliminate the potential for abuses inherent in any such programs, this remedy is overly broad because it operates inequitably to deny to female students benefits available to their male counterparts. Specifically, these benefits might include the recognition of athletic excellence and the opportunity for economic assistance to secure an education.

Therefore, DGWS believes that the appropriate solution in our contemporary society is one directed to avoiding abuses while providing to female students, on an equitable

---

[47] *Ibid.*, p. 7.

[48] James R. Ewers, "Move Over Men: The Women Are Coming," *NCPEAM Proceedings,* December 1970, p. 180.

basis, benefits comparable to those available to male students similarly situated.

   Success of financial assistance programs is dependent upon the quality of administration. To foster appropriate administrative procedures, the following guidelines are recommended.

1. The enrichment of the life of the participant should be the focus and the reason for athletic programs.
2. Adequate funding for a comprehensive athletic program should receive priority over the money assigned for financial aid. A comprehensive athletic program provides adequate funding for (a) a variety of competitive sports which will serve the needs of many students; (b) travel, using licensed carriers and with appropriate food and lodging; (c) first-rate officials; (d) well-trained coaches; and (e) equipment and facilities which are safe and aid performance.
3. The potential contribution of the "educated" citizen to society, rather than the contribution of the student to the college offering the scholarship, should be the motive for financial aid.
4. Staff time and effort should be devoted to the comprehensive program rather than to recruiting.
5. Students should be free to choose the institution on the basis of curriculum and program rather than on the amount of financial aid offered.
6. When financial aid is to be given, participants in certain sports should not be favored over those in other sports.

Women's intercollegiate gymnastics

7. Students should be encouraged to participate in the athletic program for reasons other than financial aid.[49]

Many athletic directors and leaders of men's intercollegiate sports programs have commended the DGWS's leadership in attempting to control recruiting, scholarships, and exploitation.

Since the appointment of the CIAW in 1967, our competitive society has imposed its standards on women as vehemently as it has on men. Winning is no less important to a team of young women than to a team of men. Women coaches in just a few short seasons have learned how the "game" of competitive sports actually works. Potentially great players must be recruited, a process that takes time, effort, and money. The critical questions in women's sports are: How long can the sports programs be conducted before the pitfalls of exploitation and commercialism occur? Are the ideals of the present leaders of women's sports unrealistic?

Interscholastic sports Interscholastic athletics resemble collegiate athletics, because most educational trends descend from colleges to high schools. The major difference is the absence of recruiting in secondary schools. This means that the interscholastic program can devote its time, effort, and money to the further development of the participants and other areas of the program. There is little or no dissension among athletes as a result of special treatment of individuals or groups on high school teams. No athlete receives any special compensation for his or her services. Coaches cannot replace their players with someone bigger, faster, and stronger, but must attempt to develop each prospective athlete to his utmost potential in many ways. This demands coaching talents.

The coach is usually considered to be at the bottom of the academic totem pole. In spite of his educational standing, he does something that frequently is missing elsewhere in teaching—he enters into an encounter with his pupils. Sometimes this encounter is positive and at other times negative, but it is real and the athlete knows where he stands. He is not afraid to preach the gospel of winning—that not only is it good to win but that it is not immoral to desire to win. Interscholastic athletics have a special meaning to many who have experienced the thrill of being a part of a team and have had a leader who encourages his players to succeed by their own efforts. Coach Larry Hawkins'

[49] "The Division for Girls' and Women's Sports, *Philosophy and Standards for Girls' and Women's Sports*," rev. ed. Washington, D.C.: American Alliance for Health, Physical Education, and Recreation, 1972, p. 4.

personal dedication to the inner-city boys at Carver High School in Chicago is best attested by these quotations from graduates of the program.

Hawkins made the things happening in the world, in Chicago, in the university, in the country, seem more real.
He built us up so that we thought we could perform and then followed up and tried to keep in touch with us.
We were taught not to say we didn't like anything until we had tried it. It is hard to say you don't like an apple until you have tried one.
The program made a difference between my being on a street corner and making something of myself.[50]

   Programs of interscholastic sports are expanding in many directions. Girls' programs are emerging in high schools all over the country. Junior high schools are offering interschool competitive opportunities for their students. Midland, Texas, public schools, for example, constructed a program for children in grades 4, 5, and 6 which has taken pressure off the people in the city to develop organized leagues for competition. They emphasized:

1. participation for everyone;
2. skill development;
3. a chance to learn sportsmanship, team play, and competition under more relaxed conditions than in leagues emphasizing winning.[51]

Enrichment programs

School programs of physical education and recreation are continually expanding beyond the service program, intramurals, and interschool athletics. Special programs to serve people with extraordinary needs are being accepted as a part of the responsibility of the schools. The community school and special physical education programs for the handicapped are striving to enrich the lives of as many people as possible within the communities they serve.

Community school concept

The late Lyndon B. Johnson expressed his philosophy of the community school:

I see a future in which education and training will be a permanent bridge between learning, employment, and human development. Even as we develop new uses of

[50] Larry Hawkins, "Athletics as Academic Motivation for the Inner-City Boy," *JOPER,* February 1972, p. 41.

[51] Linus J. Dowell, "Environmental Factors of Childhood Competitive Athletics," *Physical Educator,* March 1971, p. 19.

technology we recognize that people grow stale unless there is a continuous renewal of their knowledge, enrichment of their skills, and development of their talents. Tomorrow's school will be the center of community life, for grownups as well as children, a shopping center of human services. It might have a community health clinic or a public library, a theatre and recreational facilities. It will provide formal education for all citizens—and it will not close its doors anymore at three o'clock. It will employ its buildings round the clock and its teachers round the year. We just cannot afford to have an 85-billion-dollar plant in this country open less than 30 percent of the time.[52]

The concept of the community school is much more than keeping the school building open in the evenings and on weekends. It is not a program that begins when the regular school ends, nor is it a separate program added to the existing school. "The community school curriculum encompasses all the programs of action and learning from early morning until late at night and for each day of the entire year."[53]

School administrators have been requested by many church groups, scout troops, and community organizations to allow their use of the school's facilities. Frequently, the rental of the facilities is too expensive or their requests are turned down for the following reasons:

1. We have no personnel available to supervise.
2. We do not want to invite vandalism.
3. The evening hours are the only time that our maintenance personnel can clean the building.
4. We have not budgeted for the operation of the facilities in the evenings.
5. If we permit your group the use of the facilities, then we would have to make them available to every organization.

These are all very logical reasons and have been accepted for many years. However, with the rise in costs for labor, materials, and services, the taxpayer is beginning to ask how this burden can be reduced. Are we getting the best possible return for our school tax money? We are losing if our schools are locked at nights, weekends, and summers because inside these locked doors are many opportunities for a richer community life. By using the schools more and avoiding duplication of facilities and services, community schools make a much better return on our tax dollar and give more confidence to the public.[54]

[52] Quoted in D. U. Levine, "Community School in Historical Perspective," *The Elementary School Journal,* 67, January 1967, p. 192.

[53] W. Fred Totten and Frank J. Manley, *The Community School.* Galien, Michigan: Allied Education Council, 1969, p. xxviii.

[54] Roger Cox, "An Investigation and Comparison of Selected State and Local Officials' Agreements or Disagreements concerning the Community School Concept," unpublished doctoral dissertation, The University of Utah, 1973, pp. 24, 26.

Milwaukee was the first city to benefit from a state law approving a tax for the community use of schools. The Board of School directors accepted the responsibility for organizing and conducting the entire school program. In response to the voters' craving for leisure-time pursuits, the fourth "R," for recreation, became an integral part of the total educational experience in Milwaukee's public schools. Among the exciting activities included in these programs are:

1. creative experiences—arts, crafts, drama, music;
2. contemporary interests—family living, home and household, investment planning, languages for travel, driver education;
3. personal health, figure analysis, physical fitness, indoor sports;
4. recreation skills—golf, gun safety, mountaineering, watercraft safety;
5. sports and athletic contests—friendly competition, mixed activity.

Programming for the elderly is extensive, with 62 golden-age clubs and 6 "drop-in" centers, XYZ (eXtra Years of Zest). Adaptive recreation and developmental activities are provided for over 1000 physically handicapped, mentally retarded, and emotionally disturbed children in a continuous operation.[55]

Special physical education for the handicapped

"The most important accomplishment in the life of my boy was learning to swim. He can go to the public swimming pool and 'join in' with the other boys in water games. He can relate to them because he can do what they can do." These words came from the heart of a dedicated mother of a twelve-year-old mongoloid. It was easy to see that raising this boy for twelve years had taken its toll on her. She looked tired, because she was tired. Her other five children are "normal" but the father is not capable of accepting John as one of the family. Nor is John accepted by the neighborhood boys because he looks different, can't talk well enough to be understood, can't run very fast, can't throw a ball very well, can't catch a ball, and can't remember the rules of the games. Thank goodness for television, because a TV won't reject anyone. However, can a young boy spend his entire life in front of a TV?

The educational opportunities for a mongoloid are extremely limited. At the preschool age only a few private training schools are available, many with untrained, volunteer personnel doing most of the teaching. Public schools are doing their best to provide educational opportunities for the retarded after they

---

[55]George T. Wilson, "The New Leisure Ethic and What It Means to the Community School," *JOPER*, January 1973, p. 65.

reach school age. Most schools are understaffed and the necessary equipment and supplies are not available.

John has been provided with many opportunities to help him develop—more than his parents could afford. He has been to numerous camping programs, has attended the summer recreation programs at the local parks, and is very active in the YMCA. John is mentally retarded, but trainable. His mother is vitally concerned about him because she realizes that he will soon be reaching that age when he must:

1. develop some independence;
2. learn some elementary vocational skills;
3. be able to resolve some of his own personal problems;
4. be prepared to face the "cruel world";
5. have some skills to enjoy his leisure successfully.

Fortunately, John will make it, because his mother did not wait for someone to assume the responsibility of training him. She performed admirably. She made sure that he had many successful experiences. In addition to swimming, John likes to bowl with his brothers and sisters. He won a medal in the fifty-yard-dash at the "Special Olympics." He goes horseback riding. Camping is one of the family's favorite summer activities.

This true development illustrates that:

1. mongoloid children can progress to a state where they can be accepted by their peers in some areas of activity;
2. handicapped children require a lot of care, love, attention, and direction if they are going to achieve;
3. parents (or parent) must be willing to assume some of the responsibility for the educational opportunities of their children;
4. school programs for handicapped children must assume a high priority in the educational developments of the future;
5. physical education programs may be the most important subjects for many handicapped children.

Physical education activities may be the only areas where achievement is noticeable to the children. Many handicapped children tend to lead sedentary lives, having poor motor development and being rejected socially by their peers. Their life is filled with leisure time because the work that they can accomplish around the home is limited. The need for qualified personnel and outstanding programs of physical education is desperate for these extraordinary children. Fortunately, physical education and programs for elementary school children are the two fastest developing areas in this profession. There are many outstanding programs in existence and the research supports their necessity and importance.

Special physical education for the handicapped

Professional preparation programs

Professional preparation within the formal curriculum assists the candidate in developing the competencies needed for the chosen profession. As the profession of physical education broadens in scope, programs for the training of teachers at colleges and universities must be prepared to change. New areas of specialization will affect professional preparation, as will different approaches to teaching.

Scope of physical education and professional preparation

Among the developments broadening the scope of physical education that will affect professional preparation programs, the following seem to be most critical at this time:

1. Physical education service programs in the schools and colleges will move into "lifetime sports." Colleges and universities will need to offer retraining workshops for teachers already on the job. In addition, the performance and teaching skills of these carry-over sports will need to be included within the competencies of graduates in physical education.
2. More extensive programs of physical education at the elementary level definitely will require a specialist prepared in the skills of physical education with a complete understanding of the physical, psychological, and social development of this age group.
3. The addition of special physical education programs for the handicapped creates a definite demand for a preparation combining special education, recreation therapy, and physical education.
4. Three separate developments in coaching will affect professional preparation in this

area. First, the secondary administrator is increasingly hiring coaches for men's sports from teaching fields outside of physical education. In turn, this forces many male students with coaching ambitions to pursue a teaching major in another field. Second, along with the increased number of male coaches employed by high schools, teachers of different academic subjects have been appointed assistant coaches without any preparation or participation in the sport. These separate developments have stimulated the "coaching minor" which provides for those students who are seeking teaching and coaching employment. Third, the tremendous growth of girls' and women's athletics places a burden on many physical educators now teaching who neither prepared for nor participated in competitive sports while in college. Workshops, clinics, and in-service training sessions will be critical to those teachers assigned the responsibilities for coaching teams. The future teachers of girls' physical education will need to be prepared for all aspects of coaching competitive teams. In addition to the skills and techniques of coaching, sports psychology and sports sociology are meaningful preparations. ·

5. Commercial recreation facilities are being constructed in all parts of the country. The health spa, tennis club, golf club, ski resort, and boating businesses are examples of the numerous employment opportunities for qualified candidates. These private recreational facilities require some special skills that are unique to their business such as business management, accounting, public relations, and human relations skills, as well as the basic skills for teaching physical education.

6. A few selected professional preparation programs are conducted with professional athletic teams to develop qualified administrators of sports teams.

As new areas of emphasis and specialization develop, the programs of professional preparation need to become more flexible. Employment opportunities are available in more areas than ever before. In the past, most college and university professional preparation programs in physical education prepared a person to teach at the secondary level. Everyone took basically the same program, regardless of interest. If you took a job as an elementary teacher, you merely learned the competencies needed for that assignment by trial and error.

The major changes in the entire profession of physical education at this time create a degree of excitement that has never before existed. We are at the threshold of making an impact on our society which will never be forgotten. The United States has never been more ready to accept the total concept of physical education and recreation than it is now. The question remains, can it do the job? The answer must be, yes!

Summary

1. Historically, physical education programs have reflected the philosophy of the leaders in the profession and the needs of young people. Program emphases have varied from the European influence of gymnastics, through

numerous fitness movements, to sports programs dominated by team sports.

2. In 1965, the Lifetime Sports Foundation was established to help promote sports that could be enjoyed by all throughout their lifetime. Along with the AAHPER's support of the lifetime sports movement, a tremendous change is taking place in school and college physical education programs. Such activities as mountaineering, orienteering, rock climbing, snow skiing, ski touring, judo, karate, aikido, hathayoga, kayaking, canoeing, sailing, trap shooting, riflery, jogging, cycling, fishing, horseback riding, and skating appear quite frequently in college programs throughout the country.

3. The unique characteristic of many lifetime sports is that the participant is not required to possess the ability to run fast, be strong, throw and catch a ball.

4. The nonball lifetime sports are popular for the following reasons: (a) students like to be identified individually; (b) many of the activities are new and exciting experiences; (c) many do not require a level of motor-skill development to be successful; (d) many are enjoyed primarily for the merits of participation and not to determine a winner or a loser; (e) many have foreign origins that give the student the opportunity to learn sports native to other countries and cultures.

5. One of the most difficult hurdles to overcome in order to initiate innovative activities in a physical education program is the class schedule.

6. Although physical education is still a required subject in 74 percent of the colleges and universities, there appears to be a trend toward making the subject elective.

7. Among the critical problems confronting secondary school physical education programs are: (a) money; (b) large classes; (c) range of age and ability levels; (d) schedule; (e) facilities; (f) equipment; (g) faculty competencies.

8. As elementary physical education programs reveal the results of their efforts, it may not be long before physical education, under the direction of a specialist, will be an integral part of every elementary school program.

9. Perhaps the most dramatic change in the intramural program in most colleges and universities is the sports-club movement.

10. Because of the differing emphases on various sports within intercollegiate athletics programs, we need a new system for classifying these sports in order to discuss the problems within the respective programs. The terms *semiprofessional* and *amateur* would serve. All sports with less than 80 percent of their participants on full NCAA scholarship would be classified

as amateur sports. All sports above the 80 percent level would be *semiprofessional.*

11. Semiprofessional sports in colleges and universities could offer these benefits: (a) a unifying force; (b) entertainment; (c) publicity; (d) income; (e) employment of several people; (f) a laboratory of experiences for the athletes.

12. The AIAW was organized during the 1971–1972 academic year to: (a) foster broad programs of women's intercollegiate athletics; (b) assist member schools to extend and enrich their programs; (c) stimulate the development of quality leadership among persons responsible for women's intercollegiate programs; (d) encourage excellence in performance of participants in women's intercollegiate athletics.

13. The community school concept is much more than keeping the school building open in the evenings and on weekends. It encompasses all the programs of action and learning from early morning until late at night and for each day of the entire school year.

14. Physical education may be the most important subject for many handicapped children. Fortunately, programs of physical education for handicapped children and in the elementary schools are the two fastest developing areas in this profession.

Questions

1. What is the responsibility of the physical educator toward children who are physically unfit?
2. What was President Kennedy's influence on physical education in the schools?
3. Identify the main characteristics of the so-called carry-over activities.
4. Document the statement that carry-over activities are becoming more and more popular with students, especially those of college age.
5. What are the implications of approaching a physical education foundations course from a problem-solving point of view?
6. Do you believe that all physical education courses for a college population should be elective?
7. Discuss the implications of resolution 4 approved by the NCPEAM in January 1973.
8. Identify the major problems that physical education is facing in the public schools. Propose solutions.
9. Do you know of any innovative programs actually in effect? Compare their objectives to the traditional ones.
10. Do you think that physical education programs in elementary schools have proved

successful enough to serve as a persuasive argument for the schools that do not have any specialists?

11. Are there any indications that intramural sports programs are in a period of transition? Document.
12. Could you relate the historical forces that have made sports such a powerful institution in the United States?
13. Discuss some of the evils of today's athletics.
14. Are collegiate athletics programs education, entertainment, or professionalism?
15. Identify the benefits of a successful athletics program for an institution.
16. What are the main athletics associations and conferences? Enumerate some of their activities.
17. Who is a coach? What are a coach's responsibilities? Is there a difference between a physical educator and a coach?
18. It has often been said that commercial recreation facilities are exploiting people. What is your opinion regarding this matter?
19. How has the equal-opportunity concept been developing over the last few years for groups such as the handicapped and the blind?

19

CAREERS
IN PHYSICAL EDUCATION

At the beginning of a new school year, many university departments invite new and returning students to orientation meetings to help them make a successful start in their college education. The following questions are typically asked by students interested in physical education as a career.

Employment opportunities

I am interested in majoring in physical education but I have heard that the employment opportunities are extremely limited. Is this true?

That physical educators have more employment opportunities than graduates of other disciplines is a difficult statement to prove. However, physical educators who have combined their studies with health and recreation are frequently qualified and are employed in the following capacities:

437

Physical education teachers in elementary schools
Physical education teachers in secondary schools
Coaches and teachers in secondary schools
Athletic trainers in secondary schools
Physical education supervisors
Faculty managers of athletics or athletic directors in secondary schools
Physical education teachers in junior colleges
Coaches and physical education teachers in junior colleges
Physical education department chairmen and athletics directors in junior colleges
Physical education teachers in the colleges and universities
Coaches and physical education teachers in colleges and universities ·
Athletics trainers in colleges and universities
Athletics directors in colleges and universities
Administrators of professional athletic teams
Athletics trainers of professional athletic teams
Teachers of handicapped children and adults in public and private schools, institutions, colleges, and hospitals
Instructors in the YWCA and YMCA
Directors of YWCA and YMCA programs
Public park and recreation leaders
Camp counselors, instructors, and directors
Directors of religious-affiliated youth centers
American Red Cross
Boy Scouts and Girl Scouts
Boys' Clubs of America
Recreation directors for private industry
Instructors in health spas
Directors or managers of health spas
Recreation directors in state institutions such as prisons and juvenile correction schools
Recreation directors for the National Park Service
Directors of recreational programs for the armed services
Instructors in private studios of dance, gymnastics, fencing, karate, judo, and scuba diving
Instructors and directors of private gymnasiums, swim clubs, tennis clubs, golf clubs, hunting clubs, and ski resorts
Sporting equipment, manufacturing and selling
Sporting equipment design
Sports telecasting and broadcasting
Sports journalism
Sport facilities planning
Sport facilities construction
Sports information, direction, and publicity
Sports nutrition research
Sports training and paramedical practice
Sports publications and training-film production and sales
International exchange programs

Overseas educational service
International schools services
Peace Corps
Vista
Job Corps

Additionally, some physical educators enter the business world as sales people, capitalizing on their competitive background and experience in working with people.

Specific possibilities

Can you be more specific about job possibilities?

Although the above list shows the possibilities open to physical educators, it must be recognized that actual employment opportunities are extremely limited in certain jobs and in certain geographic locations. The surplus of teachers in almost every field of study extends to physical education, for the following reasons:

1. the taxpayers' refusal to support public education;
2. a leveling-off in student enrollments;
3. a reduction in teaching staff (unfortunately, athletics and elementary physical education instruction are eliminated when funds are reduced);
4. teacher preparation in colleges and universities emphasizes quantity rather than quality in the selection, retention, and graduation of physical educators.

According to Harold Regier, in 1971, 305,711 graduates of colleges and universities were prepared to teach, but only 19,000 positions were available. These alarming statistics are somewhat misleading, because the Regier report did not consider the number of vacancies created by those leaving the profession, nor did it indicate the demand for teachers by subject area. The relative surplus of teachers, however, does mean that those who get jobs, in whatever field, will be those with the highest qualifications.[1]

Other findings in Regier's report include:

1. There would be no teacher surplus if present staff workloads were adjusted and class sizes reduced to what they should be.
2. The employment of teacher aides to perform the tasks normally required of teachers has also contributed to the oversupply of teachers.
3. Recruiting minority teachers, including black, Indian, and Hispanic-American, has introduced a new dimension to the problem of teacher supply and demand.

[1] Herold G. Regier, *Too Many Teachers: Fact or Fiction?* Bloomington, Ind.: Phi Delta Kappa, 1972, pp. 1–16.

439

With these points in mind, it might be said that there is no surplus of teachers but an undersupply of money. Only 7 percent or so of the gross national product is spent on education; new means are required to fund education adequately and employ the full force of qualified teachers.[2]

Financial considerations

In view of the financial cutbacks in public school budgets, is the elementary school physical education specialist in a very secure position?

Even though it is strongly urged that physical education specialists teach only physical education in elementary schools, this is not commonly practiced. Even in districts where this has been done, physical education specialists have had to teach all subjects when budgets became strained. Hence preparing to teach physical education in elementary schools does not exempt you from teaching other subjects. It might be advisable to combine physical education with a major in elementary education to qualify as a teacher in the elementary classroom. However, an all-level certificate is available in many states if you want to teach only physical education in the elementary school.

Employment in elementary schools is expected to decline through the 1980s in proportion to the decrease in enrollment. However, increased emphasis on education for the very young (ages three to four), for children in low-income areas, and for the mentally retarded, as well as smaller student-teacher ratios may increase the need for teachers. Chances of employment may be quite favorable if you are willing to take a position in the urban ghettos, rural districts, and in less popular geographic regions.

Responsibilities and duties in secondary schools

Are the duties and responsibilities of physical education teachers the same in most secondary schools?

The duties and responsibilities of secondary school physical education teachers vary greatly with the size of the school and with such other factors as:

1. facilities,
2. equipment,
3. administrative philosophy of physical education,
4. the competency of the teacher.

[2] *Ibid.*

In a small secondary school, the faculty may include one physical education teacher for boys and one for girls. Each may have similar responsibilities, which might include:

1. teaching physical education classes, including all activities;
2. teaching in his or her minor field of study;
3. conducting intramural sports programs;
4. coaching two or three athletic teams;
5. managing the athletics program;
6. supervising the lunch room and hallways;
7. marking athletic fields.

The large secondary school might include a faculty of six physical educators who share the responsibilities of the total program. A faculty of this size makes possible the employment of physical educators with specializations, with different responsibilities for each faculty member. For example, one physical educator may teach dance, gymnastics, and other selected individual sports, one or two classes in her minor field, and coach the girls' gymnastic and tennis teams. Another may teach physical education classes in team sports, one or two classes in his minor field, and direct the boys' intramural program.

These differences between the small and the large secondary school add to the scope of employment available to the physical educator. The subject and teaching methods may be similar in both settings but the environment and the people with whom you work are vastly different in most cases. Some physical educators enjoy rural community living; others would not consider employment outside a metropolitan area.

Salaries tend to favor the larger schools. In 1971–1972, the average beginning salary in cities with population between 6000 and 11,999 was $7017 for graduates with a bachelor's degree; the average maximum was $10,192. The average beginning salary in cities of over 100,000 population, for teachers with the bachelor's degree, was $7503; the average maximum was $11,684.

Extra pay is usually available to those secondary school teachers who undertake extra duties such as coaching, based upon the extent of the additional responsibilities. Some school districts will pay as much as $1000 extra to head football coaches.

Is it true that public school administrators are willing to employ physical education teachers who assume no coaching responsibilities?

Public school administrators were asked: "Would you prefer to employ teachers of physical education who would assume no coaching responsibilities at the interscholastic level?" Forty-six percent of the administrators responded "yes," 28 percent responded "no," and 26 percent had no preference. However, when asked: "Do you employ teachers of physical education who assist with coaching duties?" 83 percent responded "yes," 8 percent, "no," and 9 percent, "not usually." One administrator responded that a good physical education teacher does not have time for anything but physical education classes and intramurals.[3]

With the pressures placed upon the administrators and the coaches to provide opportunities for athletic competition and to produce winning teams, the demand for coaches will always be greater than the number of physical educators. Therefore, most physical educators will be assigned some coaching responsibilities to accompany their teaching assignments.

The college situation

I am only interested in becoming a head football coach. Do colleges offer a major in coaching?

According to all available information, no college or university offers a major in coaching. However, numerous departments of physical education offer a minor in coaching, programs initiated when high schools began to expand their interscholastic programs. Some schoods offer ten or more sports for boys and six or more sports for girls, each sport requiring at least one coach. In these high schools, the coaching staff consists of sixteen or more coaches of whom no more than six are employed as physical education instructors. The other ten coaches teach other academic subjects. Some have had experience as varsity athletes on college teams; a few have not engaged in competitive athletics. For those without experience as player or coach, the coaching minor provides a basic understanding of this field. In many states where coaching is an area of certification, only certified personnel can join the coaching staff. To meet certification standards, the applicant must have completed at least a minor in coaching or a major in physical education.

To become a head coach in any sport, it would be advisable to major in an academic field other than physical education, and pursue a minor in coaching. Fifty-two percent of the administrators responded "yes" when asked: "Would you recommend that we discourage those students interested in coaching from majoring in physical education?" Thirty-one percent said "no," and 17 percent indicated no preference.[4]

[3] David G. Adolph, "What Academic and Coaching Preparation for Our Prospective Teacher-Coaches Will Best Fulfill the Needs of the High Schools in the Local Area?" unpublished master's thesis, University of Akron, 1965, pp. 26, 27, 35, and 36.

[4] *Ibid*, p. 36.

What is involved in college teaching?

Teaching at a college or university will also vary with the size of the institution and, more specifically, of the department. At a small college with a combined department of health, physical education, recreation, and athletics, most faculty will teach activity classes, teach in the professional preparation program, assist with intramural sports, and coach athletic teams. The professional preparation program includes a wide range of courses, such as:

1. teaching specific sports skills;
2. methods of teaching physical education;
3. administration of physical education;
4. student teaching;
5. anatomy;
6. kinesiology;
7. physiology;
8. adapted physical education;
9. tests and measurements;
10. health education;
11. recreation;
12. coaching classes.

Each faculty member is expected to be knowledgeable in all areas, but will usually specialize in one or two. Additional duties might include:

1. departmental committees;
2. college committees;
3. counseling students;
4. community service projects such as clinics and workshops;
5. attending conferences and conventions;
6. contributing articles of interest to professional journals;
7. continuously reading and studying professional literature.

Coaching responsibilities in small colleges might include serving as a head coach in one sport and assisting in one or two other sports. Most faculty members will coach at least two or three sports.

At a university, responsibilities become more specialized. Coaches do very little teaching, if any, in the physical education department. In many universities, the department of athletics is completely separate from health and physical education, and the coaches do not hold faculty appointments.

Some universities have even separated health, physical education, and recreation (leisure studies) into distinct divisions or departments. This separation is more prevalent where the departments offer graduate degrees and, therefore, have a more highly specialized faculty. The areas of specialization in physical education at a university include those offered by a college and, in addition:

1. administration and leadership;
2. curriculum;
3. research methodology and statistics;
4. mechanical analysis of activity;
5. physiology of exercise and human performance;
6. psychology of sport;
7. sociology of sport;
8. sport history;
9. motor learning;
10. physical education/recreation for the handicapped.

Nonteaching responsibilities at a university are similar to those at a college. In addition, major assignments are: directing graduate students in research work, and administering and evaluating comprehensive and oral examinations.

Employment at a university requires a doctoral degree and some teaching experience. Many colleges also require the doctoral degree for employment where teaching and/or administrative responsibilities are primary assignments. Most head football and head basketball coaching positions at colleges do not require the doctoral degree, these appointments being usually based upon successful coaching experience.

Average salaries for college and university physical educators range from $8342 for instructors to $16,684 for professors. Table 19.1 shows the mean salaries and differentials between mean salaries of men and women faculty in

Table 19.1   Mean salaries and differentials between mean salaries of men and women faculty in colleges and universities

Rank	Colleges				Universities			
	N	Mean	SD	Diff.	N	Mean	SD	Diff.
Professor								
Male	39	16,098	2,306	200	71	16,005	2,466	−679
Female	31	15,898	1,735		60	16,684	2,761	
Associate Professor								
Male	36	12,998	1,442	112	65	13,455	1,594	419
Female	33	12,886	1,370		61	13,036	2,274	
Assistant Professor								
Male	55	12,206	1,428	438	65	11,508	1,495	1,025
Female	45	10,768	1,262		107	10,483	1,451	
Instructor								
Male	19	9,386	911	595	47	8,955	1,262	613
Female	38	8,791	1,048		69	8,342	917	

Source: Rita J. Aschcraft, "Comparison of Employment Status of Men and Women in Four-Year Public Institutions," JOPER, April 1973, p. 61.

Table 19.2 Mean salaries and differentials between mean salaries of men and women faculty in colleges and universities

	Colleges				Universities			
Rank	N	Mean	SD	Diff.	N	Mean	SD	Diff.
Professor								
Male	15	18,007	2,793	931	36	19,114	4,815	1,047
Female	5	17,076	3,016		16	18,067	5,029	
Associate Professor								
Male	14	13,798	1,563	744	31	16,450	2,943	3,685
Female	10	13,054	926		12	12,765	4,547	
Assistant Professor								
Male	19	11,628	3,560	1,199	33	13,637	2,115	4,442
Female	16	10,429	1,990		17	9,195	2,503	
Instructor								
Male	7	10,995	1,542	2,119	22	10,984	3,005	3,270
Female	5	8,876	879		12	7,714	2,169	

Source: Rita J. Aschcraft, "Comparison of Employment Status of Men and Women in Four-Year Public Institutions," *JOPER,* April 1973, p. 61.

colleges and universities; the determination is by rank and covers a salary period of nine or ten months. Table 19.2 gives the same information for an eleven- or twelve-month salary period.

Prospects for an abundance of suitable jobs for those with M.A.s and Ph.D.s rest upon four related facts:

1. The basic population pattern has already reduced public school enrollments almost everywhere. The threat of zero population growth has been with us since the mid-1960s. Although population patterns may change, the changes that will affect college enrollments in the 1980s have already taken place.
2. The proportion of young people going on to college has steadily increased throughout the century. It is about 40 percent nationally and has passed 50 percent in some states. Although a large pool of prospective college students remains in the general population, it is strikingly smaller than in the past.
3. Increasing the college population significantly is dependent upon increasing the financial support for higher education. Perhaps the country could afford a continuing expansion of graduate work, but the pattern of spending in the past does not justify much optimism. The percentage of the gross national product going to higher education seems to be leveling off.
4. The expanding job market for M.A.s and Ph.D.s was largely created by the colleges and universities.[5]

[5]Kenneth E. Eble, "How To Succeed despite a Ph.D.?" *The Chronicle of Higher Education,* July 16, 1973, p. 3.

College programs

Does every department of health and physical education offer the same programs of study for the range of job opportunities available?

One of the most promising trends in preparing physical educators is the addition of specific programs of study to meet the local, state, and regional expectations of prospective employers. The offering of a coaching minor by many colleges and universities exemplifies this, as do programs for elementary school physical education specialists and for athletic trainers.

The University of Utah introduced a course in "Commercial Physical Education" designed cooperatively with European Health Spa to qualify teachers and administrators for that company. The program also develops competencies for employment in other private recreational enterprises such as ski resorts, swim and tennis clubs, golf and country clubs, and private gymnasiums. The program combines the following areas:

1. physical education;
2. health education;
3. nutrition;
4. commercial recreation;
5. physical therapy;
6. public relations;
7. business management and accounting.

Bellevue Community College in Washington has developed an occupational program in physical education to prepare its graduates to meet specific job requirements. This program consists of:

1. ski instructor training;
2. underwater diver certification;
3. marine operations;
4. recreation leadership;
5. park and recreation management.

A key element in the successful operation of this program was the establishment of an advisory committee which constantly surveys the job market to guarantee student placement after graduation.[6]

Mason[7] originated the program of preparation in sports administration, designed to prepare the student for a career at either the public school,

---

[6] Robert E. Wendel, "Occupational Programs Are the Future," *JOPER*, October 1972, p. 17.

[7] James Mason, "New Patterns Meet Changing Needs," *JOPER*, November–December 1967. p. 29.

college, or professional level. The student receives a wide variety of experiences as a sports administration intern in public relations, personnel management, media relations advertising, ticket sales, promotion, finance, accounting, purchasing, travel arrangements, scheduling, and contest management.

Some colleges and universities have added courses and field experiences in the specialized areas of adapted physical education and/or physical education for the handicapped. These programs include:

1. introduction to special education;
2. physical education for the physically handicapped;
3. physical education for the mentally retarded;
4. motor learning and the exceptional child;
5. applying motor learning theory to the handicapped;
6. laboratory experiences in teaching the handicapped.

The cost of graduate education limits the programs offered. To equip a human performance or a motor learning laboratory properly exceeds the financial resources of many universities. Sports sociology and sports psychology are both limited by lack of qualified teaching personnel.

Teaching skills, characteristics, and personality traits

Are there special skills, characteristics, and personality traits that seem to be predominant in teachers?

Professional preparation programs must be both specific and general if they are to create teachers competent in several responsibilities. Physical educators are, first of all, teachers, possessing the same skills and characteristics as other teachers in the school. Commonly accepted skills and characteristics of teachers in general include:

1. the development of an adequate physical basis—health, organic vigor, physical fitness, a state of well-being, and total fitness—for the full and abundant life;
2. the development of vocational competence to earn a livelihood and contribute to society;
3. the development of good citizenship to contribute effectively and responsibly to the democracy of which one is a part;
4. the development of desirable personality and character traits;
5. the development of social competence to participate cooperatively and constructively in group endeavors;
6. the development of knowledge, understandings, and skills to use leisure in constructive and satisfying ways;

7. the development of the ability to think and employ one's rational powers to achieve the understanding, aesthetic sensitivity, and moral responsibility necessary to a rich and complete life.[8]

Physical educators are, second, teachers of physical education with such skills and characteristics as:

1. better than average skill in the activity taught and ability to teach it with conviction, enthusiasm, and pride;
2. understanding contemporary students, their needs, interests, and characteristics;
3. giving individual attention and aid to students and knowing them by name;
4. understanding that there are many ways of achieving success, but presenting to students those methods generally considered most effective;
5. understanding the role of a teacher, but maintaining a good relationship with students;
6. understanding the role of physical education in total education and the ability to interpret this to the student;
7. believing sincerely in the values of physical education;
8. possessing sufficient conviction about these values to remain calm and optimistic amid the criticism and questions of other members of the academic community;
9. being professionally prepared to answer the "why's" as well as the "how's" of physical education;
10. ability to demonstrate and analyze skills;
11. desire to teach and work with the learner;
12. possessing a variety of good teaching techniques;
13. ability to relate to the student and recognize his dignity;
14. possessing a good sense of humor and a consistently high level of enthusiasm;
15. flexibility, to adjust to unexpected interferences and take advantage of unplanned opportunities to learn;
16. knowing the subject well enough to employ brief and colorful teaching cues;
17. keeping in clear perspective the role of the physical education teacher and of physical education in relation to each student's total education;
18. sensitivity to student feelings;
19. concern for the below-average and average as well as the superior student;
20. knowing the activity well enough to make learning simple and desirable;
21. providing a sound system of evaluation;
22. striving to perceive the world from the student's point of view.[9]

Developing these characteristics and skills requires a comprehensive program that enables you to understand man in his biological, physical, psychological,

[8] AAHPER, *Professional Preparation in Health, Physical Education, and Recreation.* Washington, D.C.: American Alliance for Health, Physical Education, and Recreation, 1962, p. 13.

[9] Barry C. Pelton, *New Curriculum Perspectives.* Dubuque, Iowa: William C. Brown Company, Publishers, 1970, pp. 65–66.

and social environments, as each relates to becoming a teacher of physical education.

Basic beliefs underlying your professional preparation should include:

1. Professional preparation should be consistent with the philosophy of a free, democratic society.
2. Professional preparation should develop broadly educated persons.
3. Professional preparation should be the responsibility of the college or university as a whole.
4. The profession, the institution, and the agencies employing professional personnel should share responsibility in professional education.
5. The profession should determine the nature of professional preparation.
6. Institutions should be granted increased authority for the certification of school personnel through state departments of public instruction and for the registration of other personnel through professional organizations.
7. Programs of professional preparation should be designed to maintain and improve professional standards.
8. Professional preparation should provide for the synthesis of all experiences that will enable the student to make significant educational decisions.
9. Five years of professional preparation are essential for the basic preparation of personnel in each of the areas of health education, physical education, and recreation education. (Not widely practiced unless it results in a master's degree.)
10. Professional preparation should be a continuous process throughout the career of the professional person.
11. A curriculum designed to prepare professional personnel for a changing society must be responsive to change.
12. The program of professional preparation should be evaluated frequently in terms of the basic concepts and purposes of the profession.
13. Professional preparation should emphasize the development of a personal philosophy which embraces a dedication and devotion for service to mankind.[10]

Certification requirements

Are the requirements for certification to teach physical education the same in all states?

Just as law, medicine, and other professions have standards of eligibility for practice, so does teaching. Hence, the term *certified* signals to the prospective employer that one is prepared to accomplish certain teaching tasks in physical education.

The requirements for the bachelor's degree do not always lead to certification as well. The broad areas within the specialization such as sports skills,

[10] AAPHER, *Professional Preparation in Health, Physical Education, and Recreation*, pp. 21–24.

Table 19.3 Basic and minimum requirements for authorization to teach
physical education

	Men		Women	
State	Basic Require.†	Minimum Require.‡	Basic Require.	Minimum Require.
Alabama	24	18	24	18
Alaska	16	—	16	—
Arizona	30	20	30	18
Arkansas	21	21	21	21
California	AC	AC	AC	AC
Colorado	18	—	18	—
Connecticut	35	35	35	35
Delaware	40[a]	40	40[a]	40
District of Col.	30	30	30	30
Florida	24	—	24	—
Georgia	24	66	24	6
Hawaii	M	M	M	M
Idaho	30	20	30	20
Illinois	20	20	20	20
Indiana	40	24	40	24
Iowa	30	30	30	30
Kansas	24	24	24	24
Kentucky	24	18	24	18
Louisiana	33– 20[a]	33– 20	33– 20[a]	33– 20
Maine	B	B	B	B
Maryland	30	30	30	30
Massachusetts	18	9	18	9
Michigan	24	15	24	15
Minnesota	M	m	M	m
Mississippi	30	30	30	30
Missouri	30	30	30	30
Montana	30	20	30	20
Nebraska	24	12	24	12
Nevada	M	—	M	—
New Hampshire	30[a]	12	30[a]	12
New Jersey	40	40	40	40
New Mexico	36	36	36	36
New York	36	36	36	36
North Carolina	36	—	36	—
North Dakota	16	16	16	16
Ohio	—	24[d]	—	24[d]
Oklahoma	30	18	30	18
Oregon	24	24	24	24
Pennsylvania	AC	AC	AC	AC

Table 19.3 (Continued)

	Men		Women	
State	Basic Require.†	Minimum Require.‡	Basic Require.	Minimum Require.
Puerto Rico	30	30	30	30
Rhode Island	36	36	36	36
South Carolina	24	24	24	24
South Dakota	15	—	15	—
Tennessee	24[b,g]	24	24[b,g]	24
Texas	24	24	24	24
Utah	42	15	42	15
Vermont	36	18	36	18
Virginia	36	36	36	36
Washington	M	m	M	m
West Virginia	39[b]	24	34[b]	24
Wisconsin	22	22	22	22
Wyoming	24	18	24	18

B—A bachelor's degree in an approved program may be accepted in lieu of the required semester hours.

M—a major

m—a minor

AC—approved curriculum

Delaware:40[a]—grades one to twelve

Louisiana: 33—20[a]—gives authorization in health, physical, and safety education; 20—gives authorization only in physical education (including coaching).

New Hampshire: 30[a]—plus 6 credits in methods of teaching the specialty on the elementary and secondary levels.

Ohio: 24[d]—40 credits for a special certificate.

Tennessee: 24[b,g]—valid for grades one to twelve and including health (12 credits) and physical education (12 credits).

West Virginia: 39[b] and 34[b]—valid for grades one to twelve.

†The basic requirement for teaching a subject full time, for a major fraction of the school day, or in the highest classification of schools.

‡The minimum requirement for teaching a subject part time, for a minor fraction of the school day, or in the lowest classification of schools.

Source: T. M. Stinnett. *A Manual on Certification Requirements for School Personnel in the United States.* Washington, D.C.: Natonal Commission on Teacher Education and Professional Standards, National Education Association, 1970.

sciences, methods, student practice, have similar requirements from state to state, but the required number of semester hours may vary considerably, as shown in Table 19.3.

Even though the number of semester hours may vary by as much as 20 from institution to institution, several general requirements must be met by the student and the institution prior to certification. Specific requirements can be provided by your particular department.

United States citizenship is usually required before certification to teach, but a declaration of intent or preliminary papers are sufficient for a temporary certificate in some states. An oath of allegiance is a requirement in about one half the states. Age limits for certification range from 17 to 65.

Most states' requirements for the specific course of study are similar. Differences in general education may vary: for example, some states require the history of that particular state and of federal government. Thus, if you are certified in one state and move to another, you may have to take a course in the history of that state before full certification is granted.

States grant emergency, provisional or temporary, and permanent teaching certificates. The exact requirements for each type must be obtained from the certification department of the state to which you are applying.

A study of practices and trends in certification reveals a move toward greater reciprocity among states which would enable a student certified to teach in Texas to move to California or New York and be certifiable without a great deal of additional college work. Another move to separate certification programs for the elementary and secondary school teachers of physical education would provide needed in-depth preparation at both levels. Professional certification is being urged for athletic coaches who may not be interested in teaching physical education but who certainly need specific training to become coaches.

Special teaching certification in health education as distinct from physical education is already granted by at least 22 states, and this number will no doubt increase. This practice should provide a long-needed improvement of teaching in both physical education and health education.

If the competency-based concept of teacher education and certification continues to flourish, then certification of teachers will be guided by three criteria:

1. *Academic proficiency.* This, the lowest level in use at this time, means that the candidate has achieved a bachelor's degree, has taken certain courses, and has maintained a minimum grade-point average.
2. *Ability to perform skills and behaviors deemed essential to teaching.* This level has three aspects. First, it prescribes that a teacher must be able to perform or demonstrate teaching tasks. Second, it requires that the candidate be able to verbalize about the teaching act. Third, it specifies that the teacher be able to effect change in student behavior. If this concept is implemented, then certification will not be tied to courses, units, and degrees, but will be granted for competencies essential to the task of teaching.
3. *Ability to produce changes in pupil behavior.* This is perhaps the most rigorous criticism. It requires that the candidate's behavior produce an acceptable level of

pupil learning under specified conditions and over a specified time. The growth of pupils must be reflected not only in cognitive achievement, but also in affective development.[11]

Professional physical education organizations

Almost every professional group has national and state organizations such as the American Medical Association for physicians. Do physical education teachers have organizations of this type?

After graduation, you will embark on a career related to physical education and find it necessary to communicate with colleagues in similar pursuits; you will also need access to disciplinary and professional literature. These are two most effective means of maintaining an up-to-date grasp of contemporary theories and practices. In an organization sponsored by physical educators, you are a member of a group of dedicated individuals who are extremely friendly and very willing to share ideas with you. You will also find the writing in the journals and monographs quite helpful and relevant to what is happening in physical education throughout the United States and abroad.

American Alliance for Health, Physical Education, and Recreation

The American Alliance for Health, Physical Education, and Recreation (AAHPER) is a service organization devoted to many facets of the fields mentioned in its title. It is a service organization because the administrative officers of the group do not devise policy to be followed by members of the three fields. Policies and guidelines for the fields are communicated through the AAHPER, however, but they are initiated and developed by the membership of the group or their elected representatives.

AAHPER was founded in 1885 as the American Association for the Advancement of Physical Education; in 1903 this group became the American Physical Education Association. Eventually, in 1937, it merged with the departments of School Health and Physical Education of the National Education Association and, in 1938, added the name Recreation. After its restructuring in 1974, the American Association for Health, Physical Education, and Recreation became the American Alliance for Health, Physical Education, and Recreation. AAHPER is no longer affiliated with NEA.

[11] Roser, et al., *The Power of Competency-based Teacher Education,* Committee on National Program Priorities in Teacher Education, Project no. 1-0475. U.S. Department of Health, Education and Welfare, 1971, pp. 17–21.

The purposes and objectives of AAHPER are stated in its bylaws:

1. to support, encourage, and provide guidance for personnel throughout the nation as they seek to develop and conduct school and community programs in health education, physical education, and recreation based upon the needs, interests, and inherent capacities of the individual and of the society of which he is a part;
2. to facilitate cooperation among these fields of education to further their ultimate and mutual improvement;
3. to improve the effectiveness of school health education, physical education, and recreation in the promotion of human welfare;
4. to increase public understanding and appreciation of the importance and value of the fields as they each and jointly contribute to human welfare;
5. to encourage and facilitate research which will enrich the depth and scope of each of the related fields and to disseminate the findings widely throughout the profession;
6. to further the continuous evaluation of professional standards for personnel and programs, as necessary to assure the improvement of these fields of education;
7. to hold such national conventions and to sponsor such conferences, institutes, and other meetings as will make effective the work of the organization; and to coordinate and support the activities of such local, state, and district organizations as may be integral parts of or affiliated with this national organization, subject to restrictions set forth herein;
8. to produce and distribute such publications as will be of assistance to persons within the profession in the improvement of education;
9. to cooperate with other professional groups of similar interests for the ultimate development of allied fields;
10. to conduct such other activities as shall be approved by the Board of Directors and Representative Assembly of the Association, provided that the Association shall not engage in any activity which would be inconsistent with the status of an educational and charitable organization as defined in Section 501 (c) (3) of the Internal Revenue Code of 1954 or any successor provision thereto, and none of the said purposes shall at any time be deemed or construed to be purposes other than the public benefit purposes and objectives consistent with such educational and charitable status.

To implement the objectives, and to foster communication among its membership, the Alliance is divided into six districts: the Eastern, Midwest, Central, Northwest, Southwest, and Southern districts.

Each district encompasses several states, each state having a suborganization of the AAHPER. Conferences and conventions are sponsored by the national organization, the districts, and the states. Of particular interest to an undergraduate major in health, physical education, or recreation is the recent emergence of strong student sections at the state, district, and national levels. These sections permit the student to become involved in Alliance service and become a part of the fields at a very early age.

454

Among the many publications the Alliance sponsors, *The Journal of Physical Education and Recreation* (JOPER), *The Research Quarterly,* and a newsletter entitled *Update* are perhaps the best known and the most widely read. Student members receive these publications, at a reduced rate, from the Alliance at 1201 Sixteenth Street, NW, Washington, D.C. 20036.

National Association of Physical Education for College Women

This important national association was officially organized in 1924. Historically, physical education was divided into men's and women's departments. This division is rapidly disappearing, but when it was prevalent, women physical educators at colleges needed an organization that would permit them to meet and discuss common problems arising in their departments.

The National Association is now composed of five district associations, the Eastern, Midwest, Central, Southern, and Western. These are relatively independent organizations, but a woman must be a member of a district to attain national membership.

National College Physical Education Association for Men

Originally the Society of College Gymnasium Directors, this organization was established in 1897. Its present name was taken in 1962; the purposes of the Association are many and varied. Among them are the definition of major problems and issues facing physical education in higher education, the interpretation of research, the development of interdisciplinary relationships, and the improvement of the public understanding of physical education. The Association convenes once a year and conducts a series of meetings, seminars, and presentations which are published in the *Proceedings.* The National Association of Physical Education for College Women and the National College Physical Education Association for Men have combined in 1963 to publish *Quest,* a monograph devoted to scholarly research and significant philosophical treatises concerning physical education.

American Academy of Physical Education

Founded in 1930, the purposes of this organization are to elevate standards, bestow honors, and advance knowledge and understanding in physical education and related fields. Membership in the Academy is limited to those elected as fellows because of outstanding professional contributions in research, service, or publication. The Academy publishes the presentations at its national meetings in the *Academy Papers,* including the memorial lecture dedicated to R. Tait McKenzie, a pioneer in the field, that is a meaningful contribution to physical education.

American College of Sports Medicine

In 1954, practitioners of medicine, physical education, and physiology founded this association. Its purposes are to promote and advance scientific studies of the effects of sports on human health, sponsor meetings of physicians, scientists, and educators whose interests are related to sports medicine, and initiate and coordinate research in the area of interest. In 1969, the association began a journal entitled *Science of Medicine in Sports,* which has made significant contributions to many fields, including physical education.

In addition to these associations are professional sororal and fraternal organizations. Delta Psi Kappa limits its membership to women who have a major or minor concentration in physical education. Chapters are located at various colleges and universities, and the official publication, *The Foil,* contains articles and information from the chapters.

Another women's sororal organization, Phi Delta Pi, dedicated to leadership in the field, publishes *The Professional Physical Educator.* Phi Epsilon Kappa is a fraternity limited to males who are students or teachers of health, physical, recreation, or safety education. The organization produces, among many publications, *The Physical Educator,* which often contains stimulating articles.

International employment opportunities

I am intrigued by the possibility of employment abroad. Would you discuss more completely international programs of physical education?

International interest in health, physical education, and recreation has increased at a phenomenal rate in the last thirty years. Several national and international governmental and educational agencies, the International Council for Health, Physical Education, and Recreation, and, to some extent, the Olympic games have aided this growth.

Professional preparation to teach physical education in foreign countries includes, in some cases, practice teaching abroad. Opportunities for professional activity overseas arise in teacher or student exchanges, summer courses, teaching assignments, volunteer programs, or travel during a sabbatical leave. In general, minimum requirements for participation include at least two to three years of teaching experience, a bachelor's degree or, in most cases, a master's degree (highly selective programs require a doctoral degree), some knowledge of the host country language, and U.S. citizenship.

The Association of Commonwealth Universities

This Association is for recently graduated students.

Central Bureau for Educational Visits and Exchanges

This Bureau serves as a national office for information, documentation, and advice on educational travel and the administration of official exchange schemes. It maintains a listing of international meetings, recreation and special activity holidays, exchange visits, group exchanges, working holidays, study courses in Britain, and accommodations.

Committee on International Exchange of Persons

The Committee bestows grants for university lecturing and advanced research, usually for one academic year of the host institution. The requirements for lectureships are: U.S. citizenship, college or university teaching experience at the level of the appointment sought, and, in some cases, proficiency in a foreign language. For research grants, one must have U.S. citizenship, a doctoral degree, or recognized professional training.

Council on International Exchange

This Council serves as a clearinghouse for information on travel, orientation, and exchange programs throughout the world and issues publications in these fields. It encourages development of exchange opportunities throughout the world for students, young adults, and teachers.

U.S. Department of Defense

One can teach in schools for dependents of military and civilian personnel overseas.

Institute of International Education

This Institute bestows grants for predoctoral study or research that enable students to live and study in a foreign country for one academic year. It conducts educational exchange programs sponsored by colleges and universities, foundations, corporations, private organizations, individuals, governments, and intergovernmental agencies; it maintains a library including catalogs of U.S. and foreign educational institutions and materials on comparative education, foreign educational systems and programs, and organizations in the field of international education, and provides information and advice on higher education in the United States and abroad. It publishes studies, handbooks, and information brochures. The requirements are U.S. citizenship, a bachelor's degree or its equivalent, proficiency in the host country's language, and good health. Enrolled applicants submit applications to the campus Fulbright Adviser by a date set by him or her; at-large applicants submit applications in New York by November 1 prior to the academic year for which he or she is being considered; travel grants should be applied for by February 1 of the academic year being considered.

International Organizations Recruitment

This office seeks qualified persons to refer to the United Nations Educational, Scientific and Cultural Organization (UNESCO) for its field positions. The requirements are an advanced degree, 5 to 10 years of teaching and/or administrative experience at the college or university level, proficiency in either English, French, or Spanish depending on the country involved, U.S. citizenship, good health, under 60 years of age, and high personal qualifications and character.

International Schools Service

The Service administers a worldwide program of curriculum and administrative guidance for overseas schools. Requirements for teaching are a bachelor's degree and two or more years of classroom experience. For an administrative position, one must have a master's degree, several years of teaching experience, as well as administrative experience in the position sought. To be a specialist, a person needs a master's degree in the specialization and 5 years teaching or administrative experience.

Overseas Educational Service

The Service recruits faculty and administrators to fill new or vacant posts, and disseminates information to interested institutions and individuals in the United States about teaching, research, and administrative posts in developing countries. It assists American scholars in solving the problems involved in extended overseas service, and provides information on institutions in Africa, Asia, Latin America, and the Middle East. Requirements are usually a doctoral degree and U.S. citizenship. Vacancy information is received by OES in the spring for teaching positions to begin in the fall. Most are two-year assignments.

Pan American Health Organization

Applications are accepted from those in nursing, public health, medical, and clinical sciences areas.

The Peace Corps

Applications are accepted in many areas of education as well as physical education; educational background requirements vary. There are teaching opportunities in elementary, secondary, normal, and vocational schools, and in universities.

Teacher-Exchange Branch

The Exchange bestows grants for teaching in elementary and secondary schools and summer seminars. Only elementary and secondary school teachers, college instructors, and assistant professors are eligible. Some grants require good health, emotional maturity and stability, and facility in the language of the host country. For teaching positions, a bachelor's degree, U.S. citizenship, and three years of teaching experience, preferably in the subject field and at the level of the position for which application is made, are required. Summer seminars require two years of teaching in the subject field of the seminar. Applications must be made by November 1 prior to the academic year being considered.

Other organizations concerned with employment abroad are:

American Friends of the Middle East
American University in Cairo
Asia Foundation
Association of Universities and Colleges of Canada
Near East College Association

Applying for a job

What are the procedures I should follow in order to find employment?

Among the procedures that might be helpful to you in seeking employment are:

1. Expand your teaching competencies in as many areas as possible. Those capable of teaching swimming, gymnastics, karate, judo, yoga, fencing, scuba diving, backpacking, and survival in addition to the team sports and individual sports of archery, bowling, tennis, and golf will enhance their employment opportunities.
2. Compile a brief resumé of your educational and teaching experiences, including the subjects and activities that you are qualified to teach.
3. File your credentials early with the placement bureau at the university. Each college and university offers a free placement service for its graduates.
4. Identify the type of job opportunity that you desire. Locate prospective employers and direct a letter with a resumé, inquiring about openings available.
5. If possible, introduce yourself to prospective employers with an office call and/or at professional meetings. Be tactful with this procedure.
6. Indicate your interests and special competencies to faculty members. Frequently, prospective employers ask faculty members to recommend qualified candidates for a specific position.
7. Check the job opportunities listed with your university placement bureau frequently and follow up those opportunities for which you are qualified. Do not apply for a position for which you do not qualify.
8. If invited for an interview, be prepared for it, be prompt, dress appropriately, listen carefully, know what questions you would like answered, and base your responses to questions on your own principles, convictions, and thoughts. Do not try to anticipate what the employer wants to hear.

Placement bureaus

Are there placement bureaus that can assist me in getting a job?

Numerous placement agencies can be helpful to you in seeking a job. The university placement bureau can help you by:

1. keeping a set of your credentials available for prospective employers;
2. sending your credentials promptly at your request;
3. identifying job opportunities in your local area.

The American Alliance for Health, Physical Education, and Recreation provides a placement service for members of the Alliance. This service's listing of job opportunities covers a much wider geographical range than does the university's placement bureau. The placement bureau is active at the national conventions of AAHPER.

Many state associations for health, physical education, and recreation provide placement services for their members. Commercial employment agencies will also assist you. However, these agencies are operated for profit and require a registration fee or a percentage of your first year's salary. A complete list of these agencies is available from the National Association of Teachers Agencies, Room 400, 64 East Jackson Boulevard, Chicago, Illinois 60604.

Summary

1. The scope of employment opportunities for health and physical education majors is very broad.
2. There is a surplus of teachers for the following reasons: (a) the taxpayers' refusal to support public education; (b) leveling-off in enrollments; (c) reduction in teaching staffs; (d) teacher-preparation colleges and universities emphasize quantity rather than quality in their selection, retention, and graduation of physical educators.
3. Regier challenges the problem of teacher surplus, stating there is no surplus of teachers but an undersupply of money.
4. The emphasis in teacher-preparation programs is on competencies rather than credits earned, degrees, or years in college.
5. Opportunities for employment in elementary schools through the 1980s are expected to decline in proportion to the decrease in enrollment.
6. The duties and responsibilities of secondary school physical education teachers will vary tremendously with the size of the school.
7. Although school administrators would like to employ physical education teachers who would concentrate on teaching and intramural programs, the vast number of coaches required to conduct athletic programs virtually demands that the physical education teachers coach athletic teams.
8. It is urged that professional certification for athletics coaches be required. In many colleges and universities, a coaching minor provides prospective coaches the opportunity to meet certification requirements.
9. Average salaries for college and university physical educators range from $8342 for instructors to $16,684 for professors.
10. Colleges and universities are continually adding new courses of study to fulfill the educational needs of more students. However, selected programs requiring expensive equipment and highly specialized personnel are only available at certain colleges and universities.
11. States usually grant emergency, provisional or temporary, and permanent teaching certificates.

12. A trend toward greater reciprocity among states would enable a student certified in one state to teach in all states.

13. Active membership in professional organizations and reading professional literature are two effective means to maintain an up-to-date grasp of contemporary theories and practices. Professional organizations which serve the needs of the physical educator are: (a) American Alliance for Health, Physical Education, and Recreation; (b) National Association of Physical Education for College Women; (c) National College Physical Education Association for Men; (d) American Academy of Physical Education; and (e) American College of Sports Medicine. These organizations publish the following periodicals: (a) *The Journal of Physical Education and Recreation,* (b) *The Research Quarterly,* (c) *The Journal of Health,* (d) *Update,* (e) *The Proceedings of NCPEAM,* (f) *Quest,* (g) *The Academy Papers,* and (h) *Science of Medicine in Sports.*

14. Opportunities for physical education abroad arise in teacher or student exchange programs, summer courses, teaching assignments, volunteer programs, or travel.

15. Employment is no longer automatic upon completion of your degree program. The task of seeking employment must be carefully planned and properly executed. A little "luck" may also be helpful.

Questions

1. Who should be responsible for telling you all the facts about manpower demand and supply in physical education?
2. Do you consider it important to be cognizant of the job market before you commit yourself to a specialization? Give examples that demonstrate the full implications of such awareness.
3. Assume that when you picked a major your advisor did not tell you anything about job opportunities. After your graduation you discover the hard way that it is virtually impossible to get a job in this area because the market has been crowded for years. Could you, or should you, take any legal action against your advisor?
4. How can one say that the surplus of physical educators will raise the quality of physical education teaching?
5. What is competency-based instruction? Do you see any future for it? Explain.
6. If institutions were to set exit standards instead of entry standards, what would be the major consequences of such an approach?
7. What is the present status of the elementary physical education specialist?
8. Enumerate some of the major problems encountered in public schools where someone has to coach and teach. Can you propose any solutions?

9. What are some of the desirable personality traits for a person desiring a physical education teaching career?
10. Should all states have the same teaching certification requirements?
11. Are there any job opportunities in foreign countries? What agencies could help you?
12. Why is it important to make yourself personally known to at least two or three of your teachers while you are a student?
13. What are some of the "rules" that you should observe when you seek employment?
14. If you were asked to provide an employee with a vita or resumé, would you know how to write one?

SELECTED READINGS

Adams, J. A. "A closed-loop theory of motor learning," *Journal of Motor Behavior,* 1971, 3, 111–149.

Adrian, M. J. "An introduction to electrogoniometry," *Kinesiology Review,* 1968, 12–18.

Allport, F. H. *Social Psychology.* Boston: Houghton Mifflin, 1924.

Amir, Y. "Contact hypothesis in ethnic relations." *Psychological Bulletin,* 1969, 71, 310–342.

Apter, M. *The New Technology of Education.* New York: Macmillan, 1968.

Auedon, E. M., and B. Sutton-Smith, eds. *The Study of Games.* New York: John Wiley & Sons, 1971.

Ausubel, D. P. *Educational Psychology: A Cognitive View.* New York: Holt, Rinehart and Winston, 1968.

———, and E. V. Sullivan. *Theory and Problems of Child Development.* New York: Grune & Stratton, 1970.

SELECTED READINGS

Barrow, H. M., and R. McGee. *A Practical Approach to Measurement in Physical Education.* Philadelphia, Pa: Lea & Febiger, 1964.

Bell, V. L. *Sensorimotor Learning.* Englewood Cliffs, N.J.: Prentice-Hall (Goodyear), 1970.

Berkowitz, J., B. Levey, and A. R. Harvey. "Effects of performance evaluations on group integration and motivation," *Human Relations,* 1951, 10, 145–148.

Bernard, H. W. *Human Development in Western Culture.* Boston: Allyn & Bacon, 1970.

Breckenridge, M. E., and E. L. Vincent. *Child Development: Physical and Psychological Growth through Adolescence.* Philadelphia, Pa.: W. B. Saunders, 1965.

Brightbill, C. K. *Man and Leisure: A Philosophy of Recreation.* Englewood Cliffs, N.J.: Prentice-Hall, Inc., 1961.

Brown, J. *A-V Instruction: Materials and Methods.* 3d ed. New York: McGraw-Hill, 1969.

Bruner, J. "The Course of Cognitive Growth," in M. L. Haimowitz and N. R. Haimowitz, eds., *Human Development: Selected Readings.* New York: Crowell, 1966.

Bushnell, D., and D. Allen. *The Computer in American Education.* New York: Association for Educational Data Systems, 1967.

Butler, G. D. *Introduction to Community Recreation.* New York: McGraw-Hill, 1967.

Calvin, A. *Programmed Instruction: Bold New Venture.* Bloomington, Ind.: Indiana University Press, 1969.

Carlson, R., T. Deppe, and J. MacLean. *Recreation in American Life.* Belmont, Calif.: Wadsworth, 1972.

Carmichael, L. *Carmichael's Manual of Child Psychology.* 3d ed. New York: John Wiley & Sons, 1970.

Clarke, H. H. *Application of Measurement to Health and Physical Education.* 4th ed. Englewood Cliffs, N.J.: Prentice-Hall, Inc., 1967.

Consolazio, F. C., R. E. Johnson, and L. J. Pecora. *Physiological Measurements of Metabolic Functions in Man.* New York: McGraw-Hill, 1963.

Cooper, J. M., ed. *Selected Topics on Biomechanics.* Chicago: The Athletic Institute, 1971.

Costello, L., and G. Gordon. *Teaching with Television: A Guide to Instructional TV.* 2d ed. New York: Hastings House, 1965.

Cratty, B. J. *Movement Behavior and Motor Learning.* 2d ed. Philadelphia, Pa.: Lea & Febiger, 1967.

———. *Perceptual and Motor Development in Infants and Children.* New York: Macmillan, 1970.

———. *Psychology and Physical Activity.* Englewood Cliffs, N.J.: Prentice-Hall, 1968.

Davis, J. H. *Group Performance.* Reading, Mass.: Addison-Wesley, 1969.

Dodson, D. W. "Integration of Negroes in baseball," *Journal of Educational Sociology,* 1954, 28, 73–82.

Easson, W. *The Severely Disturbed Adolescent.* New York: International Universities Press, 1969.

———. "The school as a community," *Theory into Practice,* 11, 1972.

Espenschade, A. S. "The contributions of physical activity to growth," *Research Quarterly,* 1960, 31, 351–364.

———, and H. M. Eckert. *Motor Development.* Columbus, Ohio: C. E. Merrill, 1967.

Falls, H. B., E. L. Wallis, and G. A. Logan. *Foundations of Conditioning.* New York: Academic Press, Inc., 1970.

"Fitness for youth," *JOPER,* December 1956.

Fitts, P. M., and M. I. Posner. *Human Performance.* Belmont, Calif.: Brooks/Cole, 1967.

Frost, R. *Psychological Concepts Applied to Physical Education and Coaching.* Reading. Mass.: Addison-Wesley, 1971.

Frye, V., and M. Peters. *Therapeutic Recreation: Its Theory, Practices and Principles.* Harrisburg, Pa.: Stackpole Books, 1972.

Garner, W. R. "To perceive is to know," *American Psychologist,* 1966, 21, 11–19.

Gilmore, B. J. Play: a Special Behavior, in R. E. Herron and B. Sutton-Smith, eds., *Child's Play.* New York: John Wiley & Sons, 1971.

Guilford, J. P. *Personality.* New York: McGraw-Hill, 1959.

Halstead, W. C., and W. B. Rucker. "Memory: a molecular maze," *Psychology Today,* 1968, 38–41.

Hamachek, D. E. *The Self in Growth, Teaching, and Learning: Selected Readings.* Englewood Cliffs, N.J.: Prentice-Hall, 1965.

Hart, M. M. *Sport in the Sociocultural Process.* Dubuque, Iowa: William C. Brown Co., 1972.

Haskins, M. J. *Evaluation in Physical Education.* Dubuque, Iowa: William C. Brown Co., 1971.

Haun, P. *Recreation: A Medical Viewpoint.* New York: Teachers College, Columbia University, Bureau of Publications, 1965.

Hill, F. *Learning: A Survey of Psychological Interpretations.* San Francisco, Calif.: Chandler Publishing Co., 1963.

Hjelte, G., and J. S. Shivers. *Public Administration of Recreational Services.* Philadelphia, Pa.: Lea & Febiger, 1972.

Hodgkins, J. "Reaction time and speed of movement in males and females of various ages," *Research Quarterly,* 1963, 34, 335–343.

Horowitz, F. D. "Research strategies and concepts of development and learning," *Merrill-Palmer Quarterly of Behavior and Development,* 1970, 16, 235–237.

Ibraham, H. "Prejudice among college athletes," *Research Quarterly,* 1969, 39, 556–559.

Jacobs, P., M. Maier, and L. Stolurow. *A Guide to Evaluating Self-Instructional Programs.* New York: Holt, Rinehart and Winston, 1966.

Kagan, J. *Understanding Children; Behavior, Motives, and Thought.* New York: Harcourt Brace Jovanovich, 1971.

Karpovich, P. V., and W. E. Sinning. *Physiology of Muscular Activity.* 7th ed. Philadelphia, Pa.: W. B. Saunders Co., 1971.

Kenyon, G. S., ed. *Aspects of Contemporary Sport Sociology.* Chicago: The Athletic Institute, 1969.

———, and J. W. Loy, Jr., eds. *Sport, Culture, and Society.* New York: Macmillan, 1969.

Kimber, D. C., et al. *Anatomy and Physiology.* 15th ed. New York: Macmillan, 1966.

Kirchner, G. *Physical Education for Elementary School Children.* 2d ed. Dubuque, Iowa: William C. Brown Co., 1970.

Kozman, H., R. Cassidy, and C. Jackson. *Methods in Physical Education.* 4th ed., Dubuque, Iowa: William C. Brown Co., 1967.

Kraus, R. *Recreation Today: Program Planning and Leadership,* New York: Appleton-Century-Crofts, 1966.

———. *Recreation and Leisure in Modern Society.* New York: Appleton-Century-Crofts, 1971.

———. *Therapeutic Recreation Service: Principles and Practices.* Philadelphia, Pa.: W. B. Saunders Co., 1973.

———, and J. E. Curtis. *Creative Administration in Recreation and Parks.* St. Louis, Mo.: C. V. Mosby, 1973.

Lansley, K. L., and M. L. Howell. "Play classifications and physical education," *JOPER,* 1970, 59, 44–45.

Latchaw, M., and G. Egstrom. *Human Movement.* Englewood Cliffs, N.J.: Prentice-Hall, 1969.

Lawther, D. *The Learning of Physical Skills.* Englewood Cliffs, N.J.: Prentice-Hall, 1968.

Mager, R. *Preparing Instructional Objectives.* Belmont, Calif.: Fearon Publishers, 1962.

Maier, H. W. *Three Theories of Child Development.* New York: Harper & Row, 1969.

Martens, R., and D. M. Landers. "Coaction effects on a muscular endurance task," *Research Quarterly,* 1969, 40, 733–737.

Mathews, D. K. *Measurement in Physical Education.* 3d ed. Philadelphia, Pa.: W. B. Saunders Co., 1968.

————, and E. L. Fox. *The Physiological Basis of Physical Education and Athletics.* Philadelphia, Pa.: W. B. Saunders Co., 1971.

McCandless, B. R. *Children: Behavior and Development.* 2d ed. New York: Holt, Rinehart and Winston, 1967.

McCristal, K. J., and W. C. Adams. *Foundations of Physical Activity.* Champaign, Ill.: Stripes Publishing Co., 1963.

Meacham, M., and A. Wiesen. *Changing Classroom Behavior: A Manual for Precision Teaching.* Scranton, Pa.: International Textbook Company, 1970.

Meyer, H. D., C. K. Brightbill, and H. Douglas Sessoms. *Community Recreation: A Guide to Its Organization.* Englewood Cliffs, N.J.: Prentice-Hall, 1969.

Meyers, C. R., and E. T. Blesh. *Measurement in Physical Education.* New York: Ronald Press, 1962.

Mitchell, E. D., and B. S. Mason. *The Theory of Play.* New York: A. S. Barnes and Co., 1948.

Morehouse, L. E., and A. T. Miller. *Physiology of Exercise.* 6th ed. St. Louis, Mo.: C. V. Mosby, 1971.

Mussen, P. H., J. J. Conger, and J. Kagan. *Child Development and Personality.* 3d ed. New York: Harper & Row, 1969.

Myers, A. "Team competition, success, and adjustment of group members," *Journal of Abnormal Social Psychology,* 1962, 65, 325–332.

Nesbitt, J. A., P. D. Brown, and J. F. Murphy. *Recreation and Leisure Service for the Disadvantaged.* Philadelphia, Pa.: Lea & Febiger, 1971.

Noble, C. E., B. L. Baker, and T. A. Jones. "Age and Sex Parameters in Psychomotor Learning," *Perceptual and Motor Skills,* 1964, 19, 935–945.

Nyquist, E., and G. Hawes, eds. *Open Education: A Sourcebook for Parents and Teachers.* New York: Bantam Books, 1972.

Olmsted, M. S. *The Small Group.* New York: Random House, 1959.

Oxendine, J. B. *Psychology of Motor Learning.* New York: Appleton-Century-Crofts, 1968.

––––––. "Emotional arousal and motor performance," *Quest,* 1970, monograph XIII, 23–32.

Pomeroy, J. *Recreation for the Physically Handicapped.* New York: Macmillan, 1964.

President's Council on Youth Fitness. *Youth Physical Fitness.* Washington, D.C.: U.S. Government Printing Office, 1961.

Ricci, B. *Physiological Basis of Human Performance.* Philadelphia, Pa.: Lea & Febiger, 1967.

Robb, M. D. *The Dynamics of Motor Skill Acquistion.* Englewood Cliffs, N.J.: Prentice-Hall, 1972.

Roberts, J. M., and B. Sutton-Smith. Child Training and Game Involvement, in E. M. Auedon and B. Sutton-Smith, eds., *The Study of Games.* New York: John Wiley & Sons, 1971.

Rodney, L. S. *Administration of Public Recreation.* New York: Ronald Press, 1964.

Rushall, B., and D. Siedentop. *The Development and Control of Behavior in Sport and Physical Education.* Philadelphia, Pa.: Lea & Febiger, 1972.

Sage, G. H. *Introduction to Motor Behavior: A Neuropsychological Approach.* Reading, Mass.: Addison-Wesley, 1971.

––––––. *Sport and American Society: Selected Readings.* Reading, Mass.: Addison-Wesley Co., 1970.

Sapora A. V., and E. Mitchell. *The Theory of Play and Recreation.* New York: Ronald Press, 1961.

Scott, G. M., and E. French. *Measurement and Evaluation in Physical Education.* Dubuque, Iowa: William C. Brown Co., 1959.

Scott, J. P. "Critical Periods in Behavior Development," *Science,* 1962, 138, 949–958.

Sherif, M. "Superordinate goals in the reduction of intergroup conflict," *American Journal of Sociology,* 1958, 63, 349–363.

Shivers, J. S. *Principles and Practices of Recreational Service.* New York: Macmillan, 1967.

Siedentop, D. "Behavior analysis and teacher training," *Quest,* 1972, monograph XVIII, 26–32.

––––––, and B. Rushall. "An operant model for skill acquisition," *Quest,* 1972, monograph XVIII, 82–90.

Singer, R. N. *Motor Learning and Human Performance,* 2d ed. New York: Macmillan, 1975.

Singer, R. N., ed. *Readings in Motor Learning.* Philadelphia, Pa.: Lea & Febiger, 1972.

————. *The Psychomotor Domain: Movement Behavior.* Philadelphia, Pa.: Lea & Febiger, 1972.

"Skill learning and performance." Special issue, *Research Quarterly,* 1972, 43, 263–397.

Skinner, B. F. *Beyond Freedom and Dignity.* New York: Knopf, 1971.

Spear, J. *Creating Visuals for T.V.* Washington, D.C.: National Education Association, 1962.

Sulzer, B., and G. Mayer. *Behavior Modification Procedures for School Personnel.* Hinsdale, Ill.: The Dryden Press Inc., 1972.

Taylor, E. A. *A Manual for Visual Presentation in Education and Training.* London: Pergamon Press, 1966.

Vernon, G. M. *Human Interaction.* New York: Ronald Press, 1965.

Vredenbregt, J., and J. Wartenweiler, eds. *Biomechanics II.* Baltimore, Md.: University Park Press, 1971.

Wartenweiler, J., E. Jokl, and N. Hebbelinck, eds. *Biomechanics I.* Baltimore, Md.: University Park Press, 1968.

Williams, R. M. *Strangers Next Door: Ethnic Relations in American Communities.* Englewood Cliffs, N.J.: Prentice-Hall, 1964.

Works, E. "The prejudice-interaction hypothesis from the point of view of the Negro minority group," *American Journal of Sociology,* May 1962, 67, 47–52.

INDEX

Prenatal development, 237
Primary groups, 271–272
Private organizations, and recreation, 317–318
Problem solving, 111–112, 175–176, 178–180
Profession, defined, 19, 318
    relationship between discipline and, 20–21
Professional organizations, 320–321, 335,
    453–459
Professionalism, and physical education, 7,
    15–16, 19–21
Programmed instruction, 134, 140–144, 173
Psychiatric hospitals, recreation programs in,
    332–333
Psychological inventories, 261
Public agencies, and recreation, 315–316
Public health educator, 358
Public-relations role of teacher, 105–106
Punishment, and learning, 113, 183

Racial attitudes, and ethnic group contact,
    280–282
Reaction time (RT), 264–265
Recreation, careers in, 322–325
    defined, 32–33, 309–310
    education in, 319–320
    historical overview of, 313–315
    personal goals for, 310–312
    professionalism in, 318–319
    relationship between physical education and,
        346–348
    See also Community recreation
Recreation leaders, functions of, 338–339
    in-service education of, 340–341
    on-the-job supervision of, 341
    orientation of, 340
    supervisory, 339–340
    traits of, 337–338
Recreation programs, activities included in,
    326–330
    availability of, 325
    coordination of, 326
    facilities for, 325, 333–336
    leadership for, 337–342
    principles for the organization of, 330–332
    in psychiatric hospital, 332–333
    role of schools in, 342
    sponsors of, 315–318
Reference group, 272
Reflective thinking, stages of, 310
Reinforcement, in behavior modification,
    167–168
Related activities model, 34–35

Relaxation, and physical fitness, 215–217
Reproductive system, 204
Respiratory system, 199–200
Response time (RT), 265
Rhythmic activities, in elementary school
    physical education program, 405
River boating, 384
Rock climbing, 381–382
Role playing, 181–182, 272, 273

School health coordinator, 372–373
School health program, see Health education
School health services, 359, 369–370
Schools, function of, 43–44
    healthful environment for, 370
    and interschool athletic programs, 413–420
    physical education programs, see Physical
        education programs
    role in recreation, 342–346
    See also Elementary school physical
        education programs; High schools,
        physical education programs in
Science, aims and method of, 299–300
Scientific research, 301–307
Scuba diving, 385–386
Sensing, 202, 248–250
Series photographs, 148
Service activities, in recreation programs, 330
Sex roles, 273
Skeletal system, 191–195, 196–197
Skill development, 120, 130, 253, 405
Slide projectors, 149
Soccer, 156, 177, 179
Social facilitation, 282–283
Social programs, in recreation programs, 329
Socialization, defined, 278–279
    and games, 279–280
    and modeling, 183
    and physical education, 53, 86–91, 93–97,
        311
    and sports, 95–97
Sociology, defined, 269
    of sport, 270
Special events, in recreation programs, 329–330
Specificity theory, and sports, 262–263
Spectator sports, in the United States, 83–84
Speed, and motor fitness, 212–213
Sport(s), in British public schools, 91–92
    for combat, 75–76
    compared with games, 31
    for competition and reward, 75–86
    defined, 28–31

479

DATE DUE